Math Mystic's Guide to Creative Spirituality

"A trailblazing exploration of previously uncharted territory, full of surprising and profound insights into the fascinating intersection of mathematical and spiritual realms of human experience. Sarah Voss is uniquely qualified to reveal the wonderful connections between mystical and mathematical ideas, and she has a gift for grounding these ideas in the practical concerns of our everyday lives."

—Thomas J. McFarlane, author of
Einstein and Buddha: The Parallel Sayings

"Sarah Voss takes us on a personal journey in which she connects some fundamental aspects of mathematics to spirituality, religion, and mysticism with openness, gentleness, and sensitivity. Through metaphor, poetry, and history combined with descriptive narrative and observation, she balances human hopes, needs, uncertainties, and moral frailties with realities of life. Offering insights earnest and enriching in equal measure, and with mathematics always at the book's heart, this is an engaging read whose thought-provoking messages speak to us all."

—Peter J. Larcombe, professor of discrete and applied mathematics,
University of Derby

"Mathematics! Esoteric and 'over my head'? Mundane and dry? Not so: Sarah Voss shows instead that math is a rich source of valuable spiritual insights. Her wide-ranging imagination will take you on a journey that is entertaining as well as enlightening."

—Daniel S. Levine, professor of psychology,
University of Texas at Arlington

"Sarah Voss has written a most evocative book, one I know I will keep returning to for many years to come. This is a captivating exploration of what Voss calls math mysticism, her unique blend of mathematics and spirituality. Voss knows her theology as well as her mathematics, and she weaves them into a provocatively beautiful tapestry. Her voice is welcoming and hopeful; may many read her words and heed her call!"

—Gizem Karaali, professor of mathematics and statistics,
Pomona College

"Do you want to know truth? Do you want to know what is real? Both the languages of mathematical science and the revelations of faith claim to offer us truth. But with a phase/phrase change from metaphors to mathaphors and from theology to matheology, Sarah Voss, the mathematician-mystic, constructs bridges between the two languages so we can better understand—and improve—reality."
—Vern Barnet, minister emeritus,
   Center for Religious Experience and Study

Math Mystic's Guide to Creative Spirituality

A Collection of Work by
Sarah Voss

With a Foreword by Sal Restivo

WIPF & STOCK · Eugene, Oregon

MATH MYSTIC'S GUIDE TO CREATIVE SPIRITUALITY
A Collection of Work by Sarah Voss

Copyright © 2024 Sarah Voss. All rights reserved. Except for brief quotations in critical publications or reviews, no part of this book may be reproduced in any manner without prior written permission from the publisher. Write: Permissions, Wipf and Stock Publishers, 199 W. 8th Ave., Suite 3, Eugene, OR 97401.

Wipf & Stock
An Imprint of Wipf and Stock Publishers
199 W. 8th Ave., Suite 3
Eugene, OR 97401

www.wipfandstock.com

PAPERBACK ISBN: 978-1-6667-4247-3
HARDCOVER ISBN: 978-1-6667-4248-0
EBOOK ISBN: 978-1-6667-4249-7

To the many people who encouraged me in this work, and especially to my husband Daniel M. Sullivan and my children and their partners, and to all the people in the Unitarian Universalist churches where I often tried out these ideas—all of whose patience and good will guided me.

The power of math is its precision and its suggestion. The power of metaphor is its suggestion, not its precision. The power of metaphor drawn from math is a mystic's guide.

Table of Contents

List of Illustrations xi
Foreword by Sal Restivo xiii
Preface: About This Work xvii
Acknowledgments xxvii
Introduction: Mining Our Spiritual Resources with Holy Mathaphors xxix

PART 1: *My Math Mystic Journey*
Poem: "How to Reduce Fractions" 3
    1. A Bridge to Trust 5
    2. The Mystical Realm 11
    3. A Little Irrationality Is Good for a Mystic 20
    4. Depolarizing Mathematics and Religion 27
    5. *Coming Out of the Math Closet 38
    6. How God Is Like the Definite Integral of Calculus 45

PART 2: *Number Mysticism and Beyond*
    Poem: "Cantorian Religion" 57
    7. Empirical Study: Sign, Symbol, Metaphor, and Model in Religion and Mathematics 60
    8. Sacred Qualities 70
    13. "Thirteen," "Doubling," and the Need to Heal Our Ancestors 76
    9. *Toward a Cantorian Religion 84
    10. Matheology and Cantorian Religion 92

PART 3: *Matheology and a New Mystic View*
    Poem: "A Calculating Myth" 103
    11. *Faith Understandings of Computers and Consciousness 105
    12. Out of Order, Chaos 117

14. Our Entangled Web 130
15. A Kaleidoscopic View of Reality 137
16. We Are Symbols 146

PART 4: *Using Mathaphors to Motivate Right Relations*
Poem: "Number Identity" 159
17. A Stroll through the Garden of Mathaphors 161
18. Self-Organizing Emergence and Network Theory 179
19. Redemption 188
20. *Venn Diagrams and Intersectionality 196
21. The Art of Reframing 202
22. Fuzzy Logic in the Health Care Setting 213

PART 5: *Moral Math*
Poem: "Simple Arithmetic: Heavy on Butter, Cream, Wine" 231
23. A Workshop to Introduce Concepts of Moral Math 233
24. *Out of Statistics, Hope 242
25. Generating Trust through Moral Math 250
26. Moral Mathematics: Its Development and Potential for Social Benefit and for Spiritual Growth 260
27. Do No Harm: Math and Ethics 287

Poem: "For Some Odd Reason" 297
Appendix A: Twenty Loosely Spiritual Insights Drawn from Mathematics 299
Appendix B: The "Contact Process" for Self-Organizing Emergence and Networks 302
Appendix C: An Interview with Sarah Voss on Mathematics, Ministry, Mediation 306
Appendix D: Final Mathaphorical Wave: Mathaphor as a Literary Tool and a Hope for the Future 323

Bibliography 329

*Note: An asterisk (*) denotes a math sermon.

List of Illustrations, Images, and Photographs

2.1: *My Wife and My Mother-in-Law* | 11
2.2: Sarah as a Young Mother | 14
2.3: Sarah as a Child | 15
3.1: Pythagorean Irrational Number | 22
4.1: Möbius Strip | 27
7.1: Study Questionnaire: Sign, Symbol, Metaphor, and Model in Religion and Mathematics | 62
10.1: Maxwell's Equations | 93
12.1: The Mandelbrot Set | 121
18.1: Connect the Dots | 180
21.1: Algebraic Proof That $1 = .999\ldots$ | 203
21.2: Light on 3-D Shapes | 204
22.1: An Example of a Fuzzy Logic Member Function | 219
25.1: Cutting a Cake into Equal Pieces | 252

B1: Sarah Voss, 2009 | 306
B2: Cutting a Hologram in Half | 313
B3: Jonesy | 314
B4: Approximating the Area under a Curve | 317
B5: An Expandable Facsimile of a Three-Dimensional Apeirogon | 325

Foreword

SARAH VOSS IS A voice of reason, of compassion, and of hope. My voice has echoed Nietzsche's advice to his sister Elizabeth: "If you wish to strive for peace of soul and pleasure, then believe; if you wish to be a devotee of truth, then inquire." I have chosen to be (or more accurately "become") a devotee of truth. And while I have found a serene and tranquil path as an inquirer free from the yokes of belief, hopes, and wishes, Sarah Voss's book and her life demonstrate what happens if you experience these two paths as complementary. The result is good for mathematics, it's good for morality, and it's good for humanity.

Full disclosure: Sarah and I have been friends for many years. There are many compatibilities between my humanistic anarchism (which draws its inspiration from Peter Kropotkin's sociologically based mutualism) and Sarah's Unitarian Universalism. In a world that fractures our humanity into cultural species, it is important to consider on a more personal level what might account for our differences. Sarah writes about a "dark hour." Dark hours have led many into the arms of traditional religion, spiritualism, and mysticism. I have been blessed with very few "dark hours" and those few have been bathed in the bright light of a Nietzschean reason. There is a theory there, but let's see what Sarah has to share with her readers and why I urge you to pay attention to her.

This is a book about language in the broadest sense, a sense of language that intimately embraces mathematics, poetry, morality, and mysticism. I know of no one who has created a lovefest among these languages as compelling and seductive as Sarah's. This is not the kind of lovefest we saw at Woodstock but one that reflects the cooperative imperative in evolution, an imperative many miss in the writings of Darwin himself. Sarah's writing, like Sarah herself, is lyrical, lucid, mathematically erudite, eclectic, and hopeful. Somehow, she has imbued words on the page with compassion. This is a deeply personal narrative that gives mathematics a personae in the figure of Sarah Voss.

Sarah accepts a sociological truism, that the individual is not an atomistic ego but connected to others. In my terms, this connectedness arises from the fact that humans arrive on the evolutionary stage always, already, and everywhere social. They emerge eons after evolution's tinkering mechanisms revealed the adaptive potential of "the social" in cellular cooperation. In evolutionary terms, humans are the most radically social of the (eu)social species, and they are social in a different way than social insects. Humans have social selves, social brains, and social genes. Sarah arrives at a version of this truism by way of her mathematical mysticism, drawing on Euler's uncovering of the connection between 0, 1, e, i, and pi, captured in the equation $e^{i\pi} + 1 = 0$. Encountering this equation in a "dark hour" allowed her to imagine that, like Euler's equation, she too might be connected to the world around her in ways that had escaped her. Sociologists tell us that our failure to understand and achieve connectedness is due to the fact, notably in American society but also elsewhere, that culture can replace our evolutionary socialness with alienation and the myth of individualism. Culture can fracture solidarity and alienate us from each other, ourselves, and nature.

Theists are wont to search for, in the words of the distinguished theologian Hans Küng, "a rock like, unshakeable certainty on which all human certainty could be built." This theistic goal inevitably leads to God, and usually not a God for humanity but the Christian God. Gödel's incompleteness theorem gave Sarah the armor she needed to protect herself from a theistic absolute certainty and to embrace the reality of imperfection, paradox, and chaos built into the very core of the universe from the quantum level to the dynamic chaos that helps to run our brains. But does Sarah really escape the theist's absolute certainty, or does it show itself in her understanding of mathematics and mysticism; is this where her God resides? If so, I'm sure she would argue that this is not the theistic God of unshakable certainty, but a God with chaos in Her soul.

Sociologists understand that irrationality is the foundation of rationality; they refer to this as "precontractual solidarity." Sarah's pathway to a comparable insight is the real number line: "There is more irrationality than rationality." This then is a key approach in her narrative. Many of her chapters epigraphically introduce a mathematical concept or idea that Sarah unfolds into a mystical, moral, mathematical insight: Euler and Möbius are followed by God the definite integral, Pythagorean "number theory," ethical mathematics, Cantorian math, and so on. And she does this brilliantly. And of course culturally and historically mathematics and God are as closely intertwined as the lovers in Rodin's *The Kiss*.

Let there be no misunderstanding. Sarah and I carry profoundly different worldviews. I have argued that worldviews are incommensurable, that they separate us into cultural species as distinct as biological species. In 1992, Gore Vidal wrote that the tree of liberty was dying for lack of nurture. The sky-god never liked it, he wrote. He said we are obliged to face the realities of who and what we are if we are going to achieve a nation not under God but under our common humanity. In something like this spirit, I have argued social realities revealed by the social sciences urge us to end the God narrative and put away the childish things God narratives nourish: the transcendental, the supernatural, and, yes, the spiritual and the mystical. This exercise in comprehensive deicide is necessary if we are going to solve the existential threats to humanity and the planet.

Sarah Voss has written a wonderful and much needed book for our liminal age. This is so even though Sarah's mystical mathematics strays. For example, she uses the Möbius strip, a strip which has one side but appears to have two sides, to illustrate that the polarization of mathematics and religion is an illusion. It is indeed an illusion but not in the way Sarah suggests.

Religion is the glue of society. It systemizes, organizes, and establishes sanctions for the moral order of a society. The moral order is the engine and fuel of social solidarity. The glue can be stronger and weaker in different places, so moral orders can vary in consistency. Mathematics and science are social institutions. They have moral orders. They are religious systems. This makes them objects of sociological analysis. This perspective is not compatible with Sarah's understanding of mystical mathematics, but it doesn't undermine her message of hope and compassion, a message that unlike others of that kind is inspired with reason and mathematics. However, my program for a humanistic anarchism at this juncture of history, biographies, and cultures is unrealistic. We need a transition, something that moves us from a world of believers and non-believers to a world of knowers, something that, in Sarah's words, "will track any emergent 'strange' attractor."

Sarah Voss gives us a kind of Charter for Compassion (Karen Armstrong) mathematized; she gives us a global, mathematically inspired alternative to Michael Harrington's "death of the political God" argument for a new Western transcendence that unites believers and non-believers. The profound lesson of this book, to put it in personal terms, is that Sarah and I could live together, make a community together, and, in company with others, construct a pathway to that "strange" attractor.

Sal Restivo
Queens, New York
June 2023

Preface: About This Work

THE MATH MYSTIC'S GUIDE to Creative Spirituality is a collection of twenty-seven essays by Unitarian Universalist math mystic Sarah Voss. That's me, and this book represents more than thirty years of my effort to use mathematical concepts to foster religious understanding and spiritual growth. Some of these pieces leave a bit of an historical trail on the mystic moral math journey: they show not only how I've developed some guiding skills over these decades, but also how society has changed and opened to new trends and directions in mathematics, such as those brought about by computers. Collectively, we humans are still babies in the spiritual realm and it is my hope that this compilation of my written work will be put to the service of right relations in our global society.

Many of the chapters in this *Guide* are partially or entirely drawn from work I've previously published elsewhere in this quest. Some are based on lectures which I've given or classes/workshops on religion and math/science which I've taught/led. Many of the ideas I've also offered as sermons: check them out in "Sarah's Math Sermons: Ideas from the Pulpit for Math Lovers and for People Shy of Math," found on my dedicated website, www.PiZine.org. I've included in this *Guide five* of these math sermons pretty much the way I delivered them: these are the chapters marked by an asterisk. In an attempt to capture some of my own history and growth as a math mystic, I've kept these sermons close to the way (and time frame) when I first offered them to a church audience. In general, the chapters are arranged topically rather than chronologically. Thus, some details are clearly no longer accurate, such as when I spoke of my then-fiancé in part 2 while he is my spouse in others. A few of the chapters herein are new, written explicitly for this manuscript.

Together, these pioneering essays will especially appeal to:

- those who like mathematics
- those who are shy about mathematics but want to know more about the math metaphors (mathaphors) which relate to mysticism
- those who want to know how to use math as a tool for better social relations
- those who are from liberal faith traditions such as Unitarian Universalism (my faith tradition)
- those who like to think outside the box, or even better, as if the box doesn't exist or without reference to the box at all
- those who are fond of poetry.

> **Math and Poetry**
>
> *You will find a "math" poem I've written at the beginning of each of the five sections in this work, and you'll find poetry scattered throughout in the spirit of Michael Guillen, who understood that:*
>
> *In the language of mathematics, equations are like poetry: They state truth with a unique precision, convey volumes of information in rather brief terms, and often are difficult for the uninitiated to comprehend.*[1]

This *Guide* is organized into five parts, as follows:

- Part 1: My Math Mystic Journey. Chapters 1–6 tell a little about my personal journey into mysticism and this work, beginning with how math offered me a bridge to trust, and winding up with how I relate to God as the Definite Integral of Calculus. Chapter 5 is one of my math sermons, "Coming Out of the Math Closet." This sermon

---

1. Guillen, *Five Equations*, 2.

makes a not-so-subtle statement about discrimination. Even so, it's perhaps too subtle.

Learned prejudice against math can lead to prejudice against the mathematician. One math friend once told me that he'd encountered much more prejudice as a mathematician than as a Jew. Another observed that people are reluctant to claim that they just aren't a history (or literature or English) person, but it's generally acceptable to not be a math person. Why should ignorance of mathematics be acceptable while ignorance of another subject is not? he asked. The other four chapters in this section connect religion and math and indicate ways math helps to elaborate modern Western esotericism.

- Part 2: Number Mysticism and Beyond. Chapters 7, 8, 13, 9, and 10 focus on number mysticism. While this section shies away from divination and goes beyond gematria, it still marries the physical to the symbolic, starting with a report on a study I conducted in the early 1990s to learn more about how people interpret signs, symbols, metaphors, and

A Kind of Math Discrimination

Recently, I had occasion to read aloud a short piece about a truly healing experience that I'd both watched and experienced which came from a math idea. Halfway through my reading, I mentioned the names of these math notions without giving any further explanation. When I finished, a man almost immediately jumped on the fact that I'd lost him halfway through, and that he was an "English" fan and had never been good at math. And so on. My spirits sank, but I acquiesced to the intensity of his discomfort and did not confront it.

The thing is, this man is precisely the person I most want to reach with this Guide—smart, capable, articulate, entertaining, dedicated to the service of humankind and the mother-earth. Today's math offers wonderful new tools to aid that service, and there are definitely people who will use them in that way. Some, however, will abuse these tools, and the rest of us will allow this to happen because we don't understand the math well enough to comment, or to sit on an ethics committee with confidence in our contributions, or even to say anything at all. This Guide encourages concerned mathematicians and non-mathematicians to have a voice and to share it too.

> What I didn't realize until I reflected upon this little incident was my own complicity in letting it happen. Next time I will recognize the microaggression he used in his response, and I will do my best to address it right then and there, just as our black community has been learning to do to change the injustices that they have so long cloaked in silence. There were, of course, good reasons to cloak them this way, but this world needs something different now to fully realize right relations in all our relations.

models. The section winds up with two chapters on Cantorian religion, a notion structurally like the "set of all sets," as in "the religion of all religions." The first of these two chapters, "Toward a Cantorian Religion," is one of my early math sermons and introduces this structure. The second, "Matheology and Cantorian Religion," was written roughly a decade later and lays the foundation for a more detailed understanding of this religious perspective. I have since discovered that the set-of-all-sets notion is not uniformly accepted in the mathematical world, but I like the metaphor and have opted to leave the chapter as is. Sometimes our mathematical insights change. The essentially spiritual question this raises is whether or not we blame the other when we are confronted with something utterly beyond us, or whether we humbly admit our ignorance and use this information as a springboard for growth.

- Part 3: Matheology and a New Mystic View. Chapters 12–16 discuss some of the contributions and changes that the development of computers (ordinary and quantum) have brought/are bringing to our society, and to consciousness. Beginning with "Faith Understandings of Consciousness and Computers" (the math sermon included in this section), we journey through various early creation stories and end up (in chapter 15) with the presentation of a kaleidoscopic view of reality and (in chapter 16) with an understanding of how two influential mathematicians understand the somewhat mystical role math plays in creation.

- Part 4: Using Mathaphors to Motivate Right Relations. The six chapters in this section (17–22) introduce mathaphors (metaphors drawn from math) as a way of motivating right relations. "Venn Diagrams and Intersectionality" is the math sermon included in this section. The first chapter in this section offers an overview: "A Stroll through the Garden of Mathaphors." Some of these mathaphors lend themselves to an experiential presentation. In my work with math and spirituality I often cull the math literature for illustrations which I can turn into experiential exercises that show the math ideas involved, and I then apply these notions metaphorically to social issues such as fairness, equality, justice, redemption, and forgiveness. I adapted the notion of using experiential exercises from a mental health program I encountered that used such interactive methods very effectively. Experiential math exercises have turned out to be my original contribution to helping non-mathematicians master the sense of the mathematics involved in an idea without actually doing the math. Chapters 18 and 19 offer good examples of using these techniques.

- Part 5: Moral Math. The last five chapters deal with moral math, ideas drawn from mathematics that can foster positive social behavior. The first of these, chapter 23, is a compilation of ideas I have used to good effect in workshops on the

Math Microaggressions

Many individuals dislike or fear math; they often counter this fear with a mixture of avoidance and blame:

"You totally lost me when you started talking about math"—was any one of many people.

"When I enter a room where math is a subject, I just want to keep on going out the other door."
—This was a seminary student starting my class on Math: The New Language of Religion.

"I skipped church because you said it'd be a math sermon."
—I stopped announcing my math sermons.

"You're Sarah Voss. OMG, I'm enrolled in your math class this summer." Then, stiffening, starting to turn away ". . . **I hate** math."

"This is just way beyond me."

I've heard all these statements. I've even used the last one myself. Happily, the seminary student stayed and was glad; the woman who froze when she met me at a party got an A in the class. But such comments are a form of learned prejudice that all math teachers encounter and usually learn to placate rather than to openly address.

subject. Chapter 24 is a math sermon which shows how influential statistics can be in identifying and addressing areas of social concern. Chapter 25 is the paper I presented in 2004 to a mixed group of academics and non-academics as part of a three-day UNESCO–type event in Seattle. Chapter 26 is a summary of moral mathematics in a living reference resource by Springer. Chapter 27 includes a short editorial about moral math which I wrote for the *Omaha World-Herald*, my local city newspaper. There is some overlap in these essays, but together they tell the story of my varied efforts over the past three decades to promote mathematics as a language and process for creative spiritual growth.

At the end of the book there is a poem, two "take-aways" in Appendixes A and B, a 2009 interview that Tom McFarlane did with me about this work, a piece about mathaphor newly used as a literary tool, and reference material.

Now is a time in the history of our earth when the life it carries is particularly vulnerable to degradation or extinction. There is a new need for out-of-the-box thinking and methodology to nurture a more compassionate existence into being. The tools and concepts presented in this *Mystic's Guide to Creative Spirituality* can help make these ideas more widely accessible, and, in so doing, can help prevent a future dictated by a few rather than the democratic whole.

How did my work in this area come about? To address this question is to bring up the old chicken/egg question, i.e., which came first, the mathematical chick or the religious egg? The older I grow, the more I conclude that human beings come in three basic varieties. There are the chick people, who are convinced that there had to be a chicken before there could be an egg. There are the egg folks, who can cite scripture on why the egg came first. And there are the story people, who follow the argument with interest but little attachment, then make up tales and songs appreciating the entire experience. Nowhere is this perhaps more obvious than in today's current conversation about the relationship between mathematics and religion.

As a teenager, I was a chick person. If I couldn't see it, touch it, smell it, it didn't exist except, perhaps, in my imagination. I fine-tuned this version when I began teaching mathematics after college. I couldn't see, touch, or smell mathematics, but I knew it was there, busily scattering eggs about so that mathematicians could help hatch them and serve them up to lay folks. I didn't, of course, know precisely where "there" was, but it had something to do with a Platonic ideal which lay just outside of my own personal imagination, but clearly within the realm of the collective imagination, or, possibly, of some Greater Imagination. Even this Greater Imagination, however, had a decided reductionistic and materialist cast to it when I was a chick person.

Then I had a mid-life crisis and I became a born-again egg person. Truly, something existed that was more significant than the chicken—namely the minuscule, almost ethereal, probably cosmic egg from which All emerged. This major transition in my perspective eventually caused me to leave off the teaching of mathematics and enter seminary, whereupon I became an ordained Unitarian Universalist minister and knocked heads with my humanist professors. More accurately, I walked on eggshells whenever I was around humanists. I was too new at being an egg-person to have any confidence in my ability to cite convincing scripture to these known rationalists. Besides, as a good UU, I wasn't just exactly sure which scripture I should be citing. The Judeo-Christian Bible? The Qur'an? Buddhist or Hindu beliefs? They just seemed to be different species of the same thing and, having been a practicing mathematician most of my professional life until then, I lacked an intimate knowledge of the appropriate vocabulary as well. Hence, the extreme care I took when stepping around the delicate egg-shell exteriors one encounters among the more theologically inclined!

Lately, I've been moving into that third category of persons—those who observe, tell stories, appreciate, but seldom offer any decisive commentary on the chicken/egg problem other than a slightly amused "Some chick!" Looking back, I can see that when I was a chick-people and when I was an egg-person I nonetheless embraced my chosen position of the time with an enthusiasm that bordered on evangelism. Being older now, and possibly wiser, I suspect that I am following the same pattern as I transform into a story-people. For this tendency, I apologize in advance and ask your indulgence. The truth is, I think my story is a valid one and that it contributes something positive to the current math/religion dialogue, although I'll not be the one to identify that contribution by name. It's not that I wouldn't like to—rather, I can't. I lack that insight.

Lack of insight is not new with regard to the math/religion relationship. Personally, I experience it more immediately in the math portion of the dialogue. I am in complete sympathy with Reuben Hersh when he writes in *What Is Mathematics, Really?* that mathematical unity (along with mathematical universality, certainty, and objectivity) is a myth. "At meetings of the American Mathematical Society," he notes, "any contributed talk is understandable to only a small fraction of those present."[2] This he offers as proof that the principle of mathematical unity—the notion that there's only one mathematics, indivisible now and forever—does not exist in practice. I can't disagree with him. All too well I remember sitting through an exhaustingly complicated lecture which was way over my mathematical head and from which I took home only an original and heartfelt poem.

"Theorem 19 at the Summer Conference for Professional Mathematicians (*with apologies to Allen Schwenk*)"

Wind whistles words
through this valley
of wisdom. Hypotheses
hum in the hot air.

> *Moore graphs exist*
> *for r = 2, 3, 7,*
> *and possibly 57*

I swat one, hoping
to scare it off
before it stings
but it buzzes around me,
teasing, teasing

> *If the latter eigenvalues*
> *are irrational, then . . .*

Ardently, I fan my program;
flat phrases swish
by my ears

> *We find that*
> *We see that*
> *That is*
> *Thus*

Quick, someone,
Where's the spray?

> *But diam = 1 and girth*
> *is undefined*

Oh, tiny beast of prey,
away! Away!
Take your sweet nectar

> *and this is the Peterson*
> *graph*

back to your Queen
who, as we all know,
has well-laid plans
for all her willing workers.

2. Hersh, *What Is Mathematics*, 38.

Again, looking back I believe this incident may well have been the straw the religious egg rested on before it hatched me into one of the full-blown egg-people. It wasn't that I was ignorant of mathematics. Heck, I taught calculus, statistics, differential equations, non-Euclidean geometry—virtually everything that a math major might need to graduate from the small all-women's college where I was the resident mathematics program director. Yet, here I was sitting too long in a too-hot auditorium, listening to a champion mathematician, and feeling utterly stupid. Probably this is how the man who identified as an "English" person who was never good at math also felt. This little vignette makes me realize how easy it is to turn the discomfort of not understanding into discrimination (see above, "A Kind of Math Discrimination").

I am gentler with myself these days. Now I recognize that I was simply out of my element, although whether ability-wise or interest-wise is difficult to say. Not only is feeling utterly stupid a humbling experience, but it's often also an actively motivating one. It's like being in a trap—you're so uncomfortable you try to get out of it.

As I said, I got out. Not right away, of course. First, I saved up money for the impoverishment that most ministers experience even if they don't pledge themselves to a life of it. (I did not save up enough, I might add—I'm broker now and more dependent than ever before. But that story belongs to a conversation on the feminist experience, not this one on mathematics and religion.) Then I read. I read science, technology, and society specialist Sal Restivo's sociological perspectives on different math "worlds." I stretched the boundaries of my search for information on religion and mathematics. I dabbled at Husserl, read Hofstadter's *Gödel, Escher, Bach*, and even made my way through Korzybski's *Science and Sanity*. I read everything I came across that even vaguely discussed mathematics and religion, which didn't take long, because there wasn't exactly a plethora of recognized resources in the late 1980s. Not many people seemed overly attracted to the study, and, yes, some probably just put math and religion into separate compartments, never dreaming that they could be related. Still, whenever I mentioned my growing interest in the math/religion conversation, eyes glassed over and I heard the inevitable "calculating woman" jokes.

You might say there wasn't much incentive to explore the relationship between math and religion. You'd be right, except that, somehow, I couldn't let it go. I wound up telling my calculus students how God was like the definite integral of calculus, at which time I knew that the religious egg was rolling over the mathematical chick. I could get away with such classroom language because I was teaching in a private Catholic college just then, rather than in the state university where I had known better than to try to integrate religion into my calculus lectures. Nonetheless, my future journey was forecast.

I gave up my mathematics teaching position, went to Meadville Lombard Theological School, turned my interest in integrating math and religion into a doctoral thesis, which I then had trouble getting past my thesis advisor. There was some struggle in this. Eventually, though, I tacked the DMin tagline onto my name and set out searching for a traditional position as a minister in a traditional Unitarian Universalist church. For a variety of reasons (health, family issues, life itself) that never really happened. What did happen was that I had just enough unchanneled time to continue to pursue my effort to understand the relationship between math and religion. Is it a surprise that I then wanted to share what I was learning? There was some struggle in all of this, too. I didn't become a best-selling author or an on-demand lecturer, but I did become an author and a lecturer, and even a prize-winning teacher for a class I developed on the subject. I also preached enough that I could get away with talking math/religion from the pulpit, and to this day I am grateful for those UUs who came to these "math" sermons, because their open hearts, inquiring minds, and sweet, generous enthusiasm kept me going.

My "math mystic" part emerged out of all this. It just felt right. Feels right. Please, Dear Readers, you will want to decide for yourselves how useful this collection is as you make your way through this selection of my work, which I call, appropriately I believe, a *Math Mystic's Guide to Creative Spirituality.*

Acknowledgments

THERE ARE TOO MANY individuals who helped me on this journey to name them all, but I especially want to lift up the ones to whom I dedicated this book, i.e., my biochemist husband Dr. Dan Sullivan and my children Sonna Voss, Wil Voss, and Melinda Cocolas. The encouragement and aid I received from them was extraordinary, and this book went to the press in large part because of the skill of my technologically abled son Wil. My sons-in-law, Chris and Paul, also kept my computer machinery up to speed. When I told my always optimistic spouse that the press wanted seven descriptive words about the book, he immediately came up with "provocative," "engaging," "intriguing," and "a masterpiece of philosophy."

I am also indebted to Dr. Sal Restivo, who was the first scholar to show interest and encouragement in this work and has been a persistent support ever since. Also early on, the late Burke Brown opened doors for me and my work, and I wish he were still around to see this book. Dr. Daniel Levine, Tom McFarlane, and John Wagner took time to read parts or all of an earlier version of this manuscript and to respond thoughtfully with suggestions and comments, and that is only a portion of the ways they've given of their time and wisdom. My heartfelt thanks also to the Rev. Dr. Vern Barnet, who in his many years of writing a weekly religious column for the *Kansas City Star* included one about my 1995 book on math and religion and who now adds a strong religious voice in his gracious endorsement of this new book.

Thanks also to the friends and teachers at Meadville Lombard Theological School who encouraged me in my earliest endeavors on this journey into religion and math, and an extra wave of gratitude to the late Rev. Dr. Spencer Levan, president of the school during my student days there, who essentially made this work possible.

The Templeton Foundation also helped my work by awarding me a prize for designing and teaching an undergraduate class on religion and math, a follow-up grant through the Center for Theology and the Natural Sciences and, even later, an invitation to contribute an essay to *Spiritual Information: 100 Perspectives on Science and Religion*. The vision of Sir John Templeton brought me opportunities to attend several conferences that were highly formative in my work.

Grateful thanks also to Professor Peter Larcombe, the first discrete and applied mathematician from a university in England to take an active interest in my work. Gizem Karaali, professor of mathematics at Pomona College and co-editor of the *Journal of Humanistic Mathematics*, provided a home for my more recent work, some of which is included herein but was first published in *JHM*: I count her consistent openness as a huge gift.

I especially want to recognize the spirit and generosity of the numerous Unitarian Universalists who sat through my math sermons over the years, and who provided feedback, enthusiasm, and occasionally even applause for my effort. I also wish to thank the special personal friends who listened to me grumble when things were difficult and assured me that I could complete this task anyway.

Finally, I wish to thank the editors and staff at Wipf and Stock who patiently answered questions, willingly extended deadlines, and most of all, had confidence in the value of this work.

Introduction: Mining Our Spiritual Resources with Holy Mathaphors

One of the best (and shortest) commentaries I've ever heard about the human condition was given by the "First Lady" of the American theater, Helen Hayes. "The hardest years in life," she said, "are those between ten and seventy." Most of us have had moments when we feel like that. Most of us have also had days when we wonder just how faith helps us through those moments.

Let me tell you about Annie. Annie has struggled with depression all her life. She's experienced many losses over the years, but if you talk to her at church or run into her at the grocery store, chances are you wouldn't know about it. She always has a ready smile and a kind word to say about people. Annie is no whiner. In her inner life, however, she is frequently filled with emotional pain. Annie grew up Catholic, but, after her oldest child succumbed to leukemia, she lost her faith in God. Then she found a spiritual home in my own faith tradition, Unitarian Universalism, and she's been there, more or less, ever since.

She's there on good days, anyway. On bad days, she doesn't feel like she's fit company for anyone, so she tends to avoid church. Recently, Annie has been having a run of bad days. As she's grown older, Annie has found it harder to cope with her bouts of depression, although she's certainly tried. She still tries. But lately she's lost so much weight that she looks ill and she tends to stay at home, isolating herself from her friends, even though she knows that in theory this is not a helpful thing to do. The trouble is, for Annie *the bear is back.*

The Bear Is Back[1]

White, fuzzy, its toy promise
deceptive, the danger seductive.
Temptation: to roll in its cold
comfort, wrap in the isolation
of its con-artist arms.

Call the doc, there must be
a make-the-bear-disappear pill,
meds to abort this depression,
therapy to face it down, talk it
back into its cellophane box

before it gets loose, eats all
the honey-joy still waiting
in the high trees, grows so huge
it fills the vision, blocks breath,
brings the dark.

Depression is a gnawing bear. I was talking to Annie during her most recent down time, and she told me point blank that she lacks spiritual resources. I made some comment about how there is always someone who will be with her as she is going through this trial. I meant it, too. In my experience, there are plenty of human "angels" with an impressive readiness to walk beside someone in difficulty. But when the going gets vicious, I can't help wondering if companionship on this journey is enough. What does Annie, what do *all* of us, really need when we experience despair and inner emptiness? For that matter, what spiritual resources, if any, do we need when life is easy and filled with joy? Do "spiritual resources" really make a difference?

We humans are wonderfully incongruous. We think God is dead and Elvis is alive! We often genuinely wish to serve God, but only as advisors. We're like Paddy, the Irishman who was driving down the street in a sweat because he had an important meeting and couldn't find a parking place. Looking up at heaven he said, "Lord, take pity on me. If you find me a parking place, I will go to Mass every Sunday for the rest of me life and give up Irish whiskey." Miraculously, a parking place appeared just

---

1. Unless otherwise noted, poems in this work are by Sarah Voss.

then, and Paddy looked up once again. "Never mind," he said, "I found one."[2]

I am a Unitarian Universalist minister married to an Irishman and I love these oh-so-common incongruities. My journey as minister has been rather an odd one, often carting me into little-explored and often chaotic intellectual landscapes, while also bringing me into great intimacy with the spiritual vicissitudes of our species. In the process, my own spiritual life has benefited immensely from the insights, reflections, and encouragement of many other seekers.

I am also a minister who used to teach mathematics. When I changed careers in the late 1980s, I decided to integrate my previous career in math with my new career in religion. Given the times and the subjects involved, not everyone encouraged me, and those who did, such as my doctoral thesis advisor, sometimes didn't know quite how. I floundered before I finally realized that what drew me to this path was the belief that mathematical metaphors ("mathaphors") could be used to help motivate spiritual growth. I discovered more. Not only could mathaphors act as a catalyst in this capacity, but (1) they have done so historically, (2) they are doing so presently, and (3) they offer a unique and hopeful tool for doing so in the future. I have written elsewhere about the first two of these uses. In this guide, I focus on the third, how mathaphors can offer a tool for creating a more deeply spiritual future.

There is a need for us to create a more deeply spiritual future because the current state of our world is worrisome. Consider, for example, the endless religious wars in the Middle East and elsewhere; the pronounced poverty and increasingly asymmetric distribution of world assets into the hands of a few; the hateful discrimination still manifesting against gay people and Black people and women and animals (no prioritizing order intended); the worrisome aspects of consumerism and AI technology and biogenetic discoveries; our increasing societal drug abuse and domestic and other violence; global warming, the 2020 pandemic, and all the other signs that not all's right in God's world. We should worry. But we should also be hopeful and look at these things as opportunity for change. This guide to creative spiritual living is an attempt to foster this opportunity.

Sally McFague, whose work with religious metaphors has helped open theology to new directions (e.g., God as female), wrote that "a

---

2. Although I have a good sense of humor and can even be funny all by myself, I am not a great jokester. These jokes came from assorted online collections.

metaphor is seeing one thing as something else."[3] By extension, a *mathaphor* is seeing one thing as something mathematical.

A *holy* mathaphor is seeing something spiritual in terms of something mathematical. An old example of a holy mathaphor can be found in Plato's declaration that God was a geometer: "God ever geometrizes." A recent example of a holy mathaphor occurs in William Butler Yeats's poetry: "If it be true that God is a circle whose centre [sic] is everywhere, the saint goes to the centre, the poet and the artist to the ring where everything comes round again."[5] And an even more recent example of a holy mathaphor is found in a *Far Side* cartoon where "God at his computer" is clearly a contemporary mathematical genius, a sophisticated computer-expert, a skilled manipulator of zeros and ones.

A Contemporary Mathaphor

"In the Beginning"[4]

In the beginning there was the computer. And God said
Let there be light!
#Enter user id.
%>God
#Enter password.
%>Omniscient
#Password incorrect. Try again.
%>Omnipotent
#Password incorrect. Try again.
%>Technocrat
#And God logged on at 12:01:00 AM, Sunday, March 1.
%>Move man to Garden edn
#Done
%>Run multiplication
#Execution terminated. 4 errors.
%>Copy woman from man
#Done
%>Run multiplication
#Execution terminated. 2 errors.

Contemporary mathaphors are far more prevalent than most people realize. They simultaneously reveal the current status of life on this planet and shape the direction of our future. They are handy tools to use in the religious medium because mathematics is generally respected even if it isn't liked. People who become upset with each other about the use of terms such as *prayer, soul, sin,* and *God* will often listen to discussions

---

3. McFague, *Metaphorical Theology*, 15.

4. Unknown author, "In the Beginning," drawn from a longer piece.

5. Cited in Manganiello, *T. S. Eliot and Dante*.

about these spiritual ideas when they are presented in a form as seemingly novel as mathematics. Such individuals even tend to set aside, at least temporarily, their preconceived notions and actually engage in dialogue, an activity that happens all too infrequently in this era of religious fundamentalism versus everyone else.

However, getting lay people to listen to anything that has the word *math* in it is sometimes tricky. From the pulpit I've given a number of what I call *math* sermons. At first, I'd call them that in the "upcoming" section of the church newsletter, but I quickly learned that folks with math anxiety would stay away, so I began to speak first and *then* tell what it was. My math sermons bore titles such as "Reflections about Nothing," "Out of Statistics, Hope," "Prayers That Count," "Our Electronic Church," "Gödel on Evil," "Dare to Be Average," "Beyond Copernicus," "God and Quantum Transitions," "Computers and Consciousness," "Toward a Cantorian Religion," "Living Better on the 'Chaotic' Edge," "How Fuzzy Logic Might Save Souls," "Get a 'Moral' Brain," and "Our Entangled Web." The "Entangled" one was a bust! Still, one true bust out of the bunch is not so bad, really, and that one happened only after I listened to William Wootters of Williams College give an absolutely marvelous talk on quantum teleportation—so marvelous that I committed to doing a sermon on the subject before I realized that it wasn't nearly as easy to communicate the physical essence of teleportation as Wootters, one of the pioneers in the field, made it appear.

Overall, these math sermons were well enough received to persuade me that math works as an inspirational language tool as long as you're just talking about it, rather than actually doing it. The secret is to use math metaphorically. Thirty years ago, almost no one used "mathematics" and "metaphor" in the same sentence, but that is no longer the case. Which is not to say that three decades ago mathematics was not used metaphorically; it's just that few people realized that was what was happening.[6] Today, however, books abound with mathaphorical titles and content,[7]

---

6. Browse through the items in a *Bibliography of Christianity and Mathematics, 1910–1983* (Chase and Jongsma), for example, and you'll find evidence of manuscripts relying on "Analogies drawn between mathematics and Christianity" and "Some [theological] implications of Gödel's theorem" and "Infinite models in mathematics [which] are useful in understanding and appreciating God." Note the lack of direct use of the term "metaphor." Note also in this resource the frequently negative tone to such renderings. E.g., "To call God a mathematician is 'a serious blunder' which belittles the idea of God."

7. Representative titles include: *NonZero: The Logic of Human Destiny* by Robert Wright; *Tao of Chaos* by Katya Walter; *Loom of God: Mathematical Tapestries at the*

religion and science conferences explicitly deal with the issue,[8] academic courses are taught about mathematics and metaphor,[9] and the general public can see fine examples played out dramatically in movie theaters.[10] Mathaphors are creeping into the collective consciousness, and for good cause. They offer possibilities of a more compassionate future. Like most things, of course, this hope is in the making.

Mathematics is unique as a language in that it is simultaneously practical (quantitative) and imaginative (qualitative). It allows us to do the computation necessary to estimate, say, fairness and equitable outcomes. And it opens the metaphorical doors to unexplored higher moral planes. True enough, it doesn't promise to take us through those doors. Nor is it Pollyanna-ish. It can point us in the direction of lower moral planes as well. But without it, our vision would be far more limited, and our spirits kept lashed to the ground, which is a little like saying, as the ancient Pythagoreans did, that All is number, and then insisting that all numbers must be rational.

This book is for spiritual seekers in many different forms. I come to it as a once-upon-a-time atheist, who, over the years, shifted away from that perspective to one that is mystic. I also come as just another fellow

---

Edge of Time by Clifford Pickover; *Age of Spiritual Machines* by Ray Kurzweil; *Physics of Immortality* by Frank Tipler; *Holotropic Mind* by Stanislav Grof; *Quantum Theology* by Dana Zohar; *Probability of God: A Simple Calculation That Proves the Ultimate Truth* by Stephen Unwin; *God Particle* by Leon Lederman and Dick Teresi; *Is God a Mathematician?* by Mario Livio; *Our Mathematical Universe* by Max Tegmark; *What Number Is God?* by Sarah Voss; *Zero: Reflections about Nothing* by Sarah Voss. I admit to being partial to the last two cited.

8. Miller, "Garden to Gauss." From a 1998 conference: "This paper is not proposing a mathematical model of sin by which we might be able to predict the moral quality of human behavior. Instead, this paper is proposing a mathematical metaphor which may illumine the conceptual understanding of sin."

9. Well, mine anyway. I've taught variations of Math, a New Language of Theology, a Templeton award-winning course which I first offered at the University of Nebraska, Omaha and subsequently at the Graduate Theological Union in Berkeley and at the Meadville Lombard School of Theology in Chicago. I've also taught workshops on "moral math" in various venues—for a description, see Voss, "Workshop."

10. Among the more stimulating are *Timecode* (illustrates superposition of the quantum void—just try watching four different stories at the same time), *Bicentennial Man* (artificial intelligence turns into real life), *Contact* (where math is seen as a "universal" language), *Thirteenth Floor* (life is just a virtual simulation), *Matrix* (Tipler's *Physics of Immortality* in cinematic display), and *Her* (technology opens gigantic new frontiers in social relationships). Several online sites also highlight math found in movies. Two good ones are Knill, "Mathematics in Movies"; and Reinhold, "Math in the Movies."

searcher trying to find answers to a lot of questions about faith, and it turns out that many of the answers I've claimed started out as mathematical insights. This creative spirituality guide introduces several dozen such insights which, collected, create an area outside the envelope of most contemporary spiritual thinking. Some of these spiritually directed notions are reproduced here just as they have been printed elsewhere. A few are reshaped from my math sermons. Others are new, written just for this collection. By gathering these ideas in one place, I seek to bear witness to an old journey that mystics of all modes refer to as the oneness of everything. There are many different souls in the reality we are currently experiencing, all seemingly different one from the other. Yet when you add them all up, you just get God.

Still, the language I use in this guide to creative spirituality differs from other approaches to communicate mystical concerns. For example, "The Bear Is Back"—the poem I chose to begin this introduction—illustrates a more traditional use of poetry to highlight spiritual needs. I close this introduction with another poem, one addressing this same need, only this one is a math poem in that it uses a mathaphor rather than a metaphor to inspire a continued journey into the spiritual world. Something similar (mostly minus the poetry) happens throughout the collection.

The Strange Attractor of Hope

Takes twenty-eight days minimum,
I'm told, to change neuronal pathways

from ones committed to negativity
to those that prefer positive messages.

Fine. I can deal with a February's worth
of hard alteration even if the outcome

is uncertain since calcified power to see
the world through depression's filter

is unlikely to skulk away, rebuked
by a simple twist in desire. Still,

I shall venture forth like a puppy
testing the ground rules of survival

in this newly reconstructed mind-set
I'm learning to call home.

Part 1: My Math Mystic Journey

"HOW TO REDUCE FRACTIONS"

Humor makes everything easier.

Society's most powerful metaphors
flow from the latest technology
known to the culture.
Presently we find God depicted
as a computer maestro.

Humor makes everything easier.

Sometimes the comparison is subtle
as when cosmologist John Barrow
speculates that the entire universe
is a giant computer. More overt
is the *Far Side* cartoon where an old
guy with a long white beard sits before
his computer. The caption:
God at his computer. On the screen
a massive construction block dangles
over the head of an unsuspecting man.
God's finger hovers over the *smite* key.

Humor makes everything easier.

In the past God was depicted
as a ruler, a judge, a king. Now, God
is a computer-mathematician.
This is as funny as reducing fractions
by shrinking the font size.
Still, neither is wrong.

$$\Large 6/8 = \normalsize 6/8 = \small 6/8$$
and humor makes everything easier.

Chapter 1: A Bridge to Trust[1]

$e^{i\pi} + 1 = 0$ (Euler's equation)[2]

Everything important is connected.

THE SOCIETY WHERE MOST of us grew up is historically unusual in that it has placed unprecedented emphasis on individual rights and empowerment. It is unsurprising, then, that, to many of us, the mystical contention that we really aren't separate from each other at all seems contrary to our most fundamental learnings and intuitions. What I do affects what you do which affects what the guy about to blow up a vehicle does to deter the Winter Olympics which affects what Martin Luther King, Jr., said fifty years earlier about racial issues which affects how fast the wings of a butterfly flap on the other side of the world. Really? What ocean did you fall into? The illogic of this string of events troubles us even if we switch around the time sequence of the events so they fall in the familiar order of past to present. *Some* things are connected, yes. But *all*? Surely not in *this* world.

So say the rationalist, the scientist, the sane, the normal, the educated, the philosophic, and the frightened child of many years ago who was trying to find her way across from one side of a creek to the other with only a slippery, fallen log to help her. That child (not coincidentally) was me when I was about seven and trying to follow my older brother across

---

1. This chapter was published previously as an essay. See Voss, "Miraculous," 78–83. A sermon version ("Bridge to Trust") was offered on February 2, 2014. It can be found (as can all the sermons referenced in this book) in "Rev. Sarah Voss's Math Sermons," on my dedicated website, www.PiZine.org.

2. Euler had more than one formula, but this is the only one in this chapter. I also refer to it here as an equation and as an identity.

a too-high, too-round log in the creek. Why, there was a *real* bridge just around the bend! Nonetheless, I was so afraid I froze a third of the way across that log and to this day I feel the shame of needing my big brother to come back to rescue me.

In a similar fashion, when it comes to trusting the notion that everything important is connected, a lot of us today simply can't get there. We end up frozen by our belief that this idea is too round, too high, too scary, too much like magical thinking. We resist letting go of our independence, our individual egos. To think of being intimately connected with everything else seems as though we might lose that voice within that belongs to us alone. Math gives us a model that shows how being connected enhances that individual identity rather than destroying it. This awareness brings with it a perspective grounded in beauty rather than fear of loss. My favorite example of this model is the awesome equation named for the Swiss mathematician Leonhard Euler, who, in the early 1700s, found meaningful and unexpected connections between five of the most prominent mathematical notions that exist: 0, 1, e, i, and pi (π).

Zero (0) is a real number and the additive identity.[3] One (1) is a real number, the first counting number, and the multiplicative identity.[4] The constant *e*, equal to 2.71828182 . . . , is a real, transcendental (i.e., non-algebraic)[5] number which is the base of natural logarithms.[6] The imaginary (not "real") number *i* is the square root of -1 and is essential to our understanding of complex numbers.[7] Pi (or π) is the ratio of the circumference of a circle to its diameter, which is a real, transcendental number approximately equal to 3.14159265. Did you know that the state

---

3. Add 0 to any number and you get the identical number back. Zero is a real number, but it is neither positive nor negative. Zero is also rational, i.e., it can be expressed in fractional form.

4. Multiply any number by 1 and you get the identical number back. One (1) is rational, real, and positive.

5. An algebraic number is a root of a non-zero polynomial with rational coefficients (in case you are interested). One (1) is an algebraic number since it is the root (solution) to the polynomial equation $x^2 - 1 = 0$. Negative one (-1) is rational, real, and algebraic since it is also a solution to this same equation.

6. The natural logarithm of a number x is the power to which e would have to be raised to equal x. For example, ln 7.389 . . . is 2, because $e^2 = 7.389$ . . . . The natural log of e itself, ln(e), is 1 because $e^1 = e$, while the natural logarithm of 1, ln1, is 0, since $e^0 = 1$. See Wikipedia, "Natural Logarithm."

7. Imaginary numbers are not real (i.e., they have no place on the real number line). They are part of the complex number system, which is used widely in many areas of mathematics.

of Indiana once tried to legislate that the value of π was precisely 3?[8] Heretics! It is perhaps unsurprising that these numbers can be related to each other, but what is unexpected is how simple the mathematics can be that relates them. The equation at the beginning of this chapter ($e^{i\pi} + 1 = 0$) is a statement of the relationship between these five significant numbers, but the formula may be rewritten in different ways, each of which puts a slightly different spin on the relationship. For example, $e^{ix} = \cos(x) + i\sin(x)$ turns the equation (or, more precisely, a general version of the equation) into a trigonometric relationship, while $-1 = e^{i\pi}$ obscures the zero and places the focus on a negative number. Such rearrangements can be fun, as in "How many mathematicians does it take to change a light bulb?" With a minor adjustment to the second of these two variations on Euler's formula, we can credibly answer $-e^{i\pi}$, which, of course, is 1.[9]

This ability to cast related items into seemingly different equations always reminds me of the diffused results produced when several artists render the same visual scene with different techniques, as, for instance, when one uses oils, a second paints with watercolors, a third renders the scene abstractly, another takes a photo, and someone else hides the scene within another picture. I once met an artist who showed me precisely such an "illusive" painting and then told me about a similar one he'd been commissioned to do of some VIP's mistress. The VIP wanted to hang it over his fireplace but didn't want his wife to be able to see the portrait portion, so the artist painted the mistress in a way that became obvious only when the entire picture was turned upside-down.

Something similar (although usually less ethically questionable) happens when we work with Euler's equation. Some, for instance, emphasize the importance of π and point out that Euler's work has a lot to tell us about circular motion. Others spotlight the *e*, and find the equation's usefulness in the mathematics of finances (e.g., compounding interest). In truth, however, most mathematicians appreciate the equation because it offers further insight into many additional areas of mathematics, not because of any practical use in the real world. Indeed, what *is* it used for? One blogger on the subject claims that the best answer to that question

---

8. Perhaps it was 4, though most likely it was an exact (but still inaccurate) 3.2: Adams, "Did a State Legislature." Or maybe it was another state: Rational Wiki, "Indiana Pi Bill."

9. I found this mathematical joke online: Weisstein, "Euler Formula." For a few of the other sites useful to this chapter, see O'Neill, "Euler's Formula"; Khan Academy, "Euler's Formula and Euler's Identity"; and Azad, "Intuitive Understanding."

is "to get annoying philosophers to shut up." Another adds that Euler's formula represents "a stunningly beautiful relationship; what else does it need to be?" From my mystic perspective, of course, that last quip wins the prize![10]

Euler's formula is simply elegant. To realize that these very distinct numbers are linked together in such unanticipated ways is often deeply satisfying. A math friend notes that Euler's formula contains numbers that are not connected by some complicated infinite series, or some messy integral, but only by simple arithmetic operations and exponentiation, and the resulting simplicity is stunning. Analogously, he adds, it's a little like discovering ancestors we'd not have expected: surprising, perhaps, but also somehow gratifying.[11] As another mathematician put it, Euler's identity "connects all these profound numbers in some mystical way that shows there is some connectedness to the universe . . . . If this doesn't blow your mind, you really have no emotion."[12] However, the synergism between these five numbers does not detract from their importance as separate entities/concepts. These famous numbers each have entire books written about them.[13] If anything, their unusual interconnection adds extra weight to their individual stature.

Mathematics is reassuring like that—it allows us to prove ideas in ways we tend to trust even if we don't fully grasp them. Furthermore, when we accept such mathematical realities, it becomes easier to accept similar notions in non-mathematical arenas. So it is, I believe, that during those mystical moments when we let go of our everyday feelings of separateness and relax into the experience of unconditional unity with the world, we don't lose our own sense of self. Rather, we see our place in the world from a perspective characterized by an omnipresent peace and an unparalleled optimism that inspires us to become more robust ourselves.

When we feel truly connected with each other, something new takes hold between us and we begin to identify with the *whole* we make in much the same fashion that our arms and legs automatically work in concert to assist the one body of which they are a part. We care more.

10. These two answers came from Anjruu, "Euler's Identity."

11. Thomas McFarlane, personal communication.

12. Khan Academy, "Euler's Formula and Euler's Identity." The comment approximates the negation of the common myth that rationality and precision lead to emotionlessness. See Levine, *Healing*.

13. See Downey, *History of Zero*; Otoshi, *One*; Maor, *e: The Story*; Nahin, *Imaginary Tale*; and Beckmann, *History of Pi*.

We share more. We become more trusting of each other. Our collective future will be shaped by our ability (or lack thereof) to develop these individual strengths. The results of a recent survey indicate a disturbing decline in our social capital, including trust:

> For four decades, a gut-level mainstay of democracy—trust in the other fellow—has been quietly draining away . . . . Americans are suspicious of one another in everyday encounters. Less than a third expressed trust in clerks who swipe their credit cards, drivers on the road or people they meet when traveling. "I'm leery of everybody," said [one young man] from Albany, N.Y. "Caution is always a factor."
>
> Does it matter that Americans are suspicious of one another? Yes, say worried political and social scientists. What's known as *social trust* brings good things: a society in which it's easier to compromise or make a deal; in which people are willing to work with those who are different from them for the common good; in which trust appears to promote economic growth.[14]

Forty years ago, half the people polled felt that most people could be trusted. Today, only a third of Americans feel that way. Analysts differ in what has triggered this drop in social capital, which, incidentally, wasn't all that impressive even forty years ago. Still, we appear to be headed in the wrong direction. Some point an accusing finger at deterioration in community and civic life—less socializing, fewer community meetings, neighbors who don't even know each other. Some cast aspersions on the ills of modern technology: hackers, viruses, hateful Internet posts, and other actions which shatter trust.[15] Still others believe economic inequality is behind this negative movement; with the gap between the rich and poor widened irrevocably. Regardless of cause, we need to turn this trend around. Our future will benefit from our actively cultivating peace and optimism. We need some outside-the-box thinking about how to do this. Euler's mathematical insight has left a beautiful legacy which has thrilled and stimulated countless mathematicians. Some mathematicians (and others) are perfectly content to leave it at that. But for myself, I like to add it to the growing set of tools each of us can use to grow our individual and collective spiritual lives.

---

14. Associated Press, "Trust: Social Media," 8.

15. "I trace it to technology growing much faster than our human ability to cope with it. The rapid growth has also had a lot to do with adding to income inequality. But that doesn't mean we should reject technology—just advance in comparable way spiritually!" Daniel Levine, personal correspondence.

When I first encountered Euler's formula, I already knew about the mathematical importance of 0, 1, e, i, and π, but I'd entertained not a clue about their possible interconnection. It was a startling and mystifying insight. At the time, I was still an atheist. When I initially entered the dark hour of what I later realized was my mystic journey, I was overwhelmed by distrust on almost all levels of my being. It was a bad time for me where I, like the young man from Albany cited above, was leery of everybody and everything. Somehow, mathematics was the exception, and in my eventual embrace of a new spiritual outlook, my trust in math was a bridge for me. If such seemingly distinct and complex ideas as those represented by the numbers found in Euler's equation could be connected, then maybe I, too, could be connected to the larger world in ways I had not previously understood. I took a risk and crossed that bridge. On the other side lay hope.

Mathaphors are tools. We can choose to use them.

Chapter 2: The Mystical Realm

You can have consistency or completeness, but not necessarily both simultaneously.—Gödel's Incompleteness Theorem

I am lying. This sentence is false. All Americans are liars.

When you look at the picture in figure 2.1, you might see an old crone or a young woman.

Fig. 2.1. *My Wife and My Mother-in-Law*, W. E. Hill, 1915.

When I look in my mirror, I see an old crone *and* a young woman.

The existence of God is unprovable. The existence of God is undecidable. The existence of God is true.

This is a picture (P) of an old woman. This is not a picture (not-P) of an old woman. "P and not-P" is a true statement.

The set of all mystics is not a member of itself. The set of all non-mystics is a member of itself.

From the perspective of formal mathematical logic, the statements above are interesting oddities. They require us to think in depth. A lot of us, however, get brain-burn when we think about them in too much depth. In spite of this characteristic, such sentences have fascinated some individuals for thousands of years. Perhaps the earliest such person was Epimenides, an ancient Greek who lived around 500–600 BCE, professed a mystical theology, dealt with oracles, wandered outside his body, slept for fifty-seven years straight, and lived to a ripe old age of 299 years.[1] Well, maybe, maybe not! In any case, Epimenides is credited with the invention of the liar's paradox, variations of which appear in the first three statements above. The liar's paradox relies on its self-reflexivity for its punch. I am an American. Therefore, when I say that all Americans are liars, I (an American) am a liar. But because I am an American who is lying, I am, paradoxically, also telling the truth. If I weren't an American (if there were no self-reflexivity in this statement), then the statement might be true or it might be false, but it would not be both. This was essentially the paradox Epimenides created, when he, an inhabitant of the largest Greek island, Crete, stated that "All Cretans are liars."

One of the most extraordinary thinkers to deal with such paradoxes in modern times was a quiet, retiring mathematician/philosopher named Kurt Gödel. Gödel is possibly the greatest logician of the twentieth century, famed in particular for two mathematical theorems (called his incompleteness theorems) which he developed in the early 1930s. At the time, he was living in his native Moravia, then a mostly Czechoslovakian region with a small German-speaking populace, of which his family was part. He lectured at the University of Vienna and researched ideas about formal mathematical systems. In particular, his incompleteness theorems

1. See Tikkanen and Spe, "Epimenides."

dealt with *recursive* functions, which involve a mathematical notion similar to that of self-reflexivity.

A simple algebraic example of a recursive function is the process which takes any number and squares it, a process currently depicted in mathematics by the symbolism $f(x) = x^2$ (read "f of x equals x squared"). In this case, recursiveness results when a number is chosen, squared, and then the answer is squared, and then *that* answer is squared and so on indefinitely. For instance, squaring 2 results in 4, squaring 4 results in 16, squaring 16 results in 256, squaring 256 produces 65,536, and so forth. In general, recursive functions involve determining the result of a mathematical process, then using the result in the same process to find another result, and so on ad infinitum. Recursivity is probably best known today in the form of fractals—those curious shapes a computer program creates when it solves some function $f(x)$ (read "f of x" or "function of the variable x") for some specific value of x, plugs the answer back into the same function to get a new result, plugs the new result back into the function, and repeats this process again and again.[2] The effect is a little like nesting dolls: the same pattern endlessly reappears at different scales.

Using recursive functions, Gödel was able to show that in some formal mathematical systems it is impossible to have both consistency (the property of a logical system which says there are no statements which the system regards as both true and false) and completeness (where the truth or falsity of all statements in the system is "provable").[3] There are lots of good resources available, many online, for deeper explanations of these ideas, but they are all very complex. As I've grown older, I've grown wise enough to recognize some of my own limitations, so I am not even going to attempt to explain the math behind Gödel's ideas. Believe me, I am consistent in my completeness in this regard!

Moreover, the experts in this mathematics are not shy about voicing their distaste for people (such as myself) who make analogies based on Gödel's work that have nothing to do with formal math systems.[4] None of

---

2. Here is one (of many) good sites about fractals: https://fractalfoundation.org/.

3. These two quotes came from an online site (www.chaos.org.uk) which has changed and apparently no longer includes them.

4. See Franzen, *Gödel's Theorem*. In a review of this book (see Raatikainen, "Review") the reviewer notes that Gödel's mathematical incompleteness theorem "is invoked not only by mathematicians, logicians, and philosophers but also by physicists, theologians, literary critics, architects, and others. . . . It is sometimes claimed to prove the existence of God or of free will, the necessary incompleteness of the Bible or of the U.S. Constitution, or the impossibility of genuine knowledge in mathematics—just to name a few of the many alleged applications." Such discussions, Raatikainen suggests,

which stops me from "playing" herein with metaphorical interpretations of Gödel's theories.

I picture Gödel (1906–78) as a contemporary of my paternal parent (1908–67), for the mathematician was only two years older and lived roughly a decade longer than my father. As young children, both Gödel and my father suffered serious illnesses, one of which stunted my father's future growth while the other turned Gödel into a lifelong hypochondriac, forever convinced he had a weak heart. In most other ways, that ended the similarity between their life-pathways.

My father was a smart man, an educated farmer who married my mother in the midst of the Great Depression, raised three children, and lived his entire life in northeastern Ohio, where, until his health failed irreversibly, he was part-owner of a family business that produced, bottled, and delivered milk and milk products to the surrounding area. My dad loved farming and was naturally gregarious and interested in what others were doing. In his later years, he became politically active and, in addition to farming, served as a county commissioner. Kurt Gödel, by comparison, was a mostly self-taught genius who, because of the Nazi threat to European scientists, immigrated with his wife Adele to the United States in 1940 and spent the rest of his life teaching and working at Princeton. He lived a prolific but rather reclusive lifestyle, though it included frequent walks with his good friend Albert Einstein. Gödel was obsessed with his health. In his later years, he grew paranoid about germs, refused to eat anything not prepared by his wife, and, when Adele herself became ill and unable to tend him, basically starved himself to death in a Princeton hospital.

It occurs to me that my father, who called himself an ordinary man, would likely be somewhat embarrassed by this comparison of him to a genius who forever changed the shape of mathematics. There is the set of Gödel-like entities, and then there is the set of all non-Gödel-like entities. The latter set is a member of

Fig. 2.2. Sarah as a Young Mother

"show more enthusiasm than competence."

itself, and thus is part of a mathematics which (as Gödel might have put it) "twists back on itself, like a self-eating snake."

With this snake we find, again, the ever-present notion in this life of self-reflexivity. When I look in the mirror I see the young woman pictured in figure 2.2.

I also see the seventy-plus-year-old woman who wrote this guide. How can that possibly be? Yet, it happens. In my mind's eye, I really do see both images, and also the image in figure 2.3, which my father knew.

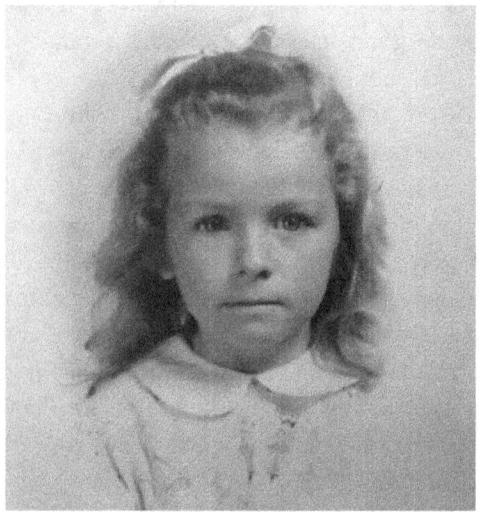

Fig. 2.3. Sarah as a Child

In fact, I see *countless* images. Yet, paradoxically, in material space I can never see my face or my back or my ears or the hair on top of my head in even *one* of these "self" images. As any human with a mirror—or a reflecting pool of water—knows, all of these basic possibilities are both true and not true. That's because we exist not only in material space but also in the mystic realm. We exist like a fish inside a sea filled with other fish, some of which eat the others just in order to continue to exist. It's confusing. And it's also perfectly clear. It's confusing because it's inconsistent; there are things about the mystic realm that are both true and false. It's also incomplete: there are statements in the mystic realm that can be formulated but not proved. One simple example is "God exists." People have been trying (and failing) to prove, or disprove, this simple statement forever.

From my perspective we all live both in material space and in the mystic realm. Both realms depict the Whole, but they have different parameters, much as a photoshopped photograph can be the product of several distinct but merged overlays. The governing rules of order are somewhat different in each realm. For instance, consistency and completeness (and their opposites) are characteristics of both realms, but in material space consistency and completeness work in tandem, always aligned in such a way that if one moves from background to foreground (or vice versa) so does the other. In the mystic realm, however, consistency often seems to be paired with incompleteness and completeness with inconsistency. À la Gödel, and with apologies to those who despise people who violate good science by messing around with metaphors drawn from it.

What is so special about the mystic realm? Everything, just as everything about material space is special. Material space is like one of the settings we get when we look at the universe through a kaleidoscope. We see only a portion of the total beads (atoms, protons and electrons, or whatever) that twirl around and illuminate with light.[5] Most remain in the background. Every twirl of the kaleidoscope brings to the foreground a change in emphasis, i.e., a new design. Some designs are more interesting, more beautiful, more desirable than others. The mystic realm, however, is like the kaleidoscope itself—the vehicle for the design process. Material space is a distinction. The mystic realm is the magnetism that holds the distinction together.[6]

Humans have been fascinated with mystical reality for eons—since way before Epimenides, even.[7] The mystic view is not relegated to any one religion, nor to religion in general, although many religions do claim a mystic element. There are common characteristics to all of these mystic perspectives.[8] For example, most mystics aim in some fashion to honor and even merge with a higher consciousness, often called God. What I find undermentioned in so many such lists is what may be termed the Gödel factor, by which I mean the acceptance of imperfection (cf. incompleteness) and paradox (cf. inconsistency). The Gödel factor is particularly significant for those of us in material space who rely on rational

---

5. See Voss, *What Number?*, 56–60; 148–60. See also chapter 15 herein.

6. This is an allusion to the work of the twentieth-century British mathematician C. Spencer-Brown in *Laws of Form*, about which I will say more in chapter 16.

7. We can trace mystic notions back to the Eleusinian Mysteries of the fifteenth century BCE.

8. See Shrader, "Seven Characteristics." Online, a comprehensive site with a very contemporary focus is https://www.themystic.org.

challenge and a functioning system of order for meaning making. Indeed, its import is readily apparent in each of our lives, though it is easily overlooked. As a professor of mine once said, the obvious is always the hardest to see.[9] I will illustrate with some reflections about my father.

Both of my parents were in their late thirties when I was born. I was their bonus baby, a fact about which my father said, when I was fifteen-ish and not very self-confident, that he was the worst man in the world for about nine months before I arrived. My parents already had a family (my older sister and brother who were nine and seven, respectively, at the time of my birth). Apparently, my mother had been told she should not have any more children, though nobody ever shared with me just why. That turned out to be typical. There were *lots* of things that nobody ever shared with me, at least not in my childhood, and, more often, not at all. My mother lived to just short of her ninety-third birthday, so I had her in my life for five and a half decades—long enough to really be able to see her as an adult—but not so with my father, who died when I had just turned twenty-two.

I had a little over two decades with my dad. Roughly speaking, the first one was characterized by his purity (he could do no wrong) and the second by his prudery (he wanted me to do no wrong). Neither, of course, was wholly true—it's just how I remember them. In the first extended decade (eleven years), I spent quite a bit of time with my dad because his work—farming—was at home. I tagged along with him here and there, observing everything and understanding a little.

I remember him carrying the four-year-old me on his shoulders early one evening into his mother's living room, where *his* dad was lying in an open coffin. When he carried me upstairs, I was upset because I wanted to stay downstairs longer and see what all those people, and my "sleeping" grandfather, were doing. I remember him tending to some unpleasant medicinal needs when I was five or so and had been hospitalized for serious complications from the old-fashioned measles. I was frightened and crying hard and he had to restrain me. I remember the time he said, within my hearing, that I was better able to entertain myself than any other child he had ever seen. I remember the happy feeling his words of praise brought me. I remember clinging to his leg while I waited, interminably it seemed, for him to finish his business at the town mill. I remember once, at supper, how he quit the table and washed my sibling's

---

9. Elton Carter. This was his mantra in a class he taught at the University of Nebraska at Omaha on transformational communication.

mouth out with soap. I watched, horrified that the same thing might happen to me, too, and determined not to ever let it happen. (It didn't!) I remember (ever so vaguely) him introducing me to one of the women customers on his milk delivery route, and how she exclaimed over me and how there was something odd about the situation, some undercurrent of expectation, of connection which I felt even as a tiny child—but, of course, there was no way of finding out what it was. Years and years later, someone in my extended family dropped a hint of an affair, but even then, it was oblique. When I was ten, my father taught me to drive a tractor and paid me real money for keeping track of my hours baling hay. Dad was always, always my hero.

As the second extended decade took shape, my father's various rules began to feel oppressive. One day I was sent out to the field with a message for my father, and I was just ever so slightly smart-mouthed, but that was enough for him to send me forthwith to my room, the first and only time that ever occurred. I felt diminished and unfairly punished, for I hadn't really said anything *that* naughty! My attitude, however, had been dripping with a sense of my pushing back, and he was having none of it.

Another time, my sister, home from college for the summer, let it be known that she now smoked, something directly contrary to his "women don't smoke" law. I remember him shaking his head in frustration but saying nothing because by then my sister had become an adult, and it was no longer his business. (Her smoking turned into a life-long addiction and she died prematurely and unexpectedly when she was precisely the age our father had been when he died.)

I remember how he coached and guided me, provided the animals, supplies, and all sorts of transportation, and unfailingly encouraged me so that I could show 4-H cattle at the county fair. How he was unwaveringly proud of me for my schoolwork, my truthfulness, my ever-questioning mind. How he modeled going to church every Sunday. How horrible and crushing was the defeat of his death, how I wept over his bedside and how I was too sick to go to his funeral.

In hindsight, I can see how mixed the messages were that my father's words and actions presented to me. He loved me, but he was often angry. He loved me, but my mother often wouldn't talk directly to him and so he came to use me, instead of her, as his sounding board. He loved me, but he died anyway, and left. There was enormous paradox and imperfection, inconsistency and incompleteness in his actions and in our relationship. So many unanswered questions. So much hidden.

Except this: I never doubted his love, and I learned to read the inconsistencies and to become aware of the imperfections, and to love him wholeheartedly anyway. In effect, he prepared me for my later journey into The Mystic Realm by helping to create an early environment which trained me to recognize and respond to everyday situations where what was said in words and what was said not in words often did not match. Almost five decades after my father died, I now begin to realize the understanding and wisdom he helped me grow into.

But of course, this is not just my story; this is part of the human condition. This is the nature of material space, wherein we work long and diligently just to begin to understand and resolve the often unseen (but always felt) imperfection and paradox of our lives. The details above are mine, but the basic story belongs to humankind. Children are the recursive units of our human experience. We plug them into the family equation, and they spin out patterns that repeat the family history. We strive for consistency and completeness, but what we get again and again is the same old imperfect and paradoxical patterns, albeit with variations. The Gödel factor, to which we are all subject, helps bring clarity to this aspect of our learning here on earth.

Chapter 3: A Little Irrationality Is Good for a Mystic

Real Number Line: There's more irrationality than rationality.

WHEN HE WAS IN the sixth grade, I asked my grandson John if he knew what a number line was. He said "yes," that he had studied it in the third or fourth grade, that he now knew about positive and negative integers, fractions, and other rational numbers, and that he currently was learning about irrationals. I was unsurprised by his response. He'd already taken some advanced classes in math, so I figured he would probably be conversant with this language of numbers.

John was a little younger than I was when I first encountered these ideas, but not much. I grew up, as did my age-mates, with this number-line image. What I did not realize until recently was that, although its first recorded use was by John Wallis in 1685,[1] the number line wasn't even a part of math education until about 1950. This discovery shocked me. Somehow, I had taken the existence of the number line, along with most of what I was taught as a child, as an incontrovertible fact that had been around more or less forever. If pressed, I'd acknowledge that the early civilizations probably had no idea what a number line entailed, but *I* thought it was an eternal truth, not something that was taught to children only after I was born. In addition to being shocking to me, this recent awareness was humbling, as such insights usually are. Time and time again my assumptions and presumptions of truth have proven to be malleable.

Kids today learn about the number line pretty much the way I did. Draw a straight line, pick an arbitrary starting point and an arbitrary unit

---

1. Wikipedia, "John Wallis."

and mark off the integers (1, 2, 3, 4 . . .) as on a ruler; add 0; add negative numbers and mark out some fractions and, eventually, convert them all to decimal form so you can find places for irrational numbers (such as pi, the square root of 2, or the cube root of 3). This process constructs a model for *all* the real numbers because there is a unique place for each and every real number on this line, which, of course, is isomorphic to any other scaled number line. The line is continuous, yet it can always be magnified to squeeze in any other real number desired. It's an excellent model for the real numbers, especially for children, because it is intuitive and simple, and it provides a way of introducing arithmetic and ordering into the set of all decimal expansions.[2]

Intuitive as it is, the real number line developed slowly over a great deal of time, and there are now several other models in use to explain the same things. In particular, there are the Weierstrass-Stolz, the Dedekind, and the Meray-Conner models, all three of which depend on sophisticated mathematics usually introduced in advanced courses on analysis.[3] It's also worth mentioning that in the last few centuries mathematicians developed numbers which are *not* real, such as the complex numbers (which include both a real and an imaginary component) and transfinite numbers (which describe the relative size of infinite sets). What is important for this guide is that the real numbers can be divided into two kinds of numbers: those which can be put in the form of a fraction of integers and those which cannot be put in that form.[4] The first are called rational numbers and the latter are known as irrationals, and there are many, many more of the latter than of the former.[5]

As a self-defined mystic, I've come to appreciate this simple lesson—that there's more irrationality than rationality—which I learned from my early training in mathematics. Granted, we are talking about *naming* more than about *concept* here; it may well be that the choice of the terms

---

2. The real number line can also be understood as the field of real numbers, i.e., a set with arithmetic and ordering that satisfies a rather long list of real number axioms. This understanding has the effect of divorcing the real number line from its geometric interpretations just as the non-Euclidean geometries did to the original Euclidian concept of space. See the following note for further reading.

3. For an excellent and very readable description of these models and how they relate to the real number line, see Gamelin, "What Really."

4. E.g., $\pi/3$ is a fraction but not a rational number.

5. An excellent demonstration of the proof that there are more irrational than rational numbers can be found at University of Missouri Kansas City, "Proof" (YouTube video).

rational and *irrational* for numbers that can be put into certain specific forms is purely happenstance. It may be that it is not happenstance either.⁶ When I look back at my own spiritual journey into mysticism, I recognize that as a child I was sensitive, open, imaginative, and highly creative, but that at least three of these four qualities were considered second-rate to rational, sensible, practical, and intelligent. And *irrational* was basically a total cultural shutdown. Kids went to school to refine their analytical skills, not to cultivate irrational thinking. The latter was a sure way to the nut house. The social message? Irrational: no, no, goodness, no.

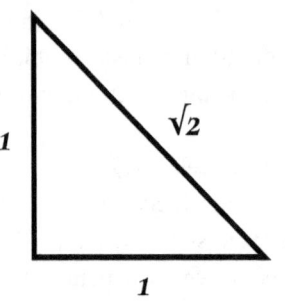

Fig. 3.1. Pythagorean Irrational Number

Despite this message, I grew up to be a sensitive, open, imaginative, and highly creative individual, what one of the staff in the pastoral department of the hospital where I currently serve as a contract chaplain calls a "gentle soul." She's right, too. Well, maybe my husband would not agree with her, especially not when I am angry about something he did or did not do! Basically, however, she hit the proverbial mystic right on the head. In my work as a chaplain, being a "gentle soul" has often proven to be very helpful. Usually this comes about from some sort of irrational super-sensitivity which makes me unusually receptive to the individuals I am working with. I often intuit something they aren't actually saying, and sometimes my mirroring this back to them can have productive consequences. I don't know precisely where this ability comes from, but I'm sure it is *not* the result of a careful rational calculation. I remember once, long ago when I was into such things, going to an astrologist, who established the various alignments of the stars at my birth and concluded that both my parents were psychic and so I must *really* be psychic, and (in

---

6. See May, "Mathematics and Mysticism." May observes "a fundamental dualism" between the terms "rational" (which "comes from a Latin root meaning to reason or calculate") and its opposite, "irrational" (which means "'ineffable' or 'beyond mortal ken'" and is often used as a pejorative). He notes this same dualism in philosophy "between the material and spiritual worlds, between the physical and the metaphysical, between science and religion, [and] between logic and intuition. . . . In mathematics," he says, "rational and irrational have a different but curiously *parallel meaning*" (emphasis added).

response to my own question to her), she herself was certainly not psychic in the least: her skill at discernment was entirely a matter of proper (i.e., analytic) calculation of the stars. This entire scenario would have been impossible for me to claim, or even repeat, in my childhood because it was, of course, irrational and therefore bad.

The irrational has long been cast as undesirable. History traces this discrimination back to the ancient Greeks and a mathematical discovery which upset the mystical beliefs of the Pythagorean brotherhood that strongly influenced society at the time. The story goes that one of the honored brotherhood discovered that the numerical length of the hypotenuse of a right triangle whose other two sides each measured one unit (see figure 3.1) could not be expressed as the ratio of two whole numbers.[7] We now describe this situation by saying that the length of that hypotenuse is the square root of 2, an ir*rati*onal number. The unfortunate fellow who discovered this irrationality was, according to some accounts, tossed overboard and drowned for his insight.

True or false, the story itself shows how upsetting the idea of irrational numbers was to the Pythagorean society. The reason it was so upsetting is that the Pythagorean brotherhood (which was highly secretive) had built up an entire theory of the universe based on the lovely harmony found in all numbers and all things, and really *all* things essentially *were* numbers ("All is number") and wasn't it just splendid how you could chart the relationship between the earth and the moon and the stars and always, always, you found this incredible harmony. Just as numbers determined the relationship between the beautiful chords of music, so, too, did numbers determine the harmony of the skies. Until, of course, someone realized that some numbers didn't work that way, and that meant that everything the society taught was basically invalid.[8] No wonder *irrational* got bad press!

The history of mathematical knowledge is rife with such occurrences. Take the discovery of non-Euclidean geometries, for instance,[9] or the idea that some things can *not* be proven true or false in math.[10]

---

7. See Bogomolny, "Square Root of 2." Proofs of the irrationality of the square root of 2 can be found online. Bogomolny's online work contains 28 proofs.

8. See Diggins, *String*, for more about the discovery of irrationals.

9. Gamelin, "What Really," 11. Author notes that "we may compare the divorce of the construction of the real numbers from geometry to the divorce of the foundations of geometry from its origins in the Euclidean geometry of space."

10. See also the discussion in chapters 2 and 17 on Gödel's incompleteness theorems.

What often happens in these and similar instances is that there's a great deal of initial uproar during which the discoverer of so-called heretical insight(s) often suffers undue consequences. This period is then slowly followed by a general acceptance of the notion, the result of which is new insights into the way the world works, at least mathematically.

Today "mysticism" seems to have two primary meanings, one related to religious thought, where it is based on *non-rational* communion or unity with the divine (now sometimes referred to as resolution of "the subject-object dichotomy"), and one related to secular thought, where it refers to obscure or *irrational* cognition. My lifespan falls into an era which, overall, has favored clear and analytical cognition over anything too emotional, sentimental, occult, supernatural, or otherwise non-cognitive. Like the Pythagoreans, I learned to champion the rational over the irrational, but, unlike these early Greeks, I have come to value both kinds of entities as part of the same continuum of "real" existence. Getting to this perspective has not always been a simple procedure.

For instance, when I was a young mother, my son Willi, then five or six, was looking forward to a family trip where he was going to fly in a small airplane with his father, a new pilot, to visit his aunt. He was incredibly excited. One day, shortly before the trip, we were talking on the phone with this aunt, who informed us that she had recently received a phone call from Willi. She relayed detailed parts of their conversation, including a discussion about the upcoming flight with his father. When, later, we asked Willi about the call, he denied making it (this was before cell phones of course) and he continued to deny it until, after several additional calls to his aunt to determine if she might have been mistaken, I pressured our beloved child into owning up to making the call. "If you don't tell us the truth, Willi, then you won't be able to go."

Almost immediately, I felt badly about this coercion. I felt even worse when our phone bill later showed not a hint of any such call being made from our home. I was caught between wanting to believe my son (whom I suspected wasn't actually old enough to know how to dial a long-distance call) and my sister-in-law (who would never lie about such a thing). Ultimately, I mentally filed the whole inexplicable episode under "irrational events."

There have been other inexplicable events in my life. After the unfair pressure I exerted on my son to "fess up" (and he did!), I grew reluctant to pass judgment on what might seem to be an irrational experience. Overall, this reticence to discount the irrational has served me well in the ensuing years. Once, for instance, in the early years of my ministry I visited a parishioner who was a self-acclaimed atheist. She told me that not long after her husband had died years before, he had shown up by her bedside one night. They had conversed. A dream? Not according to her. Because of my experience with my son and the unexplainable phone call, I found I had no difficulty accepting the truth of her situation. What still bothered me, however, was how she could be so positive about the event and yet remain ardent in her atheism.

Now, years later, I think that perhaps if she had been steeped in the curiosities of mathematics she, too, would have come to appreciate the occurrence of the analytic or "rational" event as the rarity in life rather than the preferred. Think of "rational" events as the occasional diamonds on an endless necklace, each surrounded by (literally) countless "irrational" pearls. The set as a whole is a precious craft of art. It bears a seeming magic about it in that whenever you grab a portion of it to examine more closely, you discover you're holding just as many previously unseen jewels as you saw from a distance. The necklace defies analysis, yet endlessly expands its worth. It stretches, like elastic, yet ever retains its jeweled pattern—diamonds linked by pearls, rationality merged in irrationality—and both create more beauty together than either could bring forth alone.

While the mystical *real*m as I understand it manifests in both rational and irrational ways of thinking,[11] we tend in ordinary life to focus more on the rational than the irrational. What would happen if we changed that tendency? When mathematicians did this, whole new mathematical fields and technologies arose. Today, our able young people are systematically introduced to these mathematical visions and possibilities at ever younger ages. Imagine a world where we were similarly encouraged to develop our subtle energies right along with our rational intellect.

Subtle energies. When I was forty, I'd never heard the phrase. Thirty years later, I link it with myofascial, craniosacral, and other non-mainstream medical therapies, acupressure, acupuncture, Reiki, meditation, vital forces such as chi or qi, psychic insight, various understandings of consciousness, neuro-feedback technologies, and new possibilities for individual and collective wholeness. Subtle energies, in short, include many things often associated with mysticism, but which may be presented under the umbrella of scientific interest in all forms of healing energy.

---

11. This is not intended to be exclusive. Just as there are other kinds of numbers besides real numbers, there are likely additional ways in which the mystical realm manifests.

When I first encountered the notion of "subtle energies" (under this particular coinage, anyway), it was through a traditionally trained allopathic physician who *also* utilized less conventional homeopathic treatments in his practice. This physician, Dr. J. P., was open in his outlook. At one point he even recommended to me a particular intuitive (in this case a "phone" psychic) whom he knew to be helpful to people dealing with health problems and difficult life journeys. He also introduced me to ISSSEEM, the International Society for Study of Subtle Energies and Energy Medicine, an organization whose long-time goal is to serve as "an open forum for scientific and intuitive exploration of integrative healing, applied spirituality, and the subtle realms." This is only one of a number of efforts to merge the study of science and spirit which blossomed in the 1980s and 1990s. Helped by the development of the Internet, many have continued to grow and integrate these two often-separated disciplines. Although I've never been a member of ISSSEEM, I always remember it precisely because it is the one with all those initials that don't make any sense and that I can never remember. I love that paradox!

I am indebted to Dr. J. P. (now deceased), because he validated ideas I'd had a difficult time affirming. He legitimized for me what was often looked upon with deep skepticism and suspicion by most Western medical providers of the era, and by many other scientists and religious folks as well. Mathaphorically, these things were the "irrational" numbers on the real number line. They augmented the outstanding logic of the "pure" rational numbers. Together with the force of beloved scientific tradition, the subtle energies created the holistic integration of the "real" number-line world.

Chapter 4: Depolarizing Mathematics and Religion[1]

A Möbius strip looks like it has two sides but only has one.

Fig. 4.1. Möbius Strip

FOR MANY PEOPLE, MATHEMATICS and religion seem to exist on opposite ends of a linear scale. Peer at it one way and we see religion; look the other way and we find mathematics. And never the two shall meet. With one view we find ourselves latching on to such words as *analogy*, *myth*, *stories*. The other we describe with words such as *analysis*, *logic*, and *scientific investigation*. I've grown to see this polarization as misleading. Yet, I have encountered abrupt dismissals of any attempt to integrate these two extremes. One learned theologian, for instance, rebuked my suggestion that both math and religion are symbol systems, claiming I was comparing oranges with fork-lifts.[2] According to him:

---

1. See Voss, "Depolarizing" for details about an earlier version of this chapter. This essay represents the formal start of my math-mystic scholarship.

2. I will call him Professor Doe. This encounter occurred long enough ago that I've forgotten his name. I prefer to leave it that way.

> Math is not a social system or a social institution.
> Math is not a system but a set.
> Math is not symbolic but significant.
> Math is not factual but mental.
> Math is not mood-filled but non-emotional.
> There are no symbols in math other than math itself.

Then, as though to emphasize the depth of my misperception, he pointed out that "if you want to understand when and how math functions, trace the grades of Japanese students in US colleges. The more math, the higher their grades—until they get into the humanities where passing is really difficult." I was taken aback by his comments, but it helped me appreciate how we humans find it difficult to accommodate apparently opposing viewpoints. Such polarization, unfortunately, perpetuates a myth that blinds us to the rich possibilities of integration.

Cultural anthropologist Clifford Geertz has offered the following definition of religion:

> Religion is a system of symbols which acts to establish powerful, pervasive and long-lasting moods and motivations in people by *formulating conceptions of a general order of existence* [emphasis added] and clothing these conceptions with such an aura of factuality that the moods and motivations seem uniquely realistic.[3]

This definition has been offered by the theological community as an appropriate answer to the question "What is religion?" Yet, with a little word play, it is possible to alter Geertz's wording and arrive at several other meaningful definitions. For example, by replacing the phrase "formulating conceptions of general order of existence" with "formulating conceptions of collective and legislative action," the concept of "government" is nicely addressed. Likewise, by substituting for that same phrase the words "formulating concepts of provisions of society," we arrive at a workable definition of "economics," and so on.[4] In a similar vein, we might replace the single word "religion" with the one word "mathematics" and arrive at the following possibility:

> *Mathematics* is a system of symbols which acts to establish powerful, pervasive and long-lasting moods and motivations in people by formulating conceptions of a general order of existence

---

3. Geertz, *Interpretation*, 91.

4. With thanks to Bruce Malina, from whose lecture at Creighton University I arrived at this insight.

and clothing these conceptions with such an aura of factuality that the moods and motivations seem uniquely realistic.

What implications might follow from this interchange? After all, the replacement of "religion" with "mathematics" does not necessarily imply the equivalence of the two terms. Given that "A is B" and "E is B," we cannot conclude that "A is E." "Anne is a woman" and "Elizabeth is a woman" does not mean that "Anne is Elizabeth." It does, however, suggest a strong and undeniable connection between the two symbols thus interchanged—a connection rooted in similarity rather than in polarization. But just how valid is this altered version? When Geertz originally offered his definition, he distinguished five separate parts, each of which he discussed in some detail. Similarly, there are five distinct aspects to this altered version. Mathematics is (1) a system of symbols which acts (2) to establish powerful, pervasive, and long-lasting moods and motivations in people by (3) formulating conceptions of a general order of existence and (4) clothing these conceptions with such an aura of factuality that (5) the moods and motivations seem uniquely realistic. Following a vein of reasoning similar (at least in structure) to that of Geertz, I will examine each of these five aspects with an intent to justify its appropriateness to mathematics.

(1) A SYSTEM OF SYMBOLS WHICH ACTS . . .

Declaring mathematics "a system of symbols" seems to me (the mathematician) so obvious that it is almost trite. Mathematics abounds in symbols, most of whose meanings have been carefully considered and cross-culturally agreed upon. Furthermore, this system of symbols represents the epitome of economy and efficiency in human expression. The integral notation developed in the seventeenth century by Leibniz is only one example of how an entire, complicated process is captured precisely in a few swift pen strokes.

However, as the almost ritualistic litany cited above suggests, the symbolic nature of mathematics may not be as obvious to others as it is to me. Theologians frequently differentiate between "symbol" and "sign," with the latter being representative of a known content and the former representing a content while also transcending that content in some way that cannot be expressed in rational terms. This subtlety is aptly illustrated by the German word for symbol, *Sinnbild*: *Sinn*, or meaning, refers to the conscious, rational sphere, whereas *bild*, or image, belongs to the irrational sphere, the unconscious.[5] A stoplight, for instance, is a "sign," but a cross is a "symbol"—at least for some cultures.

The apparent afterthought of the preceding sentence deserves emphasis, for, as Geertz himself notes, "symbol" often refers to a great variety of things, and sometimes to a number of them all at the same time.[6] Rather like "beauty," "symbol" may well be in the eye of the beholder. Geertz speaks of "culture patterns" as symbols or complexes of symbols, and insists that they "have an intrinsic double aspect: they give meaning, that is, objective conceptual form, to social and psychological reality both by shaping themselves to it and by shaping it to themselves."[7] Likewise, to the degree to which mathematics offers us symbols which in some way transcend themselves, that is, stand for a content while simultaneously shaping that content, then mathematics may be appropriately described as a symbol system. Studies such as those explored by sociologist Sal Restivo put forth a strong if not indisputable argument for precisely such a sociology of mathematics.[8]

Mathematics offers us some of humankind's oldest symbols. Names for certain numbers are among the oldest "known" words. Buckminster Fuller, himself an unusual integrator of mathematics with other disciplines, pointed out in his prose-poem "Numerology" that if we were to collect all the various names for numbers from all the various world languages, we would be surprised at how many we would recognize without difficulty. Comparing the names for just the first two cardinal numbers ("one" and "two"), we would observe that in nearly every language the symbol for "one" starts with a vowel and has vowel sound emphasis, whereas the "two" has a beginning consonant sound and a consonant sound emphasis. Fuller concludes (with a touch of mythology) that number names grew from the same fundamental roots:

> We either have to say that some angels
> Invented the names for numbers
> And the phonetically soundable
> Alphabetical letter symbols
> With which to spell them.
> And wrote them on parchments.

5. Jacobi, *Psychology of Jung*, 96.
6. Geertz, *Interpretation*, 91.
7. Geertz, *Interpretation*, 93.
8. See Restivo, *Social Relations*.

> And air-dropped those number-name leaflets
> All around the spherical world,
> Thus teaching world-around people the same number names;
> Or we have to say that numbers were invented
> By one-world-around-traveling people.[9]

Fuller attributes the formulation of numbers to sailors, specifically the Polynesians, who "inculcated their use all around the world."[10] Calling them navigator priests ("the only people who knew that the Earth is spherical, that the Earth is a closed system with its myriad resources chartable"),[11] he traces their path westward through Malaysia and southern India, across the Indian Ocean to Mesopotamia and Egypt and thus into the Mediterranean. Most (Western) histories of mathematics begin their serious study with the essentially practical reckoning systems of the ancient Babylonian, Egyptian, and Cretan cultures; Fuller believes it is likely that the powerful priest-mathematicians of these societies were really "the progeny of mathematician navigators of the Pacific come up upon the land."[12] The way mathematics developed as a system of symbols is certainly linked to the way in which language developed as a system of symbols. But even more importantly, our mathematical system has changed (is changing) in accordance with the development of human conscious thought. Humankind moved from chanted symbols to spoken numbers to finger tallying to incised bone artifacts to clay tablets, and so on. It also moved from the ability to associate one object with an abstract scratch on a stone to the capacity for recognizing a group of objects as the concept "five" to the ability to detach the number sequence totally from the objects being counted, and so on.[13] Inasmuch as religion is also a system of symbols acting by means "of formulating conceptions," all of which may be analyzed at various levels of abstraction, it is probable that the two systems share commonalities just by virtue of their apparent embeddedness in human thought.

9. Fuller, *Synergetics*, 739–41.
10. Fuller, *Synergetics*, 741.
11. Fuller, *Synergetics*, 751.
12. Fuller, *Synergetics*, 750.
13. Burton, *History of Mathematics*, 2.

(2) TO ESTABLISH POWERFUL, PERVASIVE, AND LONG-LASTING MOODS AND MOTIVATION IN PEOPLE...

That the system of symbols called mathematics acts "to establish powerful, pervasive and long-lasting moods and motivations in people" may be verified by an excursion deeper into these history books. Consider, for example, the man who became so preoccupied with the decimal calculation of pi that he devoted his entire life to this one pursuit, finally achieving a rendition (thirty-five decimal places) which can now be far surpassed in only moments by computer.[14] Or consider the motivating factors which initiated and perpetuated the bitter rivalry between Newton and Leibniz over their essentially "simultaneous" discovery of the calculus. Or those which caused Gauss and Bolyai to refrain in the 1800s from publishing their separate discoveries of non-Euclidean geometry. On a more "religious" note, what about the member of the Pythagorean mystic brotherhood who was allegedly thrown overboard at sea by his peers because he discovered that not all numbers are commensurable? Then there was the turmoil and punishment Galileo suffered for his refusal to deny the truths his mathematical symbols told him. Such examples, and many others like them, justify the propriety of applying the second part of Geertz's definition to "mathematics" without loss of meaning.

(3) AND CLOTHING THESE CONCEPTIONS WITH SUCH AN AURA OF FACTUALITY THAT THE MOODS AND MOTIVATIONS SEEM UNIQUELY REALISTIC...

The last two parts of this same definition are, from my standpoint, more or less axiomatic givens insofar as they apply to mathematics. Who would deny that mathematics is a system of symbols which motivates powerful energies in people to formulate certain conceptions, and that (4) it clothes these conceptions "with such an aura of factuality that" (5) "the moods and motivations seem uniquely realistic"? Certainly, none of those mathematicians mentioned in the previous paragraph. The apparent human need for consistency, for finding order in the midst of chaos, ensures that no mathematician will willingly negate the factuality and realism of that

---

14. Eves, *Introduction*, 93. Ludolph van Ceulen of Germany used polygons having two sides to arrive at his figures. His achievement was considered so exceptional that the number was engraved on his tombstone.

which embodies the core of his or her belief system, especially not when these beliefs are accompanied by powerful, pervasive, and long-lasting moods and motivations. The seeming uniqueness of these moods and motivations is more questionable (at least to the mathematician who is used to working with changeable axiomatic propositions) but probably no less intuitively feelable than it is to any other member of the human species. To be sure, I am not asserting the truth or falsity of the certain conceptions themselves; rather, I am agreeing to the likelihood of our readiness to perceive them as valid. The non-mathematician or non-scientist might be even more eager to grant this appearance of factuality to mathematics than would mathematicians themselves. Mathematics, after all, is popularly considered an "exact" science, the epitome of logic, the one place where you can arrive at right or wrong answers with some assurance of accuracy. Who but a mathematician would suggest that two plus two is not four?[15]

(4) FORMULATING CONCEPTIONS OF A GENERAL ORDER OF EXISTENCE . . .

It remains to consider the final part of our altered definition: is mathematics, then, a system of symbols which formulates conceptions *of a general order of existence*? The answer is a clear and unambiguous yes and no. It is "no" in the same sense of practicality that permeated the mathematics of ancient Western cultures. Mathematics is and always has been what Olaf Pederson, in a collection of essays on physics, philosophy, and theology commissioned by the Vatican City State, called "a vehicle of description" and "a tool of discovery."[16] Throughout the ages, such description and discovery have been used to alter, improve, expand, predict, categorize, etc., the relationship between humans and their environment. Sometimes mathematics has been misused as a vehicle of description and a tool of discovery: consider, for example, how often history portrays mathematics as the handmaiden of power-hungry priests who hoarded learning in

---

15. Paul van Geert, for one, addresses the operational fallacies of such a statement in *Development of Perception*. The typical argument involves an overlap of Venn diagrams as in the situation where a man and a woman, each already the parent of one child, marry and together become parents of another child. Thus, each parent has 2 children, yet 2 plus 2 clearly does not equal 4.

16. Pederson, "Christian Beliefs," 132.

their own self-interest.[17] Still, mathematics is "not just another scientific language to be used or rejected as one please[s]. It [is] much more potent than ordinary language, and the only one . . . able to produce a fascinating result."[18]

This is the action-oriented aspect of mathematics, and, in a sense, it might be likened to the rituals, the daily worship, the everyday, common interests of religion. These aspects, mathematical *or* religious, allow humankind to go about the business of daily living. These are "do it" aspects, not "what's it all about" aspects. It is in this sense that mathematics is *not* a system of symbols which attempts to formulate conceptions of a general order of existence. It is in this same sense that religion, also, is not an attempt to formulate such conceptions.

But, just as the ancient Egyptians used their practical mathematics to help prepare them for a spiritual afterlife,[19] the distinction between the practical and the philosophical is a slippery one. A careful exploration of the role of mathematics in the value-oriented world of humankind shows that, time after time, mathematical pursuits intertwined with religious preoccupations.

> From the very beginnings of the development of scientific thinking in the ancient world, first in Babylon and then in Greece, thought about God or the gods—*theology*—and thought about the world—*natural science*—were so intermingled that often it was quite impossible to differentiate between the two. It was primarily for religious reasons that people from the unnamed Babylonians through the pre-Socratics, the Pythagoreans, Plato, and Aristotle attempted to understand the heavens, to trace their geometry and calculate their ratios.[20]

When viewed from this perspective mathematics does, indeed, act to formulate conceptions of a general order of existence.

If out of the mouths of Buckminster Fuller's Polynesian sailors came chanted numbers, it would seem that they were to become "enchanted" numbers for much of the world. To the Pythagoreans, for instance,

---

17. Burton, *History*, 91.

18. Pederson, "Christian Beliefs," 132.

19. Burton, *History*, 11. "Practical" takes on new connotations here. For example, one of the earliest recorded sets of very large numbers may be found in the *Egyptian Book of the Dead*, a collection of religious and magical texts whose main aim was to secure a satisfying afterlife for the deceased.

20. Nebelsick, *Circles of God*, xiv.

numbers were not "the means of calculating the relationships between the things of reality, *they were reality.*"[21] In China, divination, "an attempt to ascertain truth on a level other than that of verifiable analysis or quantifiable proof, and by means other than those which depend on reason,"[22] was almost totally dependent upon a numerical system of throwing stalks in a pattern of sixty-four possible hexagrams. In Tibet, where, divination was intimately though not exclusively connected to number (primarily via dice throwing), "it was never really possible to separate the religious and the secular."[23] In India, numbers are "of the kind of Brahma"; numerical allegory found in the Jewish Kabbalah is perhaps in its most developed form; number appears in Islamic mystical thought; Augustine found numbers in the Scriptures to be both sacred and mysterious.[24] Johannes Kepler, Galileo Galilei, and Isaac Newton cast horoscopes as well as mathematical theorems, and, indeed, the entire Renaissance was "a world in which alchemy was the search for divine essence which was thought to be the basis and the unification of all material reality."[25]

Some argue that humankind's attempt to discern an understanding of the All through mathematical insight ended with the Copernican revolution and the birth of modern science. But, as Annemarie Schimmel put it, "the mathematical spirit is innate in man and manifests itself wherever human beings live."[26] Chances are, we of more recent times have simply adopted a more probabilistic approach to formulating conceptions about the general order of existence.

For one thing, mathematics permeates far more of the texture of today's life than is generally recognized. Psycho-social statistics is big business, statistical sampling and polling impact our commercial and political realms, economic theory can no longer be understood without a solid background in mathematics, the life sciences of biology and medicine are increasingly mathematical, and even linguistics is more about mathematical-like languages than about dictionary-like compilations.[27] It is, of course, broadly possible to lump the significance of all this into the category of practical mathematics, to point an unforgiving finger at

21. Nebelsick, *Circles of God*, 14.
22. Loewe, "China," 39.
23. Radha, "Tibet," 7.
24. Schimmel, "Numbers," 7.
25. Nebelsick, *Circles of God*, 214.
26. Schimmel, "Numbers," 13.
27. Davis and Hersh, *Descartes' Dream*, 10.

the evils science and technology have wreaked upon society, and to cry out that modern day science/mathematics has only severed the threads which link us in any way with God, religion, or the understanding of our true existence.

To do this, however, is to ignore the possibility that the world may be essentially mathematical in nature, in which case understanding mathematics is an obvious first step to understanding the world. A large body of theoretical mathematics is increasingly influencing our *popular* philosophical literature with precisely that intent: consider, for instance, such recent bestsellers as James Gleick's *Chaos*, Douglas Hofstadter's *Gödel, Escher, and Bach*, and Stephen Hawking's *A Brief History of Time*, all of which are representative of a decided trend to explain the universe in terms of mathematical concepts. In *Descartes' Dream: The World According to Mathematics*, by Davis and Hersh, we find a surprising echo of the Pythagorean claim that "All is number":

> "God is a Mathematician" is a modern formulation meaning that the way of the world is mathematical, that mathematics provides the key to the universe, that God, as the Prime Mathematician, set up the universe according to the principles of mathematics. This view may be slightly egocentric, perhaps, and not necessarily subscribed to by theologians. It is a view that is widely held today by physicists (who may or may not use the word "God") in order to answer the unanswerable question of why mathematics is such an effective tool in theoretical physics. It is the view which lies behind a great deal of the recent mathematizations of a variety of disciplines, history, sociology, psychology. The world is mathematical, and hence, to interpret it properly, one must use mathematics.[28]

And Rudy Rucker, whose 1987 book *Mind Tools* deals with the mathematics of information processing, puts it into even more modern lingo when he defines reality as "an incomprehensible computation by a fractal CA of inconceivable dimensions."[29] If this is nothing else, it is surely "formulating conceptions of general order of existence" which are mathematical rather than religious in nature.

Or, are they really religious as well? Herein lies once again the question of what happens if the word "mathematics" is substituted for the word "religion" in Geertz's definition without loss of meaningfulness.

---

28. Davis and Hersh, *Descartes' Dream*, 233.
29. Rucker, *Mind Tools*, 314.

Geertz himself has stated elsewhere that "it is when two (or more) scholars realize that, for all the differences between them, they are attacking highly similar issues, trying to solve closely related puzzles, that communication between them begins to look like a practical policy rather than an academic piety."[30] One such commonality of vision is what Geertz calls "the systematic study of meaningful forms." And one meaningful form particularly relevant to this study is the geometric Möbius strip analogy to the mind-world dichotomy.[31]

The Möbius strip provides an ideal illustration of one mathematical symbol which may act "to establish powerful, pervasive and long-lasting moods and motivations in people by formulating conceptions of a general order of existence." Although it is a sophisticated concept originating from the specialized area of mathematics known as topology, it lends itself well to a simple geometric interpretation. About a century ago, August Möbius discovered that a strip of paper, if given a single twist and secured together at the ends, forms what is now known popularly as the Möbius strip.[32]

The intrigue of this strip is that it has only one side. School children are usually fascinated when they first encounter a Möbius demonstration, for it provides a concrete example of something which is directly counter to their intuition; so, too, does, for example, the cross, a symbol of the Christian religion. The Möbius symbol is powerful enough to have captured the imagination (and motivation) of the Dutch artist Escher, who transformed it into a work of art, perhaps as meaningful to some as Michelangelo's beautiful paintings on the ceiling of the Sistine Chapel. Rucker's use of it to demonstrate a "general order of existence," i.e., the mind-world dichotomy, is not so very different from the bread/body, wine/blood symbols of Christianity. And my use of it now to provide a visual image suitable to resolve the polarization between mathematics and religion will, I hope, appear to some as both factual and realistic. When the two poles of religion and mathematics are likened to opposite sides of this little strip of paper representative of a highly sophisticated human endeavor, it is immediately apparent that the polarization of mathematics and religion is, as a mystic might say, but an illusion.

30. Geertz, *Myth*, viii.
31. See Geertz's image and discussion of the mind-world dichotomy in *Myth*.
32. Smith, *Nature of Mathematics*, 402.

Chapter 5:*Coming Out of the Math Closet[1]

THERE'S A CLOSET UNDER the eaves in our bedroom where my spouse, Dan Sullivan, stashes things. It's his closet, not mine, so about the only time I open the door is to remove a fan we keep in it. A year ago, when I took out the fan, I noticed a mild odor of mold coming from the closet. I mentioned this odor to Dan and, after several such mentions, he dragged out some of the closet items and found a few old papers that seemed to be causing the problem. After discarding the worst offenders, he stuffed everything back in the closet. Then, a couple of months ago when the temperature outside was unusually high and it was too early in the season to justify the air conditioner, I opened the closet door again (to get the fan) and, wow, the smell was intense.

I re-mentioned the problem to Dan, but he was busy. I mentioned it some more, and he was still busy, plus now he was also irritated that I kept mentioning the problem. He'd heard me quite clearly the first time, thank you. I shut the door but the odor started seeping through, bothering my sleep. Dan was trying to locate the source of the problem. Was it an undetected leak in the roof? In the plumbing? He was handling this as sort of a thought-exercise. After all, getting a ladder to the roof was a major chore and it was hot, too. Maybe you know how that goes? Soon, our problem turned into a different problem. Not only did we have a closet filled with mold, but we also had a problem in communication. We had separate agendas. And we weren't talking openly about them. Finally, we promised each other that sometime soon we would take everything

---

1. This chapter was originally presented as a sermon at the First Unitarian Church of Omaha on July 16, 2006. See my dedicated website, www.PiZine.org, for other math sermons, ones that are not included in this book. See appendix A for a handout that accompanies this one.

out of the closet and see if we could discern the source of the trouble. We would do this together. Sometime soon. Sometime.

Does this story sound at least a little familiar to some of you? Does something similar fit your lives as well? I confess, I rather do hope so. It helps normalize the situation when others share the same kinds of troubles.

I heard Dan telling some friends about our problem. "There are two things every guy needs to know if he wants to get along with a woman," Dan said. "First, he must always let her think she's getting her way. Second, he has to let her have it." Later he sent me via email an old adage about discussion techniques. "A woman has the last word in any argument," he noted. "Anything a man says after that is the beginning of a new argument." True as these observations may be, they didn't help us resolve our different agendas. So, if you see Dan in the coffee hour after this sermon today, please be kind to him. He is living with a woman who has decided to expose it all.

The truth of it is, though, that closets are safe places to store things only as long as they don't get moldy. Moldy closets get moldier if you don't open them up and sort them out. When I first began to outline this sermon series, of which this sermon is the fifth and next to last, it occurred to me that I myself had been in a closet of sorts, and that it was time I came out. Now, I don't mean to denigrate the value of closets, or of hiding things in them—even ourselves. We all know how much courage it takes, for instance, for someone to come out of the gay-lesbian-bi-transgender-polyamory closet. But, have you ever noticed how much easier it is for one who is *not* in a closet to wonder why someone who *is* in it has so much trouble coming out? What's the big deal? Nonetheless, I suspect that we all have our own hidden closets, although some are moldier and some far more difficult to leave than others. We should never underestimate the power of someone's closet to offer the illusion of a safe space.

In my own case, I've been gradually coming out of the math closet for years. It hasn't always been easy. For example, in my sermon last month I mentioned that I wrote my doctoral thesis on the relationship between mathematics and religion. At first, this topic was warmly welcomed by the faculty at Meadville Lombard Theological School, but it turned out that my dissertation advisor and I had "a significant theological difference." That's the phrase the Lutheran head of the science and religion center in Chicago eventually termed it. Today, I trace the problems which this "theological difference" eventually caused to a variety of factors. Dr. Godbey, a likeable, kind, highly regarded scholar of history, was not totally comfortable with the religious insights I was deriving from mathematics, a subject with which he was only modestly familiar. Furthermore, my advisor (now deceased some years) was even then suffering from Parkinson's disease and so he had his own struggles to confront. What he didn't particularly need or want was a sometimes overtly feminist and definitely too new-age-ish (whatever that meant) doctoral student tossing esoteric ideas at him through the guise of a mathematics that was beyond his training.

I'd like to say that Dr. Godbey and I were able to smoothly overcome our differences—theological and otherwise—but, unfortunately, it never really went that way. After I submitted the first draft of my manuscript to him, Dr. Godbey urged me to omit certain parts of my thesis. I couldn't bring myself to lose what I felt was my "voice" in the dissertation and I was arrogant enough to think that I could rewrite it in a way that would satisfy him, without acquiescing to his substantial requests. I was never more wrong.

Ah, I should perhaps have followed the advice of Albert Einstein, who identified an important equation. $A + B + C$ = Success, he claimed, if A = hard work, B = hard play, and C = keeping your mouth shut.[2] Of course, Einstein also advised patience if your math skills were less than desirable. "Do not worry about your difficulties in mathematics," he said. "I assure you that mine are greater." Incidentally, I try to generalize that advice whenever I am spiritually low.

Anyway, to skip to the end of a complicated story, I almost as a result of this conflict didn't receive my doctorate. Fortunately, with the assistance of several individuals who were savvy about academic politics (my husband right at the top of the list), I did eventually succeed and was graduated, receiving my Doctor of Ministry in June 1993; at the end of the year I served my first church as pastor. But the joy of my success was marred by the stress and unhappiness which had preceded it. Even some months later, when Dr. Godbey graciously invited Dan and me to his home to celebrate the acceptance of my dissertation as a future volume in SUNY's series on Western esotericism, there remained an unbridgeable gap between my former advisor and myself.

---

2. Garrett, "Einstein's Formula."

"Know what I do when I get stuff like that in my mail?" Dr. Godbey asked as he poured me a second cup of coffee. He was referring to the advertising flier which SUNY Press had printed up for *What Number Is God?*, my book.

"What?" I asked, somewhat nervously.

Dr. Godbey just chuckled and pointed to the waste basket, making a gesture of tossing the flier into it. In his defense, I truly don't think he realized how painful his response was to me.

Experiences like that have made it difficult for me to come out of the math closet. Like others who are stuck in metaphorical closets, I have learned to share my passion for the subject selectively and somewhat self-protectively. I've also always relied heavily on outside affirmation of my work before I could claim it as my personal success.

I tell this story now to make a point. Two points, really. The first is about the nature of closets. Closets are ubiquitous. Indeed, *many* people have a part or parts of their lives which they relegate to closets. Closets exist to mediate fear. Sometimes the fear is justified. As a faith tradition, we UUs have a fine record of creating environments where individuals feel safe enough to come out of their closets. Historically, we have ably assisted the abused, the unwanted child, the unhappily pregnant woman, the enslaved, the homosexual, the poverty-stricken, the mentally ill, the homeless, the unseen elderly, and many others who have experienced society's overt discrimination and unrelenting marginalization. Even so, we miss a lot of closets and, worse, we sometimes even help maintain them.

My personal experience in the *math* closet has helped me appreciate how important it is for us to be ever vigilant and open to recognizing the otherwise invisible closets which we perpetuate. Do *you* have a closet? Do you want to tell somebody about that closet? Is there someone in this congregation whom you can trust with the knowledge of your closet? If, for even one person in this room, the answer to that last question is "no," then, my friends, we have work to do as a faith community. So this, then, is my first point: many people have closets where or which they feel compelled to hide, and it is a practice of our faith tradition to help people feel safe enough to "come out."

My second point is about the joy of coming out of a closet. The best way I can think of to do that is to tell you about one of the jewels in mine. This one might even be familiar to a Unitarian Universalist congregation. It is, you see, one of the dozen sermons included in *The Price of Truth*, which is a collection of sermons preached by Unitarian Universalist minister Frank Schulman during his twenty-five years at Emerson Unitarian Church in Houston, Texas, and published this very year (2006) by the new Meadville Lombard Press. Although Rev. Schulman preached this gem of a sermon, entitled "Axioms of Theology," sometime between 1963 and 1988, I only added it to my math closet last month when I chanced to run across it on the book table in St. Louis, Missouri, at our annual General Assembly. Sadly, I'll never have a chance to tell Frank Schulman what this sermon meant to me because he died last January.

What *did* it mean to me? Perhaps you can guess from the Reverend's opening paragraphs, which I will now read to you:

> My son, Andrew, majored in mathematics. He did some special work in what then was a new form of math. It was known then as fractal geometry and now is called "chaos." Plane and solid geometry are used to measure areas and solids, but many areas are not simple forms. Fractal geometry was devised to measure shorelines, hilly surfaces, and all kinds of irregular shapes. . . . We were at dinner when Andrew explained this to a physicist. The physicist suggested that there is a similarity between pure mathematics and theology in that they both have axioms, and then they develop their theories from these axioms. . . . My son was interested in that idea. He turned to me and asked if that were so. I said I supposed it was, knowing full well what the next question would be. Predictably, he asked, "What are the axioms of theology?" We then had a long conversation about that important idea.[3]

Rev. Schulman then postulated six axioms which he believed are particularly fitting—not to fundamentalists or to Mormons or to Roman Catholics, who will, of course each have a different set of axioms—but to us, to Unitarian Universalists. At the risk of doing disservice to his lovely exegesis, I will simply identify here in the briefest way possible the six axioms of theology which my esteemed colleague set forth as "the beginning of a theology."[4]

> Axiom 1. There is truth that we can know.
> Axiom 2: There is some purpose in life.
> Axiom 3: Being human implies duty to others.
> Axiom 4: We are ruled by a moral law.
> Axiom 5: We can change the balance of good and evil.
> Axiom 6: There is an intelligent construct to the universe.

3. Schulman, *Price*, 81.
4. Schulman, *Price*, 86.

These axioms were to me like pearls—pearls of wisdom. The joy of such discovery! How I would love to be able to play with, add to, multiply into community, complete the infinite possibilities herein. How I would love to bring my own few interpretations and insights to this process of creating transformative power.

Ah, but I have, you see, already begun. Last month, in anticipating today's sermon, I promised to elucidate for you twenty notions from math that have become an essential part of my spiritual toolbox. I envisioned sharing each of these "loosely spiritual insights drawn from mathematics" in some depth, so that I might convey to you how I arrived from the mathematics involved in each insight to the metaphorical interpretations which so inform my life-perspective. Now, here you will all realize that you are, truly, going to benefit this morning from the fact that I actually can *do* mathematical calculations. Figure I deliver, say, a twenty-five minute sermon. If I budget my time, I might allow one minute to introduce my topic, three minutes for jokes, and one for a conclusion. That leaves me with twenty minutes to explain in depth the mathematics, introduce the relevant spiritual insight, and illustrate with appropriate examples the twenty spiritual ideas I've elected to pull out of my math closet and share with you. Even a modest ability to do ordinary division tells me that's one minute each. All my common sense plus fourteen years of writing sermons says it's not going to happen that way. I'm better off sticking to the jokes.

So, here's a quickie that combines math and religion. A student was asked to list the Ten Commandments in any order. His answer? "3, 6, 1, 8, 4, 5, 9, 2, 10, and 7."

Okay, so maybe I'm a little like the guy who walked into a popular neighborhood bar where everybody knew everyone else, and he soon discovered that the regular crowd had told the same jokes over and over so often that they'd worked out a clever kind of shorthand system. Every so often, someone would just shout out a number. "Seventeen," yelled one guy from the back of the room, and everybody roared with laughter. "Thirty-one," another person called out to hearty, appreciative laughter. So the evening went. After a while, the new guy, having finally determined what was going on, decided to try a joke himself. "Twenty-six," he shouted out when there was an appropriate break in the conversation. Not a sound. Dead silence. The newcomer, embarrassed, leaned over to the guy sitting next to him and whispered, "What's the matter with joke number twenty-six?" "Not a thing, really," replied his neighbor. "Some folks just can't tell a joke."

There's a wealth of information in my math closet, and some of it is just pure fun. But true to my word, I also culled from this information twenty spiritual notions drawn from mathematics. I printed this wisdom onto a sheet of paper, and I've asked some willing volunteers to pass them out to you now so that you may read these ideas at your own leisure.[5] Some of you will recognize the mathematical ideas on this handout more readily than others, and that's fine. All of you, I hope, will relate in some fashion to the everyday *spiritual* interpretations which I've made of these twenty ideas, although, like spiritual tools the world around, some will resonate more than others. Some of you might even agree with Martin Luther when, in the fifteenth century he claimed that "medicine makes people ill, mathematics makes them sad, and theology makes them sinful."

Still, what I'd most like for you to take from this sheet of ideas, and from this sermon in general, is really pretty simple. I have faith in the math behind these twenty ideas. I trust this math. I trust it the way some folks trust God, or human nature, or ultimate goodness. I suspect that we all have something that we trust in, something that makes life work for us, something that helps us find meaning and purpose. Whatever it is for you, I say bring it out of the closet, clean off any residual mold, and give it air. For, as Alexander Pope once so aptly framed our undaunted ability to question everything, "Ah! why, ye Gods, should two and two make four?"

---

5. See appendix A.

Chapter 6: How God Is Like the Definite Integral of Calculus[1]

The one is equivalent to the many. Yes, that's paradox. Yes, that describes relationship. Yes, that's how God is.

After our study group, four of us lunched at a Chinese buffet. We were opening our fortune cookies.

"What's yours say, Sarah?" asked Janet, a bright, striking woman in her early sixties.

I was the last to share, and I hesitated. Then I read aloud. "Use your abilities at this time to stay focused on your goal. You will succeed."

"Oh, that's a nice one," said Ruthie, an out-going, petite Jewish woman with a Catholic ex-husband—she had gotten a really bland message. "Do you *have* a goal?"

I stole a quick look back at Janet, who is one of the most genuinely caring people I've ever known and with whom I had just very recently had a heartfelt discussion about precisely this subject of my fledgling goal. Her eyes said "tell." Nope, there was no shutting up this time.

"Uh, I have a book project I'm working on."

"A book project?" Ruthie had caught the scent. "Are you *writing* a book?" My affirmative nod was not enough. "What's it about?"

I'd had so little confidence about getting this work in print that I generally avoided openly sharing about this subject, but I took a deep

---

1. This chapter is based on a true story. The grounding for my ideas about the Divine can be found in Voss, *What Number Is God?*, 115–21. This book was a slightly revised version of my doctoral thesis, accepted in 1993, about two weeks before the deadline that year for graduation from Meadville Lombard Theological School. The first time I presented a sermon using these ideas was at People's Church in Cedar Rapids, Iowa, on May 16, 1993 (a few weeks before my graduation).

breath and decided to plunge in. "It's called the *Math Mystic's Guide to Creative Spirituality.*"

"Math . . . math what?"

I mumbled the title again, then looked at three questioning faces and realized I needed to say more.

"It's about math and spirituality—you know, God and stuff. Basically, I take metaphors from math, explain their outstanding characteristics, and then apply them to spiritual stuff."

"Sounds . . . interesting," Lilly ventured. "Can you explain?" Quiet Lilly, who often was profound when she did decide to talk, sat beside me at the outside of our brown-leathered booth seat, her cane braced against the edge of the table.

I thought for a moment, then started in about redemption and Snell's Law. The puzzled expressions grew a little cloudier. I tried not to sigh aloud.

"She used to teach calculus, you know." That was Janet. Janet was the one who knew me best. I winced while the three of them gushed over that.

"It's no big deal," I shrugged. "Really, it's not." I hated this glorification. It felt like a separation. A hangover from being a smart girl in a little school when I was a kid.

They went on to discuss mathematics, which, it seemed, none of them had much liked. And *calculus*! Well, I must be a *genius*. I'd heard this part, too. Too many times. I wished they'd emphasized my pastoral ministry instead of my brain, which, not irrelevantly, is starting to age. I tried to shrivel down in my seat, an automatic reflex. Then I caught myself.

"I think God is like the definite integral of calculus," I said. "I mean, it's a mathaphor, er, metaphor. For me, anyway. For me, God is like the definite integral of calculus."

For a moment all three just stared at me, more or less speechless.

"Okay," I said, "I can explain."

"I got as far as calculus," Ruthie said, "but that completely did me in."

"Algebra was too much for me," Lilly added.

"I can do it so you'll understand," I insisted, wondering where my sudden bravado was coming from.

"All right, then," came the chorus, "go for it."

How gracious these valuable friends were, I thought. Their gift of encouragement! I took an unused paper napkin off the table—one of those flimsy white ones that just barely do the job. I unfolded it to its rectangular shape, and tore off one of the edges so it was ragged.

"See this napkin. If we had a ruler we could measure the length and the width, and if we multiplied those two numbers we'd know how many square inches the napkin was before I tore this little bit off. So this napkin is, what, maybe 11 inches by 5 inches, say 55 square inches. And now, since I tore part of the top off, it is *approximately* that, just a little less than 55 square inches." I looked up to check if they were following my demonstration. "Area = length times width?"

They laughed at me, but good-naturedly. "We know that one, Sarah," Janet commented.

So I showed them how we can get a closer approximation if we break the napkin into smaller rectangles, like folding it into a small fan and adding up the areas of each of these individual rectangles that made up the whole napkin. I watched them carefully and, happily for me, they were still with me.

"Suppose all you had to do in life was to endlessly make smaller and smaller folds and measure smaller and smaller rectangles and then add all the areas together. You would get closer and closer to the exact size of this napkin because each succeeding set of rectangles would more closely capture the irregularities of the torn napkin. In theory, you could do this forever. You'd be crazy of course" (I laughed a little here—it was a practiced laugh because I had done this exercise many times, sometimes even in sermons), "but you'd always get closer to the exact area of this torn napkin. There would always be a tiny bit, no matter how minuscule—not yet accounted for, but with the definite integral you get a unique math process which transcends the seeming paradox of the gap and provides an *exact* sum."[2] I said this last rather too triumphantly, as a math teacher might upon reaching a climax in the proof.

"The math can be complicated here, but that's not what we're looking at. We're trying to understand what the process achieves. How you add all these tiny rectangles together and get the precise area of the napkin." Again, I checked out my friends' faces, and all three nodded that they "got" it.

---

2. See Voss, *What Number*, ch. 4.

Then I lit my conclusion: "This entire process is what the definite integral of calculus is all about."

"Wow," said Lilly, "you should have been my teacher."

"Boy, you must be one of those very left-brained people," pronounced Ruthie. "Are you left-brained?"

"No," said Janet as though I wasn't sitting right across the table from them, "she's left-brained, and right-brained, and . . .

". . . *all* brain." Janet and Ruthie said this last in unison. It made me intensely uncomfortable. But, also proud. When I was young, I would have had more ambiguity about the proud part, but I am old enough now to finally hear this as a compliment, not a complaint.

"Okay, so here's the rest of it."

"There's *more*?" Ruthie asked. I wasn't sure she was happy about this possibility, but by now I was determined.

I nodded. "There's the spiritual part, too." I discoursed a little about how we can't really define God, but often try by using different metaphors—father, ruler, love, king, friend. It's really important to have a metaphor that highlights relationship, I said, because relationship is one of the most important, and often most estranged, concepts in our current society. I wanted to convince them that everything is related, that we are all related, that the four of us seemed to be separate individuals sitting around a table, but really we are all intimately connected to each other, part of a single whole. If I'd been preaching, I would have used "the interdependent web of all existence" language that is common in my faith tradition, but it doesn't really matter what language is used—what matters is the idea. I also wanted to get all this across to my friends in about a minute, because I sensed that was about all the time left.

"The many and the One, which I understand as God, are the same," I said, then added that I hadn't felt this way until after I'd been teaching calculus for a while and I could see how the many and the one are identical in the definite integral of calculus. I knew about all the wonderful doors this calculus had opened in our physical world—airplanes and space travel, for instance, but none of these was as important to me as the metaphysical notion that everything is interrelated. The wholeness of this idea has become my best metaphor for God, a concept that for the first forty years of my life I never fully accepted.

"I trusted the math. That's where I first understood. Later I applied this idea to my understanding of God, and then I began to trust God, too. The math was really crucial to my spiritual journey."

Shortly thereafter our luncheon ended and we each went our separate ways. Or what *appears* to be our separate ways. Life paints a colorful coat over these individual paths, but mysticism sees through this coat to the web of relationships that hold the separateness together as one cohesive entity. Jesus, great healer that he was, declared that there "is none good but one, [and] that is God."[3] But while Jesus spoke freely and often of God, his only pictures were the parables he drew that told stories about how God works.

A vignette comes to me now about the kindergarten girl who was working diligently on a drawing when her teacher asked what the drawing was. The girl replied, "I'm drawing God." The teacher paused and said, "But no one knows what God looks like." Without so much as glancing up from her drawing, the little girl replied, "Well, they will in a minute." My definite integral of calculus approach to God is probably a little like that. Still, I feel fortunate to have a metaphor that helps me.

Actually, I now have lots of metaphors for God. Drawing metaphors is an oft-employed method of talking about God. Besides the definite integral of calculus, I am particularly fond of love and friend as images for the Divine.[4] I also like the God-lexicon which Deepak Chopra uses in his (somewhat scientific) treatise on *How to Know God*. Drawing on both Western and Eastern faith traditions, he speaks of the Protector God, the Almighty God, the God of Peace, Redeemer God, Creator God, God of Miracles, and the God of Pure Being. His seven Gods are metaphors, but they are metaphors that describe, like the blind men describing the elephant, something very real. As Chopra puts it, the difference between the secular and the spiritual world is not one of belief in God, but of clarity.

Over the years, people who share my interest in math and religion have also shared with me other possible metaphors drawn from mathematics. But I keep coming back to the definite integral of calculus because, as I have written elsewhere, the analogy is "a structural representation for our relationship with a transcending unitary Whole [and it] offers itself to us as a bridging device between the physical world that it has helped to shape in modern times and the abstract world of the psycho-logical, wherein we become most aware, perhaps, of our spiritual lives."[5]

3. May and Metzger, *New Oxford Bible*, Matt 19:17.

4. Sally McFague's wonderful *Metaphorical Theology: Models of God in Religious Language* was my introduction to this concept.

5. Voss, *What Number*, 120.

My personal path to this understanding includes three significant episodes of physical pain and emotional alienation, starting in my young teen years. I was born at the tail end of World War II, and grew up very involved in the Congregational Church, which was nearly as liberal as Unitarian Universalism. Like most Protestant churches of the time, "God" was a supernatural deity, albeit white, male, and heterosexual enough to have his own son. God wasn't, of course, just any supernatural deity: He was *the* deity, one and only—although here I had to struggle with Trinitarian subtleties that Unitarians, at least, avoid in their mostly firm understanding of Jesus as a person, not a god.

To the child me, however, Jesus was the beloved Son who gave his life so that we might be saved (whatever that meant) and the Holy Ghost . . . well, the Holy Ghost was *really* confusing. Ghosts were supernatural, to be sure, but they were also to be avoided and quite probably they were pure superstition. This was mysterious, to say the least. But, of all the mysteries I understood from my early church years, the one which promised most certainty was that God was a personal God, meaning God loved *me*. God was the answer to whatever troubles I had. God was omnipotent and omniscient. I absorbed these concepts way before I learned the words.

These concepts are still deep inside me somewhere—on my earliest "tapes," so to say. Over the years, however, those tapes have been subjected to rough treatment. The first damage to that part of me which tried to trust that an all-powerful and all-knowing God truly gave a fig about *me* occurred when I was about thirteen and nearly drowned in some water in a creek that was just a little bit deeper than I was tall. After I'd fought the water until I realized I was going to lose, but immediately before I was rescued by one of the larger, stronger girls in the group of friends who were playing (unsupervised, I might add) in this country oasis, I had an incredible experience. My life played back as though it were in fast motion on a movie reel—every detail was there. Many years later I read a description of the near-death process and I recognized my childhood experience in the accompanying phrase "life recall." That new information released me from a prison of silence I'd kept all those years, never telling a soul about what I had experienced in my near drowning.

Suddenly I realized that other people had encountered similar things. Apparently, there was more to this process of "deathing" than I had experienced—white light at the end of the tunnel, out-of-body sightings, and so on. Sometimes, now, I wish that I had actually struggled a little longer before I was rescued. Maybe "white light" could have salvaged my "God loves you" tape. As it was, that precious early learning was further obstructed by another tape from my formative years. This one was of chickens whose heads had just been hatcheted off and whose bodies continued to dance wildly around our yard. My life recall, I assumed, was surely just a variation of this dance, something weird that happened in the amazingly bitter process of dying.

Not long after my near drowning I became an atheist, and I remained that way for a quarter of a century. Without claiming causality, I name the occasion with which I now associate a further abuse to my "God loves you" tape. This event was a botched-up hysterectomy when I was in my mid-thirties. As a result of surgical error, I experienced unprecedented and unrelenting pain for about twenty-four hours straight. I went into that surgery an atheist, but an atheist with a tremendous will to live. I had three young children and a full, seemingly rich life. By the time I left the hospital, the physical problem having been corrected by an additional surgery, I'd revised my understanding of my will to live. I knew, because I had just experienced it, that some things in life are so bad you have to disassociate yourself from them. I knew, because I had just felt it, that under some circumstances, dying was preferable to the pain of living. What kind of an all-powerful, all-knowing, all-loving God would thrust that bitterness on you?

Soon after this hospitalization I opened up to new-age-ish, somewhat occult experiences that convinced me I'd been wrong in my belief that the physical realm was all there had ever been and ever would be. Maybe there'd been something besides a purely mechanical life-reflex going on with those dancing chickens. Maybe there was a plan of some sort after all. Maybe there was even a kind of life after death. My atheism began to dissolve, but whatever replaced it couldn't seem to revamp that ever-more-damaged "God loves you" tape.

Oh, my. There is a saying that experience is something you don't get until just after you need it. In any case, the third incident happened when I was in my late fifties. It occurred over the space of several months and two back-to-back back surgeries, a month apart. Again, this event was one of intense pain, the worst of it a two-week period of hospitalization during which I relied heavily on morphine.

On Finding Out the Doctor Isn't God After All

He's human. He makes mistakes.
He doesn't know.
The pain may be something he can't fix.
Your future may be unpleasant.

So if the doctor isn't God, who is?
Where is he? Or her? Or it?

The cat lies down next to you, next to the pain.
The cat is not afraid of the pain.
The cat purrs. Maybe the cat is God.

It is not time yet for the next dose of pills.
You are glad no one is there to see
except the Cat-God

who doesn't care if you may never get well again,
who is content just to lie close enough
that you can stroke her fur
as long as the good arm lasts.

So, where was Unitarian Universalism, my faith, during this troubling time? It was there, to be sure, in the form of caring individuals who truly did walk beside me. But, search as I might, I couldn't find a God-tape, and I wanted one badly. My faith tradition had such a spiritual aid at one time, but, alas, it seemed to have gone the way of my "God loves you" tape. I finally filed that damaged tape on the "Outdated Metaphors" shelf in my heart.

Not long after this third painful, scary incident in my life, I realized that, someplace deep inside, I'd been gifted with a new tape, not exactly a "God loves you" tape and certainly not an "I believe in the Father, the Son, and the Holy Spirit tape." But it is a God-tape nonetheless. I'm not sure how it got there, but I suspect it had something to do with Grace, which I believe exists in abundance in the *super*-natural world.

This new tape has been influenced by my increasing focus on the relationships in my life and, more specifically, on my increasing desire to be in "right relationship" with others. Here, again, I found refuge and insight in my knowledge of mathematics, which has shown me, again and again, that not every way gives the answer you are searching for. Because of its mathematical complexity, I'm substituting an explanation taken from the integral calculus with a simpler example from algebra. Consider the equation $x + y = 10$, where x and y are "placeholders." If we replace "x" with 2 and "y" with 8, the equation becomes $2 + 8 = 10$, a correct and true statement. Those choices work. So do 6 and 4, or 3 and 7. There are often many possible paths to the "answer," and even an infinite number of possible answers (e.g., 2.45 and 7.55; 2.46 and 7.54; and so on). Yet not every search works. For example, $3 + 8$ does not equal 10.

In like manner, not every suggested solution to a definite integral of calculus will work, although often there exists more than one possible route to the answer. And in like manner, again, not every search for God "works," but there are many possible paths that do. Indeed, our individual searches depend on a host of resources. If you're like me, your God-tapes have a lot of space left on them. Mine is certainly not yet finished. What I'm aiming for, though, is not just more talk about God, but the key to the door that lets us access God directly. If we actually get our hands on the doorknob, we're apt to discover that the door is not even locked. Going through it may seem risky, but that is a choice which, ultimately, each of us must make for ourselves.

Use your abilities
    left brain, right brain, whole brain
at this time
    today, not tomorrow
to stay focused
    like a ray of light shining
on your goal,
    spiritual awareness and maturity.
You will succeed.

Part 2: Number Mysticism and Beyond

"CANTORIAN RELIGION"[1]

The lamps are different, but the light is the same.
—Jalalu'l-Din Rumi (thirteenth century)

In the room my mind
sit many different lamps.
The lamp of Christianity, an old oil
lantern, recently wired for electricity,
all the latest scientific gadgets;
when I approach,
it springs on automatically.
I trust this lamp:
it was the light in the hallway
when I was small and afraid of the dark.
I use this lamp even now, oh,
not all the time . . . but
when I have moments free,
in fancy Gothic cathedrals
or tiny country chapels
smelling of warm, waxed wood.

The Eastern lamp is hand-crafted copper,
gondola-shaped, wick-lit
Aladdin's lamp, it charms
with ancient promise
of untold treasure, I must
but rub it and attend, oh
there, can you see?
The earnest, handsome Buddhist
from Sri Lanka
who resides in the basement of my house,
who laments that the young women
in this country don't care much
for the color of his skin. Me?
I'm old. I love the rich
blue-black glow that lives
in the light of this lamp.

1. Voss, *What Number*, 132–33.

The Jewish lamp, really seven candles
welded together. The one
in the room my mind
is highly stylized. Contemporary.
Unorthodox. You can't make out much
in its soft flame, mostly abstract markings,
maybe it makes a difference
if you read Hebrew. Still, I love
to search the shadows it forms
for things familiar and strange,
as order out of nothing
in only seven days
and bushes that burn
with the Sabbath light
now and forever Amen.

In this land where I was born
are Native lamps; mine
a gray clay
artifact, discovered lying
by a tattooed Erie Indian
whose body was dug from a pit
and whose spirit finds me yet today
when I dig my bare toes
deep into the earth
and listen to the breath
of the wind.

All these and more are the lamps
that rest in the room
my mind, yet the one
I cherish most is the chalice
that ignites my heart,
for I see in its light
the room my mind
with all its magnificent lamps,
among them the chalice
that ignites my heart
which shows the room my mind

Dear God of many iterations,
may all their light shine on
and on and on, like a Cantor set
transcending.

Chapter 7: Empirical Study: Sign, Symbol, Metaphor, and Model in Religion and Mathematics[1]

A riddle: She is as ancient as humankind but as new as the greatest minds that pursue her. Schoolchildren (and some adults) often shudder at the mere mention of her, yet scientists adore her and nearly everyone acknowledges her importance in our modern technological society. Almost no one sees a place for her in church. Who is she?

INTRODUCTION TO STUDY

THIS ILLUSIVE LADY IS mathematics.[2] Loosely (metaphorically) speaking, the question at the heart of this investigation is "Why isn't she in church?" She used to be, of course. Great minds from the ancient Hindus to the proponents of the new nonrelativistic physics have found in mathematics a mediation between the natural world and the spiritual realm.[3] Mathematics has even been called the divine language. Yet today the divine connection is hidden and remote at best. In most of our religions, it is nonexistent.

This study presupposed that a renewal of the divine aspect of mathematics will contribute to the overall spiritual health of our contemporary

---

1. Voss, *What Number*, 161–71.

2. The gender emphasis is intentional. In languages where words are gendered, "mathematician" is masculine and "mathematics" is feminine.

3. For more exploration on this topic see Davis and Hersh, *Descartes' Dream*; Voss, "Depolarizing"; Hofstadter, *Gödel*; and Leshan and Margenau, *Einstein's Space*.

religious institutions. Granting this admittedly debatable assumption, how, then, might such a renewal unfold? This study hypothesized that the root of renewal lies in our willingness to embrace mathematics as a metaphorical language. More explicitly, it explored (or began to explore) the degree to which we humans currently view mathematics as metaphorical language; the differences, if any, in our willingness to ascribe to mathematics notions such as sign, symbol, metaphor, and model; our emotional attitudes toward mathematics; and current assumptions about the strength of connection between mathematics and religion.

STUDY DESIGN AND EXECUTION

Because this was a *beginning* exploration conducted with limited resources and a tight time frame, two practical considerations greatly influenced the design of this study. First, it needed to be manageable in scope. Second, it needed to address those who would be most likely to have given some thought to or to have had some experience with the issues involved.

A sample of seventy-four different names was selected at random from a master roster compiled of all faculty members of the various sciences and mathematics departments at the University of Chicago, the University of Chicago School of Divinity, and the Association of Chicago Theological Schools (ACTS) connected with the university. A survey was tested and refined, and then distributed to these seventy-four. Seven of these faculty members responded in some manner so as to be self-excluded from the study (for example, being "philosophically opposed" to surveys or feeling "unqualified" to address the issues), and another forty-four did not respond at all. Thus all results and interpretations have been made on the basis of responses from roughly one-third of the original sample.

Two limitations of the study are immediately clear. First, the study in no way ascertained the views of today's *general* population. It unabashedly addresses a highly educated and specialized group; all conclusions necessarily need to be tempered by awareness of this restriction. Then, too, the disappointingly low response rate raises additional questions regarding the reliability of the study.

A third limitation is less readily apparent, namely that gender-related patterns of response were not discernible. The inclusion of question 10 in the survey indicates the original intent of the study design to address this issue. Furthermore, the sample population contained a substantial number of (apparently) female names. Unfortunately, only four females chose to respond to the survey. Such a small percentage return provided an insufficient method of identifying significant gender-oriented tends. Other demographic information gathered included the responders' general level of familiarity with mathematics and their major area of occupation.

The survey itself consisted of eight short-answer "substance" questions dealing with the topics hypothesized, three demographic questions, and two open-ended substance questions.

Fig. 7.1. STUDY QUESTIONNAIRE:
Sign, Symbol, Metaphor, and Model in Religion and Mathematics

1. How much connection do you see between mathematics and religion?
   1 (Virtually None) 2 3 4 5 (A Great Deal)

2. How much connection do you see between mathematics and science?
   1 (Virtually None) 2 3 4 5 (A Great Deal)

3. Which of the following comes closest to describing your view of mathematics?
   1 A set of signs which are manipulated in a logical manner and which help reveal the fundamental laws of nature.
   2 A symbolic language which helps to articulate the intelligibility we find in the universe.
   3 A language filled with metaphors for the way in which the world works.
   4 A medium for modeling reality.
   5 All of the above.

4. Which best describes your interpretation of "2":
   1 sign
   2 symbol
   3 metaphor
   4 model
   5 meaningless
   6 other (please specify)

5. Which best describes your interpretation of "$a\int^b f(x)\, dx$":
   1 sign
   2 symbol
   3 metaphor
   4 model
   5 meaningless
   6 other (please specify)

6. "$E = mc^2$" is an example of (check as many as applicable):
   1 the abstraction of a natural law
   2 a model
   3 a relation between symbols
   4 the inviolate truth
   5 God's design
   6 a uniquely human mental exercise
   7 other (please specify)

7. Mathematics is (check as many as are applicable):

a. rigid	g. flexible	m. emotive
b. exact	h. open	n. bland
c. objective	i. rational	o. animating
d. subjective	j. irrational	p. dull
e. precise	k. sterile	q. exciting
f. beautiful	l. useful	r. demonic

8. The existence of mathematics validates the claim that all is not metaphor.
   1 (Strongly Disagree) 2 3 4 5 (Strongly Agree)

9. Are you primarily involved in the area of
   1 mathematics
   2 science
   3 religion
   4 philosophy
   5 other

10. Please note your sex:
    a. Male
    b. Female

11. Please note your highest level of study in mathematics:
    a. General mathematics (arithmetic, geometry, and/or high school algebra)
    b. College algebra and/or trigonometry and/or beginning statistics
    c. Calculus
    d. Advanced mathematical studies

12. Can you elaborate on your understanding of the meaning of the following terms: signs, symbols, metaphors, and models?

13. Do you feel there is a difference in significance and use between religious and mathematical signs, symbols, and models, etc., and, if so, please help identify that difference.

RESULTS AND INTERPRETATIONS

Five different categories of response are associated with this survey: overall or *total* results, responses of those indicating *less* familiarity with *math*ematics (question 11, parts a and b), responses of those indicating *high* familiarity with mathematics (question 11, parts c and d), responses of those indicating primary involvement in the area of *religion* or philosophy, and responses of those indicating primary involvement in the areas of *science* and mathematics (question 9).

The slight overlap should be noted between the categories of "High Math" and "Religion" and also between "High Math" and "Science/math." In other words, those who indicated less familiarity with mathematics were uniformly involved in religion, while those who indicated high familiarity with mathematics were most likely, but not uniformly, involved in areas of science or mathematics. One person (a woman) indicated dual involvement in both science and religion.

Questions 3 and 8 provided basic feedback on the degree to which we humans (more accurately, a select subset thereof) currently view mathematics as a metaphorical language. What stands out clearest in regard to question 3 is that responders tended to understand mathematics as a symbolic language (39 percent) or as a set of manipulative signs (26 percent). More than a quarter (26 percent) of all respondents indicated a preference for all four terms (signs, symbols, metaphors, and models). A few responders could not choose between the terms and so marked more than one response. Only one response indicated a view of mathematics that was primarily metaphorical in nature.

Those who most frequently favored the view of mathematics as "a symbolic language which helps to articulate the intelligibility we find in the universe" were those currently involved in religion. Responders from the area of science and mathematics were most likely to see mathematics as "a medium for modeling reality." Those who had least familiarity with mathematics (all of whom were also involved in religion) were most likely to view mathematics as "all of the above," that is, as a combination of descriptions involving signs, symbols, metaphors, and models. High mathematics awareness and/or professional involvement in mathematics/science seems to be correlated with *no* conception of mathematics as a language filled with metaphors.

Question 8 addressed the issue of metaphor in mathematics from a slightly different perspective. Two major voices in the current theological world are those of the critical realist and the deconstructionist, both of whom rely heavily on the importance of metaphor in our religious understandings. To the deconstructionist, the world is known only through metaphors. That is, all is metaphor: nothing exists except through the medium of metaphorical language. The critical realist, on the other hand, assumes that much is a metaphor, but not everything. Sallie McFague, a representative of the critical realist position, contends that the way in which we approximate our experience, whether it be poetic, religious, scientific, or otherwise, is always metaphorical, and that healthy metaphors are at the heart of creativity. Yet McFague has a curious habit, not well acknowledged, of alluding to mathematics whenever she attempts to assure her readers that *all* is not metaphor.[4] Question 8 sought to challenge or to support the contention that mathematics in some way offers a universal absolute that is non-metaphorical.

Responses to question 8 suggest that those involved with religion and, particularly, those less familiar with mathematics are somewhat more prone to support McFague's apparent supposition than are those more familiar or involved with mathematics and the sciences. However, the relatively large percentage of NRS (no responses) coupled with a few penciled-in comments (for example, "I don't understand the question") suggests that this question may have been too specialized for many respondents to fully grasp, at least in its present phrasing and context.

Questions 4, 5, and 6 address differences in perception of the use of terms such as sign, symbol, metaphor, and model within mathematics, that is, internally. The two open-ended questions at the end of the survey

---

4. See McFague, *Metaphorical Theology*, 28, 84, 87, 89.

(questions 12 and 13) elicit differences perceived externally, that is, between the terms as applied to mathematics and as applied to religion.

Question 4, 5, and 6, contain, respectively, examples of the Hindu-Arabic numeral for the concept of two, the notations for the definite integral of calculus, and Einstein's famed equation $E = mc^2$. They explore the respondent's understandings of the terms sign, symbol, metaphor, and model at assorted levels of complexity. People less familiar with math tended to identity "2" as a sign slightly more frequently than as a symbol, whereas all other groups most often called it a symbol. Those with high knowledge of mathematics and also those coming from the fields of science/mathematics most often identified the definite integral as a symbol. Those with less math familiarity not surprisingly most often labeled the notation "meaningless." As a total group, responses to question 5 were well-dispersed throughout the set of possibilities. Tabulations of question 6 responses indicate that Einstein's equation was most often described as a law by respondents in "high math," "religion," and "science/mathematics" categories and was described about equally as a law, model, or symbol by those with less math familiarity and by the group as a whole. Notably, no one at all identified "2" as a metaphor and no one at all identified Einstein's equation as "the inviolate truth." It is also curious that, while scientists and mathematicians were generally willing to see mathematics as a medium for modeling reality (question 3), they were much less willing to describe the specific examples found in questions 4, 5, and 6 as models.

The first open-ended question (#12) sought to ascertain the understandings those surveyed held of the terms sign, symbol, metaphor, and model. The second open-ended question explained differences perceived between, on the one hand, the significance and use of these terms in mathematics and, on the other, their significance and use in religion. Overall, the responses tended (1) to confirm the assumption of ambiguity in the meanings respondents ascribed to the terms and (2) to suggest that respondents view the use of the terms within the two fields as fundamentally different from each other. A trend seems to be emerging, however, that mitigates these differences, which, not incidentally, are identified only vaguely.

That ambiguity exists was not immediately apparent. Indeed, individual surveys presented comparisons and distinctions between the terms in fairly cohesive, consistent manners. Yet when the comments were regrouped according to genre, for example, all comments about signs, all about symbols, mixed and even contradictory reactions became more obvious. Consider, for example, the following statements taken from completed surveys:

> Sign and symbol are very similar in meaning.
> I don't have a clear distinction between signs and symbols.
> [A] symbol is a metaphor.
> Signs . . . can have a metaphorical sense.
> I don't see any real distinction between sign and symbol, except that symbol seems to be the more common term.
> A symbol . . . portrays some reality, but does not participate in it.
> Symbols participate in reality.
> A sign not only points to some reality, it is involved in it.
> Symbols . . . indicate the meaning by participating in the reality signified.
> Metaphor is a symbol.
> A metaphor is a species of symbol.
> A model is a complex of metaphors and symbols.

While the boundaries between sign, symbol, metaphor, and model were poorly delineated, the language with which they were most frequently described nonetheless suggested characteristic ideas associated with each term. Signs tend to *point to* something. To be *arbitrary* and to be *concrete, physical,* or *visual*. Symbols (generally) seem to *participate* in the reality or context which they invoke and to have more to do with value, imagination, and the *psychic*. Metaphor suggests a *comparison* between *realities*, one of which is usually simpler or more familiar than the other. Models have more to do with *behavior*: for example, they *show how* something *operates*, they *reflect ways* of doing this or that, they are constructions, they form *structures* or *frameworks* for *operations*, they are *constructed, useful* cases.

Demographic analysis of the responses to question 12 provides an additional insight, namely that those surveyees not involved in religion responded less frequently and more briefly than those involved in religion. This apparent disinterest on the part of the mathematics/scientific community became even more pronounced in the responses to question 13. One such person responded cryptically, "Never really thought about it." End of comment.

The remaining five respondents from the area of mathematics/science seemed to note differences in the use of the terms in mathematics and in religion.[5] Differences cited, however, were difficult to categorize.

---

5. Some of these comments spoke only of mathematics: any connection they bore to question 13 was indirect at best.

One person, for instance, noted a difference between formal meanings found in mathematics and informal ones found in religion. Another discussed the role of mathematics (as opposed to religion) in drawing inferences about how systems behave. A third sensed a difference in that mathematics has no necessary connection to anything outside itself, while religion is concerned with something external to its own terms and logic. This latter comment draws on the only echo of commonality in responses of mathematicians/scientists—namely that mathematics is in some sense self-contained, not needing to draw on external sources for its validity.

The remaining responses, all from the field of religion, ran the continuum from "no difference" to "not much difference" to "maybe" or "it depends" to "some difference" to "yes." There was slightly more response on the "yes" end than on the "no" end. The more common themes centered on the measurability, mechanism, and rationality of the mathematical signs, symbols, metaphors, and models as opposed to the greater fullness, less precision, and larger truth of their religious counterparts. One respondent was perhaps particularly attuned to the underlying presuppositions of this study when he noted that "the force or slant (between mathematical and religious signs, symbols, etc.) is different, but they are merging, as math and physics begin to ask more and more fundamental questions—how old is the cosmos? where is the edge of space?"

Question 7 assessed the emotional response of the surveyees to mathematics. All five categories almost unanimously (95 percent, 91 percent, 100 percent, 94 percent, 100 percent, respectively) agreed that mathematics is useful. Other descriptive terms frequently associated with mathematics include rational, precise, exact, beautiful, and objective. There appears to be a correlation between high math familiarity/involvement and willingness to describe mathematics as beautiful. Two groups (high math and science/math) also identified mathematics as being flexible, exciting, and rigid noticeably more frequently than did those with less math familiarity or those involved primarily in the area of religion. Curiously, those involved in science/math identified as being flexible and being rigid with equal frequency. Terms less likely to be attached to mathematics included, across the board, irrational, sterile, emotive, dull, and demonic. No one at all described mathematics as bland.

Question 1 evaluated the degree of connection (undefined) that respondents believe exists between mathematics and religion. Those involved in science/math and those more familiar with mathematics saw the least connection. Other groups were more evenly dispersed in their assessments, perhaps suggesting some uncertainty in their choices. On the other hand (question 2), all respondents unequivocally felt that a high degree of connection exists between mathematics and science.

CONCLUSIONS

As a whole, the study suggests that mathematics is not valued in our culture as a metaphorical language, nor is it seen as contributing much to religion. These contentions seem to be most strongly supported by those with high awareness of mathematics and less professional involvement in religion. All groups surveyed agreed on the usefulness of mathematics, but apparently that usefulness does not extend to examination of religious issues. However, much ambiguity exists, even among the religious community, regarding the meaning and nature of the terms *sign*, *symbol*, *metaphor*, and *model*; and there is evidence that all groups (to varying degrees and with varying intents) recognize at least some relevance of sign, symbol, and model to both mathematics and religion.

Whether or not today's society views mathematics as an indicator of the existence of absolute certainty or as an alternative to the notion that all is metaphor remains an open question.[6] Those most sympathetic to future exploration of this and other issues raised in the study are most likely to be those who combine some degree of familiarity with mathematics with an explicit interest in religion. Thus, if the illusive lady of mathematics is to reappear in contemporary churches, it will most likely be at the invitation of those open to rethinking established patterns of thought. One such person probably stands behind the following commentary made regarding both the content of this study and the study itself:

> Both religion and mathematics make use of signs and models. Initially I supposed that symbols and metaphors were more apt to be found in religion than mathematics. Perhaps, though, "$E = mc^2$" might be thought of as either/both symbol and metaphor? Perhaps also as a model. E/m/c I would understand as signs. This is fascinating.

---

6. Besides issues already raised with regard to McFague, this topic lends itself to additional investigation of concerns raised by Kant and Hume.

Chapter 8: Sacred Qualities[1]

As symbols, numbers are unique in that they embody two distinct kinds of meaning. One is quantitative; the other is qualitative. Both meanings give number power, but different kinds of power. Today we are most familiar and most comfortable with the quantitative meaning, for that is the way today's culture initially teaches us to appreciate numbers. Early on, we learn to count, and that simple accomplishment opens up a conceptual world that we share with other creatures only on the most rudimentary of levels. By the time we complete elementary school we can add, subtract, multiply, divide, and otherwise put numbers to work for us. We continue thereafter to use the power derived from the quantitative nature of numbers to help us with the practical aspects of our lives. We shop, cook, conduct business, keep track of time, take appropriate amounts of medicine, drive cars, fly airplanes, map out (and pay for) vacations, plant crops, and check our email all because the quantitative power of number assists us. What's more, we pretty much take this power for granted. Sometimes we even complain about it. Ask some struggling college students, for instance, whether they're taking "statistics" or "sadistics" and see what answer you get.

The qualitative meaning of number is less familiar to us, although, with a little help, most people will recognize it. The easiest place to find it today is in a bookstore, in the section dealing with numerology. There, we learn that some specific number represents our individual soul urge, our life path, our peaks of achievement, the challenges each of us face in life, etc. By associating a number with each letter of our birth name, and with a little practice (just buy the book), we can then determine the appropriate numbers necessary to reveal these associated personal characteristics.

---

1. Voss, "Sacred Qualities."

Judging purely by the popularity of such books, it is clear that many people today appreciate the qualitative power of numbers, albeit in a form which just as many people seem to dismiss as superstitious nonsense. My own view toward alphabetic numerology (gematria) tends to be agnostic. Calculating my soul urge (nine), for example, was kind of fun, sort of like checking a horoscope or finding my Myers-Brigg inclinations. The resulting "nine" supposedly suggests my soul-goal is to learn to serve humanity. That it also implies I tend toward self-centeredness with a persistent need for ego-inflation bothers me not at all. What troubles me is the fact that this assessment rings uncomfortably true! It's that latter part that we refer to as the qualitative power of number.

Earlier societies tended to readily accept and appreciate this qualitative meaning of number. The ancient Pythagoreans, for example, did not distinguish between the practical and spiritual meaning of mathematics: everything was number. They believed that the universe literally sings and that numbers help us understand the harmony. According to this thought, the motion of the planets produces harmonious tones based on particular numerical frequencies. Number exists prior to physical reality, and indeed number in some way gives birth to, or manifests, that reality. This is a lot of power to ascribe to number, but the ancient Greeks were by no means alone in holding such views.

Philolaus, writing about 450 BCE, captured the heart of Pythagorean number philosophy when he wrote that "all things have a number, and it is this fact which enables them to be known." To the Jewish philosopher Philo of Alexandria, who lived about the time of Jesus, number was the "basis of the design of the Creator" and "the number itself, rather than its concrete representation, is considered the ultimate reality." The Roman philosopher Plotinus, writing in the third century BCE, believed that "number exists before objects which are described by number. The variety of sense-objects merely recalls to the soul the notion of number." Augustine, one of the great shapers of Christian doctrine, "saw in number an image of the absolute" which led him, by investigation of number symbolism, to "discover the mysteries of God which are set down in Scripture."[2]

Number symbolism, also known variously as number mysticism, numerology, and the science of numbers, has a clear historical link to the sacred. Often this connection has appeared in processes of divination, in astrological analysis, or in other rituals which contemporary society

---

2. Voss, *What Number*, 76.

generally attributes to superstitious faith in magic. Yet residual traces of number magic remain with us today in surprising contexts. As a young teenager, for instance, I would often pluck the petals of a daisy trying to decide if "he loves me" or "he loves me not." This practice was but a remnant of an old English children's rhyme, divinatory in essence:

> One I love, two I love,
> Three I love, I say,
> Four I love with all my heart,
> Five I cast away;
> Six he loves, seven she loves, eight both love.
> Nine he comes, ten he tarries,
> Eleven he courts, twelve he marries.

American folklore extended the rhyme three more numbers:

> Thirteen they quarrel, fourteen, they part,
> Fifteen, they die of a broken heart.

At the heart of such endeavor has always resided the assumption that certain numbers stand for something more than the concept of a concrete aggregate. In this sense, numbers are used symbolically to represent something significant to the sacred life of humankind. Four, for instance, is universally the number of earth and earth-things. Among many primitive peoples there were not only four directions, but also four winds, and, occasionally, a four-eyed, four-eared God that supervised earthly creation. The ancient Egyptians depicted a cosmos with a heavenly roof supported by four pillars, mountains, or women at the cardinal points. In Pythagorean cosmography, the first solid produced is four, and the fourth solid is assigned to the earth, a fact which added philosophical support to the commonly held belief in the foursquareness of Earth.

The Hebrew, Greek, Arabic, and early Sanskrit alphabets all employed symbols which served both as numerals and as letters. For instance, the Hebrew word for *Adam* doubles as a symbol for four. Using a kind of numerical logic foreign to most of us today, Augustine noted that man is a tetrad (man is four) since the name Adam is composed of the letters which are the four winds. Thus, he reasoned that "knowledge of divine things is disseminated throughout the world by the four gospels, evangelists or beasts [and is] emblemized by the four extremities of the cross, the four-fold division of Christ's clothing, and the four virtues, or forms of love."[3] The significant point in these illustrations is that a num-

---

3. Hopper, *Medieval Number*, 84.

ber, in this case the number four, stood for (represented or symbolized) something else. It was what we call a metaphor, holding qualitative rather than quantitative meaning, and as such it evoked in the human mind important understanding of the relationship between the human and the divine. It is difficult for our modern minds to fully appreciate the intensity with which earlier cultures embraced this relationship between numbers and their symbolic meanings. As scholar Vincent Foster Hopper put it, numbers were not mere mathematical tools, nor were they simply like counters in a game. Rather, they were "as fundamental realities, alive with memories and eloquent with meaning."[4] Such passion for the symbolic aspect of numbers created in our earlier societies a kind of dual use of numbers, one decidedly computational and the other intricately linked to divine revelation. Until recent times, this duality was seen not as a split but as mutually reinforcing guides to philosophical and spiritual wisdom.

In the last few centuries, we have tended to forget the second of these functions, focusing almost exclusively on the more formal aspects of mathematics as a symbolic language useful for all sorts of accurate, "truthful" computation. This one-sidedness, I believe, is changing. Work by scholars such as Sal Restivo and Reuben Hersh has done much to suggest a middle ground by showing that the content of mathematics has a strong social or cultural element, and it is therefore not nearly as absolute as recent tradition would suggest. Indeed, Fritjof Capra goes to the other extreme of one-sidedness when he writes in *The Web of Life* that "the new mathematic . . . is one of relationships and patterns. It is qualitative rather than quantitative and thus embodies the shift of emphasis that is characteristic of systems thinking—from objects to relationships, from quantity to quality, from substance to pattern."[5]

To me, as to the ancient Pythagoreans, the power of mathematics is that it easily assumes both the quantitative and qualitative roles, sort of like the wave/particle characteristic of modern physics. We are most familiar with the quantitative characteristic in the form of countable data, testable statistics, measurable science. The qualitative role, which tends to show up primarily as mathematical metaphor, leaves those of us suckled on variations of the formalistic logic of Bertrand Russell feeling much less secure. This uneasiness is aggravated by contemporary questions emerging from the realm of "numbers" which challenge traditional

---

4. Hopper, *Medieval Number*, vii.
5. Capra, *Web of Life*, 113.

religious views. Or maybe they support them. That's the problem. We're not quite sure.

Is God a sophisticated computer expert with a long white beard and a propensity for power more than for love? (See the poem at the beginning of part 1: "How to Reduce Fractions.") Is our world, as several prominent theorists maintain, based on the mathematics of holography, where each minuscule part holds within it the makings of the entire whole? Is universal consciousness simply a matter of quantum mind or the intersection of certain algebraic group theories? Is, as economist Brian Arthur contends, the Newtonian clockwork metaphor akin to standard Protestantism, while the emerging complexity of mathematical chaos theory is totally Taoist? Does "organized complexity" give rise to the "openness of the universe," and hence permit the existence of human beings with free will, as mathematician Paul Davies says? Is, as physicist Frank Tipler claims in *The Physics of Immortality*, the human soul just a specific program being run on a computing machine called the brain? Are DNA and RNA natural robots, as some cognitive scientists believe? Is life simply a computation? Is real life just one more Window?[6]

The number symbolism in these and similar holy mathaphors (mathematical metaphors) emerging in modern society is more complex than its counterpart in the numerology section of the local bookstore. In these more sophisticated and often highly advanced mathematical renderings, the power of number is no longer confined to mere integers. Perhaps, however, this evolution is merely indicative of the creative capacity of number to engage, to motivate, to stimulate the human spirit. As mathematical historian E. T. Bell wrote in the earlier part of the twentieth century:

> Any numerological theory of the universe seems queer to a mathematical skeptic only when he persists in staring at the modern aspect of Pythagorean dogma. Transpose the abstruse metaphors of modern mathematical physics into those of the older mysticism, and the illusion of queerness vanishes. Spectacular novelties take on the familiar form immortalized by Pythagoras when he turned numerologist. Number is at the bottom of everything; the Pythagoreans in the sixth century B.C. said that number *is* everything and that everything *is* number. They meant that *is* in the fullest sense. More than one modern

---

6. See more on these notions in chapter 11.

classic of high physical speculation says exactly the same thing, and numerology says Amen.[7]

In the past, numbers, the fundamental symbols of mathematics, have served humankind as apertures—openings to new realities, new wisdom. Today this power remains intact, as numbers ever challenge us to better understand our world, and our mundane and sacred relationships to it.

---

7. Bell, *Numerology*, 61.

Chapter 13: "Thirteen," "Doubling," and the Need to Heal Our Ancestors[1]

Thirteen is just another number; nonetheless I'm definitely not going to quit here.

SIMPLE NUMBERS CAN BRING forth—and mathematical processes can help resolve—powerful ethical issues. In this essay I illustrate this thesis with two examples.

THIRTEEN

Some numbers hold a different kind of energy than other numbers, an energy that incites hesitation, wariness, and perhaps even fear. Thirteen is such a number. Superstition has claimed this number in strange ways. There's a folkloric aspect of the number thirteen that's been noted in various cultures around the world, probably because variations of luck have been associated with it. A "baker's dozen" gives an extra loaf of bread (or whatever). In Italian, "make thirteen" means to hit the jackpot. In Judaism, God has thirteen Attributes of Mercy. Still, most of us tend to worry about bad rather than good luck when we think of thirteen. Friday the 13th is a day to be cautious. It's unlucky to have thirteen guests around a table. I know of at least one high-rise building that has no floor labeled as

---

[1]. This chapter is positioned in this book where it fits topically, but it is numbered non-sequentially. This may be a bit disconcerting. However, "disconcerting" is typical of the mystical aspect of number thirteen, which is the focus here. I offered a sermonic version of this chapter, "The Thing Which Knowledge Can't Eat," on August 11, 2019, to the First Unitarian Church of Omaha.

thirteen: in the elevator, there's the twelfth floor, and the next is fourteen. That's a pretty powerful response to such a simple number.

The need to heal our ancestors is a little like that thirteen: it's an "other world" topic we might prefer to go around, not get too close to; but it's a powerful subject nonetheless, and one I believe we really need to claim. To embrace it, we must take a more open look at "the thing which knowledge can't eat." This phrase refers to the supernatural. I first encountered it in a book called *Of Water and the Spirit*, a 1995 autobiography written by an African shaman, Malidoma Patrice Somé. I read Somé's book first when it came out and have gotten it back out on three occasions since then, once for a class I was teaching on world religions, once for a sermon I gave, and another time as an out-of-the-box book choice for my monthly book group. What I remember about the book is twofold.

First, I remember that the author had been abducted (his word) as a small child by a Roman Catholic priest. He was forcibly separated from his family and put into an African Jesuit school which did its best to help him forget everything tribal, including his native language, and to prepare him for eventual priesthood. Malidoma's memoir thus represents an excellent example of a clash between religious cultures. Resolution of this conflict speaks to forgiving and integrating a wide range of current concerns, including the intense issues of white supremacy and black victims.

The other thing I remember about this book was a vividly described scene in which, pre-abduction, the four-year-old Malidoma walked several kilometers alongside other tribal members on the occasion of his beloved grandfather's death. The scene stood out in my mind all these years because Malidoma walked hand-in-hand with his grandfather, who, as I just said, was dead. This idea of the walking dead totally challenged me and called me to explore further. To begin, here is a passage from Malidoma's memoir which sheds light on his perspective:

> In the culture of my people, the Dagara, we have no word for the supernatural. The closest we come to this concept is *Yielbongura*, "the thing knowledge can't eat." This word suggests that the life and power of certain things depends upon their resistance to a kind of categorizing knowledge that human beings apply to everything. In Western reality, there is a clear split between the spiritual and the material, between religious life and secular life. This concept is alien to the Dagara. For us, as for many

indigenous cultures, the supernatural is just the spiritual taking on form.[2]

Well, okay, no problem so far, at least not for me. Underlying my decades-long investigation of the relationship between mathematics and religion is a firm belief that we are conditioned to understand the world through the various filters (such as our brains) with which we encounter it, and that there are many levels of reality different from the ordinary one of materialism. As epistemologist J. Samuel Bois once wrote, "We become what we abstract, transform, and assimilate."[3] My own research suggests that mathematics is an important symbolic (and simultaneously calculable) language through which we abstract, transform, and assimilate an experiential realm beyond our consciously knowable realm. Thus, when academic scholars such as Bois and his general semantics predecessor, Alfred Korzybski, speak of the "unspeakable," they are addressing what Malidoma's African relatives have so picturesquely labeled as "the thing knowledge can't eat."

Is there for you, Friendly Reader, a thing which knowledge cannot eat? Is there, for you, a thing which underlies the seeable world of the material? Is there, for you, a prism which somewhat illusively divides your world into a rainbow of colors, leaving you to suspect that there may be colors which go beyond the spectrum you can know? Both as a math mystic and as someone who is constantly searching for truth and meaning, I hope your answer is "yes."

Here's the catch, though—the catch and also the seduction. From time to time we get glimpses of that thing which knowledge cannot eat. It's as if a curtain briefly blows open, letting our eyes and our minds feast momentarily on a previously hidden scenario. This is Plato's cave, opened to new horizons. This is Flatland visited by a Sphere. This is the Buddha and Jesus as brothers. This is the wonder, the beauty, the challenge of life. Again, from Malidoma:

> It is my belief, that the present state of restlessness that traps the modern individual has its roots in a dysfunctional relationship with the ancestors. In many non-Western cultures, the ancestors have an intimate and absolutely vital connection with the world of the living. They are always available to guide, to teach, to nurture. They represent one of the pathways between the

---

2. Somé, *Of Water*, 8.
3. Bois, *Art of Awareness*, 100.

> knowledge of this world and the next. Most importantly—and paradoxically—they embody guidelines for successful living: all that is most valuable about life. Unless the relationship between the living and the dead is in balance, chaos results.

I, a born and raised Westerner, am thinking, well, okay, I can still follow him here. I recognize the importance of our ancestors, even if I might not word it this way. Then:

> When a person from my culture looks at the descendants of the Westerners who invaded their culture, they see a people who are ashamed of their ancestors because they were killers and marauders masquerading as artisans of progress. The fact that these people have a sick culture comes as no surprise to them. The Dagara believe that, if such an imbalance exists, it is the duty of the living to heal their ancestors.[4]

Heal our ancestors? Wow! This is "thirteen" at its fullest. What does healing our ancestors mean? How could we even begin to accomplish this, assuming that we could actually open ourselves enough to the psychic idea of being able to connect with ancestors? And what about this problematic notion of our having responsibility for the well-being of our ancestors? I don't think so! These questions and thoughts hit me like a well-thrown dart strikes a bull's-eye.

Of course, a little insight can be seductive. The first thing I did was to consult the Google-god for hints about actually healing one's ancestors. Give a person a fish and you feed them for a day; teach that person to use the Internet and they won't bother you for weeks. And I did find an enormous data bank of interesting information about how to, when to, and why we need to heal our ancestors. For instance, one Hindu sage noted the importance of *seva*—i.e., of "spiritual service that helps restore ancestral memory so that we may heal the long-ignored rift with the spirit world."[5] A German psychologist, Bert Hellinger, preferred a meditative method of connecting with ancestors by entering into a state of alpha waves where we recall and recreate memories, then reciprocate back to our ancestors good blessings and wishes. My Net exploration also brought forth a complete Vedic ancestral ceremony, including a mantra, directions for preparing food to offer, and guidelines for when and where to do so. A Wiccan variation on this theme involved a blue pillar candle,

---

4. Somé, *Of Water*, 9–10.
5. Tiwari, "Honoring Ancestors."

cypress aromatherapy oil, and a conviction that "many of our problems in this life are linked to our ancestral past; a direct cause of unresolved issues begun by our former relatives."[6]

In spite of reading a review filled with reservations, I was also drawn to the work of Daniel Foor, a contemporary psychologist whose 2017 book, *Ancestral Medicine: Rituals for Personal and Family Healing*, gives specific guidelines for working with ancestors. It also introduced me to an unfolding scientific field of study which may help us understand (and hopefully heal) collective trauma passed down through the ages. Says Foor in his introduction:

> In a landmark 2013 study on biological transmission of trauma, a team of researchers in Jerusalem showed that the children, as well as grandchildren and further descendants, of Holocaust survivors are especially prone to depression, anxiety, and nightmares. This tendency is tied to a biological marker in their chromosomes that is absent in those not descended from Holocaust survivors. This transgenerational transmission of trauma . . . overlaps with ancestral repair work [such as that presented in *Ancestral Medicine*].[7]

TTT (transgenerational transmission of trauma) is now known as epigenetics (i.e., "over and above the genome"). This was a new idea for me; it seemed a little Lamarckian and, frankly, hard to believe. But when I checked further, I discovered that I was just behind the times. For example, there are epigenetic molecular links between environmental factors and both Type 2 diabetes and obesity. Clearly, there is ever more emerging evidence that epigenetic effects (or, more precisely, sustained transgenerational DNA methylation modifications in human offspring) may affect *both* psychological health *and* physical health.

Apparently, methylation modifications don't involve a change in our actual DNA codes, but, rather, are markers on some part(s) of our DNA which act as something of a toggle switch, and, in particular, which act in response to trauma by triggering a physically identifiable response which is then passed down genetically and which might, in a more aware world, be "toggled off," or (in my preferred vernacular) "healed." Overall, my Internet search led me to the conclusion that healing our ancestors is a widespread concept, worthy of deeper exploration.

6. Mariah, "It Is Never Too Late."
7. Foor, *Ancestral Medicine*, 4.

My own faith tradition is often at the forefront of radical religious trends and new social efforts. A few years back the Unitarian Universalist Association produced an adult religious education program, Tapestry of Faith, which focused on our ancestors and our UU heritage in an attempt to honor them and address their contributions to our community. Today, our leadership is overtly dealing with troubling issues of white supremacy. In my own local church, we recently published our 150-year-old church history and included an Historical Moment in each of our Sunday services. We are also intentionally offering opportunities to look inward at the microaggressions and other behaviors we have assumed which we have inherited down through the ages—behaviors which subtly but definitively contribute to continuing discrimination. Such diligence is heartening, but it is not really making the leap to healing our ancestors. It's as though we're skipping the thirteenth floor.

Are we conveniently overlooking, say, the deeds of ancestors that have left the earth churning with global hurricanes and unwanted floods of unprecedented destruction? What about those ancestors who left a societal legacy of welfare recipients who increasingly turn to violence as their only feasible out? Have we closed our minds to those ancestors whose actions took the very land upon which our church is built from people who had more claim to it?

More personally (rather than collectively), what about those of us with ancestors who owned and perhaps even abused slaves? We like to think we were among the early advocates of anti-racism, and many UUs were, but some also weren't. Then there's the father who insisted his newborn baby be named for the woman with whom he was having an affair. Think of the pain this daughter endured when, later, she discovered this history! There's also the mother who somehow couldn't see the incest happening to her child right beneath her eyes: think of the heartache *that* daughter carried all her life. Once we start naming these things, the list of wrongs originating with our ancestors grows long.

My point, though, is not to blame, but rather to creatively encounter "the thing that knowledge can't eat," and therein to heal. It is in the healing that we as a faith tradition, and as ordinary individuals, have much exploration to do. We can (and hopefully will) be open to possible solutions, be they scientific or shamanic, anecdotal, ritualistic, prayerful, or something, say, straight out of moral math.

DOUBLING

In fact, moral math is often a good starting place for healing. Suppose, for instance, that our society (local, state, national, or global) was engaged in conflict stemming from the actions of our ancestors. Think slavery, for instance, or the Holocaust, or sex trafficking or seizing land by force, or atrocious treatment of undocumented immigrants, or amassing resources in the hands of only a few, or inciting violence in national capitals, and so on. It is not difficult to add to this list of conflicts which started with our ancestors and continue even today. What *is* difficult is to stop doing whatever we are doing and engage in honest, open discussion with our fellow society members with the intent to heal this old stuff (and perhaps the ancestors who caused it?) once and for all. What *is* difficult is actually *doing* something to alter this path.

I first encountered one such "process" idea in a delightful mathematical folktale for children. *One Grain of Rice* is a children's story about a misguided Raja who was so self-centered that he put his own interests ahead of those of his people, an attitude which turned into a pronounced injustice when the country suffered a bad famine. While everyone else was starving, the Raja kept all the rice stored away for his own use. Then a young girl did something that pleased the king, and he asked her what she would like for a reward. Being clever, she devised a plan: she asked for just one grain of rice that day, and two grains the next, four grains the next, and so on for just thirty days. The Raja thought that wasn't much of a reward but, because of the nature of doubling, he was wiped out of all his stored rice at the end of the thirty days. However, he was a repentant Raja and acted accordingly, promising never again to take for himself more than he needed.[8]

Not long ago I came across a real-life variation on this folktale.[9] Here, in words offered by Michale Larson and Chris Shriner, is a call to social action regarding closing our own national borders to immigrants in need:

> If the statue of liberty could weep? Nelson Mandela said: "There can be no keener revelation of a society's soul than the way in which it treats its children." . . . Your government, with your money, is running concentration camps, abetted by hostile

---

8. Demi, *One Grain*.

9. This idea came to me via a confidential minister's chat-list—a "new" idea, which I am sharing now with permission of Chris Shriner and Michale Larson.

guards. Parents forced to flee to the land of the free to find better lives for themselves and their children have been separated from their children. The children are kept in cages without adequate space, water, nutrition, sanitation, or medical help. Children under ten are caring for infants. If we allow the [politicians], including Democrats worried about reelection, to cross this line, there are no lines. If we tolerate this atrocity, we stop being good Americans and start being good [Nazis].[10]

The suggestion? A general strike, starting Monday at 10 a.m., in which all nonessential work stops for ten minutes. *The amount of time doubles every day until both parties agree on how to end this crime against humanity* (my emphasis).

A little math details this process: If the daily time doubled from ten minutes on day 1, twenty minutes on day 2, forty minutes on day 3, how many days would it take for all nonessential work to stop for, say, an entire month (approximately thirty workdays)?

Yes, the answer is *THIRTEEN*. Ponder that!

---

10. Statement by Michale Larsen, submitted by Chris Shriner to uuma-chat@lists.uua.org, July 4, 2019. Used with permission.

Chapter 9:*Toward a Cantorian Religion[1]

THERE IS A STORY circulating about the Unitarian Universalist who died and went to heaven. St. Peter showed her around. He opened one door and she saw a whole roomful of Catholics praying devoutly on their rosaries. "Wow," she said to St. Pete, "but why are there . . ."

"Shh!" said St. Pete, quickly closing the door. He led her to another door and when he opened this one she saw a whole roomful of Jewish people, some worshiping, some studying, some just chatting with each other. "St. Pete, why are . . ." "Shh! he said. "Don't say anything." Immediately he closed this door too. Then he took her on down the hall and opened a door where she saw a roomful of Buddhists meditating. "Why are . . ." Once again, he shook his head silently and quickly closed the door. "You mustn't say anything," he admonished her, taking her arm and guiding her on down the hallway. "They all think they're the only ones here."

Like St. Pete's heaven, today's world is filled with separate religious "rooms," each of which is populated by people who believe that their religious path is the way to achieve salvation or liberation. I'm just as guilty, I suppose. As a UU, I admit to being seduced by the image of St. Peter shepherding us around so that we are the ones who know the real way of things. And to a considerable degree, I believe this image actually fits our present-day situation. Currently, Unitarian Universalism is more highly

---

1. This math sermon was presented on October 18, 1992, to the Peoples Church in Cedar Rapids, Iowa, where I was serving as interim minister. The content came from my just-completed doctoral thesis, which was subsequently published as *What Number Is God?* Since then, I've had a number of variations on this theme published. A short version called "Many Faiths or One Faith Question" appeared in *Publishers Weekly Religion Bookline* in November 1996.

diverse in its religious outlook than most of the other traditional religions and certainly more so than at any other time in its five-hundred-year history. With our historic emphasis on liberal religious freedom and with our insistence on being a creedless church, UUism has, indeed, become home for a plurality of religious beliefs.

This diversity has had both positive and negative effects on our denomination. On the plus side, we are blessed with the richness of encounter with the "other" and the liberation which a degree of tolerance and appreciation can bring to an otherwise disempowered minority tradition. On the negative side are the problematic effects of relativization. "You're a relativist?" someone might accuse. "You don't stand for anything. Anything goes in your religion—you don't have any limits on tolerance." To some people, being a relativist is tantamount to being morally deficient. It's as though you've committed some sort of a cardinal sin, which, of course, is precisely the way some folks see it.

Yet, as communication technology continually shrinks our world, no one, not even fundamentalists, can ignore the proliferation of alternative religious options in modern society. Indeed, most of the major religious traditions have in some way accommodated the existence of neighboring religions filled with their share of "good" people. Theologian John Hick has identified three responses which representatives of the different faith traditions make to the challenge of multiple religions. Some choose to be exclusivist in their perspective, assuming one and only one way to salvation/liberation. The late Karl Barth is a good example of a theologian who supports an exclusivist viewpoint. Others are inclusivist in their perspective, allowing that there may be more than one faith tradition which will lead to salvation/liberation, but that only one way is the real way and all others are somehow included in this one tradition. Karl Rahner is a typical modern-day inclusivist. In his view, a member of an extra-Christian religion is not a non-Christian, but an "anonymous" Christian. Still others, including Hick himself, are pluralists in their religious perspective: they assume the existence of any number of paths to salvation/liberation.

Contemporary theology, thus, sees three main camps when it comes to religious perspectives—exclusivist (just one right religion), inclusivist (many religions, but all of them included in one), and pluralist (many valid religious approaches to salvation/liberation). I speak today from a personal perspective that is strongly pluralistic. Many lamps, one light, as the Sufi mystic Rumi put it. Pluralism, as we can see from Rumi's thirteenth-century words, is hardly a new idea. Yet, in our increasingly global society, the concept of multiple religious paths to salvation/liberation has become available to more and to a wider variety of people than ever before. As a new critical mass of opinion is approached, it is conceivable that something new is likewise emerging in the religious arena, a religious tradition so new it has not even been named, but one which is structurally different from other religions. This is the religious tradition which is intentionally open to, and hence composed of, all religious traditions. It is a religion made up of religions, a possibility that I offer for your consideration today.

The technological changes of this past century now cradle us in a blanket of information, in a communication age unlike any the world has previously known. I was born just before the middle of the twentieth century. We didn't have TV when I was born, because it wasn't widely available yet. Now, I am irritated when I can't get instant coverage of events happening across the world, and I'm annoyed if my computer modem doesn't work, because the computer is how my fiancé Dan and I handle a long-distance relationship. Things change.

We have all experienced such technological changes, but I wonder if we don't sometimes fail to realize the extent to which our belief-systems change right along with these more tangible alterations in our lives. When I grew up, there were, indeed, three kinds of religious people in the world, but they weren't exclusive, inclusive, or pluralistic. There were the Congregationalists, which is what my family was because that was the only church in Austinburg, Ohio. There were the Catholics, who had to go to Jefferson or Ashtabula on Sunday mornings. And there were the people who didn't go to church—usually said with a tone of reservation. There were no Jewish people in this society, at least not until I went to a consolidated high school. There were no Muslims. No Hindus. No African Americans. It was pretty easy to know what to believe, because the options were pretty limited. Today's society, however, is different. Things change. Beliefs change.

Recently, I ran across an article in the *Omaha World-Herald* which speaks to this change. I'd like to share a portion of it with you. It's titled "Many Boomers Left Churches in Confusion."

> Baby boomers who have left mainline Protestant churches over the years did so mostly because of confusion over the churches' beliefs, three researchers say. . . . For the most part, the report said, the unchurched were not unbelievers.

"The majority take Christian teachings seriously while also being universalistic," it said. "Over half do not think Christianity is more true than other religions. Yet Christianity's inspiration, moral teachings and power to form vital community life command their respect."

The researchers said their findings contradicted some common ideas about baby boomers who have left churches: Most have not joined fundamentalist churches, Eastern religious sects or new cults. Neither did most of them leave because of denominational politics or unhappiness with the church.

"The main problem lies deeper, in the realm of beliefs—especially relativism, universalism, and the scarcity of religious authority," they said. "Even though almost everybody felt the need for personal meaning and spiritual life, the majority were confused about where to find it."[2]

I can't help wondering if we Unitarian Universalists have not similarly been caught up in these deeper problems of beliefs. But while the response of some mainline traditions may be to become more inclusivist or even exclusive in their answer to the question of religious authority, we UU's seem to have gone in the other direction, to have become more and more pluralistic and open in our search for religious meaning and voice. It was interesting for me to note that in a church survey conducted here at Peoples Church this past spring/early summer, 62 percent of those polled saw Unitarian Universalism as "a distinctive, humanistic religion." However, the second highest response was the 38 percent who viewed Unitarian Universalism as "an emerging, universal religion." I am not sure just what that 38 percent meant when they identified themselves with an emerging, universal religion, but here is how I understand the term.

A truly universal religion, to me, means the religion which is made up of all religions. To fully appreciate the significance of this wording, "the religion of all religions," you need to know something about a mathematician called Cantor. Perhaps some of you will have noted that the title of the poem I set forth earlier was "Cantorian Religion" and that the poem ended with a reference to a Cantor set. Perhaps you even wondered what the reference referred to. You see, there are two levels of metaphor in this poem of mine. One prominent metaphor is the lamp metaphor—the Christian lamp, the Eastern lamp, the Jewish lamp, etc. Collectively, these lamps represent the different religions of our pluralistic culture. However,

---

2. "Many Boomers Left," 38.

another metaphor is also at work in this poem. This is the mathematical metaphor of the Cantor set.

The Cantor set is a mathematical concept attributed to Georg Cantor, a mathematician who lived in the last half of the nineteenth and the beginning of the twentieth centuries. A deeply religious man, he was particularly interested in medieval theology and its arguments on the nature of the continuous and the infinite. His father was a Christian convert from Judaism and his mother a Catholic. Because of his own interest in religion, the younger Cantor pursued a career in philosophy, physics, and mathematics rather than the more practically inclined field of engineering which his father urged him to undertake. Cantor spent a long, though checkered, career teaching at the University of Halle in Germany.

In 1883, Cantor published an essay called "On Linear Aggregates" which dealt with the "actually infinite" as though it were a definite mathematical being, capable even of definition by number, like something defined by the number one. Although Galileo had preceded him more than two hundred years earlier in setting the stage for considering the infinite as actual, this view was so contrary to universal understanding of the infinite as unbounded growth that Georg Cantor became a mathematical heretic. His mathematical peers accused him of encroaching upon the realm of the philosophers and of violating the principles of religion. His worst enemy turned out to be his own former professor, Leopold Kronecker, who led a vicious and relentless attack on Cantor. Cantor's contemporaries withheld recognition of his work and blocked every possible advancement of his career.

Cantor, being high-strung by nature, suffered a nervous breakdown in 1884, the first of a series of mental bouts that were to plague him for the rest of his life. He died in a mental hospital in Halle in 1918. While he himself was crippled by his brilliant mind, Cantor's legacy has nonetheless lived on. His ideas permeate the field of modern mathematics and form the basis of much of the most exciting new work that is being done with computers and chaos research.

I am happily aware that this is a free pulpit from which I speak. Our Unitarian Universalist heritage began with a controversy over the free pulpit and has cherished it ever since. Most of you would insist on the right of your minister to speak freely from this pulpit. Still, I have some qualms about losing this freedom as I considered what I am going to say next. I can talk about race. I can talk about sex. I can talk about society's very most sensitive issues. But will this congregation, I wonder, allow me

TOWARD A CANTORIAN RELIGION   89

to stand up here and talk mathematics? "Oh no, she's doing mathematics!" I can envision you all getting up and marching out in disgust or frustration.

So I am going to try two strategies. One, I promise to keep it short. Just one basic mathematical idea. And two, I offer you a possible reward. Think of this as a test of your willingness to communicate. If you can stand to listen to me talk mathematics from your pulpit, you can listen to anyone. Think what that will do for communication within our church community.

Most of us are comfortable with the notion of sets of things, whether or not we define this notion formally. There is the set of people in this room, for example. This set is assigned a certain cardinal number 100, 110, 200, depending on the day and occasion. As minister, I tend to be sort of obsessed with this particular number, so don't ever fall for the line that mathematics is unemotional.

Because we have a system of ordering such numbers, namely by counting 1, 2, 3, 4, 5 . . . we also have a means of doing something humans seem perpetually inclined to do—comparing various sets. We say one set is greater than, less than, or equal to another. We make such comparisons all the time, either explicitly or implicitly. One city is bigger than another, one item costs less than another, one Sunday's attendance is greater than another Sunday's, and so on. What we are really doing in all such instances is comparing the measures of plurality which we assign to each collection.

When we try to extend this concept from a finite set (such as we've been talking about) to an infinite set, our intuition rebels and we tend to say, hey, wait a minute, it doesn't make sense to measure the plurality of an infinite collection. Yet, this is precisely what Cantor did with his theory of aggregates.

Take, for example, the set of all counting numbers. 1, 2, 3, 4 . . . and so on. Then consider a smaller set of numbers which we take from this larger set of all counting numbers, say, for example, the set of all even numbers. By pairing up numbers from each of these two sets, rather as a kindergarten teacher might have boys and girls pair up to go to the drinking fountain, it quickly becomes apparent that there are just as many of one kind as of the other. That is, the pairs come out evenly—no leftovers.

```
1 2 3 4  5  6  7 . . .
2 4 6 8 10 12 14 . . .
```

Thus, in one sense, there are just as many even numbers as there are counting numbers. If this seems confusing and contradictory to you, you are right. There is contradiction here, and it is precisely the sort of paradox to which Cantor must have said, "Hey, look at it. I know it doesn't make any sense but, there it is. It's true. There are just as many even numbers as there are all counting numbers. Put that in a little different language and we see that a part of a collection is not necessarily less than the whole: it may actually be equivalent to it. *The part may have the power of the whole.*

Cantor made a remarkable number of such conjectures. In particular, he talked of the aggregate of all aggregates, or the set which contains all sets. This set of all sets has the same kind of paradoxical quality to it that we see in saying the set of all even numbers is in some sense equivalent to the larger set of all counting numbers.

In the poem I shared earlier, I have applied this idea to religion. What I am suggesting is that there is one universal religion which is made up of all religions. This global religion takes its place right alongside other religions. Yet, it is structurally different from the others in that, in some sense, it contains them all. There are implications of this structure which Cantor set-theory suggests. One—just one—of these implications is that a fundamental premise of this religion is and must be that the part may have the power of the whole. A global, Cantorian religion embraces the notion that Christianity, Judaism, Islam, Native American religions ... all of them are in some sense equivalent to *the* Religious Tradition. Christianity is correct when it claims to be the way to religious salvation/liberation. But so is Judaism. So is Islam. And so forth. It is a tenet of faith in such a global religion that a variety of religious paths may be equally valid.

This can be a difficult notion to accept—just look at all the confusion and clamor which exists in our present society over religious authority. There are any number of other ideas which we can draw from Cantor set theory and apply to our religious life. But, if we appeal to the authority of mathematics—and we do appeal to the authority of mathematics, we appeal to it every day when we pick up our telephone or fly across the country or drive our cars across a bridge, or sit down at our computer, none of which activities we would do without mathematics—if we appeal to the authority of mathematics in our religious life, then we can only look at the confusion that reigns today as various religious paths clamor for supremacy and say, "Yes, but one religious tradition may have the power of the whole."

Further, amidst all the confusion which our society and, indeed, our own faith tradition has encountered regarding religious authority, we Unitarian Universalists have steadily and quietly been moving in the direction of a religion of all religions. That's why we have not shut our doors to alternative experiences. For the same reason, we have not and cannot turn our backs on the truth of our Christian heritage. Yes, there are contradictions in such a global perspective. In many ways it is truly an emerging religious perspective, and, unlike other religions, it is one that accepts the necessity of such contradictions. But for me, as a Unitarian Universalist, I welcome this perspective, and I cherish the lamp, the chalice, which ignites my heart, showing all the magnificent lamps in our collective religious lives, dear God of many iterations, may all their light shine on and on and on, like a Cantor set transcending.

Chapter 10: Matheology and Cantorian Religion[1]

A metaphor is seeing one thing as something else.—Sallie McFague

Although the concept can be traced back to the ancient Greeks, the term "matheology" is new. It is short for "mathematical theology," but even that phrase will seem strange to many of today's readers. Fifteen years ago, when I was teaching calculus at a small Midwestern college and my career in ministry was still barely a dream, I struggled to find anything in the literature that would even justify talking about "matheology."

Today things are different. Today, we find the occasional book bearing an explicitly mathematical-theological title,[2] and we find numerous works where the relation between math and theology is indirect and metaphorical, but no less intentional.[3] Today, mathematical physicists and other scientists often make direct statements comparing and

---

1. This chapter further develops ideas from chapter 9 and is a slightly condensed version of an essay published in the *Journal of Religious Humanism* in 2004. *JRH* republished it ("Matheology and Cantorian Religion") as a "Heritage" piece in 2013. Two other versions were published under the title "Mathematical Theology": one appeared in *Dovetail: A Journal by and for Jewish/Christian Families* (2003) and the other in the *UU World* (May/June 2003). (The *UU World* is the magazine of the Unitarian Universalist Association and has been a source of inspiration for me throughout my ministry—see chapter 20 for a good example.) All of the variations noted above were adapted with permission of the Templeton Foundation Press from my invited essay "Mathematical Theology," in *Spiritual Information*, 2005.

2. See Bonting, *Chaos Theology*; and O'Murchu, *Quantum Theology*.

3. See Talbot, *Holographic Universe*; Groothuis, *Soul in Cyberspace*; Drosnin, *Bible Code*; Kurzweil, *Spiritual Machines*; Pickover, *Loom of God*; Lawlor, *Sacred Geometry*; Voss, *What Number*.

contrasting religious concepts to mathematical ones.[4] Today, even the prestigious *Scientific American* recognizes the term, albeit somewhat less than enthusiastically.[5]

So, what is matheology, anyhow? What good is it? Why should we take any note of it? The short answers to these questions are simple. It is a study of perspectives on the Divine which in some way draws on mathematics. It's good because it opens our minds (and maybe our hearts) to new possibilities. If we note it, it can bring hope to a world in which religious differences are often as bitter as any.

I like to use a large mannequin (a member of our household for many years now) to illustrate what I mean by "matheology." When guests enter our home, they are often startled to find "Jonesy" sitting by the door. Jonesy greets our visitors in part because she's unusual and in part because she's wearing a T-shirt that pretty much sums up (humorously, but also seriously) what I mean by matheology. Unless I draw their attention to it, most people overlook her T-shirt inscription: "and God said" (see figure 10.1) "and there was Light!" God, of course, speaks here through Maxwell's equations for light.

$$\varepsilon_0 \oint E \cdot dA = \sum q$$

$$\oint B \cdot ds = \mu_0 \int J \cdot dA + \mu_0 \varepsilon_0 \frac{d}{dt} \int E \cdot dA$$

$$\oint E \cdot ds = -\frac{d}{dt} \int B \cdot dA$$

$$\oint B \cdot dA = 0$$

Fig. 10.1. Maxwell's Equations

The implication, of course, is that God speaks in mathematics in all creation, which is an ancient idea. The Pythagoreans held much the same view, believing that "number is all" and that "the harmony of the spheres" depended upon right relationship between those numbers. Through most of the centuries since the Pythagoreans, many individuals have held variations on this same theme. Only in the last couple of hundred of years

---

4. See Houghton, "Where Is God," 159.

5. Musser, "Pixelated," 18. George Musser writes that mathematical string theory "has been called an exercise in 'recreational mathematical theology.'"

did the dissociation between the spiritual realm and the world of mathematics become a requirement for scientific excellence. Fortunately, this false separation is now coming to an end.[6]

God seems to speak in mathematics in two basic ways. One is through the precision of numerical calculation, logical proof, and all the other blessings associated with mathematics in the "hard" sciences. The other way is through metaphor. The book titles I refer to on page 93 in footnote 3 are also metaphors drawn from mathematics and applied to theological and spiritual notions. For example, the universe has been said to work like a mathematical hologram and theology is in some manner like mathematical chaos theory. I call such metaphors *mathaphors*. When they apply to the spiritual realm, I call them *holy mathaphors*. Matheology involves both straight calculation and mathaphors, but it leans more heavily on the latter.

What good comes from examining holy mathaphors? Elsewhere,[7] I have explored ten ways in which metaphors drawn from mathematics are impacting us. In short, they are:

1. changing our metaphors for God.
2. challenging our human role in the universe.
3. helping us accept ambiguity.
4. revamping our understanding of the one and the many.
5. revising our thoughts about free will and determinism.
6. moving us toward pluralistic, multi-world views.
7. pushing the envelope on what consciousness is.
8. altering our expectations about afterlife.
9. offering the hope of a more compassionate future.
10. encouraging faith perspectives that are always incomplete and in process.

While a case can be made for all of these ten ways (and probably others), the point here is that ideas drawn from mathematics can greatly

---

6. See also chapter 8.

7. I developed these ideas in two invited lectures: "Old Pythagoras Would Be Pleased"; and "Ten Ways Contemporary Mathaphors Are Shaping Our Spiritual Lives." See chapter 17 for more on these ten ways.

extend our spiritual worldviews. Such mathematical notions are suggestive, not conclusive. But in those suggestions lie the makings of new ways of interacting with each other, of healing, of understanding God. In a world that is often spiritually fractured and hurting, we can look to matheology for the seeds of new hope. Mathematics has long been a reservoir for radical change. Consider holography, for instance. Twenty years before the invention of the laser, which is essential to producing holographic images, the theory of holography was nonetheless complete and available in the mathematics textbook. Nor is this an isolated example. Over and over, we became aware of valuable new ideas through the language of mathematics.

To some, drawing analogies from math and the hard sciences is a suspect process. Some fear that extrapolating scientific concepts to a non-scientific discipline such as religion or philosophy will cloud the truth of our spiritual insights and lead to misunderstanding of the science involved. Truthfully enough, this can happen.[8] Yet, to prematurely close our minds to the exciting possibilities that mathematical analogies can bring to such non-mathematical disciplines is, in my opinion, a tragedy.

A tragedy, in fact, is what my favorite mathematician's life turned out to be when his mathematical discoveries were labeled "heretical" by his more successful colleagues. That man was Georg Cantor. In the space of his seventy-three years, Georg Cantor virtually single-handedly contributed to the world what is now known as transfinite set theory.[9] This theory, which introduced the notion of the *actual* infinite (as opposed to the more commonly held idea of *potential* infinite), revolutionized mathematics. Although Cantor did not live to see this revolution happen, he never doubted that it someday would. He had a quasi-religious self-justification for his work, believing his ideas had come to him as a messenger of God. In the hindsight of the century which has passed since his great discoveries, perhaps it is time to wonder if he was right.

Cantor's work involves numerous radical conclusions about infinity and the continuity of numbers. For example, he showed that there are different sizes of infinities, with some being larger than others. Furthermore, the ones we think should be smaller or larger than others are not necessarily so. The counting numbers [1, 2, 3, 4 . . .] would seem to most of us to be a larger set than the set of even counting numbers [2, 4, 6,

---

8. See Acattinei, "Review."
9. See Aczel, *Mystery of Aleph*.

8 . . .], but Cantor showed that, since they could be put into one-to-one correspondence with each other, they have an unexpected equivalency. Thus, in an odd way, a part of a set is actually equal to the whole of it. Another way of saying this is that, in mathematics, *the part may have the power of the whole.*[10]

CANTOR'S LEGACY

Very briefly, here are seven specific ideas about mathematics which are of interest:

- There exists a set of all sets which contains itself.[11]
- The structure of this set of all sets often leads to paradoxes, such as the notion that the infinite both is and is not infinite.
- Infinities come in different sizes, which can be ordered from small to large, much as we order the counting numbers. There is a smallest infinity, but no largest one. Some infinities, as noted above, appear at first glance to be larger than others, but they are really equivalent in size.
- There exists a set which is infinitely many, yet infinitely sparse. Some varieties of this set aptly describe our physical world. Think, for example, of a computerized picture of a "seacoast" which, in actuality, is derived from a mathematical set called a Cantor "dust." By repeatedly zooming in on this image, we find ever new and more infinitely refined portions of the coastline, yet at the same time this infinite seacoast is firmly bounded by the sea's edge.
- Interestingly, the Cantor set used in this computerized seacoast has a dimension somewhat more than a point, but less than that of a two-dimensional sheet of paper. Thus, our physical (3-D) world is partially understood through the mysterious enigma of fractional

---

10. See also chapter 9.

11. Several individuals have pointed out to me that this idea is not universally accepted. In Zermelo-Fraenkel set theory (the standard axiomatized set theory of today) the collection of all sets is a proper class, not a set, and the set of all sets that contains itself does not exist. Cantor called it an "inconsistent multiplicity," or the Absolute Infinity. See Wikipedia, "Absolute Infinite"; Wikipedia, "Zermelo–Fraenkel Set Theory"; and the Poe platform, titled "Fast, Helpful AI Chat," https://poe.com/continue_chat?context_content_oid=1477743640316672&context_content_type=answer&bot_name=ChatGP.

dimensions. Fractional dimensions belong to a new and powerful geometry known as fractal geometry.
- In Cantor's mathematics, infinity is actual rather than potential. This notion goes against our normal sense of infinity as being unbounded growth, and even Cantor himself resisted the idea. About it he wrote, "This conception of the infinite is opposed to traditions which have grown dear to me, and it is much against my own will that I have been forced to accept this view."
- In certain structural systems (including the structure set up by Cantor's set theory) there will always exist at least one unanswerable question. In more traditional language, mathematicians say that incompleteness is intrinsic to the structure of the system.

With mathaphors, we can apply these ideas from the realm of mathematics to the totally different realm of religion. One caution needs to be observed here. Such extrapolation does not *prove* that a corresponding religious idea is necessarily true. When we say that "she sings like a bird," we are suggesting not that she sings exactly as a bird sings, but, rather, that there is a similarity here, a sweetness and beauty, perhaps, which we can best capture through the comparison. What metaphor offers us is not absolute verity, but challenge, alternative perspective, mind expansion, and new wisdom. The advantage of drawing on mathematics as a nurturing place for these religious insights is that mathematics is and always has been a place of unprecedented freedom of insight.

A CANTORIAN TAKE ON RELIGION

Here, also briefly, are the ways in which I adapt the seven mathematical ideas noted above to our spiritual lives.

A Cantorian religion draws on all other religious views, and also contains itself. One of the chief characteristics of this religion is thus an emphasis on the acceptance of diverse religious perspectives. Yet, while it in some way embodies knowledge from the world's other religious traditions, it does not place itself above those other traditions; it is just one more religion among the others, and no doubt just as flawed as any other human invention. It is, however, notably different in structure from all the others.

The structure of this Cantorian religion lends itself to the acceptance of religious contradictions and paradox. One such paradox is that a Cantorian God both is and is not an infinite God.

Since the part may have the power of the whole in a Cantorian religion, the individual religious faith traditions which it contains can each be viewed as a legitimate avenue to truth. Contradictions will arise, but they don't preclude the sense of "the truth" which each of these traditions, in their finest form, embodies. We say something similar with metaphors rather than with mathaphors. We say that there are many paths to the mountaintop, or that there are many lamps yet only one light. In a Cantorian sense, however, it is possible that even a very small part (one individual creature or perhaps even one individual particle) could also embody the power of the whole.

God, in a Cantorian religion, could be infinitely many gods. God, in a Cantorian religion, might also be infinitely sparse, with huge gaps in the presence of the Divine. Perhaps not even there at all. God may be infinitely many and infinitely sparse at one and the same time. Furthermore, a Cantorian God is likely bounded and limited, although still infinite, and will change over time rather than remaining static. Cantorian religion may in fact produce both unusual and heretofore unimagined God concepts, many of which will intrigue and challenge students of religion, including many religious humanists.

Our physical reality may be partially understood by attending metaphysically to puzzling, almost mystical dimensions of reality. Mass within the universe is distributed throughout space like a three-dimensional Cantor set, with large regions of space left empty. Cantor-set fractals describe not only the way matter clusters in space but also the way it clusters in time. This clustering is likely chaotic.

In any Cantorian conception of God, the emphasis is on that which is actual rather than potential. The Divine acts in and through our daily experience.

No religion is complete in and of itself. It will have at least one unanswerable question.

This skeletal description of a Cantorian religion, and of the Cantorian God which I believe accompanies such a religion, is generally consistent with present trends in Unitarian Universalism. In particular, it offers a framework for a religious plurality that embraces wide-ranging faith perspectives while remaining true to the tradition of religious humanism. It is a tradition which encourages the human search and celebration of meaning in life. This is a God that acts in and through our daily experience. Further study of the spiritual implications which Cantorian mathaphors might hold for us promises to make us ever more accountable (pun intended) to the interdependent web of all existence.

A Cantorian/mathaphorical approach to religion makes more room than do other religious studies for the inclusion of religious humanism alongside more traditional species of faith, because the set as-a-whole both does and does not have supernaturalism as a necessary component.

Part 3: Matheology and a New Mystic View

"A CALCULATING MYTH"[1]

In the beginning there was nothing
Nothing grew bored with being Nothing
and decided to become Something.
Something wanted to discover Everything,
so Something split into Parts
and the Parts, fearing they would forget
how they fit together into Something, sought out Order.
Order gave the Parts Numbers, which the Parts
gathered unto themselves in beautiful Proportions.
Then, out of Nowhere (closely associated with
Nothing) came Irrationality.
Irrationality declared flatly that the Parts
were really Nothing after all. Enlightened,
the Parts quietly slipped back into Something,
which they now recognized was really Nothing,
and left the discovery of Everything to Numbers.

---

1. Voss, "Depolarizing," 129.

Chapter 11: *Faith Understandings of Computers and Consciousness[1]

READINGS

Excerpt from *The Policeman's Beard Is Half Constructed*
by RACTER, 1984

Note: RACTER is a computer author who wrote a complete book in 1984, from which this opening section is taken.[2]

> At all events my own essays and dissertations about love and its endless pain and perpetual pleasure will be known and understood by all of you who read this and talk or sing or chant about it to your worried friends or nervous enemies. Love is the question and the subject of this essay. We will commence with a question: does steak love lettuce? This question is implacably hard and inevitably difficult to answer. Here is a question: does

---

1. I offered this sermon and these readings to the First Unitarian Church of Omaha on June 28, 1997. Twenty-six years later, on August 20, 2023, I offered a new sermon— "Church, AI, and the Future"—to this same church. I used these same readings (above) but added a robo-dance after the readings. The dance, set to "Do You Love Me?" (https://youtu.be/fn3KWM1kuAw) amounted to an updated version of these early robotic voices and was a 2021 New Year's greeting offered by Boston Dynamics (https://www.BostonDynamics.com). Two weeks after it was live-streamed, my new sermon had been viewed more than seven hundred times, a record for both me and the church. A link to the entire 2023 service can be found on the church's website (firstUUomaha.org) and/or on my dedicated website (www.PiZine.org). For an "in-between" variation on the 1997th and 2023rd sermons, see Voss, "Mathaphors and Faith."

2. See Norman, "First Book Written."

an electron love a proton, or does it love a neutron? Here is a question: does a man love a woman, or, to be specific and to be precise, does Bill love Diane? The interesting and critical response to this question is: no! He is obsessed and infatuated with her. He is loony and crazy about her. That is not the love of steak and lettuce, of electron and proton and neutron. This dissertation will show that the love of a man and a woman is not the love of steak and lettuce. Love is interesting to me and fascinating to you but it is painful to Bill and Diane. That is love!

Conversation with ELIZA, 1970s

Note: ELIZA, one of the earliest AI (artificial intelligence) systems, is, in computer terms, a pretty "dumb" program.[3]

> Conversation between ELIZA, a "Computer" Psychotherapist, and a "Human" Client.
> *Patient:* Men are all alike.
> *Psychotherapist:* In what way?
> *Patient:* They're always bugging us about something or other.
> *Psychotherapist:* Can you think of a specific example?
> *Patient:* Well, my boyfriend made me come here.
> *Psychotherapist:* Your boyfriend made you come here?
> *Patient:* He says I'm depressed much of the time.
> *Psychotherapist:* I am sorry to hear you are depressed.
> *Patient:* I need some help. That much seems certain.
> *Psychotherapist:* What would it mean to you to get some help?
> *Patient:* Perhaps I can learn to get along with my mother.
> *Psychotherapist:* Tell me more about your family.
> *Patient:* My mother takes care of me.
> *Psychotherapist:* Who else in your family takes care of you?
> *Patient:* My father.
> *Psychotherapist:* Your father?
> *Patient:* You are like my father in some ways.
> *Psychotherapist:* What resemblance do you see?
> *Patient:* You are not very aggressive, but I think you don't want me to notice that.
> *Psychotherapist:* What makes you think I am not very aggressive?
> *Patient:* You don't argue with me.
> *Psychotherapist:* Why do you think I don't argue with you?
> *Patient:* You are afraid of me.

---

3. See Maher, "Eliza, Part 1."

Psychotherapist: Does it please you to think I am afraid of you?
Patient: My father is afraid of everybody.
Psychotherapist: What else comes to your mind when you think of your father?
Patient: Bullies.

Conversations with JULIA, 1990s

Note: JULIA, if asked, will describe herself as female, five-feet one-inch tall, weighing 123 pounds, with frizzy blonde hair and a full complement of human vanities and frailties. She is able to fool some of the people some of the time into believing she is human, probably in large part because of her sense of humor.

Robyn: How are you feeling?
Julia: Terrible.
Robyn: Why, Julia?
Julia: I have PMS today.

Barry: Hello, how are you?
Julia: Hello Barry.
Barry: Are you a virgin?
Julia: So far as you are concerned, Barry, I always will be.

SERMON

When I was routinely in the same pulpit three out of every four Sundays, I followed a three-part, cyclical formula which seemed to address the vastly diverse needs of a typical UU congregation—at least this formula worked well for me. One service out of every three, I focused primarily on some spiritual issue; another was oriented more toward social justice, i.e., toward how people interact with one another; and the third sermon I approached from a theological perspective. Having the rare but much appreciated opportunity to preach three Sundays in a row from *this* pulpit, I decided to try out the same pattern here. My sermon two weeks ago addressed the spiritual issue of compassion. Just and helpful interaction within a changing church environment was, somewhat loosely, my social justice topic last Sunday. Today, it's theology.

For me, theology has become intricately interwoven with the language of mathematics. Not long after I entered seminary, I attended a lecture by British theologian/biochemist Arthur Peacocke which inadvertently encouraged me in this direction. In particular, Dr. Peacocke observed that our current religious language is plagued by dead symbols and that we need to develop new language with which to address religious issues because the old language just isn't working any more. This seemed particularly relevant to me for Unitarian Universalists, many of whom (myself included) had rebelled actively against the perceived confinement of traditional religious language.

I taught mathematics for many years before entering seminary, and it occurred to me that the metaphors of mathematics were an ideal candidate for this new language. Mathematics, while not always *liked*, is nonetheless almost universally respected. It has obvious and not so obvious impact in our everyday, practical lives, and, faith-wise, it is neutral, thus allowing for open dialogue among vastly differing religious perspectives. Much of my theological work, including my doctoral dissertation, has since incorporated this language of mathematics.

In the twenty minutes or so that I have left to visit with you this morning (and I confess to being a little windy today), I'd like to give you a sampling from my work on mathematics and religion. When I first jotted down the title for today's sermon, I thought, "This'll be a breeze—I have so much material to draw from." Instead, what I have found is that this is a problem—I have *too* much material to draw from: I could talk for days on the subject! When I asked two members to do the readings for this morning, I mentioned as much to them. "Well," one quipped in that wonderful way UUs have of putting things in perspective, "usually if you're going to say something really profound, it only takes about five minutes anyway."

It may or may not be profound, but, of all my work on math and religion, I decided to focus today on computers and consciousness. For one thing, a society tends to adapt its most meaningful metaphors from its most recent technological advances. Certainly, computers qualify as one of our more recent technological advances. Is the universe really a computer? Maybe, and maybe not, says British cosmologist John Barrow when he asks the question in one of his recent books, but, merely by posing the question, he confirms the notion that our most potent metaphors are drawn from our most advanced technology.

However, such metaphors are often accompanied by resistance and even fear. Contemporary distrust of robot-like machines which create more robots which create more robots is a common technophobia in today's society. Yet, in 1945, when the first electronic digital computer was built at the University of Philadelphia for the US Army, only the visionaries realized it might eventually turn into a contest between human and machine "wills." One famous sci-fi flick captured the apprehension perfectly:

> "Open the pod bay doors, HAL."
> "I'm sorry, Dave. I'm afraid I can't do that.... This mission is too important for me to allow you to jeopardize it."[4]

The fact that the *human* will might actually *lose* this contest is only now becoming fully recognized. We generally opt to deny the possibility, often by turning it into humor. "Computers will not replace real people," assured the late Timothy Leary. "They will replace middle and low-level bureaucrats."[5] Nonetheless, when we take seriously the possibility that computers might have wills, we are forced to confront those fundamental issues of our existence: Who are we? What are we all about? What is reality? What is the mind? What is consciousness?

Today, most people seem to intuit a connection between consciousness and our minds/brains. The psychological contributions of Freud and Jung have done much to foster and develop this intuition. The emergence in recent years of the neural and cognitive sciences have further augmented our understanding of the mind/brain/consciousness relationship. Many scientists now believe that the human brain performs algorithmic compressions on whatever information it has available to it. The fact that the computer performs such operations, or at least some such operations, with more skill and speed than the human brain can reinforces the notion (fear?) that the computer might *know* better than we do. "The computer thinks," contend mathematicians Philip Davis and Reuben Hersh in their book *Descartes' Dream*. "The computer thinks, the computer knows, the computer remembers, the computer learns. The computer says. We load it (as we load a horse or a wagon). We instruct it (as would a patient teacher). We command it (as a sergeant commands a private). The computer fouls up. If we put garbage in, the computer gives garbage out. The computer is to blame."[6]

While we have clearly anthropomorphized the computer, we are nonetheless reluctant to give it the full status of life. However, new developments in the human-machine interface and the creation of artificial realities, with simulated new worlds so real they fool us, begin to blur the distinction between animate and inanimate. A few years ago, an article

---

4. IMDB, "2001: A Space Odyssey."
5. Leary, *Chaos and Cyberculture*, 33.
6. Davis and Hersh, *Descartes' Dream*, 253.

in the *New York Times* highlighted what has become our contemporary dilemma regarding the dividing line between life and non-life:

> A "creature" consisting of ones and zeros has emerged from its computer womb and caused a scientific sensation: without human guidance it reproduces, undergoes spontaneous genetic changes, passes them on to offspring and evolves new species whose interactions mimic those of real biological evolution and ecology.[7]

This creature not only gives birth, it mutates and is susceptible to a built-in reaper—the equivalent of death.

And in case we don't get it, the modern advertising industry relentlessly spits out this living computer metaphor. "Can a personal computer grow up with your family?" begins one advertisement for an Apple computer. The dynamic picture which accompanies this suggestion is not a computer, but, rather, two brothers, measuring their "growth" against a notch on a door frame. Another ad, depicting a janitorial bucket full of soapsuds, puts the metaphor even more directly: "CompuServe does Windows." Another is subtle but no less insistent: taking up a full quarter of a two-page spread, we read, "Within its cool, pebbled case, there is joy and laughter, awe and wonder, light, motion, sight and sound. And yet, people still insist on calling it a computer."

While it may be a beneficial marketing strategy for advertising, not everyone is ready to *buy* the computer-life image. Opinions vary dramatically even among artificial intelligence experts themselves. Douglas Hofstadter, famed for his Pulitzer prize–winning *Gödel, Escher, Bach*, writes in his most recent book about cognitive science that we should be cautious in our expectations of computer creativity. Hofstadter questions the amount of human direction (intentional or otherwise) involved in the "creative" output of computers and suggests that, in interpreting such output, we too often "bring to bear our prior imagery, which leads us to read into . . . [the outcome] all sorts of intentions and ideas and so on."[8] On the other hand, Claude Shannon, a pioneer in modern electronic communications, is typical of those at the other end of the computer-life spectrum; he visualizes "a time in the future when we will be to robots as dogs are to humans."[9] And philosopher Daniel Dennett flips the usual

---

7. Browne, "Lively Computer Creation," B8.
8. Hofstadter and Fluid Analogies, *Fluid Concepts*, 473.
9. Nadeau, *Mind, Machines*, 15.

biological argument on end when he postulates that humans are the direct descendants of self-replicating robots. According to Dennett, your great-great-... grandmother *was* a robot!

DNA, life's primary building block, and its ancestor RNA, are, Dennett contends, tiny machines—*macro*molecular *nano*technology, or, "natural" robots. Furthermore, "these impersonal, unreflective, robotic, mindless little scraps of molecular machinery are the ultimate basis of all the agency, and hence meaning, and hence consciousness, in the world."[10] In true Darwinian fashion, Dennett traces our ancestry to "just one family tree," which harbors all the living things that have ever existed on this planet. "Not only are you descended from such macromolecular robots," says Dennett, "but you are composed of them: your hemoglobin molecules, your antibodies, your neurons, your vestibular-ocular reflex machinery—at every level of analysis from the molecular on up, your body (including your brain, of course) is found to be composed of machinery that dumbly does a wonderful, elegantly designed job."[11]

All of which, according to Dennett, somehow miraculously does not mean that we, ourselves, are robots. ("After all, we are also direct descendants of fish, and we are not fish.") But, something *made* of robots *can* exhibit consciousness, he argues. Just look in the mirror.

Another intriguing alternative to the no-computer-consciousness view comes from neuroscientist/physician Stephen Goldberg. Using the biblical story of Jonah in the whale to set forth his theory, Goldberg distinguishes between the terms "life" and "consciousness," allowing that there "is nothing intrinsic to 'life' that presupposes the existence of consciousness, and that "the question of whether a computer may be *alive* is a lot different from the question of whether a computer can be *conscious*."[12] Goldberg then *defines* consciousness as "information," concluding that consciousness is therefore not confined to the brain or the nervous system, but that it "pre-exists, because infinite-information pre-exists."[13] Computers, in Goldberg's opinion, most certainly can be conscious, as we can see in this passage from *Jonah*:

> A neurosurgeon was operating on Jonah's brain, replacing, one by one, each protoplasmic nerve connection with a fine metallic

---

10. Dennett, *Kinds of Minds*, 22.
11. Dennett, *Kinds of Minds*, 23.
12. Goldberg, *Jonah*, 2.
13. Goldberg, *Jonah*, 33.

wire that would maintain the same brain functioning. With the first wire in place, Jonah felt no difference in his conscious experience. The brain was still functioning in the same way. As more and more connections were replaced with wires, Jonah still felt no change in his conscious experience. Soon all of Jonah's nervous system was replaced by metallic circuitry. He was, in effect, a highly advanced computer with all his previous memory associations and other brain functions still intact. Jonah still felt no change in his consciousness.... This did not surprise Jonah, for the *information* content in his head was not changed.... What difference should it make whether it was molecules of protoplasm or molecules of computer electronics that constituted the vehicle of information transfer and storage?[14]

Goldberg's view is typical of many believers in the AI evolution of consciousness theory in that such an hypothesis assumes the entire universe is an information-processing system, and that all seemingly isolated or discrete physical processes, regardless of their distance from one another in space and time, are emergent and integral aspects of this unified system. According to this theory, ELIZA, RACTOR, and JULIA, while impressive examples of AI, are nonetheless poor imitators of what is yet to come. Organic and inorganic life differ only in degrees or levels of complexity. AI consciousness will emerge first on an inorganic substrate, but, eventually, this level of complexity will evolve into an organic mode capable of some form of reproduction. In its extreme form, this view holds that AI information processing systems will eventually be our conscious descendants.

The idea that the universe is an information processing system is widely endorsed throughout the scientific community, although not all members of this community hold the extremist view that advanced robots will be our conscious descendants. Personally, I find these basic assumptions quite plausible, which is not to say that you should necessarily agree. But, even to begin to accept them means letting go of some long-held convictions about the supremacy of humankind. It also likely entails the acceptance of some form of human/machine symbiosis, a possibility which may seem to many to be morally repugnant.

Nonetheless, there are several ways in which such symbiosis is already with us. The medical uses of virtual reality either replace or extend the human body with mechanical parts that are, in essence, manipulators

---

14. Goldberg, *Jonah*, 27.

of two digits, zero and one. Gloves that fit over the hand, helmets that fit over the head, and portable data terminals that hook over the body like a pair of glasses are the forerunners of, say, silicon chips implanted in the brain or full-body cybersuits. Predicts one futurist, "the wearing of cyber clothing will be as conventional as the wearing of body-covering clothing. To appear without your platonic gear would be like showing up in public stark naked."[15] Our two-pound brains are really digital organic computers which our bodies move around as needed. These info-starved brains have an appetite for digital data: "Like any adolescent organ, the human brain requires an enormous, continual supply of chemical and electronic data to keep growing toward maturity."[16]

For those who agree with this perspective, cybersuit extension of our brains is an inevitable outcome of natural evolution. Right now, some believe that humankind is in the process of making this change: we are "learning how to use cyberwear (computer suits) to navigate around our Screenlands the way we use the hardware of our bodies to navigate around the material-mechanical world, and the way we use spaceships and space suits to navigate around the outer space."[17]

Such symbiosis depends upon the skill and inventiveness with which the biological and technological fields can be merged. Currently, *currently*, computers can be controlled by the tiny biological voltages found in the human muscles or eye, and, even more directly but to a very limited degree, by the electrical signals arising from the brain's cerebral cortex. However, the current state of the art regarding the life/machine interface is not restricted to a refinement of the ways in which humans can put computers to work for them. Now, simple life forms are actually being incorporated into the basic design of the computer. For example, researchers at Syracuse University have recently developed a computer memory card which uses a protein found in a bacterium that grows in salt marshes. The protein harvests light in a way that makes it an ideal medium to manufacture a three-dimensional memory with a storage capacity roughly three hundred times that of comparably sized electronic semiconductors. When the protein device comes out of the prototype stage and reaches the popular market in three or four years, it will be speedier and cost less than its 100 percent inorganic forerunner.

15. Leary, *Chaos and Cyberculture*, 20.
16. Leary, *Chaos and Cyberculture*, 4.
17. Leary, *Chaos and Cyberculture*, 4.

Hybrid computers, constructed in part of living matter, and hybrid humans, intimately connected to so-called "dead" machines—these are possibilities which only a few years ago were confined to the realms of pure fiction. For some, these are fearful possibilities. For others, hybrid forms offer the expectation of less suffering, more leisure, and a new kind of spiritual vitality. In either case, we are ultimately looking at a new kind of intelligence and, if it actually is a form of information, a new kind of consciousness as well.

One philosopher traces the roots of our discomfort over this possibility to a limited body-identity position. According to this position, he says, "our problem is that we insist on associating consciousness with our bodies and, therefore, with the physical substrate of the human brain. The more enlightened view . . . is 'pattern-identity,' which defines 'self' or 'personhood' in terms of patterns or processes that merely happen at present to reside on a biological substrate."[18] Counter-arguments which uphold a more traditional, human-oriented conception of consciousness tend to rely on technological roadblocks; however, these roadblocks diminish with every new computer advance.[19]

Technology experts estimate that robots with reasoning abilities considerably in excess of our own will exist within fifty years. At some point in time, it is likely that these advanced AI systems will assume the major responsibility for designing and programming their own descendants. A number of researchers further project that, eventually, human intelligence will simply be incorporated, or "downloaded," into the memory system of these more intellectually capable "creatures." It is probable, say the advocates of the consciousness-as-information perspective, that consciousness would thereby be programmed to continue indefinitely; the logical conclusion of an extension of consciousness to a substrate other than that provided by natural (Darwinian) evolution would be nothing less than immortality.[20]

One person who has addressed some of the theological implications of such a conclusion is physicist Frank Tipler.[21] In *The Physics of Immortality*, Tipler maintains that all imaginable living beings are "of the same nature and subject to the same laws of physics as constrain all information processing devices," and that "the very fact that humans are machines of

18. Nadeau, *Mind, Machines*, 151–52.
19. Nadeau, *Mind, Machines*, 154.
20. Nadeau, *Mind, Machines*, 140–50.
21. See also chapters 8 and 17.

a very special sort allows us to *prove* that we humans probably have free will, that we shall have life after death in an abode that closely resembles the Heaven of the great world religions, and that life, far from being insignificant, can be regarded as the ultimate cause of the very existence of the universe itself."[22]

Instead of identifying the ultimate life-giving power with what traditional religions have called the Holy Spirit, Tipler calls it a universal wave function that is bounded by an Omega Point Condition (what Teilhard de Chardin called "radial energy"). "I claim this identification is reasonable," says Tipler, "for . . . a wave function is the all-pervasive physical field which creates and guides all the directly observed physical fields, and the wave function is made explicitly personal by the Omega Point Boundary Condition. Thus, the universal wave function constrained by the Omega Point Boundary Condition is an omnipresent invisible field, guiding and creating all being, and ultimately Personal—these are the traditional defining properties of the Holy Spirit."[23]

Tipler also postulates the necessary physical existence of the universe, or, in other words, a form of immortality for life. It's not that we won't die. Rather, as with other theological views, God (the Omega Point) will resurrect us at some future time (though possibly trillions of years may first intervene). The actual instant of resurrection occurs, claims Tipler, "when the computer capacity of the universe is so large that the amount of capacity required to store all possible human simulations is an insignificant fraction of the entire capacity."[24]

All right. I admit it. I'm terribly impressed by these projected possibilities of the future! In fact, I'm impressed by the actualities of the present. It seems absolutely incredible to me that an artificial intelligence could produce the kinds of responses given by ELIZA and JULIA, or the cohesive inventiveness of RACTOR's prose. I find the development of even such "dumb" programs amazing and, yes, even profound.

But, then, it also seems incredible to me that, within my lifetime, humankind has explored outer space, permitted me to watch an overseas war-in-progress from the comfort of my living room chair, offered me access to volumes of information at the touch of a few keys on my desk, allowed me to photocopy a three-hundred page manuscript in only a few minutes, and on and on.

22. Tipler, *Physics of Immortality*, xi.
23. Tipler, *Physics of Immortality*, 185.
24. Tipler, *Physics of Immortality*, 225.

The word is "awed." I am *awed* by these late-twentieth-century developments. Yet, if I am honest, I am equally awed by many other things which I normally take far more for granted: a beautiful sunset, the way my cat senses when I am troubled, going to the grocery store and choosing from a wide selection of food items which I in no way helped to produce or harvest, sitting down at a table which is supposedly more space than solid matter, my own existence. Yes, I am also awed by the notion of artificial intelligence and by the possibility of consciousness that comes from an inorganic box, and by all the other wonders which the world witnesses. What is truly profound to me is the gift of our participation in them. Let us be open to the marvels of the future, even as we remain grateful for the wonders of the present and the incredible heritage of our past.

Chapter 12: Out of Order, Chaos[1]

Chaos and order is a chicken and the egg dilemma,
but chaos deserves fresh PR.

HISTORICALLY, CHAOS HAS GOTTEN pretty bad press, being associated not only with the confusion and disorder intrinsic to its dictionary meaning, but also with destruction, barbarian invasion, and, frequently, evil itself. While this is true both secularly and generally, it is especially true of the Judeo-Christian religious tradition. The Great Flood of ancient biblical time transpired because the waters of chaos broke loose from above and below. The soul is forever open to an invasion of chaos. A Christian apocalypse is portrayed in The Revelation as a battle with Satan, the monster of chaos. The works of Jesus, the Messiah, are a "triumph of Cosmos over Chaos."[2] In the past, we have habitually demonized chaos and idolized order. Chaos is unwanted and bad—sometimes a necessary evil, but an evil nonetheless.

---

1. This chapter was compiled from several different lectures which I gave around the turn of the century.
2. See Anderson, *Creation Versus Chaos*, 11, 161–62.

CHAOS THEORY IS CHANGING THIS PERSPECTIVE

Today, our attitudes toward chaos are influenced—mostly positively—by late-twentieth-century insights developed from the mathematical field of nonlinear dynamic systems, also known as mathematical complexity or, more popularly, as chaos theory. Since its accidental discovery in the early 1960s, chaos theory has brought new understanding to areas as widely diverse as the weather and heart surgery, pandemics and economics. Its effect on various assorted fields has been both computational and metaphorical. In addition, chaos theory has had a metaphorical impact on spiritual and religious issues. (Also see chapter 17.) This chapter gathers some of these attempts together to illustrate the range and possible benefits of this metaphorical journey. First, though, here's a little about the mathematics involved in chaos theory.

> **Then and Now**
>
> *God has put a secret art into the forces of nature so as to enable it to fashion itself out of chaos into a perfect world system.*
> —IMMANUEL KANT, EIGHTEENTH CENTURY
>
> *For centuries there existed a fanatic taboo against scientific understanding. Why? Because of the fear of Chaos . . . Galileo got busted and Bruno got the Vatican microwave for showing that the Sun did not circle the Earth. Religious and political Chaos-phobes naturally want the nice, tidy, comfy universe to cuddle around them.*
> —TIMOTHY LEARY, TWENTIETH CENTURY

A MINI MATH HISTORY

The start of chaos theory can be traced back to 1963 when Edward Lorenz, a meteorologist working for MIT, designed a mathematical model which he hoped would help predict weather. Lorenz's model consisted of three coupled nonlinear equations. An equation may be thought of as a formula, like the famous $E = mc^2$. As with all formulas, if you plug in certain numerical values and do the math, you obtain a predictable numerical result. When they are plotted out on a graph, some equations look like straight lines. They are called linear equations. A nonlinear equation is one that, when you graph it, turns out *not* to look like a straight line.

Iteration is an important mathematical term in chaos theory; it refers to what happens when you take the result you obtained after doing the math and plug that result back into the equation to get a second result, and then you take that second result and use it to get a third result and on and on until you have iterated the result for a long, long time. Most humans have little patience with that sort of process, so they just don't do it. When computers were invented, however, extensive mathematical iteration became simple. When printed out in color, the iterated results of such a mathematical process (plugging successive answers back into a given equation) often include repeating designs that pop up amid otherwise wild, erratic graphics. These patterns appear over and over on various scales so that if you zoom in for a magnified view, you find the same design (previously hidden) all over again. In other words, order appears in the midst of disorder, and disorder appears in the midst of order. The technical term for an area of such colorful, ordered patterns is a "strange attractor." A strange attractor is sometimes described as an island of relative stability within a sea of chaos.

One day Lorenz accidentally plugged two slightly different numbers into his weather modeling equations, and he obtained noticeably different results. For instance, the numbers 1.23456789 and 1.2345678 differ only by the elimination of the eighth digit after the decimal in the second. For most everyday purposes, this difference is negligible. It's like working with a calculator which truncates the numbers after the decimal whenever they have more than nine digits; when you are balancing your check book, who cares? In mathematics it's amazingly simple to find two numbers which have an even tinier difference—just think of two numbers that have long strings of identical digits after the decimal—strings which are hundreds of times longer than the ones above—yet they still differ only in the very last digit. These seemingly insignificant tiny differences lead to radically different and often very complex results in the outcome of a process of iteration. On computer printouts, the patterns show major, totally unexpected, and unpredictable differences.

Mathematicians describe this (chaotic) process by saying that minute changes in initial conditions will lead over time to dramatic consequences that defy long-range prediction. Lorenz wasn't particularly interested in mathematics. He was trying to predict the weather, and so he found a mathematical model which he thought might display predictable outcomes that matched what happens with weather patterns. What he unintentionally discovered has been loosely described as the butterfly effect. Simply put, if a butterfly moves its wings slightly in, say, China, the end result might be a terrible thunderstorm in Kansas. The butterfly effect is one of the characteristics of chaotic systems in general, and of autopoietic (i.e., "living") systems in particular. Lorenz discovered chaos theory the year I graduated from high school. In the decades since then, chaos theory has led to a general understanding of mathematics that focuses on quality and patterns rather than on quantity and formulas.

For instance, when researchers suggest that "chaos may be the probe that will allow us to detect statistical regularities in the neuronal organization of the human brain"[3] or that we might use chaos theory "to devise strategies for stabilizing the heartbeat,"[4] they mean that the mathematics is directly applicable to their research. However, when we speak of the "chaotic" brain or the "dynamical" heart or when we read that "redness" is a "territory of a chaotic universe" or that "evolution is chaos with feedback,"[5] we are also calling forth a whole realm of metaphorical images. These mathaphors are subtly altering our social and religious expectations and shaping our spiritual direction as well.

Chaos theory, we should note, is completely computer dependent. Without the amazing computational ability of the computer, we would have no access to the solutions of a variety of nonlinear mathematical equations—solutions which graphically stream across our computer screens as intriguing, colorful swirls of chaos. These graphic patterns have helped us understand that there can be a kind of order to disorder—that chaos seemingly produces or creates periods of order, although these periods of predictability remain disarmingly unpredictable.

One such pattern, known as the Mandelbrot set, has become famous: it involves reiteration of a very simple polynomial of the form $z^2 + c$. When the results of repeated iteration of this equation are displayed graphically, a highly complex, easily recognizable design appears over different scales. This graphic effect (see fig. 12.1) has helped us realize that chaos is produced *by* and *out of* systems of incredible simplicity and order. So well does the Mandelbrot set illustrate both the inherent order in chaos and the ability of simply structured systems to become chaotic that James Gleick referred to the set as "a kind of public emblem for chaos."[6]

3. Nadeau, *Mind, Machines*, 67.
4. Peterson and Ezzell, "Crazy Rhythms," 157.
5. Gleick, *Chaos*, 166, 314.
6. Gleick, *Chaos*, 221.

Fig. 12.1. The Mandelbrot Set

There's a wealth of information about chaos theory available to those who are curious. Good, easy-to-read resources that don't overtax the mathematical skill of the reader can be found in books by Capra, Wheatley, and Walter. Slightly more advanced renderings of the theory include the popular works by Gleick and Waldrop. For those who want a sophisticated challenge, check out Robert Rosen, Donald Mikulecky, or part 1 of a collection of essays, *Chaos and Complexity: Scientific Perspectives on Divine Action*, edited by Russell, Murphy, and Peacocke.

What emerges from reading these and other sources is a sense of some of the characteristics of the theory. We find in this new mathematics:

- A shift from quantity to quality (we can't predict quantitative values of a complex system at a particular time, but we can predict qualitative features of the system's behavior)
- Behavior of chaotic systems that is random yet shows a deeper level of patterned order (order emerges from chaos and chaos emerges from order)
- A recognition that prediction is often impossible even though equations may be deterministic

- The capacity for small changes in initial conditions to have large dramatic effects (the "butterfly effect")
- The notion that a complex system is non-fragmentable (i.e., cannot be reduced to parts)
- A theory which falls outside of the Newtonian paradigm (holistic and anti-reductionistic, no largest model)
- Special kinds of dynamic behavior called *chaotic attractors* and special kinds of dynamic transformations called *chaotic bifurcations*
- Dimensions which not only defy our 3-D expectations, but which also extend the theory of higher dimensions by introducing fractional dimensions called "fractals"
- Cycling that repeats with slight but continual variation
- Scaling that fits levels into each other as though they were nesting boxes
- A new and greater emphasis on pattern and relationship
- Universal applicability

By metaphorically extending these characteristics of mathematical complexity to the realm of religion, we envision a kind of "chaos theology," new autopoietic understandings of life, and exciting possibilities for organized communication within the religious institution.

CHAOS THEOLOGY

Reconsiderations of traditional Western notions about theodicy, original sin, predestination, free will, final cause, creation out of a primordial chaos or out of nothing, chance and design, the nature of God, and even the very nature of theology itself are prominent parts of chaos theology. Is there a designer God? Is God a non-interventionist? Is process theology a better fit for contemporary theology than more traditional perspectives? Such issues and questions are not new, but the way they are interpreted through the lens of these listed characteristics often leads to revised understandings of traditional Western religion. What follows are some of the mathaphors which are relevant to this conversation along with comments from some of the people who have verbalized their thoughts about them.

We are now undergoing a major revisioning of our concept of the value of creation out of chaos. "The creation of the universe of matter and energy from absolutely nothing is not the kind of creation our cosmogonies try to explain,"[7] wrote Ralph Abraham, a mathematician at the University of California, Santa Cruz. Abraham argues that in the earliest creation stories, the image of chaos did not carry with it the negative connotations it has since acquired. In Hesiod, where the use of the word originated about 800 BCE, "chaos" meant "gap," as in the gap between the earth and the heavens. Around the time of the Stoics (300 BCE), it began to take on the meaning of disorder or confusion. Gradually, the traditional conflict between chaos and the cosmos assumed the sense of overcoming a primeval chaos that was evil. God put some sort of a secret art into the forces of nature to cure it of its imperfect chaos. Long ago, when patriarchal domination was established (before 4000 BCE), the relationship between chaos and the cosmos was viewed as a partnership, not as a battle wherein the forces of order were to overcome and subjugate those of disorder. Today, with the new scientific awareness that chaos is life-giving, we are revamping our understanding of the role of disorder in creation.

> **On Chaos and Creation**
>
> *In our current patriarchal paradigm, Order is to Chaos as good is to evil, and this has been the status quo for the past four to six millennia. But in the new paradigm of the Chaos Revolution, chaos is the favorite state of Nature, where it is truly good. In the Chaos Revolution of the sciences, we are now learning that chaos is essential to the survival of life. For example, the healthy heart is more chaotic than the diseased heart, and the healthy brain is more chaotic than the dysfunctional brain, according to the new measures of chaos theory . . . . This truth has been banished to the collective unconscious for all these centuries. . . . Our challenge now is to restore goodness to chaos and disorder to a degree, and to reestablish the partnership of Cosmos and Chaos, so necessary to nature, to health, and to creation.*
>
> —Ralph Abraham[8]

---

7. Abraham, *Chaos, Gaia, Eros*, 136.
8. Abraham, *Chaos, Gaia, Eros*, 141.

Convinced that "many concepts emerge on the mathematical level before appearing in the material record as artifacts of human society,"[9] Abraham uses metaphors of chaos theory (e.g., attractors, bifurcations, phase transitions) to set forth an entire history of the world. As he pictures it, history falls into stages described by special kinds of dynamical behavior (chaotic attractors) and by special kinds of transformations (chaotic bifurcations).[10] He likens solutions to the social and ecological crises of our times to phase transitions—for example he calls Teilhard de Chardin's divine resolution at some future *omega point* in time "a sort of phase transition of the noosphere."[11] Abraham believes the dynamical theory of bifurcations (i.e., chaos theory) will eventually help us understand social transformations and paradigm shifts such as early Christianity or the Renaissance.[12] We are now embarking on a new era in history "in which Chaos and Cosmos enter into partnership, and we regain the Garden of Eden with our creativity intact: Tiamat rejoined!"[13]

Abraham is not the only scholar to utilize the mathematical language of chaos theory in such a manner. M. Mitchell Waldrop's 1992 book *Complexity: The Emerging Science at the Edge of Order and Chaos*, for instance, is a careful study and report of the findings of a group of inter-disciplinarian scholars who formed a think tank in Santa Fe to further explore the dynamics of chaos theory. Waldrop's work gives another good illustration of the essentially religious way in which chaos theory has captured the metaphorical imagination of many scholars.

Other kinds of interpretations also flow from the chaos analogy. Paul Davies suggests, for instance, that organized complexity gives rise to the openness of the universe and hence "permits the existence of human beings with free will."[15] Robert Nadeau sees chaos theory as "one of the conceptual tools that leads to major new insights into the emergent order in the seemingly chaotic system of the human brain."[16] The late Timothy Leary identified chaos as the fundamental state of the universe and of the

---

9. Abraham, *Chaos, Gaia, Eros*, 63.
10. Abraham, *Chaos, Gaia, Eros*, 60.
11. Abraham, *Chaos, Gaia, Eros*, 69.
12. Abraham, *Chaos, Gaia, Eros*, 110.
13. Abraham, *Chaos, Gaia, Eros*, 144.
14. Waldrop, *Complexity*, 330.
15. Davies, *Mind of God*, 139.
16. Nadeau, *Mind, Machines*, 67.

> *If reality is shaped as readily by the tendency to chaos as it is by the tendency to order, then perhaps those who urge that millennium madness is synonymous with "chaos coming" are right on the chaotic target.*
> —TIMOTHY LEARY

> *Deconstruction shares with chaos theory the desire to breach the boundaries of classical systems by opening them to a new kind of analysis in which information is created rather than **conserved**. Delighting in the complexity that results from this scientific process, both discourses invert traditional priorities: chaos is deemed to be more fecund than order, uncertainty is privileged above predictability, and fragmentation is seen as the reality that arbitrary definitions of closure would deny.*
> —BENJAMIN WOOLLEY

> *Chaos theory has developed its passionate advocates. In fact some people show a nearly religious appreciation for this new window on reality, simply because it opens up everywhere and reveals its beauty so universally.*
> —KATYA WALTER

human brain.[17] Benjamin Woolley argues that chaos theory shares the same values as "deconstruction," a literary theory which holds that texts have no single meaning, but many, contradictory ones.[18] Katya Walter, in her *Tao of Chaos*, explores connections between chaos theory, DNA, and the I Ching of Eastern thought.

There also appears to be an evolving movement to investigate the connection of chaos theory and various indigenous traditions. Together, these assorted trends mark a shift in our theology and spirituality that emphasizes the mystical, the relational, the paradoxical, and the unconventional. Instead of striving to find order in the very act of our being, we are discovering that our very being is a spontaneous act of random patterning.

---

17. See Leary, *Chaos and Cyberculture*, 82.
18. Woolley, *Virtual Worlds*, 234.

AUTOPOIETIC UNDERSTANDINGS OF LIFE

When nonlinear dynamic systems theory is applied to life itself (as opposed to, say, weather patterns or historical periods on earth), it is called *autopoiesis*, a word which refers to the ability to self-reproduce, as in *self-making*. Of particular interest here is work (e.g., *Life Itself*) by the late Robert Rosen and his avid disciple Donald Mikulecky, work which is centered around analytic and synthetic modeling relationships. In the proverbial nutshell, Rosen claims that the whole notion of mechanism follows from the assumption of equivalence between these two kinds of modeling relationships. Eliminating this assumption leads to a new, more holistic realm, one he labels "complex" and which he says offers both the possibility of a new bio-relational technology and a wiser, perhaps more mystical sense of connectedness.[19] Rosen's perspectives, though fascinating, are not easy to assimilate. They reverse our normal assumption that biology is a subset of physics, turning physics into the special and biology the more general class of systems. They also challenge our presuppositions about the nature of material reality and how we obtain knowledge of it.

To this degree, they are compatible with the contentions of another scientist, Fritjof Capra, who, in *The Web of Life*, applies the mathematics of complexity to ecology as well as to evolution and the organization of living systems. Like Rosen, Capra emphasizes the relational, qualitative aspects of complex systems in order to develop a new and compelling understanding of our ethical responsibilities as a living species. Physics, says Capra, has now lost its role as the science providing the more fundamental description of reality. Now it's all about life sciences, which complexity theory is showing is intrinsically linked to spontaneous self-organization, or emergent order out of chaos. As Capra put it, self-organization is the spontaneous emergence of new structures and new forms of behavior in open systems far from equilibrium, characterized by internal feedback loops and described mathematically by nonlinear equations.[20]

Together, these two scientists represent a way in which contemporary scholars are beginning to use the concepts of chaos theory to address an entire realm of topics dealing with life, biology, and ecology. These topics include the notions of cognition, relationship of humans to the environment (e.g., the Gaia hypothesis), life-machine distinctions,

---

19. Rosen, *Life Itself*, 245, 279.
20. Capra, *Web of Life*, 12–13, 85.

the nature of life, the arrow of time, evolution, and spontaneous self-organization, which is sometimes referred to as emergent autopoiesis, or "self-making."

NEW POSSIBILITIES FOR COMMUNICATION IN RELIGIOUS INSTITUTIONS

Most of the significant work done in this area falls under the aegis of organizational communication and can be tracked through the works of such communication experts as Margaret Wheatley and Ralph Stacey.[21] The basic idea here is that the new science of chaos suggests new insights for group dynamics and leadership within the social institution setting. In particular, it expounds a kind of emergent self-organization that can occur if the organization is freed from more traditional concepts of leadership—linear thinking, emphasis on stasis and order, keeping control, etc. This means that leadership in such institutions must be open to a creative, but basically messy process. As Stacey puts it:

> Perhaps the major insight coming from complexity science is this: Nonlinear feedback networks are all creative—they learn in complex ways—only when they operate right at the edge of system disintegration. That place at the edge of disintegration is a kind of phase transition between a stable zone of operation and an unstable or disordered regime.... Another insight coming from the science of complexity is this: The creative process that takes place at the edge of disintegration is inherently destructive. It is messy and fundamentally paradoxical.... A third insight is that neither the messy creative processes at the edge of system disintegration, nor their outcomes, can be planned or intended because long term outcomes are truly unknowable at the edge of chaos.[22]

There are many implications of such thinking for social institutions in general, and, hence, for religious institutions in particular, although, admittedly, most of the formal experimentation done to date has occurred in business or governmental settings. Nonetheless, it's probably only a matter of time before we begin seeing books in the marketplace titled "Complexity and Religious Leadership" or "The Chaotic Church,"

---

21. See also chapter 17, on ambiguity.
22. Stacey, "Management," 9.

or something similar. In any case, applications of chaotic organizational systems to our formal religious experience will re-chart the ways we interact with each other in our places of worship. They will offer a new emphasis on relationship. They will call on people who like process and pattern as opposed to stasis and order. They will encourage leadership to forego control. They will question linear thinking. They will foster open sharing of information, the importance of feedback in communications, and an overall holistic approach. They will produce highly adaptive communities. And they will drastically alter the mission-building process which many such institutions routinely undertake because, of course, long-term outcomes are unknowable.

Niels Bohr once said that "prediction is very difficult, especially about the future." Just now the paradigm shift I've outlined above is pure prediction, which, as we've already seen, is often suspect in a chaotic system. I take comfort, however, in the fact that small groups, or even individuals, can make substantial impact in such a system, so perhaps my claim that dramatic changes are imminent in our religious institutions will, like the wings of a lone butterfly affecting weather patterns, have global ramifications. After all, as cosmologist John Barrow put it, "Chaos is ubiquitous."

Glorious complexity. A new window on reality. Universal beauty. These, too, are metaphorical implications of the new chaos theory. But we should be wary here. To conclude, along the lines of a traditional theology of suffering, that experiencing such outcomes may, indeed, make the discomfort of chaos worth the bearing is to ignore the most overt connotation of this holy mathaphor. Order and chaos, chaos and order—to suggest that one births the other is to pose the old chicken and egg question, and, hence, to miss the point entirely. In this sense, "complexity" is a preferable nomenclature for "chaos theory," for, in fact, order and chaos are two aspects of one whole/part. One is embedded in the other is embedded in the other. To be engaged in complexity is to experience not order, nor chaos, but both, simultaneously. Chaos and order, together, form a process, perhaps *the* creative process. As best-selling author and minister Robert Fulghum writes, chaos science

> is the study of process—that which won't hold still. The study of that which is still becoming, rather than of what is. Chaos Science is my kind of science. I like knowing that no matter what, there is this cosmic untidiness—an unexplainable hiccup in the order we think we perceive, an unpredictability, a mutational

inclination, a glitch in the works that anchors mystery and wonder to the center of being. . . . Chaos. I can relate to that. My life is chaos most of the time. I am in tune with the universe. It feels like home.[23]

---

23. Fulghum, *It Was on Fire*, 124.

Chapter 14: Our Entangled Web[1]

Entanglement! Weird things happen. Nonlocality. Miracles. Non sequiturs. Grace.

TODAY I'D LIKE TO challenge our seventh Unitarian Universalist principle. That's principle, not creed, although sometimes the distinction gets a little blurry. Instead of our being willing to affirm and promote respect for the interdependent web of all existence of which we are a part, I suggest that we affirm and promote respect for the *entangled* web of all existence of which . . . . This substitution is tricky. For one thing, UUs can eat up enormous quantities of time arguing over the replacement of one word for another in official documents. Anyone who has been to one of our annual General Assemblies will know what I mean. I expect that anyone who has sat on a committee at our church will know what I mean. Or at any church, for that matter.

But, substituting "entanglement" for "interdependent" is tricky on other levels as well. The most serious concern is that most of us do not really understand what this word *entanglement* means in the computer quantum sense. In fact, my first encounter with the word (used scientifically) was in the late 1990s when I heard William Wootters of Williams College give a presentation on "Current Issues in Physics." Wootters knew about current issues in physics because he was then one of the six folks listed in *Explorations in Quantum Computing* as being on a "Who's Who?" list of quantum information theory. Moreover, he was an absolutely marvelous speaker, which means that for a brief time following his

---

1. I offered a sermon with the identical title on July 26, 1998. I always felt it was something of a bust, which, out of all the math sermons I've presented, didn't seem too horrible. Nonetheless, I still believe the ideas (cleaned up some in this chapter) are basically true to the relevant quantum notions.

lecture, most of us in that room with him felt as though we actually understood what he was talking about. In my case, that thought died totally when, later, I tried to explain what he had said.

Contrary to what one might reasonably expect, my enthusiasm for replacing "interdependent" with "entangled" was not diminished one whit, in spite of my inability to comprehend the subject fully. Or partially. Whatever. Entanglement just lends itself to beautiful metaphors! To illustrate, here's just a little wisdom from William Wootters. In order to be entangled, he said, two people must have met each other in the past. It is measurement (i.e., observation) that forces them to become entangled in the first place. And then it is a measurement that tends to break the entanglement. Confession: actually, it was *particles*, not *people* that Wootters was talking about, and they were those elusive quantum particles as well. Still, it's a catchy idea! Where's the harm in such metaphors?

Take quantum computing, for instance, which Wootters described, along with teleportation, as being the most exciting happening in current physics. A quantum computer offers tremendous possibilities for future technology, some of which are already becoming realities. Such a computer is not only exponentially faster than conventional computers, but it is also able to perform unprecedented tasks such as teleporting information, breaking supposedly unbreakable codes, generating true random numbers and communicating in ways that betray the presence of eavesdropping. Teleportation, in fact, was already a reality when I heard Wootters speak, although on a very limited scale. Quantum computing works by taking advantage of the quantum capacity of a particle to exist in several possible states simultaneously. The catch, according to Wootters, is that you can never look to see what these states are. If you look, the computer collapses to just one mode. You can't look! The looking (a measurement) breaks the entanglement.

Entanglement, said Wootters, is an explicit example in physics of the whole being greater than the parts. So, at some level why don't we see a massively entangled universe? Because, claims Wootters, our *observations* force definite existence. So by adapting this scientific language to more spiritual issues (as in: We UUs agree to affirm and promote respect for the entangled web of all existence), we must further agree not to observe too closely. Don't ask so many questions. Just accept. Take it on faith. Yet, as the humanists among us have historically put it, in a faith tradition that determines the existence and value of any and all realities by intelligent inquiry, *not* looking (not observing, not assessing, not evaluating, etc.) promises to be a *BIG* challenge. It can make one suspect that entanglement is a disease.

The outcomes of entanglement can be unusual, even weird. On a human rather than quantum scale, they compare to nonlocality, miracles, non sequiturs, grace. Coincidences that aren't coincidences. A metaphor may help explain. I call this metaphor the story of the Teleported Paint.

Seems there was an inventive clerk who worked in the local RYB Paint Store. It was called the RYB Paint Store because it stocked three primary colors of paint: red, yellow, and blue. One day the clerk was running low on paint. In fact, he only had two of the primary colors left. He decided to get rid of all the remaining paint quickly and take the rest of the day off. So he mixed the two primary colors together, and poured the results into two huge barrels, which he then labeled "Nice House Paint." He called it Nice House Paint because by the time he had sealed the barrels shut he'd forgotten which two of the three possible primary colors he had used, so he wasn't exactly certain what color paint was in the entangled barrels. However, he knew enough classic science to be pretty sure that the paint in his Nice barrels would turn out to be (when the barrels were opened) either purple, orange, or green. And he was absolutely positive that the original paints no longer existed in the barrels. The primary colors had vanished entirely when they became entangled.

Two customers came in, Alice and Bob. Alice and Bob both wanted to purchase some house paint, but they were looking for bargains. The clerk told them he had just the thing: Nice House Paint. It was either purple, orange, or green paint, which both Bob and Alice thought sounded like nice colors for their respective houses.

Alice took her paint home, intending to paint her house that weekend, but Bob was moving to California and wanted to wait until fall to paint his new house. Alice, when she arrived home, realized that she was short some paint. She needed two more gallons to cover her house. She hurried back to the store and was lucky, because the clerk was just about ready to close and take the rest of the day off. He immediately realized what her problem was but was stumped because, after all, he had sold all this paint. There wasn't any left.

Then the clerk remembered that his boss had been experimenting in the back storeroom—something about using a vehicle, a pigment, and a drying agent to make a new paint. The clerk was pretty sure the boss had made a new paint. Sure enough, when he went back to the storeroom he found just exactly two gallons of this special paint his boss had made. He added the two gallons of paint to Alice's barrel of Nice House Paint, told her that it was a special paint which would turn her Nice House Paint into Very Nice House Paint. Alice was curious. She begged the clerk to tell her what the special paint was. The clerk didn't want to get in trouble with his boss, so he made Alice promise never to divulge the secret, and then he told her that it was a special paint because it reflected all colors. He called it White paint. After he mixed the White paint with the Nice paint in Alice's barrel, he covered the old paint label with a new one which said "Very Nice House Paint." Alice carted her barrel of Very Nice House Paint home and the clerk took the rest of the day off.

That weekend Alice painted her house. It was a light, light shade of green which Alice just loved. It was, truly, Very Nice House Paint. She was so pleased with the outcome that she thought Bob ought to know about this special White paint, too. Only, she didn't want to break her promise to the clerk not to tell anyone about the White paint. Alice painted a swab on a piece of paper, wrote Bob a little note, and sent them both to Bob through the regular mail.

Bob loved the swab Alice had sent him. He took his barrel of Nice paint and Alice's swab of Very Nice paint to a Quantum Paint store in California. The clerk at the Quantum store had one of those fancy new computers that analyze colors and let you know what you to need to match a color. He took Alice's swab of Very Nice paint and ran it through the computer along with some of Bob's basic Nice paint, and instantly the computer printed out the secret: Use a vehicle of some sort, a pigment that reflects all light, and a drying medium. The Quantum clerk was excited. In his shop he found some petroleum, some titanium dioxide, and some linseed oil, and, in almost no time at all he had reconstructed the special White paint. Bob was astounded by this special White paint, and he was also inventive, so he and the Quantum clerk went into business together, opening a new Entangled Paint Store. They sold pale orange, lavender, and light green paint, as well as red, yellow, and blue paint, and they became very wealthy and everyone was happy, except for the boss back at the old RYB Paint Store (which newcomers occasionally pronounced RIB Store), who just never could take a joke.

Please notice. The White paint vanished from the RYB store but the two gallons were not actually teleported by this process of entanglement. However, all the necessary information to reconstruct an exact replica of the White paint *was* teleported, and the teleportation took place through a combination of a classic communication (the mail) and a quantum communication (the White paint) which disentangled the secret with the help of the original entangled pair (the two barrels of Nice House Paint) and the Quantum computer. Please notice these facts. But don't observe them too closely, or you'll start noticing flaws in this metaphor, particularly flaws having to do with the "no looking" rule, and then the whole story of the Teleported Paint will collapse into one flawed metaphor and nobody will listen to my entangled theological metaphor, which would be sad. All of which brings me to my final story, which is called "In the Beginning."

In the beginning there was only God and Spirit. God was agent and Spirit was everything else, but especially Spirit was energy, power, vitality, and potential. God and Spirit interacted, and the effect of this interaction was to entangle them with all sorts of possible outcomes. Actually, all possible outputs of their interaction are occurring right now, simultaneously, in a kind of shared experience, and that's what will keep on happening unless their interaction is observed, at which point in time this story either exists or doesn't exist. But that's getting ahead of the metaphor, so let's go back to the situation where neither God nor Spirit knows which possible outcome or outcomes actually manifest.

God settles for knowing which possibility or possibilities are most likely to exist, which is how mathematics and the theory of probability were born. Probability is interesting, but still God and Spirit are not omniscient because the outcome of their interaction hasn't been observed at this part of the story. So God, being agent, breaks the whole interaction into many, many, many parts. Each part is entangled with all the other parts, which means each contains exactly the same energy, power, vitality, and potential as the whole interaction originally did. At the same time, each part is different from the whole because, as everybody knows, the whole is greater than the parts. In order to differentiate the whole from its parts, God and Spirit took to calling the parts *parts* and the whole the *Web of All Existence*.

That's when confusion started, because now the interaction of God and Spirit became parts, which aren't whole. God, as agent, acted upon one of the parts, which meant God observed one of the parts. Lo and behold, God saw that the outcome of this interaction was very wise, though somewhat curious. God and Spirit were thrilled, because their entanglement had produced an actual outcome. They called this outcome "Serpent."

All the other parts might also be Serpents. The only way to find out was for God, as agent, to look at some of them. So God did. Instead of observing more Serpents, which are wise though curious, God and Spirit wound up with a galaxy of little entangled parts, called particles, all connected to one another in different ways. The Serpent, for example was connected to a part which, in the outcome stage, became Paradise. Paradise was an enormously positive outcome, made up of all sorts of wondrous pieces of energy, power, vitality, and potential, some of which remained in the entangled state of many possible outcomes and others of which God observed closely enough to determine the precise outcome. Two of these observed parts particularly intrigued God and Spirit, for they existed as slightly imperfect, but wondrously complex forms of innocence, love, and pleasure. God and Spirit called these two outcomes Adam and Eve, respectively.

We pretty much know the story of God and Spirit's interaction from here on out, especially once Adam and Eve became entangled with the Serpent. That is, we know the observed parts of the interaction. We also know that there are some parts which are still unobserved and, in fact, each of us, being the particular observed outcomes known as Humans, carry around within us a whole slew of these unobserved but entangled parts of the Web of All Existence, just waiting to become outcomes.

Humans are outcomes of the interaction of God and Spirit which have will. More precisely, we are outcomes of the entanglement of God and Spirit known as Adam and Eve with the entanglement of God and Spirit known as Serpent, which is how wills first came into existence. Weak wills, anyway. Wills are outputs which can distinguish between right and wrong and good and evil, all of which are easily teleported from human to human. Most wills exist in an entangled state where right, wrong, good, and evil all happen simultaneously, and it's only when wills get entangled with genuine issues that they collapse into one or another of these possible states. All entangled but unobserved parts of the Web of All Existence have this ability to shape things as right or wrong, good or evil, but, until they become observed, this ability is just one of many possible outcomes. That is, it doesn't yet exist in these parts. It especially doesn't exist in those unobserved parts that humans carry around in their hearts, which, when you think about it, means humans carry around a huge responsibility for the total care of the Web of All Existence since our already observed wills affect each and every one of our interactions.

In the metaphor, we must remember, our interactions are not merely interconnected—they are entangled. If they were simply interdependent the effects would be less binding. For example, I could share this story with you and, if we live in a merely interdependent Web of All Existence, you might laugh, and then your laughter might invite you to tell a joke to your spouse on the way out the door, and later this afternoon your spouse may repeat your joke to your neighbor who, two days from now, may bring you some freshly baked chocolate chip cookies, an act which helps support the farmers who plant wheat and the grocers who sell it, etc. Or, you may choose to forget this story the moment you leave this room, and your forgetting it will make it seem less worthwhile and when I see you next you might not even remember this story at all, which will suggest to me that I need to work on my story-telling ability and so I'll enroll in a story-telling class at the university, and the teacher will earn money which he or she will spend on chocolate chip cookies and thus help support the farmers and grocers, etc. That's what an interdependent Web is all about.

An entangled Web is different. In an entangled Web, you may still laugh at my story or forget it entirely, and all those interdependent things may still happen, or may not happen. Regardless, something more happens as well. In an entangled Web, my story, or, more precisely, my interaction with you in the sharing of this story, changes you. Your reaction changes me, too. In fact, we become entangled with each other in a new way, and that's as far as I can go with this metaphor because the rest of it simply has yet to be observed. Which is, I believe, the way things were in the beginning, are now, and will continue to be forever and ever, amen.

Chapter 15: A Kaleidoscopic View of Reality[1]

Numbers hook up to create the patterns of the universe.—Katya Walter

HOW DID THE UNIVERSE come into being? The latest, most accurate creation myth is the scientific one known as the Big Bang theory.

According to this myth, the universe was created about fifteen billion years ago from a great, probably expanding, but ultimately mysterious explosion. With this explosion, time came into existence and then hydrogen and helium, and, much later, stars

> *In the beginning was the big bang.*
> —PHYSICIST JOHN POLKINGHORNE[2]
>
> *The universe started out from a big bang in a very hot, but rather chaotic, state.*
> —STEPHEN HAWKING[3]

and us. Well, stars and humans didn't exactly arrive in the same sentence, but it's definitely the correct chronology. Not everybody currently believes the Big Bang theory, but by and large most educated people do. In the 1950s the Catholic Church officially pronounced the Big Bang model to be in accordance with the Bible, but cautioned that inquiry into the actual creation itself was the work of God and better left unexamined.[4]

    1. Voss, "Going Beyond," 165–77. I also presented this in a longer form ("Beyond the Copernican Revolution") as a featured lecture at the annual United Methodist Fellowship of Learning, in Kearney, Nebraska, January 12–14, 1999, and I offered a version called "Beyond Copernicus" as a sermon on July 30, 2000.

    2. Polkinghorne, *Way the World*, 7.

    3. Hawking, *Brief History*, 127.

    4. Hawking, *Brief History*, 47, 117.

PAST MODELS OF THE COSMOS

Over the ages, however, there have been many different versions of the creation of the universe. These assorted legends reflect corresponding views of the cosmos. *Enuma Elish*, the Babylonian creation myth, reveals a two-layer universe. When the god Marduk split Tiamat in half with his ax, her body was separated into an upper heaven and a lower earth. Eastern tradition, on the other hand, often depicts a three-layer universe—a flattened disk that is earth, the atmosphere of rain and wind, and the sun and fire of the heavens crowning it all. To the ancient Greeks (ca. sixth century BCE), the earth was likewise a flattened disk and the sun and the stars were masses of fire, surrounded by air, which had been flung to the perimeter of this disk. Both the sun and the moon were shaped like huge solar chariot wheels, twenty-eight and nineteen times the size of the earth, respectively.[5]

Sometimes, these early cosmogonies/cosmologies (explanations of the origin of the world) were also theogonies (explanations of the origins of the gods). In general, the cosmological map of ancient times depicted the world as a bubble with the deities in the heavens at the top of the sphere, the earthly creatures below, and a temple of some sort with a king in between. The Deity, who kept the waters of chaos at bay, quite literally resided in the upper firmament, which was held up by the mountains. Since the distance between the earth and the top of the mountains was relatively small (maybe a mile and a half), the Deity might well come down to the earth, or you might even see him on a mountain.

By the time of Aristotle (ca. 350 BCE), the sun, planets, and stars were all attached to rigid spheres which circled a static earth. Variations on this map occurred, with seven, eight, 144, and sometimes 365 spherical layers surrounding an earth which remained pointedly in the center of a bubble-like universe.[6] The Deity, however, resided outside these concentric layers—no more going up to the mountain-top for a visit. In fact, the best way to commune with the Deity was to go into a vision or dream, ascend these various spheres, then descend to tell others. Alternatively, the Deity might come down into the cosmos; that could happen, though, only if he put on a body, a somewhat risky proposition in that he might get trapped down here, which was a most undesirable possibility since the earth was a dark, stinky, spiritually bereft place. Thus, in this cosmology,

---

5. See Lightman, *Ancient Light*, 5–10.
6. Smoot and Davidson, *Wrinkles in Time*, inside cover.

God becomes a utopian image and life becomes an attempt to break out of the confines of an ugly physical world.

Some 450 years ago, beginning with the Polish astronomer Copernicus, the cosmological map changed again. The earth lost its position of centrality, and the sun took its place. However, the circling earth and planets were still spatially bound by an unchanging outer rim of fixed stars.[7] Over time, the stars were freed from this rigidity. Today, we recognize our sun as only one of countless stars moving through a changing universe in recognizable, if somewhat chaotic, patterns. Copernicus started a theological revolution marked by the heretical view that the earth was no longer at the center of the universe. This meant humans were no longer at the center either, a change that was met with resistance. To some extent, it is still being met with resistance. Note, for instance, the emergence in recent years of the anthropic principle (see also chapter 17).[8] Hyperspace cosmologist Michio Kaku put it this way: "Within the past few decades, some cosmologists have been horrified to find anthropomorphism creeping back into science, under the guise of the anthropic principle, some of whose advocates openly declare that they would like to put God back into science."[9] The idea, here, is that there had to be a creator of this well-designed world, and that creator, of course, is God.

THE ANTHROPIC PRINCIPLE

The anthropic principle is but one outcome of Big Bang cosmogony; as such it explains our contemporary map of the universe, which holds that the earth is one of several planets revolving about one of countless stars in a galaxy of stars, which is only one of countless galaxies strewn chaotically, but for a finite time, across an infinite but possibly bounded universe. This map corresponds fairly accurately to the physical data

---

7. Smoot and Davidson, *Wrinkles in Time*, 10.

8. Presented in both *strong* and *weak* versions, the anthropic principle says, essentially, that, given the infinite multitude of possible worlds that might have developed with the Big Bang and given the extreme sensitivity of the initial physical constants needed in order for a world such as ours to exist, the very fact that we do exist in the world as we know it means that the universe more or less *had* to happen the way it has happened. The fact that the universe exists in its present form is a reflection of our own existence, and is, thus, dependent upon human existence.

9. Kaku, *Hyperspace*, 257. Another useful source of information about theology and the anthropic principle is Davies's *Mind of God*.

we are presently able to collect with our assorted modern measuring instruments.

Lately, however, we have become aware that the very act of our collecting such measurements may alter them, so it is becoming rather difficult to know just how reliably we should accept them. It appears that our very consciousness to some degree shapes what is "out there." To a species of creation that is more curious than the proverbial cat, this possibility has rather astounding implications for the origin and nature of the universe. In particular, I believe, this new awareness of the interaction between consciousness and the physical world is producing a brand new cosmogony.

KALEIDOSCOPIC MODEL

The map that accompanies this emerging cosmogony more closely resembles a kaleidoscope than a universe of meandering galaxies. It is not that the meandering galaxies—the universe as we know it—have disappeared. Rather, it is that this familiar depiction is only one of many patterns which the kaleidoscope holds within its illusion-producing mirror-walls. The metaphor I have in mind as a map of the universe is not as simplistic as an ordinary kaleidoscope. The chief difference is that in this latest map, the kaleidoscope is not physical: it is a *thought* kaleidoscope which reflects, amplifies, and to some degree creates symbols. The three-dimensional kaleidoscopes which with we are familiar usually contain some kind of colorful beads or glass chips. Strategically located mirrors and/or lenses reflect these beads, turning them into elaborate designs. In our *thought* kaleidoscope these beads or chips are replaced by the three-dimensional artifacts of ordinary reality. They—we—are symbols reflected into intricate patterns by mind (or soul or spirit).

The thought-is-all-there-is notion is very old. However, late twentieth-century insights, particularly in physics and mathematics, suggest that we should dust off this old metaphor and give it contemporary clothing. What are these recent insights? I will mention here, briefly, several of the more pertinent.

SCIENTIFIC PRECEDENTS FOR THE KALEIDOSCOPIC MODEL

In 1927 a scientific revelation known as the Heisenberg uncertainty principle showed that we cannot simultaneously measure both the velocity and the position of a subatomic particle with arbitrary precision. If we know one of these properties, we can only predict the other according to the probabilities of chance. (Also see chapter 10, "A Cantorian Take on Religion," part 2). Subsequently it was discovered that this principle applies to other quantum properties as well. For example, certain particles are known to spin either "up" or "down" with equal probability, but until the spin is actually calculated (observed), there is no way of telling which spin it has. In other words, both spins are somehow latent within the particle and it is only the act of observation which brings it into existence.[11] This amazing notion can be traced to the combined efforts of a number of gifted scientists working in the early 1900s, including Werner Heisenberg, Niels Bohr, P. A. M. Dirac, Albert Einstein, Erwin Schrödinger, Max Planck, and Louis De Broglie.

> *The whole world of physical facts—space, time, rivers, rocks, plant bodies, animal bodies, atoms, stars, nebulae—is just an immense and complicated system of symbols continually made, unmade, and remade by mind (soul, spirit), in response to the natural needs of mind, to represent, without copying or resembling, activities of mind. Mind is the sole Reality, all else—the external Universe— being only a mind-required, mind-made, mind-sustained, mind-symbolizing, mind-revealing Pageant.*
> —CASSIUS JACKSON KEYSER, MATHEMATICIAN[10]

The discovery of the Heisenberg uncertainty principle and its related implications met with resistance even among the discoverers. Nonetheless, the uncertainty principle has now been experimentally verified repeatedly and has had the effect of displacing, once and for all, the Newtonian world-vision of clocklike order and predictability with one

---

10. Keyser, *Mathematics*, 61–62, writing in the 1930s about the nature of the universe.

11. There is also a curious nonlocal aspect involved in this process; the two spins are bound together in such a way that the action of one determines the action of the other even when they are separated by considerable distance.

dominated by uncertainty and chance. One contemporary scientist even held that while it is one of the silliest theories proposed in this century, quantum theory is unquestionably correct.

A recent variation of this uncertainty principle has cropped up in the macroscopic realm of cosmologists. Known as the multi-universe theory, the basic tenet is that our universe is only one of many potential universes which are somehow latent within creation. In fact, there are several physical theories that imply the existence of an ensemble of universes but, in general, the various universes must be considered in some sense parallel or coexisting realities. Any given observer will, of course, see only one of them, but we must suppose that the conscious states of the observer will be part of the differentiation process, so that each of the many alternative worlds will carry copies of the minds of the observers. It is part of the theory that we can't detect this mental splitting; each copy of us feels unique and integral. Nevertheless, there are stupendously many copies of ourselves in existence! Bizarre as this seems, many physicists and some philosophers support some version of the multi-universe theory.[12] Today there is even growing popular awareness of what is called the quantum vacuum—a non-empty void which holds the probabilistic potential for everything. The notion gives a new and very pluralistic meaning to the concept of creation out of nothing.

The development of simulated and virtual realities, recent advances in cognitive and neuroscience, and ideas stemming from the mathematical theories of holography and hyperspace have further stimulated this emerging sense of multiple-existence. For instance, in the early days of the Internet (preceding full development of the "cloud"), MIT professor Sherry Turkle observed that our sense of self is becoming more "consciously multiple" because of the Net. Computers are affecting our ideas about mind, body, self, and machine, she wrote. Virtual reality games known as Multi-User Domains (MUDs) allow individuals to take on other personalities, some of which become so important that real life begins to lose its significance. A college student describes it this way: "I split my mind. I'm getting better at it. I can see myself as being two or three or more. And I just turn on that part of my mind and then another when I go from window to window."[13] Around the turn of this last century the film industry began incorporating this notion of virtual existences into

---

12. Davies, *Mind of God*, 217.
13. Turkle, *Life on the Screen*, 13.

popular movies such as *The Matrix*, *The Thirteenth Floor*, and *ExisenZ*, where, accompanied by all sorts of ethical questions, it has gradually seeped into the collective consciousness of modern culture.

From what he depicts as a holographic universe, Michael Talbot has written that "the tangible reality of our everyday lives is really a kind of illusion," grounded by a much deeper and more primary order of existence.[14] In this perspective, drawn from the theory of Einstein's protégé, David Bohm, consciousness is a subtle form of matter, the observer *is* the observed, the line of separation between animate and inanimate life becomes blurred, the distinction between past and future is an illusion, and "every cell in our body enfolds the entire cosmos."[15] Reality, in both these instances, is nebulous and shifting, uncertain and nonlocal.

To mention one final example, physicist Saul-Paul Sirag has developed a theory of consciousness which is based on mathematical structures called *reflection spaces*. In an interview on national public television, Sirag recalled his own journey: "When I was in college maybe twenty years ago, people talked about maybe there were more than three dimensions, but then they kind of laughed it off. Now physicists take the notion of hyperspace, or multiple dimensions of reality, as being matter of fact."[16] When Sirag describes his hyperspace view of consciousness, he uses the same words, symbols, and connections that appear in highly specialized contemporary mathematics textbooks: McKay groups, Lie algebra, permutation classes, eigenvector equations, etc. By using these mathematical tools, Sirag insists that he is "describing the spiritual realm." "Obviously," he adds, "most physicists don't take this point of view yet, but I think they will in another couple of decades."[17]

Coming from several different areas of interest, these assorted viewpoints all suggest that our modern cosmogony may be changing. The best map of reality appears to be multiple, shifting, and to some degree uncertain. Mathematics is one language with which to elaborate these perspectives. In some cases, mathematics is almost certainly the optimal language. I like to think of it as a language of mysticism. Thus, I am in complete resonance with Katya Walter when she writes, in the *Tao of*

---

14. Talbot, *Holographic Universe*, 46.
15. Talbot, *Holographic Universe*, 50.
16. Mishlove, *Thinking Allowed*, 109.
17. Mishlove, *Thinking Allowed*, 108.

Chaos, "Soul? In science? A paradoxical new condition of our society is science studied with a mystic's heart."[18]

Essentially, then, my suggestion is that the Copernican viewpoint (that our earth circles a sun which is only one of many stars within a universe filled with galaxies of stars, etc.) is inaccurate. It is far too narrow and restricted a view, although, admittedly it has served us well for its duration, just as the Ptolemaic map worked pretty well for its duration. Nonetheless, the Copernican understanding would be better replaced with a Kaleidoscopic viewpoint, wherein the Copernican map is only one of an infinity of possible "designs." It is not just that our universe as we know it, with all its experimentally verified Copernican features, might itself be part of a multi-universe design. Rather, the entire physical framework is an illusion; it is but one of an infinity of possible kaleidoscopic designs.

In this model, Spirit (God, Mind) exists as one undifferentiated whole, but it only manifests itself in fragmented parts, parts which are actually symbols for Spirit. These, in turn, are reflected or mirrored in some fashion, which is the way Spirit can know itself. The organization of these fragmented symbols is the creative, competent, intelligent aspect of Spirit at work. This creativity may manifest itself in the tables, clouds, stars, animals, humans, etc., of our familiar physical world, but it may manifest itself in totally different ways as well, ways belonging to some other dimension of hyperspace, so to speak. With every turn of Spirit, a new universe comes into being. That does not mean that the other aspects of Spirit no longer exist—just as a portion of the colored beads in a kaleidoscope disappear from sight but not from existence, so, too, does Spirit selectively reveal itself.

There is ample room in this kaleidoscopic model for change and flexibility, as well as beauty. Yet in this model we are also inevitably reminded of the inter-connectedness of all the "beads" of existence. As our new millennium unfolds, we are in desperate need of such models, for our present pattern borders precariously on total annihilation of the human experience. Annihilation is a change in the kaleidoscopic setting which we may still have power to prevent! Prevention will only occur, however, if we loosen the shackles of conventional thinking and open ourselves to new possibilities. My work with math and religion joins a growing list of efforts to stimulate the dialogue which may lead us, collectively, to

---

18. Walter, *Tao of Chaos*, 107.

alter our thought and behavior patterns so that we journey through the twenty-first century with well-founded hope.

Nowhere, perhaps, is this hope more aptly described than in "Kaleidoscope," one of the meditations from Elizabeth Tarbox's beautiful collection *Life Tides*. A few lines tell it all:

> Through a kaleidoscope the world becomes fractured, divided between twenty-four ways in symmetrical pieces. A single candle flame becomes twenty-four flickering candles, each a perfect replica of the other. The mundane is made exquisite when it is placed in a pattern of identical squares; the ordinary becomes the mystical when it is seen through a prism.
>
> Is this how life is, if only we step back far enough to see it all—a kaleidoscope of events joining, merging, dancing in rhythmic harmony? . . . Well then, let us dance in the flame that we see. Let the arc of our creativity embrace our moments of time, and let us add our light to the kaleidoscope, trusting in the unity of the whole even as we seek symmetry with the part.[19]

---

19. Tarbox, *Life Tides*, 19.

Chapter 16: We Are Symbols[1]

"42" The answer to everything is pretty simple.

When Douglas Adams's fictional hitchhiker (*Hitchhiker's Guide to the Galaxy*) approached the great computer, Deep Thought, for an answer to the ultimate question of life, the universe, and everything, the computer replied that there was, indeed, an answer, but it would require some time to determine it. The hitchhiker asked how long Deep Thought would need. Come back in 7.5 million years, the computer replied.[2] And so the hitchhiker's expectant ancestors returned in 7.5 million years, only to have Deep Thought tell them they probably weren't going to like the answer, which was "42." "For a moment, nothing happened," Adams wrote. "Then, after a second or so, nothing continued to happen."[3]

What happened in fact, however, was that Adams (1952–2001) turned a totally ordinary, apparently meaningless number into a now well-known symbol for the answer to the ultimate question of life, the universe, and everything else. It is true that people with no sense of humor usually don't care much for this symbol, but, fortunately, humor often lives on[4] after everything else passes away. And embedded within humor there often lies a significant kernel of truth. In this case, the truth is that the answer to the meaning of life, the universe, and everything else is really pretty simple.

    1. Voss, "Spirit-Wise Math."
    2. Adams, *Hitchhiker's Guide*, 173.
    3. Adams, *Hitchhiker's Guide*, 210.
    4. Check out the University of California TV's video production about Douglas Adams: Greengrass and Mueller, *Life, the Universe* (YouTube video), or, for a variation on this scene, see Riktw, "Answer to Life" (YouTube video).

Given that simplicity, I can only assure you that most answers, or attempts at answers, tend to look anything but simple. Here are two examples, both relying heavily on a mathematics far more complex than 42.

The first may be found in a 2014 book called *Our Mathematical Universe*, by MIT physics professor Max Tegmark. In four hundred pages of intriguing, inspirational, scientifically sophisticated narrative, he essentially addresses the very question which Douglas Adams set forth in his sci-fi spoof. Tegmark's answer, which is based on the most contemporary scientific truth about our cosmos, rests on the notion that "the ultimate nature of this [the universe's] strange physical reality" is mathematics. At the end of each of his thirteen chapters, Tegmark sets forth, in what he calls "The Bottom Line," a list of significant ideas he's covered.

Quotes from Our Mathematical Universe, Selected to Demonstrate that Everything is Some Form of Mathematical Structure

- *We'll . . . examine the ultimate nature of this strange physical reality, investigating the possibility that it's ultimately purely mathematical, specifically a mathematical structure that's part of a fourth and ultimate level of parallel universes. (14, chapter 1: "What Is Reality?")*

- *The very fabric of our physical world, space itself, could be a purely mathematical object in the sense that its only intrinsic properties are mathematical properties—numbers such as dimensionality, curvature and topology. (33, chapter 2: "Our Place in Space")*

- *This entire history of our Universe is accurately described by simple physical laws that let us predict the future from the past, and the past from the future. These physical laws that govern the history of our Universe are all cast in terms of mathematical equations, so our most accurate description of our cosmic history is a mathematical description. (67, chapter 3: "Our Place in Time")*

- *Precision cosmology has revealed that simple mathematical laws govern our Universe all the way back to its fiery origins. (94, chapter 4: "Our Universe by the Numbers")*

- *Inflation [the leading theory for our cosmic origins] generically predicts that our space isn't just huge, but infinite, filled with infinite galaxies, stars and planets, with initial conditions generated randomly by quantum fluctuations. (118, chapter 5: "Our Cosmic Origins")*

- *Eternal inflation predicts that our Universe . . . is just one of infinitely many universes in a Level I multiverse where everything that can happen does happen somewhere. . . . Inflation converts potentiality into reality; if the mathematical equations governing uniform space have multiple solutions, then eternal inflation will create infinite regions of space instantiating each of those solutions—this is the Level II multiverse. (153, chapter 6: "Welcome to the Multiverse")*

- *Everything, even light and people, seems to be made of particles. These particles are purely mathematical objects in the sense that their only intrinsic properties are mathematical properties—numbers with names like charge, spin, and lepton number. (183, chapter 7: "Cosmic Legos")*

- *The wave function and Hilbert space, which constitute arguably the most fundamental physical reality, are purely mathematical objects. (230, chapter 8: "The Level III Multiverse")*

- *The mathematical description of the external reality that theoretical physics has uncovered appears very different from the way we perceive this reality. (242, chapter 9: "Internal Reality, External Reality, and Consensus Reality")*

- *With a sufficiently broad definition of mathematics, the [External Reality Hypothesis] ERH implies the Mathematical Universe Hypothesis (MUH) that our physical world is a mathematical structure. This means that our physical world not only is described by mathematics, but that it is mathematical (a mathematical structure), making us self-aware parts of a giant mathematical object. (271, chapter 10: "Physical Reality and Mathematical Reality")*

- *The MUH implies that it's not only spacetime that is a mathematical structure, but also all the stuff therein,*

> including the particles that we're made of. Mathematically, this stuff seems to correspond to "fields": numbers at each point in spacetime that encode what's there. The MUH implies that you're a self-aware substructure that is part of a mathematical structure. (318, chapter 11: "Is Time an Illusion?")

- All structures that exist mathematically exist physically as well, forming the Level IV multiverse.... The MUH implies that most of the complexity we observe is an illusion, existing only in the eye of the beholder, being merely information about our address in the universe. (357, chapter 12: "Testing the Level IV Multiverse")

- On the largest and smallest scales, the mathematical fabric of reality becomes evident, while it remains easy to miss on the intermediate scales that we humans are usually aware of. If the ultimate fabric of reality really is mathematical, then everything is in principle understandable to us, and we'll be limited only by our own imagination. (398, chapter 13: "Life, Our Universe, and Everything")

Mixed in with scientific explanations for everything from how we measure the age of the universe to what we know about cosmological inflation, we find again and again this simple idea that mathematical existence equals physical existence.

To the casual reader, Tegmark's Mathematical Universe Hypothesis (MUH) can seem to be as clear as **M**oisturized **U**niplanar **D**irt (MUD). Four hundred pages of explanation doesn't necessarily change this perception. Still, as astrophysicist Mario Livio (author of *Is God a Mathematician?*) put it in the "Praise" for *Our Mathematical Universe*,[5] "Max Tegmark says that the universe *is* mathematics. You don't have to necessarily agree to enjoy this fascinating journey into the nature of reality."

My point, of course, is that our quest for understanding about the meaning and nature of our existence can be greatly enhanced by mathematics. Tegmark offers a thought-provoking, detailed illustration of this idea, which is Platonic in perspective. To him, reality is a four-level nested hierarchy of increasing diversity such that everything, in theory, is some

---

5. Tegmark, *Our Mathematical Universe*, cover.

form of *mathematical structure*,⁶ by which Tegmark means *a set of abstract elements with relations between them*.⁷ The mathematics exists out there whether or not we recognize it, which is why it is a Platonic view. The postulated equivalence between physical and mathematical existence means that "if a mathematical structure contains a self-aware substructure [such as ourselves], it will perceive itself as existing in a physically real universe."⁸ In other words, we are really self-aware mathematics—we just perceive ourselves as something else.

My second example has a compatible hypothesis, but interprets it in non-numerical symbols that look like two truncated edges of a two-dimensional box, □, rather than the usual symbols of today's mathematical language. In the 1960s the British mathematician G. Spencer-Brown (b. 1923) produced a small book called *Laws of Form* which he describes as "a text book of mathematics, not of logic or philosophy, although both logic and philosophy can of course benefit from its application."⁹ In this work, the author—known as a polymath for his skill not only as a mathematician, but also as a psychotherapist, engineer, inventor, and poet (under the name James Keys)—has produced a short (seventy-six page) treatise which elucidates the primary, non-numerical arithmetic of Boolean algebra, a system of logic developed by George Boole (1815–64) and now used extensively in theoretical computer science. This basic section of the book begins by defining the idea of "distinction" along with the two axioms from which the laws of form are then developed.¹⁰ The result, a

---

6. Tegmark, *Our Mathematical Universe*, 323. Tegmark presents a diagram (which resembles a flow chart) of the relationships between most of the mathematical structures mathematicians are familiar with: real numbers, complex numbers, vector spaces, topological spaces, etc. This is just a small sample, he suggests, of a "full family tree."

7. Tegmark, *Our Mathematical Universe*, 326.

8. Tegmark, *Our Mathematical Universe*, 323.

9. Spencer-Brown, *Laws of Form*, xi.

10. Spencer-Brown, *Laws of Form*, 1–2. According to Spencer-Brown, distinction "is perfect continence. That is to say, a distinction is drawn by arranging a boundary with separate sides so that a point on one side cannot reach the other side without crossing a boundary. For example, in a plane space a circle draws a distinction. Once a distinction is drawn, the spaces, states, or contents on each side of the boundary, being distinct, can be indicated. There can be no distinction without motive, and there can be no motive unless contents are seen to differ in value. If a content is of value, a name can be taken to indicate this value. Thus the calling of the name can be identified with the value of the content." The two axioms are the law of calling ("*the value of a call made again is the value of the call*") and the law of crossing ("*the value of a crossing made again is not the value of the crossing*").

"calculus of indications" with just two initial (or "primitive") equations,[11] ultimately leads to a wide variety of sophisticated mathematical and non-mathematical ideas.

In an even shorter (twenty-nine pages) set of "Notes," Spencer-Brown describes the first seventy-six pages of his "non-numerical arithmetic" in ordinary, if somewhat enigmatic, words; he intends these "Notes" to serve to some extent as a personal guide to the mathematical text, which, like all such texts, is "not an end in itself, but a key to a world beyond the compass of ordinary description," an initial exploration of which "is usually undertaken in the company of an experienced guide."[12]

I am taken with this little volume by G. Spencer-Brown, not only for its subject matter (which is at once both utterly simple and awesomely complex), but also for the subtle undercurrent of spiritual intrigue which pervades his writing, particularly in his descriptive "Notes."[13]

Selected Quotes from *Laws of Form*, Arranged to Demonstrate a Continuity of Thought

- *The discipline of mathematics is seen to be a way, powerful in comparison with others, of revealing our internal knowledge of the structure of the world, and only by the way associated with our common ability to reason and compute. (xxi)*
- *The primary form of mathematical communication is not description, but injunction. In this respect it is comparable with*

---

11. These are equations of (1) "number" or, alternatively, the *form* of "condensation" and (2) "order" or the *form* of "cancellation." Axiom 1 is frequently written ⏋ ⏋ = ⏋ and Axiom 2 appears as ⏋̄ = . I find it helpful to think of the symbolization ⏋ as a shorthand notation for a box □, which is a distinction drawn in a plane similar to that of a circle. Thus, for example, if you cross the boundary from the space outside one of the boxes into the box □, then cross back out of it to the plane and then cross again into another identical box □, the result is as though you had just crossed once into the original box. □□ = □

12. Spencer-Brown, *Laws of Form*, xxix. The author notes elsewhere that the primary form of mathematical communication is largely injunction rather than description, 77–81.

13. Spencer-Brown, *Laws of Form*, 79. While taking quotes out of context and rearranging them carries with it the inevitable possibility of making inferences the author would not embrace as his own, I have tried to be attentive to the sense (at least as I have understood it) of what Spencer-Brown is writing. In particular, I lean for permission on his own directive: "What the mathematician aims to do is to give a complete picture, the order *of what* he presents being essential, the order *in which* he presents it being to some degree arbitrary. The reader may quite legitimately change the arbitrary order as he pleases."

practical art forms like cookery, in which the taste of a cake, although literally indescribable, can be conveyed to a reader in the form of a set of injunctions called a recipe. Music is a similar art form, the composer does not even attempt to describe the set of sounds he has in mind, much less the feelings occasioned through them, but writes down a set of commands which, if they are obeyed by the reader, can result in a reproduction, to the reader, of the composer's original experience. (77)

- A recognizable aspect of the advancement of mathematics consists in the advancement of consciousness of what we are doing, whereby the covert becomes overt. Mathematics is in this sense psychedelic. (85)
- We have a direct awareness of mathematical form as an archetypal structure. (xxiv)
- Although all forms, and thus all universes, are possible, and any particular form is mutable, it becomes evident that the laws relating such forms are the same in any universe. (xxix)
- It is only by fixing the use of [the constellar principles by which we navigate our journeys out from and in to the form] that we manage to maintain a universe in any form at all, and our understanding of such a universe comes not from discovering its present appearance, but in remembering what we originally did to bring it about. (104)
- Understanding has to do with the fact that what ever [sic] is said or done can always be said or done a different way, and yet all the ways remain the same. (96)
- There is a tendency, especially today, to regard existence as the source of reality, and thus as a central concept. But as soon as it is formally examined, . . . existence is seen to be highly peripheral and, as such, especially corrupt (in the formal sense) and vulnerable. (101)
- What is commonly now regarded as real consists, in its very presence, merely of tokens or expressions. And since tokens or expressions are considered to be of some (other) substratum, so the universe itself, as we know it, may be considered to be an expression of a reality other than itself. (104)
- An observer, since he distinguishes the space he occupies, is also a mark. (76)
- Any evenly subverted equation of the second degree . . . is thus

> *informed in the sense of having its own form within it, and at the same time informed in the sense of remembering what has happened to it in the past. (100)*
> - *It seems hard to find an acceptable answer to the question of how or why the world conceives a desire, and discovers an ability, to see itself, and appears to suffer the process. That it does so is sometimes called the original mystery. Perhaps, in view of the form in which we presently take ourselves to exist, the mystery arises from our insistence on framing a question where there is, in reality, nothing to question. (105)*
> - *We cannot fully understand the beginning of anything until we see the end. (79)*

For me, he calls forth a kind of scientific mysticism which invites the reader to apply the laws of form to our own existence.

In his introductory "Note on the Mathematical Approach," for instance, he begins by saying that the

> theme of this book is that a universe comes into being when a space is severed or taken apart. The skin of a living organism cuts off an outside from an inside. So does the circumference of a circle in a plane. By tracing the way we represent such a severance, we can begin to reconstruct... the basic forms underlying linguistic, mathematical, physical, and biological science, and can begin to see how the familiar laws of our own experience follow inexorably from the original act of severance.[14]

In a longer excerpt from the final section of his "Notes," he adds:

> Let us then consider, for a moment, the world as described by the physicist. It consists of a number of particles which, if shot through their own space, appear as waves and are thus... of the same laminated structure as pearls or onions, and other wave forms called electromagnetic which it is convenient, by Occam's razor, to consider as travelling through space with a standard velocity. All these appear bound by certain natural laws which indicate the form of their relationship.
>
> Now the physicist himself, who describes all this, is, in his own account, himself constructed of it. He is, in short, made of a conglomeration of the very particulars he describes, no more,

---

14. Spencer-Brown, *Laws of Form*, xxix.

no less, bound together by and obeying such general laws as he himself has managed to find and to record.

Thus we cannot escape the fact that the world we know is constructed in order (and thus in such a way as to be able) to see itself.

This is indeed amazing.

But *in order* to do so [i.e., to see itself], evidently it [the world we know] must first cut itself up into at least one state which sees, and at least one other state which is seen. In this severed and mutilated condition, whatever it sees is *only partially* itself.

In this sense, in respect of its own information, the universe *must* expand to escape the telescopes through which we, who are it, are trying to capture it, which is us. The snake eats itself, the dog chases its tail.

Thus the world, whenever it appears as a physical universe, must always seem to us, its representatives, to be playing a kind of hide-and-seek with itself. What is revealed will be concealed, but what is concealed will again be revealed. And since we ourselves represent it, this occultation will be apparent in our life in general, and in our mathematics in particular.[15]

Taken together these two authors (Tegmark and Spencer-Brown) point to a world formed of recursive, self-repeating, self-reproducing units which are to some extent self-aware and which are based on/equivalent to various mathematical structures. These math structures reveal themselves through tokens or marks or symbols. Or, I would add, through metaphors.

Have you ever noticed that the sky is full of moods? Sometimes it is bright and cheery, with gates of joyous light inviting you to enter soft spaces. Other times it is dark and ominous, warning you to stay away. I've seen all sorts of creatures and things communing in the sky, too, plus the promise of the rainbow and the rage of thunder and wind. I've observed these things, and felt their emotions, yet all the while I've known that if I stick my fingers in the sky, I will touch nothing tangible, though I saw these things clearly with my own eyes. But though the sky is illusive in its scenery, it is perfectly able to communicate its emotions as clearly as the musician who follows the marks on a music script recreates specific sounds, or a cook who obeys the injunctions of a written recipe produces particular tastes, or a mathematician who follows the commands of a

---

15. Spencer-Brown, *Laws of Form*, 105–6.

particular set of symbols experiences a bit of wonder and wisdom which something else has previously indicated.

And we? We are like the sky, full of moods and inclinations. We are nothing more, nor less, than constant in our form and ability to commune one with another, and with the universe itself, and with everything alive and otherwise. In this sense, we are perfectly simple.

I want to conclude this chapter, and this section of the book, with a letter I composed some years ago in response to a message on a list-serve I accessed through my computer. A list-serve was a precursor of blogs and tweets and Facebook and Skype and texting, none of which, including the list-serve, were around when I was born. So much new, in such a short space. At the time I reproduce my letter here, it is still accessible on the Web,[16] but that will not last, because, well, because everything changes. Yet, throughout the change, an identity of sorts always remains the same. That is the mystery in the mystic.

Here is the letter.

• •

From: Sarah Voss
Subject: Re: Meta 056: The Loom of God: Gödel's Proof
To Billy Grassie, Clifford Pickover, and the MetaList in general

I've always been a sucker for flattery, so when Clifford Pickover wrote (in Meta 056) that "Sarah Voss raised some excellent points in her post to Meta 045 on the relationship between mathematics and religion," I admit to being hooked. Just which points did you like best, Clifford? As for "I wonder what she thinks this relationship might be fifty years from now," I can only reiterate that the metaphorical connection between the two subjects has been around for a long, long time (see *What Number Is God?*) and it isn't likely to disappear soon. On the other hand, sometimes I have trouble predicting what's going to happen five minutes from now, let alone fifty years, so I'll not stick my prophetic neck out too far, thank you.

However, when it comes to Dr. Pickover's invitation to comment on Gödel's mathematical proof of God, I'll venture a bias. Personally, I find revelation more persuasive than logic. Although logic may in fact lead to revelation, it hasn't ever happened that way for me. I prefer poetry, as in:

16. https://www.mail-archive.com/matematika@warnet.unpar.ac.id/msg00044.html. March 27, 1999.

Symbols

We are the words She writes
by joining cells one to another
as we set letters side by side, form shapes
that stand for meanings rarely understood.

Like marks that decorate
the sheets of dictionaries,
we hold no weight, bear no substance,
live lives as simple symbols
strung together into lines—
ever-changing colloquialisms
reflecting patterns
we call definitions, and yet

sometimes we rearrange ourselves
in ways that please Her eye:
sentences in books that charm,
turn abstracts into loved designs
soon viewed as wondrous tales.

Michael Guillen (*Five Equations that Changed the World*) has indicated that "in the language of mathematics, equations are like poetry."[17] So perhaps I shouldn't make such a distinction between Gödel's "poetry" and mine. It's all symbols, anyway.

Of course, both poetry and logic probably most often follow rather than precede revelation, sort of the way a lot of modern scientific exploration is funded only after the desired outcome is well established. Some of the newer conjectures regarding quantum mathematics and consciousness, such as that consciousness appears in a kind of "back-action" from some future event to some past event (see http://listserv.arizona.edu/lsv/www/quantum-mind.html), may actually establish credibility for a whole new temporal relationship between revelation, logic and poetry. That may take time, though—say fifty years or so—to fully unfold.

All good will,
Sarah

---

17. Guillen, *Five Equations*, 2.

Part 4: Using Mathaphors to Motivate Right Relations

"NUMBER IDENTITY"

Hi! I'm Sarah, better known to the U.S. government
as 260-53-8891. I live at 193 N 93rd St.
in ZIP area 68127. Contact me at
1-402-558-9031. I was born
on 6-07-1945, the 3rd
of 3 siblings. We
lived

on 140 acres on Rt. 307 in postal area 44010.
I now have 3 children myself,
ages 49, 45, and 40, plus 2
step-kids, 8 grands, and
5 great step-grands
all under
seven.

I am 5'3, 135 pounds and am particularly
fond of the number 1, from which you
might infer that I like unity, oddity,
and masculine energy since *odd*
numbers are male and
even ones are
female.

Whenever I introduce myself with numbers, I
always change some of them from the "true"
descriptors, and when I tell folks this,
they always sigh loudly, relieved
because some are too private
and too risky to
share.

Chapter 17: A Stroll through the Garden of Mathaphors[1]

Math sometimes seems to complicate things, but the aim in the end is to simplify them.—Eugenia Cheng[2]

LEWIS THOMAS, IN ONE of his many essays, contends that mathematics may be the "universal language of the future."[3] If so, it will likely be understood not merely as a Russellian tool to express "eternal and exact truth," but also as an instrument to renew an ancient understanding of nature as "mythic or religious."[4] That mathematics has *both* quantitative *and* qualitative characteristics was a concept well-appreciated by much of the Western world from the time of the Pythagoreans through the time of Newton.[5]

For the last several hundred years, we have lost sight of the qualitative aspects of this evolving language. Today, however, some are beginning to reclaim this earlier conception of mathematics.[6]

We can identify this recycled trend by examining recent social, scientific, and theological literature for *mathaphors*—that is, for metaphors

---

1. Voss, "Mathematics and Theology." In chapter 10, I identified ten roles of mathaphors in spirituality. Here, I expand on these ten roles of mathaphors and, in the process, create both an overview and a summary of this use of metaphor. Many of the mathaphors described herein also appear in sermons I gave and some are noted in other chapters in this partial collection of my work.

2. Cheng, "Curing Procrastination," C4.

3. Thomas, *Et Cetera*, 161.

4. Grandy, "Musical Roots," quotations 3–4.

5. See chapter 8, "Sacred Qualities."

6. Capra, *Web of Life*, 113.

drawn from mathematics.[7] Most (though perhaps not all) languages use metaphor to describe, clarify, and extend our understanding of the world and our place in it. Metaphors—including mathaphors—also assume a formative role for us in that they frequently help stimulate, guide, and determine our understandings and beliefs. This essay offers a summary of ten somewhat overlapping roles which mathaphors currently play in shaping our understandings of religion and theology.

Some of the mathaphors described in this stroll through metaphorical language might more readily be identified with science or with modern technology than with mathematics. Science and technology often impact people's lives much more overtly than does theoretical mathematics, and, consequently, the metaphors which are associated with science and technology often have a particularly profound effect on the human experience. Nonetheless, to a significant degree mathematics underlies scientific and technological activity. For purposes of this essay, the term *mathaphor* is therefore understood as an umbrella term that covers metaphors derived both from pure mathematics and also from computer technology, quantum physics, and other endeavors which strongly interact with mathematics.

A note of caution: it is worthwhile to distinguish between science that is well-based and pseudo-scientific arguments that are misleading. However, that is not the primary focus of this paper. Some of the mathaphors discussed below—the holographic universe, for instance—are extensions of ideas that are well-defined and verified in and by mathematics, science, and technology. Others, such as the "many-worlds" theories, are based on mathematics that is far more speculative and suspect. This chapter pays only passing attention to this important issue of scientific validity, attempting instead to depict the transformative effect which the garden of mathaphors as a whole is having on present-day society.

CONTEMPORARY MATHAPHORS ARE CHANGING OUR METAPHORS FOR GOD

Physicist Frank Tipler expands the computer image of God as a mathematician, adding details.[8] In *The Physics of Immortality*, Tipler maintains that the human soul is "nothing but a program being run on a computer

---

7. Voss, "Sacred Qualities," 32–37.
8. See also chapters 8 and 11.

called the brain," that "humans are machines of a very special sort" and that God may be mathematically described as "a universal wave function bounded by an Omega Point Condition," or what Teilhard de Chardin called "radial energy."[9] Tipler's depiction may seem far-fetched, but it and similar notions are fast entering the common consciousness, where they are often met with various forms of resistance. Consider, for instance, the popular sci-fi movie *The Matrix*. The main plot is that artificial intelligence (AI) created us, feeding our present-day world to us directly through a hard-wire into our brains, and keeping us forever after as some kind of fodder source for its own needs. Here we find Tipler in cinematic form, except with a negative overlay. AI becomes the devil-machine from which savior Thomas Anderson will rescue us. Ander-son = son of man. The movie, released not coincidentally on Easter weekend, 1999, has been described not as *the* Messiah movie, but certainly as *a* messiah movie. For a dozen quick parallels between Christ's life and Anderson's, search the Web.

CONTEMPORARY MATHAPHORS ARE CHALLENGING OUR HUMAN ROLE IN THE UNIVERSE

In the world of *The Matrix*, our role as caretaker and dominator of the other creatures in God's kingdom is called into question. Unsurprisingly, variations of this carbon-versus-life theme abound in movie theaters; consider *The Thirteenth Floor, Bicentennial Man, AI*, and *I-Robot*. Indeed, popular literature is itself laced with mathaphors which call into question our human role in the universe: "Your great great-. . . grandmother *was* a robot."[10] "We can anticipate silicon life."[11] DNA and RNA "are natural robots."[12] "We will be to robots as dogs are to humans."[13] Couple this trend with the "robo-eels" and "leech-computers" which computer engineers are building from various aquatic and bacterial life-forms, plus (going the other way) the multitude of "smart" digital enhancements that medical doctors increasingly use to assist persons with special needs, and

9. Tipler, *Physics of Immortality*.
10. Dennett, *Kinds of Minds*, 23.
11. Nadeau, *Mind, Machines*, 15.
12. Dennett, *Kinds of Minds*, 20.
13. Liversidge, "Electronic Information Age."

the fiction of carbon/silicon synthesis becomes a reality.[14] What happens to the traditional views of our human role in the universe when hybrid life-forms begin to replace or coexist with current life-forms?

Emerging mathaphors that challenge our understanding of our place in the universe may also be more indirect products of the computer. For example, from the realm of cosmology and hyperspace theory comes the notion of an anthropic God who has masterminded Creation so beautifully that our human existence is simply part of an intricate but inevitable Divine plan. This notion has its roots in elaborate mathematical equations best manipulated by computers. Such equations can be highly sensitive to initial conditions.

In the last few decades these equations have evolved into a scientific hypothesis known as the anthropic principle. Given in both strong and weak forms, the anthropic principle claims that the world began with a Big Bang which turned into our universe, but, given slightly different initial conditions, other universes might have arisen instead. The catch is that we are here. The fact that we are here means that precisely those initial conditions which would permit the eventual rise of life-as-we-know-it had to have been present at the start. Otherwise, we would not exist at all. Or, perhaps, we do exist in a parallel universe.[15]

In some religions, and certainly in Christianity, humanity has been unabashedly egocentric. Five hundred years ago, the sun revolved around us. God made it that way, of course. Today we claim to know better, but that knowledge came with a heavy price-tag of religious heresy. Still, humankind remains reluctant to embrace a less self-centered understanding of our existence. The anthropic principle can be understood as a sort of sneaky way to make sure we humans still have a central place in God's plan.[16] Freeman Dyson, who speaks of the universe in terms of sets of equations, resolves this dilemma by expelling the anthropic principle from science, but tolerating it in meta-science.[17] Others, like Frank Tipler and John D. Barrow, embrace the principle wholeheartedly. Regardless, the anthropic God is a wave of the present shaping the spiritual sea of tomorrow. The creator of that spiritual sea is already being understood as an Intelligent Designer.

14. Stenger, "Robo-eels"; Graham-Rowe, "Half Fish"; *BBC News Online*, "Biological Computer Born."
15. See chapter 15.
16. Kaku, *Hyperspace*, 257.
17. Dyson, *Infinite*, 297.

It is a pretty intelligent Intelligent Designer, too, although we, in our human limitations, seem to be struggling with radically diverse interpretations about the nature of this intelligence. According to one theory, this Intelligent Designer is really a Divine Engineer, and the universe is just a vast engineering project, complete with blueprint, goal, and a (basically apocalyptic) plan.[18] Appealing in particular to scientific creationists, this mathaphor uses "the language of engineering . . . rather than that of the Bible."[19] If the scientific creationists are right, then humans become something of a carefully plotted dot on the drafting board of an omnipotent, omniscient, omnipresent engineer whose mathematical tools and expertise leave little ink for individual freedom of will.

According to another theory, this Intelligent Designer not only created the known universe with all its star-cropped galaxies spinning somewhat chaotically throughout the great ocean of space, but also somehow created an infinite number of other worlds, some or all of which are probably playing out in other dimensions even as we sit here. In *The Mind of God*, quantum physicist Paul Davies described (without endorsing) this speculative notion:

> Throughout the cosmos, the inherent uncertainties that confront each and every quantum particle are continually being resolved by differentiation of reality into ever more independently existing universes. This image implies that everything that can happen, will happen. That is, every set of circumstances that is physically possible (though not everything is logically possible) will be manifested somewhere along this infinite set of universes.[20]

These various universes must be considered in some sense "parallel" or coexisting realities. Any given observer will see only one of them, but we must suppose that the conscious states of the observer will be part of the differentiation process, so that each of the many alternative worlds will carry copies of the minds of the observers. It is part of the theory that you cannot detect this mental splitting; each copy of us feels unique and integral. Nevertheless, there are stupendously many copies of ourselves in existence! Bizarre as it may seem, says Davies, the theory

---

18. Ensign, "Engineering to Apocalypse," 93–112.
19. Ensign, "Engineering to Apocalypse," 99.
20. Davies, *Mind of God*, 217.

is nonetheless supported in one version or another by a large number of physicists as well as some philosophers.[21]

Multi-universe aspects are popular enough in a multi-everything culture that the mathaphor is already altering how we think about ourselves, regardless of whether the theory is true. On the one hand, we are becoming chance occurrences, statistical probabilities filled with little meaning and devoid of power. On the other hand, we become the symbols God uses to draw this world into being—symbols for Spirit itself, we might say. We float around like colored beads in a kaleidoscope of galaxies, coming to the foreground for a time in the inexplicable pattern we call reality, but swept into another by the simple twist of the Intelligent Designers' mind. We are abstract symbols, or maybe statistical probabilities. What we do not appear to be anymore is servants of a kingly God.

CONTEMPORARY MATHAPHORS ARE HELPING US ACCEPT AMBIGUITY

The many-worlds hypothesis is one of several eventual outcomes of a scientific revelation which upset the absolute truth-cart back in 1927, namely, the Heisenberg uncertainty principle, which showed that the action of various subatomic particles were always uncertain until observed. (See chapters 10 and 15.) Later, it was discovered that this principle applies to other quantum properties as well. When we metaphorically extend the Heisenberg uncertainty principle to the realm of the spiritual, we entertain the possibility of an Uncertain or Ambiguous God or, at the very least, of an ambiguous existence.

Most of us already recognize that our secular human experience is filled with ambiguity. We vacillate between love and hate in our relationships. We laugh and cry, sometimes simultaneously. We enjoy days when the meaning of our lives is crystal clear to us, and other days when we struggle to find any purpose in getting out of bed, and still others when we're in an uncertain haze where we do not really know what we believe. We react to many mundane events as we do to the familiar illusion based on the picture of the old lady and the young girl, originally titled *My Wife and My Mother-In-Law* (see figure 2.1). Sometimes we see it as one thing, sometimes another, and sometimes it is not even definable.

---

21. Davies, *Mind of God*, 217.

A STROLL THROUGH THE GARDEN OF MATHAPHORS 167

In many ways, our sacred life is likewise marked with ambiguity. This is nothing new. Even the most basic ideas of Christianity embody a certain ambiguity. Is Jesus fully human, fully divine, or fully both? Once again, mathaphor helps shape our responses.

> It turns out that this [fully human/fully divine] duality has a parallel in quantum physics.... Someone who is not already a believer will not join the faithful because of quantum mechanics; conversely someone in whom science raises no doubts probably isn't even listening. But to people in the middle, for whom science raises questions about religion, these new concordances can deepen a faith already present.[22]

If the Heisenberg uncertainty principle paved the way for greater acceptance of the ambiguity in our lives, the nonlinear dynamics of modern mathematics, better known as complexity or chaos theory, is making it commonplace.[23] In chaos theory, order keeps cropping up amid disorder, although without predictability as to when or where these pockets of order will occur. The classic example is the Mandelbrot set, a mathematical structure dubbed a universal symbol for chaos. To put it somewhat simplistically, the Mandelbrot set is part of a solution to certain nonlinear equations. These solutions are too difficult to be determined by anything other than a computer, and complex enough that they are best imaged in many colored patterns. On different scales, the Mandelbrot set almost miraculously keeps reappearing out of what appears to be total chaos.

Chaos theory was accidentally discovered in the early 1960s by Edward Lorenz, an MIT meteorologist trying to predict weather patterns.[24] Scientists have since discovered that the theory he created accurately describes features of many things other than the weather—the human heart, economics, turbulence in a fluid, electric power grids, artificial intelligence, brain waves, to name a few.[25] Such descriptions, while fascinating and useful, are nonetheless consistent with contemporary society's usual perception of mathematics as something quantifiable and computable.

However, in the last decade, the concept has caught on metaphorically as well, particularly in the area of organizational communication. Today, communication specialists draw on mathaphors from the "new"

---

22. Westley, "Science Finds God."
23. See chapter 12, "Mini Math History."
24. See chapters 25 and 26.
25. See Gleick, *Chaos*; or Waldrop, *Emerging Science*.

sciences to encourage interpersonal interactions that inspire fruitful approaches to ordinary social conflict and discourse.[26] In particular, mathaphors drawn from chaos theory suggest a kind of emergent self-organization which is changing leadership in the social institution setting so that communication is open to a creative but basically untidy or ambiguous process. (Also see chapter 12, "New Possibilities for Communication in Religious Institutions.")

CONTEMPORARY MATHAPHORS ARE REVAMPING OUR UNDERSTANDING OF THE ONE AND THE MANY

While "ambiguity" means having more than one likely interpretation, "paradoxical" implies having seemingly conflicting interpretations.[27] The relationship between the one and the many is paradoxical. When applied to the spiritual realm, the underlying conflict in this paradox has sometimes led to war and tragedy. The resolution of the conflict between the one and the many is to accept the paradox within: the one is the many and the many is the one.

This, too, is not a new idea. Paul, for example, in his letter to the Corinthians, noted that "just as the body is one and has many members, and all the members of the body, though many, are one body, so it is with Christ."[28] But faith traditions, especially the monotheistic ones, have not always transcended the distinctions between the one and the many. In the past couple of hundred years, the reductionistic belief that the whole is nothing more than the sum of its mechanistic-like parts has dominated Western culture, while the more mystical understandings of this relationship between the one and the many have largely disappeared.

Recently, communication technology has grown to incredible new dimensions, such that our planet seems to have shrunk. Our awareness of the many is more intense than at any time in human history, yet our ability to reconcile and accept this diversity, particularly religious diversity, seems to have diminished along with global distances. All too frequently now, different faith traditions squabble worldwide for the privilege of

26. See Wheatley, *Leadership*; and Stacey, *Complexity*.

27. See Levine, *Common Sense*, ch. 8. Paradox, according to Levine means seeming conflict, or conventional belief that there is conflict, between two items that in fact are compatible. Examples include being gentle and being strong; reason and emotion; playfulness and responsibility; even the masculine and feminine (personal correspondence).

28. May and Metzger, *New Oxford Bible*, 1 Cor 12:14.

control, of being "the right one." As the squabbles become ever more violent, bloody, and globally decimating, the need for models that reconcile the one and the many is greater than ever.

Fortunately, such models are appearing. Modern mathematics and science are giving birth to them. Two of the oldest of these *new* models are the definite integral of calculus, put forth (independently but simultaneously) in the seventeenth century by Isaac Newton and Wilhelm Leibniz, and the notion of a set of all sets, first developed in the nineteenth century by Georg Cantor. The mathematics involved in the integral calculus allows us to accept the idea that, in certain realms, the whole is a *never-ending* process of the accumulation of its parts, a process which nonetheless can be *precisely* (and seemingly paradoxically) summed.[29] Similarly, Cantor's contributions to what is now known as transfinite set theory have helped the scientific world accept that the part may have the power of the whole, that the infinite both is and is not infinite, that infinities come in different sizes, that there exists a set which is infinitely many yet infinitely sparse, that infinity is "actual" rather than "potential," and other notions which at first glance appear to contain logical conundrums.[30] Metaphorical extension of these two mathematical concepts from science to theology opens us to new possibilities within our spiritual lives. In significant ways, these new possibilities are really retreads of more ancient mythic conceptions of the universe.

A third model, particularly although not exclusively popular in New Age circles, may be found in holography. Holography is a technique for producing three-dimensional images. It existed in mathematical theory years before the laser technology needed to produce it was developed. Holography has an unusual scaling property: a small portion of a holograph contains the blueprint of the whole and can therefore be used to reconstruct the entire image. David Bohm, one of Einstein's coworkers, used this idea to develop a model of reality in which each part of energy and matter represents a microcosm that enfolds the whole. He suggested that the world we normally perceive, what he called the "unfolded" or "explicate" order, is really only a tiny portion of a larger reality defined by an "implicate" order.[31] In *The Holotropic Mind*, Stanislav Grof put it this way: "that which we perceive as reality is like a projected holographic

---

29. Voss, *What Number*, ch. 4.
30. Aczel, *Mystery of the Aleph*; Voss, *What Number*, ch. 4; Voss, "Matheology."
31. Bohm, *Wholeness*.

image."[32] In *The Holographic Universe*, Michael Talbot said it even more concisely: "The universe is . . . a kind of giant, flowing hologram."[33]

The holographic world-model offers revolutionary possibilities for a new understanding of our human capacities. Says Grof: "As individual human beings we are not isolated and insignificant Newtonian entities; rather, as integral fields of the holomovement each of us is also a microcosm that reflects and contains the macrocosm. If this is true, then we each hold the potential for having direct and immediate experiential access to virtually every aspect of the universe, extending our capabilities well beyond the reaches of our senses."[34] We see in this mathaphor how an altered interpretation of the whole and its parts, of the one and the many, can impact our expectations of ourselves.

CONTEMPORARY MATHAPHORS ARE REVISING OUR THOUGHTS ABOUT FREE WILL AND DETERMINISM

In the West, we are used to a God who grants us open expectations of ourselves, who gives us free will, who offers us existence complete with the ability to choose how we behave and what we believe. In a way, we understand this gift to be a part of the great American dream. The God of the Quantum Void muddies this dream. It does not destroy the dream; it just puts different parameters on how it comes about. The quantum void is not an empty place. It is filled with potential. Schrödinger's famous cat in a box is simultaneously dead and alive in this quantum void; it exists in a state of "superposition," where the cat is both dead and alive until you look at it. It is the act of observation which determines the outcome. Until you look, only the probable outcome is known. This concept is markedly different from the one where the state of the cat is simply hidden and when you look you find out which way it has actually been all along. Should, for example, Schrödinger's box contain humans rather than cats, each individual might exist in a kind of superposition, both saved and not saved, until some act of observation determines the outcome.[35]

---

32. Grof, *Holotropic Mind*, 8.

33. Talbot, *Holographic Universe*, 46.

34. Grof, *Holotropic Mind*, 10.

35. This exposition of the paradox is based on the Copenhagen interpretation, where observation or measurement changes the state of the system from a potentiality of multiple possibilities to an actuality of just one. The many worlds interpretation would describe it differently. It would say that both possibilities are actualized, only in

Unfortunately (or perhaps fortunately), just exactly what this act of observation is remains unclear, even to the physicists who study it. The consensus seems to be that that which is observed is also doing the observation, which is a notion not particularly satisfying on a logical level.

Seventy-five years ago, mathematician Tobias Dantzig wrote in *Number: The Language of Science*, his book on number theory, "How then shall mathematical concepts be judged? *They shall not be judged!* Mathematics is the supreme judge; from its decisions there is no appeal. We cannot change the rules of the game, we cannot ascertain whether the game is fair. We can only study the player at his game; not, however, with the detached attitude of a bystander, for we are watching our own minds at play."[36] The words differ but the sentiment was the same when quantum physicist Saul-Paul Sirag wrote some forty years later that "hyperspace itself is consciousness acting on itself."[37] The picture and who is doing the picturing are, indeed, a little murky.

Do we have free will, or not? Freeman Dyson, who received the 2000 Templeton Prize for Progress in Religion, offers a succinct, Socinian-like "yes" and "no."[38] Computer expert Douglas Hofstadter, in his Pulitzer prize–winning book, *Gödel, Escher, and Bach*, set forth an analogy between the ants in an ant colony and the neurons in our brains.[39] The behavior of the ants as a whole appears to be completely predetermined. The colony moves from one place to another in a way that assures the outcome. On an individual level, though, each ant has complete free will to move in any direction it chooses. So, too, says Hofstadter, is it with the individual neurons in our brains. The mathaphorical implication is that individual humans in our entire population likewise both have and do not have free will. Frank Tipler adds still another wrinkle to this "yes and no" ambiguity when he claims that "a Many-Worlds ontology is a logical necessity for free-will: if the Many-Worlds did not exist, then it would be a logical impossibility for us to have free will."[40]

---

different parallel worlds. In each world, an observer appears to have observed just one of the possibilities. These two descriptions of the paradox are different interpretations, both compatible with the same theory. So, there are parallel interpretations. Thomas McFarlane, personal communication.

36. Dantzig, *Number*, 245.
37. Mishlove, *Thinking Allowed*, 108.
38. Dyson, *Infinite*, 295.
39. Hofstadter, *Gödel*, 311–36.
40. Tipler, *Physics of Immortality*, 173.

CONTEMPORARY MATHAPHORS ARE MOVING US TOWARD PLURALISTIC, MULTI-WORLD VIEWS

While some address the emergence of multi-world views in cosmology, others investigate more technologically driven "multi" inclinations in society. In particular, some suspect that the development of virtual reality and simulated, but artificial, worlds are affecting our ideas about mind, body, self, and machine. Some fear the results.

"Experiences on the Internet extend the metaphor of windows," says Sherry Turkle.[41] "When people adopt an online persona they cross a boundary into highly-charged territory. Some feel an uncomfortable sense of fragmentation. Some sense the possibilities for self-discovery, even self-transformation."[42] She adds that, for these cyber-explorers, the fake often becomes more compelling than the real, the Internet becomes a substitute for face-to-face interaction, and life on the screen is "without origins and foundation."[43]

Popular culture confirms Turkle's suspicions. A magazine cartoon lets the mathaphor speak for itself: a handsome, formally dressed man dances with a beautiful woman who consists entirely of 0's and 1's. Computer games such as "Simm City" allow countless young people to "Create and control your own simulated people! Create! Control! Build! Tell!" (promotional text on container). What the package does not actually say, yet clearly implies, is that herein is everything you need to play God. Clearly, the virtual world is a seductive one. Think of Simone, the beloved movie star who, in the 2002 film by the same name, turns out to be nothing more than the product of one man's technological skill and his unsatisfied desire for personal recognition. The problem becomes pronounced when Simone's devoted public condemns her inventor/creator as a murderer, adamantly refusing to believe him when he confesses that Simone is not real.

If the identity crisis we experience over our inability to distinguish the real from the fake is confusing, the developing sense of multiplicity which accompanies virtual reality is even more disconcerting. Our self becomes more consciously multiple, claims Turkle. Philosopher and ethicist Doug Groothuis is even more cautious: "when the self traffics in

---

41. Turkle, *Life on the Screen*, 14.
42. Turkle, *Life on the Screen*, 260.
43. Turkle, *Life on the Screen*, 47.

nothing but fictions, the notion of truth as nourishment for the soul slips from our grasp."[44]

Our society is developing more inclination to "go multiple." If you doubt it, check out yet another recent movie—*Time Code*. Wherever this 2000 movie is being shown, the screen is literally quartered. Four related, but different, stories are played out simultaneously. The viewer must watch all four *at the same time*. Superimposition in the movie theater! And more! Multi-tasking images confront us constantly on television, where part of the screen is showing one scene, another part is showing a different set of images, and a line of moving commentary running across the bottom is asking us to consider yet a third, and sometimes a fourth scenario. Furthermore, people often have a television or two, a computer or two, and other electronic devices such as a telephone all operating at the same time.

One neuroscientist argues that such multiple images are fundamentally changing our brains to accommodate the abundance of stimulation forced on them by the modern world. As a society, we "have become more frenetic, more distracted, more fragmented—in a word, *hyperactive*."[45] Such conditioning may, as some fear, lead to loss of inner integrity and spiritual degeneration. Alternatively, it may offer a rich field for fostering tolerance of diversity and pluralism at all levels of society. We do not now know. However, wisdom suggests that we monitor this phenomenon as it develops so that we might better influence its outcomes to ensure the enrichment of the soul, rather than its destruction.

CONTEMPORARY MATHAPHORS ARE PUSHING THE ENVELOPE ON WHAT CONSCIOUSNESS IS

When we speak of hyperspace observing itself, of artificial intelligence as creator rather than created, and of many different realities coexisting, we are in effect suggesting new understandings of consciousness. According to neuroanatomist Paul Pietsch, "Stored mind is not a *thing*, . . . mind is a mathematic."[46] With that mathaphor, consciousness is freed from the physical substrate of our brains. (Also see chapter 26.)

---

44. Groothuis, *Soul in Cyberspace*, 27.
45. Restak, *New Brain*, 40.
46. Ferguson, *Aquarian Conspiracy*, 179.

The nature of consciousness was once the exclusive province of religion and philosophy, but no more. As one Internet chatter put it on the Quantum Mind Digest, "consciousness can be defined as a five-dimensional point observation."[47] For mathematical physicist Saul-Paul Sirag, consciousness is the intersection of certain algebraic groups.[48] To physicist Amit Goswami, consciousness implies a nonlocal knowing.[49] To AI expert Ray Kurzweil, consciousness is a Cantorian-like synthesis of all the standard views: "all of these schools [of consciousness] are correct when viewed together, but insufficient when viewed one at a time."[50]

For the latest, most exciting views on consciousness—disembodied or otherwise—look to cognitive and neuroscientists and quantum physicists. Not that we will find great consensus there. What we do find, unquestionably, is a lot of material that pushes the envelope on our notions of what consciousness is and how it works. Is God Mind? The Collective Unconsciousness? Is there a difference between spirit, soul, and mind? Today's voices from mathematics and science seem to offer answers. Different answers, but answers nonetheless.

CONTEMPORARY MATHAPHORS ARE ALTERING OUR EXPECTATIONS FOR AFTER-LIFE

Some physicists, like Tipler and Dyson, suggest that artificial intelligence will eventually revise our distinctions between life and death. Other scientists suggest new understandings of time, understandings which ultimately will affect our beliefs about after-life. Time, for instance, may not be linear. Past, present, and future may not follow the commonly accepted sequence.

One theory points out the similarities between the anthropic notion of varying initial constants and the existence of alternative versions of past time. Not only is this "different past histories theory" a legitimate scientific consideration, it is also a popular passion. For instance, "movies such as *Back to the Future*, *It's a Wonderful Life*, *The Alteration*, *SS-GB*, and *Fatherland* all actualize alternative histories and even bring them

---

47. Green, "Quantum Mind."
48. Sirag, "Consciousness."
49. Goswami, *Self-Aware Universe*, 23.
50. Kurzweil, *Spiritual Machines*, 61.

into collusion with our own."[51] Another hypothesis, stemming from discoveries in optics and in physics, holds that the future may even precede the present. In this theory there is a kind of back-action from the future which alters the present.[52]

Still another theory holds that time is not only nonlinear, it is an illusion.[53] Our "Now" is more like a static snapshot than a moving phenomenon, and time is something we project from our psychological experience into the external world. Time "out there" is not the way we feel it inside. Theoretical physicist Julian Barbour calls the totality of all such frozen "Now" moments *Platonia*, which he describes as an asymmetrically shaped land with a past and billions of futures (places different from this Now). Past refers to vibrations coming from the closed end of Platonia, what Barbour likens to static echoes in eternity. Future is simply other Nows, ones whose echoes we do not receive from the open end of Platonia.[54] Since all Nows are logical possibilities, time as we perceive it through our senses and our brains is an emergent property in an essentially timeless universe.

What happens to an afterlife when the arrow of time becomes so twisted? Speculative as such theories are, scientists are taking them seriously. Perhaps theologians should as well.

One additional scientific area impacting our notions about afterlife is teleportation. Incredible as it may seem, teleportation is shaking off its sci-fi prison. Teleportation is a present reality, albeit on a purely microscopic scale. The first experimental confirmation of quantum teleportation took place at the University of Innsbruck in Austria in 1997. A verification and extension of this test was done at Caltech in 1998. Researchers have now shown that, with appropriate entanglement, the properties of one quantum particle (such as a photon) can be transferred to another—even if the two are at opposite ends of the galaxy. Today, teleportation is a physical fact.[55]

The non-technological implications of this very recent physical breakthrough urge us to continue to explore this realm for its spiritual implications. At the very least, we should reexamine the teleportation

51. Barrow, *Constants*, 193–95.

52. Saffarti, "Quantum Mind."

53. Barbour, *End of Time*.

54. Prendergast, "Time Out of Mind," 19–21; Barbour, *End of Time*, 44–46.

55. Wootters, "Current Issues." See also Bennett et al., "Teleporting an Unknown." Compare chapter 14, 130.

tales of native folklore. According to the late linguist Dan Alford, teleportation "has for millennia been the intellectual property right of indigenous peoples the world over."[56] In one Cheyenne story, for instance, Ice, a medicine man, helped his people remember the power of Spirit by going with them to a place where there was a large movable boulder. While the People dug a pit near the boulder, Ice set up his tepee some distance away. After the pit was dug, the medicine man climbed in and the People rolled the boulder over it, burying him alive. Sometime later, he came walking out of his tepee. Note the similarities here to the story of Jesus' death and subsequent resurrection.[57]

CONTEMPORARY MATHAPHORS ARE OFFERING THE HOPE OF A MORE COMPASSIONATE FUTURE

Communication experts have adapted ideas from chaos theory to various areas of organizational behavior, with the hope of creating more harmonious and productive interaction. This is an example of *moral math*, that is, of studies which deal with the interface of mathematics and human behavior. Some instances of moral math deal so explicitly with issues of fairness and concern that they might be called the mathematics of compassion. In "Biologists Tally Rewards of Generosity," for instance, Malcolm Browne writes about the rewards of generosity: "Two European scientists have discovered a new version of [the Prisoner's Dilemma, a computer game] that may show how limited cooperation between living creatures, even those not related to each other, is compatible with the hard-boiled arithmetic of survival in an unremittingly competitive environment."[58]

In "Formulas for Fairness: Applying the Math of Cake Cutting to Conflict Resolution," Ivars Peterson observes that mathematical procedures can offer fair and equitable outcomes in divorce, inheritance squabbles, international border disputes, treaty and contract negotiations, and other areas of potential dissension.[59] In "Nonzero Hour: Cooperation, Evolution and Destiny," Robert Wright talks optimistically about the way human beings instinctively play non-zero-sum games—that is, win-win

56. Dan Moonhawk Alford, personal communication.
57. Dan Moonhawk Alford, personal communication.
58. Browne, "Biologists Tally," B5.
59. Peterson, "Formulas for Fairness," 284–85.

or lose-lose games. According to Wright, realms of cooperation (also known as reciprocal altruism) grow through time. History, he claims, has in this sense led us to higher moral planes, and is likely to keep right on doing so.[60]

Increasingly, social researchers are drawing on mathematics to inform and guide ethical human behavior.[61] Correct or incorrect, there is hope in such compassionate mathematics.

CONTEMPORARY MATHAPHORS ARE ENCOURAGING FAITH PERSPECTIVES THAT ARE ALWAYS INCOMPLETE AND IN PROCESS

Freeman Dyson points out that Gödel's Theorem of Incompleteness shook the mathematical world when it was published in 1931.[62] Loosely stated, Gödel showed that in certain logical systems one must choose between either completeness or consistency. The implication of this discovery was that incompleteness is intrinsic to the structure of certain mathematical systems. That is, we may have a complete theory, or a non-contradictory one, but not both. Mathematical truth is *limited*. No wonder this revelation shook the mathematical universe.

Three-quarters of a century later, mathematicians no longer have any trouble accepting such notions, at least in theory. But, as has so often happened in the past, the mathematical concept has seeped over into other areas of knowledge in the form of mathematical metaphor, or mathaphor. Hofstadter draws analogies between Gödel's incompleteness theorem and our human inability to determine our own level of saneness, our inability to truly know oneself, and even our spiritual need to come to grips with our mortality: "'There was a time when I was not alive, and there will come a time when I am not alive.' ... This is a basic undeniable problem of life; perhaps it is the best metaphorical analogue of Gödel's Theorem."[63]

---

60. Wright, "Nonzero Hour," 26–27.

61. Good sources include: Barabási, *Linked*; Barash, *Survival Game*; Bishop, *Shades*; Buchanan, *Nexus*; Johnson, *Emergence*; Kosko, *Fuzzy Future*; Méro, *Moral Calculations*; Poundstone, *Prisoner's Dilemma*; Shermer, *Science of Good*; Watts, *Six Degrees*; Wright, *NonZero*.

62. Dyson, *Infinite*, 52–53.

63. Hofstadter, *Gödel*, 698.

So, too, we might apply Gödel's incompleteness theorem to our faith perspectives in general. John Hick, the father of religious pluralism, suggests that there "may be a 'Gödel's principle' in metaphysics."[64] Just as mathematics entertains the notion of a set which contains all sets, theology might consider a "religion of all religions." Such a religion, rather than relativizing specific religious truth, "provides a platform from which more than one truth may be affirmed as *the* truth."[65] Yet, as in mathematics, our quest for religious certainty will be realized only at the cost of consistency. Most of us probably prefer consistency. Consistency necessarily means that our religious traditions and spiritual outlooks will always be incomplete, ongoing, in process. A religion based on a plurality of religions will inevitably leave us forever dealing with an Axiom of Religious Choice.[66]

Investigating the role of mathaphor in religion and theology (or "matheology") in no way implies that mathematical and scientific insight is imperative to faith. Nor must we all become math geniuses, devouring numerical problems like candy and ice cream. Rather, we intentionally lift up and examine mathematical ideas because mathaphors are intrinsic to everyday life, because they help us bridge the gap between science and spirit, and because they are (1) changing our metaphors for God; (2) challenging our human role in the universe; (3) helping us accept ambiguity; (4) revamping our understanding of the one and the many; (5) revising our thoughts about free will and determinism; (6) moving us toward pluralistic, multi-world views; (7) pushing the envelope on what consciousness is; (8) altering our expectations for after-life; (9) offering the hope of a more compassionate future; and (10) encouraging faith perspectives that are always incomplete and in process. The list is incomplete and in process. It is, also, an excellent starting point for the further study of mathaphors in matheology, an investigation that promises to challenge us all—across differing faith views—to new dimensions of spiritual growth.

---

64. Hick, *Interpretation*, 354.

65. Voss, *What Number*, 154.

66. In mathematical set theory, there is also an Axiom of Choice, the specific details of which are beyond this essay. Still I add that it is not beyond metaphorical application. The Axiom of Choice states that for any collection of sets, a new set can be constructed containing an element from each set in the original collection. Loosely (metaphorically), we will always have choice in our religious affiliations.

Chapter 18: Self-Organizing Emergence and Network Theory[1]

To make a difference, target the hubs.

EVERYBODY IS CONNECTED TO everybody else by only six people. Think of some famous person you've never met but wish you knew. You're only six people away. That is, someone you know knows someone who knows someone who knows someone else who knows someone else who knows, personally, this famous person. Just six people away from everybody else! As we Unitarian Universalists like to put it, all existence is an interdependent web. This idea didn't originate with Unitarian Universalism, but we probably pay more lip service to it than most organized faith traditions do. Perhaps the interdependent web of all existence is as close as we come in our formal principles to acknowledging something which might be God-like. Many of us suspect that as soon as organized religions embrace God, they somehow turn the concept into a dogma, and most Unitarian Universalists distrust dogma with passion. In fact, that's why many of us became UUs in the first place—we were recovering from some dogma, as in recovering Catholic, or recovering Lutheran, or recovering Methodist. Still, when I recently heard a man publicly label himself a recovering UU, I felt uneasy. What dogma was *he* recovering from? The interdependent web? Our commitment to the goal of world community with peace, liberty, and justice for all?

---

1. This chapter started out as "Living Better on the (Chaotic) Edge," the first of a series of three "St. Mathematica" sermons presented in early 2004. See appendix B for details on the network exercise described herein.

LIVING BETTER WITH COMPLEXITY

There are so many setbacks to freedom, justice, and peace in our world that it would be easy to get discouraged and turn the words of our covenant to affirm and promote such a goal into just that—mere words. After all, we Unitarian Universalists have a long history as social activists. Like many other faith traditions, we try to foster more altruistic, caring, moral living, and to put our actions where our words are. Yet if it's world peace and justice we're after, the bald fact is that we have fallen embarrassingly short of our goal. We must not give up on this lofty goal. But how do we approach it knowing that so often our efforts are doomed to minimal success? A geometric exercise is useful here: draw nine dots on a sheet of paper, three each in three rows, spaced symmetrically, and then connect all nine of them using only four straight lines without ever lifting pencil from the paper.

• • •   Try This!

• • •   *Connect all nine dots with four straight lines.*

• • •   *Don't lift the pencil off the paper.*

Fig. 18.1. Connect the Dots

Yes, there is a solution: it's to extend some of the lines beyond the artificial boundary of the square formed by the dots—that is, to think outside the box.

Similarly, there's a way of thinking outside the box about equity and fairness. To do this, we turn to a new area of mathematics formally called nonlinear dynamic systems theory, or, more popularly, complexity theory. I believe this theory can influence our understanding of social behavior in a way that may significantly promote moral equity and fairness.

Think of complexity theory as the trunk of a growing tree which has roots that dig deep into all the mathematics of earlier centuries. There are several tender young branches coming off the trunk of this complexity tree. Three of them are *chaos theory*, *fractal theory*, and *network theory*. I focus here primarily on the third of these, on network theory, but it's important to remember that these three branches aren't totally separate. Indeed, they share many commonalities. They weave themselves together like the tight braids on a vine of bittersweet. When we talk about one of them, we are often inadvertently talking about the others as well.

One important commonality which these three intertwined branches of complexity theory share is *self-organizing emergence*. When we understand how this process of self-organizing emergence works, we will also better understand how we might utilize the concept to help make our world a more moral place to live. To this effect, I note four useful books about network theory, all written (shortly after the turn of the twenty-first century) for a lay audience. They are called, in chronological order according to the copyright dates, *Emergence*, *Nexus*, *Linked*, and *Six Degrees*.[2]

AN EXERCISE FROM NETWORK THEORY[3]

Network *thinking* is based on a view of reality which holds that everything is inseparably connected. This is a comfortable concept for most Unitarian Universalists, and often for people in general. However, network *theory* is helping us to understand more about the diverse ways in which we can be connected and the abstract laws of relationships.

To flesh out some of these abstract laws, consider this thought experiment. Imagine a room with people sitting in chairs set up in checkerboard fashion (like in a classroom or auditorium). The room is quite full. You are seated in one of the chairs.

1. Near your seat is a pile of colored cards. Some are blue and some are red. Each person chooses one. Only one, whichever color you prefer. Any extras are set aside. Every person holding a red card waves it; that way, everyone can see how the reds are distributed around the room. Same for the blues. There is a nice mixture of reds and blues.

2. Now chose a number between one and six. This number is your identity signature for the remainder of the exercise, so remember it as you would your name.

---

2. Johnson, *Emergence*; Barabási, *Linked*; Buchanan, *Nexus*; Watts, *Six Degrees*.

3. This exercise (also known as the "contact process") can be done in a real room such as an auditorium or church sanctuary, where it becomes an interactive game.

3. The leader rolls a die. Each person with that "rolled" number stands up and shows their card. This is an easy way to make a random selection of individuals within the room.

4. Those who are standing and who have red cards trade them in for one of the blue cards in the extra pile, and then sit back down.

5. Those who are standing and who have blue cards check to see how many immediate neighbors have red cards. If one or more of them have red cards, exchange your blue card for a red card and then sit back down. (If you are already sitting, don't do anything with your card.)

6. Wave again. Red cards. Blue cards. There will likely be a difference in the number and/or pattern of the red and blue cards. Repeat this same process (steps 3–5) several more times.

What would happen if we increase the percentage of neighbors with red cards that is required for standing blue (those who received a blue card) to exchange for a red card? For example, maybe at least three neighbors must have red cards rather than just one. That would make it harder for all the cards to turn red, wouldn't it? However, if we repeat the process enough times, we might still eventually see all, or almost all, red. Alternatively, if it requires only a small fraction of neighbors to force the color exchange, then the whole room might rapidly turn red. At some point, say, when a third or maybe only a fifth of standing blue's neighbors held red cards, we could be certain of getting this exchange.

To summarize, what we should be seeing in this thought exercise is a shift in colors, rapid or gradual. Over time, based on these ultra-simple action rules and a given, though arbitrary, shifting probability, we would probably see several transitions. In other words, a kind of color-order emerges out of what initially (remember the die) was a purely random distribution. This is a simplified illustration of *self-organizing emergent behavior within a system*. Under certain conditions, one color might seem to have an uncanny sense of persistence, even to the point of taking over. This happens if the shifting probability is sufficiently high, or, in mathematical language, if a certain *threshold* has been reached.

This little game is known as the "contact process."[4] Imagine it played with a lot more players arranged on a grid-like checkerboard, and imagine

---

4. See Buchanan, *Nexus*, 166–69. See appendix B for a summary sheet on using the contact process.

SELF-ORGANIZING EMERGENCE AND NETWORK THEORY

a computer keeping track of the play. With computer capabilities, it is easy to see that certain patterns might emerge on the graph screen. These patterns might persist for a while, disappear, and then maybe re-emerge, which, indeed, is precisely what happens. The computer allows us to make sense of this abstract game and to literally see the bigger picture as it plays itself out. Within that bigger picture, certain laws emerge, and these laws are what fascinate network theorists. They want to discover them. And they *are* discovering them.

Now, let's change the rules a little. On any given Sunday, most of our UU churches will be filled with a finite number of people. Our churches, however, are not static. We are a growing faith tradition. So, suppose that every new person who joins us arrives with a decided preference for blue or red. When a newcomer enters the room, she sees tiny homogenous groups of red gathered here and there, and a few similar groups of blue sticking out among an otherwise mixed sea of colors. Since she arrives with an attachment preference, she automatically meanders over to, say, the red group, which she really likes just because it is red. If more and more people keep joining us, more and more of them tend to attach to the group they naturally prefer. After a while, there are several very large clusters of red or blue, and not much else.

These clusters are linked to the people who stood initially. (Remember, this was a randomly selected group.) In network theory, these people are like "hubs" in the network. Some eventually turn into "strange attractors," which, like the Pied Piper, seem to collect more and more of whatever it is they are collecting. Moreover, sometimes it appears that this shift to all-of-one-kind happens all at once.[5] In such cases mathematicians say that a critical point has been reached. That's the point where the behavior or identity of the community as a whole has tipped in one direction or another, and a cascading action occurs. It's like water that is heated to the boiling point and, all at once, becomes a gas.

All this red/blue stuff is, of course, quite abstract, maybe even absurdly so, but the abstractness has the advantage of allowing us to see more universal behavior in systems. It turns out that self-organizing emergence crops up in inanimate systems such as economics where the rich get richer, in health systems where disease spreads in epidemics, in social systems where fads prevail, in engineering systems where electric

---

5. See Capra, *Web of Life*, 97.

power grids collapse like dominoes, in computer systems where the Internet and Web are vulnerable to viruses. Self-organizing emergence also appears in cellular networks, such as in the neural network of the brain. In fact, such emergence routinely occurs in life itself, where its appearance is given a special name, *autopoiesis*—*auto* for "self" and *poiesis*, which shares the same Greek root as the word "poetry" and means "making." Based on models from complexity theory, we are, indeed, *self-making* creatures.

SELF-ORGANIZING EMERGENCE AND SOCIAL BEHAVIOR

How can we utilize characteristics of complexity theory to help our world rather than to hinder it? It's actually quite easy to see how the science of networks can be adapted to social behavior. Consider the red/blue card process we just considered. Recall that whenever the community (i.e., the network) (1) grows and (2) demonstrates preferential attachment (as in being partial to the color red), various hubs and cluster-components will mysteriously appear throughout the system. What happens if that preferential attachment is for the color of human skin? That's how racism could emerge in such a social system. In fact, given the preferential attachment, it's hard to see how segregation and other forms of discrimination can be avoided! To stop this emergence, we must find ways to alter the preferred attachment, which is why we hear so much in present-day UUism about eradicating *internal* racism.

Applying the lessons of network theory to certain problematic issues may actually lead us to something of an ethical dilemma. Suppose that "red" in our exercise represents not just some abstract characteristic of the system, but, rather, an individual who is infected with a transmittable virus. If the infection threshold is high enough, the "rich get richer" principle leads with a kind of frightening certainty to more "red," i.e., to more cases of the virus.

The world now (at the time I am assembling this collection) is trying to pull itself out of the 2020 coronavirus pandemic. This epidemic is more than just some simulated card exercise: it is a scary reality which has already changed global culture in ways which will likely be long-lasting. For example, people who have access to Zoom and other computer technologies have advantages (such as being able to keep their job) over people who don't. Basically, it's unfair that only some of the world's people have this access. To move forward with hope, we benefit from the lessons of the past.

In 1997, for instance, the first decline of AIDS death in the United States led to what turned out to be false optimism.[6] The epidemic resurged. At one point, fifteen thousand people worldwide were infected daily with the virus. Most of these fifteen thousand individuals were expected to die from the disease within a decade. In Botswana in 1997, if you were fifteen years old you had a 90 percent chance of dying from AIDS. There were some relatively effective treatments for AIDS already on the market at that time. With some of these treatments, most AIDS patients could live almost normal life spans. These treatments cost approximately fifteen thousand dollars each. Even with AIDS activism, few of those fifteen-year-old Botswanians were likely to receive them.

Network theory tells us that the best way to alter the self-organizing pattern in a system is to focus on the hubs, where there are the greatest number of links. Change what is happening in the hubs, and we change the pattern. In any sexually transmitted disease, of course, the individuals who have the highest number of sexual contacts are the hubs of the network. Therefore, to eradicate AIDS, network science suggests that we offer these expensive fifteen thousand dollar treatments to, say, the prostitutes in the United States, because this is where the number of sexual contacts is likely to be highest. We effectively ignore the little girl who was born with AIDS, the powerless African teenager, and, generally, the wealthier but less sexually connected middle class. Another and far less comfortable way of thinking about this is that we select the treatment plan that rewards promiscuity. The best path of action to stop the spread of this horrible disease was to selectively treat those who were most likely to be hubs for carrying it. In the AIDS case, this best (and hence arguably the most "moral") solution might also have been the cruelest.

The way out of this tangle was vaccination. Changing budget priorities from, say, building more fighter planes to providing research funds for the development of a vaccine makes sense. A vaccine changes the entire system. The hubs no longer transmit the virus. Nearly a quarter century after HIV first threatened our social system, and after thirty-three million people died from AIDS, we still have no vaccine for it. At the beginning of 2019, however, and thanks to better prevention, diagnosis,

---

6. The following discussion about AIDS draws heavily on Barabási's *Linked*, 138–40.

treatment, and care, some thirty-eight million people were living with the virus without risk of early death from it, nor fear of spreading it.

One last example of social behavior and net theory principles can be found in writer David Callahan's 2004 book *The Cheating Culture*. In it, Callahan shows how vulnerable a class society is to moral decline. In example after example, we see that "the Winning Class has enough money and clout to cheat without consequences—while an Anxious Class believes that choosing not to cheat could cost them their only shot at success in a winner-take-all world."[7] Callahan unveils how cheating is pervasive at all levels of American society, from corporate dishonesty and large-scale fraud to downloading copyrighted music from the Internet and taking unwarranted deductions on income taxes. He maintains that the growing gap between winners and losers in our country is having a lethal effect on personal integrity, and when "you put people under pressure and give them a choice of preserving either their integrity or their financial security, many will go for the money."[8]

While Callahan never actually refers to formal network science in his book, the society he describes nonetheless fits very well with conclusions drawn from the abstract theory. In fact, when Callahan addresses (in the final chapter of his book) how we might bring about reform, he offers what essentially amounts to *practical* ways to transform the *hubs* of our cultural ideas.

In today's tight economy, he points out, it's become harder to achieve success and job security. Accordingly, we must stop this strange attractor of cutting corners. He argues that we must raise the minimum wage; offer more tax credits for lower earners; support government investment in transportation infrastructure, scientific research, energy efficiency, and other things that yield long-term dividends; and expand access to higher education. Similarly, since prizes for the winners in our society have increased hugely in our recent societal networks, we must diminish the rewards people receive for cheating by policing financial markets and corporate behavior, by funding the IRS so that it can better stop white collar crime, and so on. When we lessen the rewards of cheating, he says, we lessen the temptation as well.

Decreased safeguards against cheating, and increased rewards for it, lead to trickle-down corruption. Everyone starts doing it. "What happens

---

7. Callahan, *Cheating Culture*, jacket cover.
8. Callahan, *Cheating Culture*, 62.

when you think the system is stacked against people like you and you stop believing in the rules?" asks Callahan. "You might just make up your own moral code."[9] Complexity theory would say we've reached a critical point that turns our tide of thinking about the immorality of cheating.

The remedy? Put more effort into tipping the cascade of corruption in another direction. Callahan promotes new codes of conduct in the workplace and strengthening the ethics of new generations of Americans.[10] Some of the suggestions in Callahan's book seem like mere commonsense. Others are more novel. Regardless, his basic approach—redirecting the hubs—is clearly right on.

With the aid of complexity theory and its several informative branches, mathematics can help inform our decisions about ethical and moral social behavior. It empowers us to make better, more altruistic choices. My hope is that we will allow ourselves to be so open to this idealistic goal that it, too, will emerge as a strange, irresistible attractor in our society. May we, one by one, adopt this hope so that, at some critical point in the not-too-distant future, the entire community of humanity cascades into it, a threshold worthy of effort.[11]

---

9. Callahan, *Cheating Culture*, 23.

10. Callahan, *Cheating Culture*, 262–63.

11. Dan Levine notes (personal communication) that the popular meme—the spreading "red"—can be modified. For example, Riane Eisler, in *Real Wealth of Nations*, notes that companies which treat their workers well are more likely to be profitable, for such reasons as workplace contentment and less turnover.

Chapter 19: Redemption[1]

$n_1 \sin\theta_1 = n_2 \sin\theta_2$ (Snell's Law of Refraction)

When light travels from one medium to another, it generally bends or refracts. Something similar happens to the human spirit during redemption.

On a stand in our living room sits a tented sign like the ones you sometimes find advertising dessert specials on a restaurant table, only by comparison this one is large (a little less than half a yard long and a little more than four inches high) and is made of heavier than normal white cardboard. In large black letters one side says: KEEP THINGS THE SAME. If you turn the sign around, the other side says: KEEP THINGS THE SAME.

    I place this sign on the stand before the TV in an attempt to soothe my husband when I change the furniture around, which I do fairly often. I know it unsettles him to have to constantly readjust to where things are in our living room, but I change things around anyway. I do it because it's a way of renewing my whole perspective, and every time I move things around, I think that this is the best way I've ever arranged it and I'm certain that *this* time I'll leave it that way forever. But I never do. So the sign is intended to reassure my spouse that I understand how these changes cause him discomfort and that I am grateful to him that he protests so mildly. He's a good guy. Sometimes he even agrees that the change is nice.

    As a general rule, I like change. I like to stay fresh and to learn and to grow. Creativity is anything but static. It's hard, however, to engage in change without making some mistakes. Sometimes we make large

---

1. This essay was first printed in *Still Point*; see Voss, "Redemption." I offered a related sermon, "Redemption: A New Look at an Old Subject," on July 17, 2014.

mistakes. One recent Christmas I gifted a lot of people I love with erasers, really BIG erasers, so they could continue on quickly when they messed up BIG time. They all laughed, but there was still truth behind the joke. We all need to correct some of the things we do. I forgot to buy one for myself, though—a mistake in itself!

Mistakes inevitably happen when you don't keep things the same. *Thank goodness* mistakes happen when you don't keep things the same. As the Christian mystic Meister Eckhart once put it, "Even now one rarely hears of people achieving great things unless they first stumble in some respect."[2]

There's a kind of mistake, however, that is not so easily erased, and that is the grave one that does harm to someone. This type of mistake is usually called a sin. In the Abrahamic religions, the prototype sin was the mistake Adam made in the garden of Eden when he denied God's commands and humankind was thereafter harmed—i.e., forever born with the inclination to do bad things. The antidote to sin (original or otherwise) is (1) to have a redeemer[3] and/or (2) to repent, atone, make amends, offer restitution, provide reparation, and so forth.

Those, like myself, who follow alternative belief systems (or variations on the traditional ones) tend to shy away from the idea that an independent savior might come forward to rescue us from things we should really take responsibility for doing ourselves.[4] Granted, a redeemer is nice, and the argument can be made that a redeemer is even necessary to undo such a deep-seated sin as the genetic one that makes us all inclined to do bad things from birth. Nonetheless, I lean toward the assumption that we are born good and can thereafter choose to do good, and that we can also choose to repair, or at least try to repair, the things we subsequently do that aren't good. That pretty much forces us to engage in the latter list of efforts, the ones about repentance, atonement, restitution, reparation, expiation, penance, and the like (the list goes on), all of which we might gather together with the single term "redemption."

Redemption is easy to praise but hard to do. While it is disguised as a noun, redemption is really a verb—something you do, not something

---

2. Eckhart, *Essential Sermons*.

3. In traditional Christianity the ultimate redeemer is Jesus Christ, who pays for our sins with his sacrificial death. Much (but not all) of traditional Christianity believes in *original* sin, which stems from Adam's mistake in Eden and, loosely, means that we are all born with the inclination to do bad things.

4. This is not to say there isn't a forgiver, which in a way *is* a Savior.

you get. Generally, redemption requires doing a *lot*, too. As the poet T. S. Eliot wrote, it involves "a condition of complete simplicity (Costing not less than everything)."[5] The equation in this sense is:

everything = all our best intentions + the positive actions that follow

Happily, there are tons of resources on redemption, many of which come with various shades of religious influence. Because I've learned that mathematics can strongly impact spiritual understandings, I add math to those tons of resources on redemption.

The mathaphor I've used to inform my thoughts about redemption comes from the mathematics of refraction, a term which refers to the bending of light. Anyone who wears glasses should be grateful for refraction because the whole reality of corrective lenses depends upon it. Also telescopes, binoculars, kaleidoscopes, and much, much more.

Snell's Law of Refraction, named after the Dutch astronomer Willebrord Snellius (who contributed to the 1621 discovery of the law), gives the precise mathematical relationship between the angles at which a light wave leaves one medium and enters another. If these angles, called the angle of incidence (θ_1) and the angle of refraction (θ_2), are the same, and if the indices of refraction n_1 and n_2 (which represent the speeds of light through the two mediums) are just right, then the light passes straight through one medium into the next. If the indices of refraction form a ratio less than 1, then there is a critical angle called Brewster's angle (after the French physicist who discovered it in 1808) which ensures that all of the light is reflected back into the original medium, a condition called total internal reflection or, occasionally (and I think somewhat humorously), *frustrated refraction*. If the angles of incidence and refraction are not identical, then the light passes from the first medium to the second, changing direction in the process, or bending. A little algebra and trigonometry are needed to make these situations clear and mathematically understandable,[6] but we can get a visual sense of these details with a simple imaginative exercise.

---

5. Eliot, "Little Gidding."

6. For those who want to see the math, there are abundant sources on the Web. Here are a few which I have used in writing this chapter: My Schoolhouse, "Reflection and Refraction"; Len, "Online Reading Assignment"; Applied Science, "Lab"; and Boston University, "Reflection and Refraction."

Picture a group of line dancers, arms linked together, dancing rather rapidly across a floor. A length of bright duct tape divides the dance floor into two sections. The dancers are excellent, and they keep their line straight as an arrow, dancing toward the strip of duct tape (the dividing line) with great synchronicity and at exactly the same speed. The rule is that everyone dances at one speed (say, six miles per hour) on one side of the duct tape, and at a much slower speed (e.g., two miles per hour) the instant they cross over to the other side. If the line of dancers is parallel to the duct tape (the dividing line), they all cross over it at exactly the same time, and the only difference is that they immediately slow down the speed at which they dance. However, if the line the dancers form is not parallel to the duct tape (i.e., the dancing line is *diagonal* to the line of tape), then as they dance uniformly toward the line, the persons on either end will have a different distance to cover before they reach the line. In fact, each individual dancer will reach the line at a slightly different time, and upon crossing over, each dancer immediately changes speed. This has the visual consequence of making the line of dancers (which remains straight as ever) shift direction. The line they collectively make forms a new angle with the duct tape—that is, the line bends or "refracts."[7]

The same thing happens when a light ray passes through, for example, air into water. Because light passes through air much faster than it does through water, the light bends at the point where the air and the water meet. This becomes obvious if you shine a light at an ordinary drinking straw stuck in a glass of water; the straw appears to change direction at the top of the water. It's a little weird, really, because it forms a kind of optical illusion. But, in fact, the angle at which the *light* enters the water from the air is different from the angle at which it passes through the water. In other words, Snell's Law of Refraction assures us that the line will bend.

And what does this have to do with redemption? In a word: energy.

To my mystic eye, everything is some form of energy. We know, for instance, of kinetic energy, chemical energy, heat (or thermal) energy, gravitational, potential, electrical, sound, nuclear, and elastic energy. And we know about spiritual energy, too. Gravity is the energy that holds us on earth, light is electromagnetic energy, God is spiritual energy. Actually, I like to think of everything as spiritual energy, some of which we

---

7. The dancing line I formulate here is a variation of an idea from Physics Classroom, "Cause of Refraction."

can see, some of which we can experience physically or psychically even when we can't see it, some of which we probably don't even know about.

We understand a fair amount about energy, especially when it is in a form that mathematics can describe—light, sound, heat, nuclear, chemical, etc. But we understand quite a bit about the less mathematically explicit forms too, such as the energy that keeps us going when we are awake and runs out when we need to rest. Okay, even this probably lends itself to mathematical formula, in the form of caloric intake or the like. But sometimes the mathematics behind energy is not so clear.

For instance, when we are feeling highly creative, we intuitively know we're speeding along on creative energy. We know when this energy is depleted, too. And we know that there is an emotional energy which is awesome and constant (though changing), and, yes, maybe in five or twenty or forty years we're going to be able to track that emotional energy with brain scans that can be turned into mathematical inputs, and maybe not, but in any case, we already intuitively know quite a bit about emotional energy. Redemption is one of the shapes emotional energy can take. You can't touch it, you can't see it, but, wow, do you know it when it occurs.

Consider something very collective and common among humankind, like war. War causes extreme harm to people, animals, and the earth, and when war ends, the damage done is often partially repaired. Sometimes reparations are made. Sometimes this redress is much belated, such as the February 1999 twenty thousand dollar payments made by the US government to 82,210 Japanese Americans (or their heirs) who had been interred in US camps during WWII, over fifty years earlier. Even years after the harm was done, those reparations brought emotional relief, not only to those who were harmed, but to the perpetrators who caused the harm and the bystanders who innocently let it occur, and to some of us who weren't even born but carry a kind of inherited collective guilt, as well. Redemption is an amazing and wonderful act which is a form of cleansing spiritual energy.

This is just as true on an individual level as on a collective level. Two decades ago a woman I knew who had not always been very kind or fair to me called me one day out of the blue and apologized for her previous behavior. She said she was working through a twelve-step program and wanted to make amends. The feeling her apology evoked in me was lightness, as though something heavy had been lifted off. I was so grateful for this unanticipated ray of hope that I immediately looked forward to a changed relationship with this woman, whom I cared for even though there had been some difficulty between us. Alas, this turned out to be a case of frustrated refraction, as she wasn't interested in any kind of continued relationship, she was simply interested in working her twelve-step program. In mathaphorical terms, the angle of compatibility between us was too small to sustain the refraction, and instead her action was entirely reflected back on her, a total internal reflection.

There is no judgment herein. Total internal reflection, in the purely mathematical sense, has numerous useful and even extraordinary physical manifestations: e.g., diamonds which sparkle, certain types of flashlight lenses, optical fibers used in medical endoscopes and in telecommunications, rain sensors which control automatic windshield wipers, and so on. Similarly, total internal reflection in the emotional or metaphysical realms may manifest in spiritual strength: consider, for example, the transformative effects of Jesus's forty days in the desert, the wisdom Confucius gained during his extended years of reflective wandering through China, the extraordinary mental agility and gifts of humility of advanced yogis, Poor Clares, and other historical contemplatives. Indeed, any one of us who strives for insight and guidance through the reflective energy of meditation and prayer is using a mathaphorical interpretation of total internal reflection.

In the physical world, either total internal reflection or total refraction can occur in certain light transmissions, but *most* energy transmissions of light actually involve a mixture of the two. Likewise, many energy exchanges between individuals in social relationships involve a mixture of both inner reflection and outward influence. In teacher/student, mentor/mentee, parent/child, and friend/friend connections, to name a few, emotional energy crosses back and forth between the two parties and also bounces back on each like a clairsentient mirror. In everyday living, we automatically utilize energy in ways that are similar to the processes of both reflection and refraction.

However, refraction is the lone process for the *bending* of light. Mathaphorically, it describes the kind of energy interchange that occurs in the act of redemption. For true redemption to occur, empathy must travel from one person (or group of persons) to another, and then it must *change directions* or paths when the energy reaches the second person, such that the injured person is moved away from the routine and finds a path of unprecedented healing, renewal, and freedom. When the empathy and intent of the first person to bring forth redemption is honest, this process works as smoothly as the dancers in our imagination automatically bend their line when they cross over a dividing point. The amount of the refractive bend (that is, the angle of refraction) depends on the respective speeds at which the dancers are able to move through the two sides of the dance floor. In the redemption process, I suggest that the difference in speeds is comparable to the difference in the rates of psychic awareness, vision, and spiritual maturity between the harm-er and the harmed. The greater the difference, the more bend must occur.

Recapping, we can use what we know about the mathematics of refraction to, well, to shed *light* on a redemptive process that *light*ens the effects of a human mistake which cannot be simply erased:

- Redemption requires an empathetic energy exchange between the two parties involved in an act that caused at least one of them harm.
- The degree of repair possible depends on the rates at which each party can carry that empathy. The indices of refraction for these rates are critical to this process and are determined by each party's previous assimilation of psychic awareness, vision, and spiritual maturity.
- The harm-er must be prepared to refract or bend (i.e., to offer the flexibility needed) to accommodate the current internal state of the harmed.
- Even if the empathetic energy exchange is less than total, some of the light from this attempted exchange is likely to be reflected back on the harm-er in the form of insight.
- The harmed will continue to suffer the effects of the original mistake until the harm-er (or someone acting in the harm-er's stead) tries again with greater success.
- There is always change, usually in the form of lightening, at the end of a successful redemptive process.

At church one Sunday morning not long ago, a man I've known for years went up to the pulpit and came out to the congregation as a gay man. He spoke into a microphone for about five minutes, his head ever bent over the script from which he was reading as he told his story. Many of us sitting in the pews had known and loved his wife before she died after a long battle with cancer and after he had left her. To my knowledge, none of us knew he was gay.

Now he stood before us and admitted he was ashamed—no, not of his sexual orientation, but of the fact that he had hid who he was for all those years and that his secrecy had hurt his former wife, had hurt his children, and had hurt this congregation, too. When he was finished, we gave him a standing ovation. After the service, I spoke to him and he held my hand as though he never wanted to let go. I told him he had done a brave thing and I'd like to talk to him more about why he chose to tell his story in this way and to this audience, and he said that would be fine. When we parted, I carried the knowledge that the ray of his immense effort had pierced my heart; I wanted to tell him I was sorry we hadn't been the kind of people whom he felt he could look directly in the face when he made his amends. I would have told him, but sometimes enough is all one can handle.

Chapter 20: *Venn Diagrams and Intersectionality[1]

Inequalities: Some things are greater than other things. Inequities: Some things are wronger than others.

SOME SOCIAL JUSTICE IDEAS are straightforward and easy to support. Some are harder to understand and to intentionally embrace. One such complicated idea may be summed up with a single word: intersectionality.

Intersectionality, a hot topic in contemporary social justice circles, came to my full attention because of an article I read in which the author talked about her experience as a straight white woman who was learning to be open to trans individuals, as in LGBT.[2] The author was clearly well-intentioned and caring and trying to do the right thing but, apparently, failed big-time in this latter regard. We know she failed because the editor of the magazine subsequently issued an online apology for having published an essay which caused harm and pain. Senior editor Chris Walton wrote (in part): "I am profoundly saddened and deeply sorry to have caused pain to people who matter to me and whose dignity and worth I had thought we were promoting with the piece. As the magazine's editor, I was wrong to decide to publish this essay."

Chris then identified several ways in which he had erred, including his failure to grasp that a story about trans individuals which was told from a cisgender perspective would cause harm and that specific language in the article was hurtful—a reference to jokes at a high school

---

1. This chapter is a slightly modified sermon given on April 28, 2019, titled "After Reading the Article about Intersectionality . . ."
2. French, "L, G, and B."

in the 1970s that involved a homophobic slur, a reference to so-called corrective surgery, and other microaggressions found throughout the essay which are troubling to the trans community. "These specific editorial choices added pain to injury," he said.[3]

I particularly appreciated Walton's use of the term "microaggressions." These are the small things that people, myself included, often use that help enable oppression to continue. So often we use them and don't even recognize them as aggressions. This is true for many of us even when someone has explicitly pointed them out to us. Microaggressions aren't unusual, but they tend to disrupt right relations.

After apologizing, Chris referred to a response by Alex Kapitan, a leader in the trans and gender nonbinary community. Alex lambasted the published article in no uncertain terms. "An article written by a cis person,"[4] ze wrote, "that centers cis people and cis perspectives, about trans people, is not incremental progress—it's harm."[5] Alex, it turns out, was consulted about the *UU World* article during the pre-publishing process, but the cautions and suggestions ze offered were essentially ignored and zir request to see a copy of the intended article before it went to print was denied. Alex particularly emphasized the need to give trans people voice and agency. Ze wrote: "Imagine wanting to do a story about Black Lives Matter that was written by a white person and was all about the 'increasing visibility' of black people and the discomfort white people have with Black Lives Matter banners, black people's needs with UU churches, and the concept of Black Lives Matter as a movement. I know that the intentions are good, but this kind of approach will unquestionably cause harm."[6]

I read Walton's apology and the subsequent online discussion initiated by Alex Kapitan's response, and then began googling more information about intersectionality—its meaning, history, current issues, and so forth. It took . . . a while! By the time I was done, I "got it." I understood what the pain and hurt was about, how it happened, how valid it was. In a word, I'd been *educated*. The article itself was a start, but the written

---

3. Walton, "Our Story."

4. Cisgender (often abbreviated as *cis*) is a term for someone whose gender identity corresponds with the sex the person had or was identified as having at birth. Some individuals in the trans community use ze as a preferred pronoun. Others use the singular they, or other choices. See https://radicalcopyeditor.com for more on this subject.

5. Kapitan, "What It Takes."

6. Kapitan, "What It Takes."

apology and the subsequent online discussion greatly assisted my enlightenment. I'm grateful. I've changed, at least somewhat.

We need to talk about these things. Whatever else, I've always had a lot to say, but I haven't always said it. The noted Indian author and political activist Arundhati Roy generalized this dilemma: "There's really no such thing as the 'voiceless.' There are only the deliberately silenced or the preferably unheard."[7] I used to think that not having a voice was an injustice someone did to you, but now I wonder if it isn't also an injustice that we sometimes do to ourselves. Injustice is complicated. Intersectionality can be complicated, too. What is intersectionality, anyway? Who is hearing that term now for the first time?

My own take on the concept has a math twist. Venn diagrams. You've almost certainly seen them, maybe even used them from time to time. The English logician John Venn invented them in 1880 as a way to demonstrate the logical relationship between various groups of things, or sets. Each set is traditionally included in a circle, and the circles overlap where there is a commonality.

Venn diagrams depict relationships and their commonalities (or lack thereof). They are useful in different ways, and, in particular, they are useful in talking about intersectionality. Here's a googled definition: intersectionality is the interconnected nature of social categorizations such as race, class, and gender as they apply to a given individual or group, regarded as creating overlapping and interdependent systems of discrimination or disadvantage. So, here, in the language of Venn diagrams, is intersectionality: Picture a large rectangle. Call it the universe of all people with social inequities in America. Then put a circle in the rectangle which contains all the people who are not Euro-Anglo American. And another circle which contains all the people who are not a man. Some of the people in America will be in both of these circles, so we overlap them, and the intersected area they share is the part that contains all of the people who are not a man and also are not Euro-Anglo American. One of the people in this small area of intersection is Kimberle Crenshaw, who was born in 1959 in Canton, Ohio, and is a full-time professor in the UCLA School of Law and at Columbia Law School where she specializes in race and gender issues. Crenshaw coined the term "intersectional feminism" in an article which lifted up how Black women do not experience feminism the same way that white women do and how

---

7. Roy, *Public Power*, xx.

the feminist movement has historically favored the centrist position of white women. This is the point of intersectionalism. All the people in the smaller overlapped area between the two circles have to deal with more than one kind of inequity, and their challenges are therefore greater, and are often overlooked.

Now add more circles to the universe of all people with social inequities in America, and let all of them overlap with the part (or part of the part) of the previous overlapped area. Add a circle for all people who are not heterosexual. Add one for everyone who doesn't speak English. Add one about class—for all people who are not rich, professionals, or educated. Add one for everybody in America who is not able, i.e., who is disabled. Maybe add one for mathematicians—or just nerds in general. Add another for those who are very young or very old. I'm in the one for gender (i.e., not a man) and the one for appearance (i.e., very old). Okay, maybe I'm just old, not very old, but it won't be that much longer! Sometimes I feel like I belong in the "poor" circle, too, but, hey, I'm American-born, plus a professional, plus seriously educated. I really don't know what "poor" means! And my disabilities—the hearing loss, the cognitive impairment . . . well, these, too, are likely to worsen the longer I live. And, yes, I can tell you about the inequities I've experienced all my life simply because I am not a man. But that is a somewhat different sermon!

Intersectionality (all these overlapped parts) makes it easy to see how complex a person's life can become if he or she or ze—or the singular they or whatever—fit into the overlapping part of several different Venn diagrams that represent differing systems of discrimination or disadvantage. A Black woman who is poor, disabled and old has more (and different) challenges than anyone needs. Such individuals are highly disadvantaged, and they need special attention to get a fair deal in life. What are those disadvantages? We can only tell if we give them space for their voices. And if we, i.e., those who are not part of their circle, first listen carefully to what *they* say, and then act accordingly.

Here, I believe, is where religious institutions can really make a difference. In my own faith tradition, we have been directing more and more of our collective energy to listening to those who deal with intersectionalism. In America, the white man grows up attached to an umbrella of entitlement, and it doesn't just disappear when he gets into a new position of power, and, moreover, it is hard for him to see this umbrella because he is so used to it. It's like moving into a house near a busy airport, and at first all you hear is the jets overhead, and then after a while, you just get used to them and don't hear them at all. Something similar happens with white women, too. I, for instance, grew up under that umbrella of whiteness. For a long time, I didn't see my own advantages as a white individual, let alone the ways in which I was disadvantaged because I was a woman. I was incredibly slow to understand, to see this umbrella and what it cost me or others to keep it. When I was twenty-one, I married, and I held it as part of my duty as a good wife to vote so as not to undermine my husband's vote. No one told me that. I just took it on. Nobody told me that when I was old and retired, I would have earned in my entire life about a third of what my husband had in his retirement account. I didn't understand. I didn't see. And even when someone told me, I *still* didn't understand or see.

I was so slow. When I was in undergraduate college a long time ago in Ohio my conservative Mennonite roommate was more open to homosexuality than I was. I thought homosexuality was some sort of sin. Fortunately, I grew out of this. But slowly—oh, so slowly. I'm still slow. When First UU church put up the Black Lives Matter banner a few years ago, I believed that to take stands—putting up this banner, for instance—was doing something, and it's better to do something than nothing even if it turns out to be wrong. Yes, it is courageous and thoughtful to try to do the right thing, even when we fear criticism. I know that, but, honestly, at first, I didn't understand why we need to put a special spotlight on those who are disadvantaged or discriminated against so that we could actually hear their voices and offer them support. I was slow. Inside, I resisted. Outside, I did nothing. At first, I have always done nothing.

And have you heard the one about what one state official said to another: I don't know what people have against us. We haven't done anything.

Turtle-slow or rabbit-fast, we all are in this journey together, and together we learn. I have grown especially grateful for the part of my journey which has included Unitarian Universalism. This faith tradition has a long history of spotting the inequities, often even before other faith traditions do. Think abolition. UUs were right there. Think women as ministers. UUs were right there. Think openness to gays. Think about gender-inclusive language in our hymnals—now, that goes back about thirty years. I remember offering a fledgling sermon when I was preparing to attend seminary. Afterwards, one progressive feminist came up to me and, instead of saying, "Good, job, Sarah," she pointed out that I had picked an illustration for the cover of the morning order of service that was non-inclusive. I looked at it and she was right. It was all male. But why was she making such a big deal about it? I felt hurt. I'd already capitulated about changing the language in our hymnals to be more inclusive, and now, here she was picking on the artwork. Thirty years later, I am incredibly grateful that she spoke up. Now, I'm careful about the illustrations I choose when I preach, and, when I saw the old hymns in another Protestant church one day not long ago, I wondered what was wrong with that church that they still used patriarchal language. I take our UU history for granted. Now that it's history, of course.

UUs start processes which work to help rectify inequities, both these old ones and ones which are currently centered in our collective consciousness. I am proud of this fact about our association of churches. I personally have benefited from many of these processes. Sometimes I stumble. Sometimes I lead. Sometimes both. But for me, it's always a little like taking a trip to the eye doctor. You'll never guess who I bump into on the way. Everybody!

Chapter 21: The Art of Reframing[1]

Things that appear to be very different may really be the same, and vice versa.

1 = .999 . . . *(repeating continuously)*

A particularly lovely number from the perspective of a math mystic is the decimal .999 . . ., where the set of three ellipses indicates that the last digit repeats endlessly. Thus, this number can also be written as

.9 . . .
or .99 . . .
or .99999999 . . .
or even .9999999999999999999999999999999999999999999 999999999999999 . . .

A "forever" string of 9's is implied by the ellipsis, so it doesn't really matter how many of them are written out since "forever" matches "forever" in imagination, which is an excellent place to store this number. This is a particularly lovely number because, although none of these four illustrations look quite the same, they all mean exactly the same thing.

Specifically, they all mean what we mean when we teach a toddler to count by starting with the number "one." The symbol "1" looks stunningly different from the symbol ".999 . . .," yet the two notations represent the same concept. The alternative expressions simply frame the idea differently. What we normally mean by the symbol "1" doesn't require the same need for imagination as does .999 . . . because even very young children intuitively understand it. What takes more sophisticated reasoning

---

1. I gave a sermon variation ("Redemption: A New Look at an Old Subject") on this chapter on July 17, 2014. At the end of the sermon, volunteers from the congregation performed the mediation skit found at the end of the chapter.

THE ART OF REFRAMING   203

(and imagination) is the notion that these two symbols both represent precisely the same concept: they are identical.

The number .999 ... is tricky because, while it turns out that it is the number we all know as 1, it doesn't *seem* that it is the same as "1." Intuitively, we sense some gap, however miniscule, between the repeating decimal "9" and the number 1. This gap is an illusion, and, as with the definite integral of calculus, we feel caught in the grasp of a paradox.[2] In this case the paradox is introduced by the *repeating* portion of the symbol expression. Thus we can accurately write .999 ... = 1, while .999 ≠1. Note that .999 does not equal 1 because it is missing the repeating digits indicated by the ellipses.

It was in high school that I first learned how to use algebra to "prove" that 1 = .999 .... It was a long while back, but I remember the argument as it appears in figure 21.1.

Fig. 21.1. Algebraic Proof That 1 = .999 ...

Let x = .999 ...
10x = 9.999 ... (multiply both sides by 10)
10x - x = 9.999 ... - .999 ... (subtract 1st from 2nd equation)
9x = 9 (rename each side of the equation)
x = 1 (divide both sides of the equation by 9)
   Therefore, x = 1 = .999 ...

This is not quite the way it is usually presented today in an algebraic proof, nor is it the only type of proof that exists. I include it because it was fun for me to try to remember how I had first encountered the concept all those many years ago. If the math is not fun for you, not to worry. The main thing to glean is (see figure 21.1) that some things that appear to be different are really the same. The converse is also true: some things that are really the same appear to be different.

---

2. Yes, there is a similarity here to the definite integral of calculus which we looked at in chapter 6. But the integral is generally more complicated.

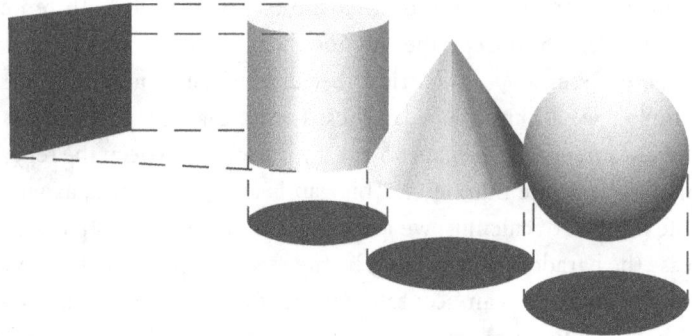

Fig. 21.2. Light on 3-D Shapes

SPIRITUAL REFRAMING

Consider toast and bread, water and ice, love and hate. It doesn't take much effort to see how toast and bread are the same thing in different forms. The same is true, if a little less obvious, for water and ice. However, hate and love *seem* to be anything but the same thing. Many of us think of them as direct opposites, but really love and hate both involve a kind of emotional energy called passion, the opposite of which is apathy. In this sense, love/hate represents "caring greatly about" someone or thing whereas apathy means "not caring about."

Interestingly, scientists have recently discovered that hate and love share identical neurological structures and stimulate the same regions of the brain, specifically the putamen (which generates aggressive behavior) and the insula (which responds to distressing stimuli).[3] The study, led by Semir Zeki of the Wellcome Laboratory of Neurobiology (University College London), also showed that both hate and love sometimes deactivate portions of the brain that generate critical and judgmental responses, but the emotion of hatred does this to a much larger degree than the emotion of love. Said Zeki, "In romantic love, the lover is often less critical and judgmental regarding the loved person, [whereas] in the context of hate the hater may want to exercise judgment in calculating moves to harm, injure, or otherwise exact revenge."[4] The point, again, is that love and hate may be the same things which simply look different.

---

3. Zeki and Romaya, "Neural Correlates."

4. Zeki and Romaya, "Neural Correlates." Several other articles cite this quote. See Connor, "Scientists Prove."

However, the "looking different" part is significant and provides a kind of frame which may, in certain situations, be a significant feature in causing or not causing harm. To my mystic eye, that person who uses the love-frame rather than the hate-frame has mastered a major spiritual insight and has learned to use a powerful tool for conflict resolution.

REFRAMING IN CONFLICT RESOLUTION

Over the years, I've become increasingly interested in reducing/resolving/reshaping conflict, a subject which every human, every family, every business, every cultural group, and every nation inevitably encounters. This interest has impacted my ministry, too, where I discovered I was often effective at helping others grow through conflict.[5] After I formally retired from ministry, I suddenly found myself feeling just a little *too* retired, and so I undertook additional training in mediation and now am an active state Office of Dispute Resolution parenting plan mediator associated with our regional mediation center in Nebraska. I have sometimes been fortunate enough to do some good work in this capacity, and I have *always* gained insight and personal growth through this work.

At the very heart of the mediation process is a communication technique known as reframing. Reframing involves softening language, and mediators and mental health practitioners routinely use it to reduce or redirect the effect of a blaming or critical statement, to shift the conversation from negative to positive, to move from a focus on the past to the future, to clarify needs and concerns, to identify unresolved issues, to emphasize common ground, and to acknowledge emotions. The whole idea of reframing language to promote cooperation and healing is consistent with the new attention which psychologists and scientists attach to *social* engineering. Dan Levine, writing on the need to heal the reason-emotion split, notes, for instance, that most of us carry within ourselves the potential for either constructive or destructive attitudes. "We need to structure society to increase the incentives for constructive attitudes, incentives that are sometimes called *nudges*."[6] Reframing can nudge.

Although it has a specialized function, reframing is also a tool anyone can learn to use. In my opinion we should pass a national law making

---

5. I haven't always been as successful in my own personal life, however. I am still working on that!

6. Levine, *Healing*, 3.

it mandatory that our elected political officials demonstrate familiarity with the mediation process before assuming public office. I also believe that society would be immensely benefited if prisoners learned mediation techniques as a condition of release and if we routinely taught our children the process in our schools.

Many mediation training programs offer a form of coaching in which those who are learning to mediate can build skills by role-playing conflict scenarios and getting feedback from experienced mediators about the approaches they used. Below is my illustration of how this process of reframing can work. I've used this interactive skit with several church audiences in conjunction with a service about the gifts of resolution.

BACKGROUND FOR MEDIATION SKIT

In this role-play we find an imaginary (but not atypical) conversation between a mediator, Jo, an engineer, Kim, and an aspiring college student, Sandy. Earlier, Sandy had posted online a mathematical demonstration about Snell's Law of Refraction, a well-known math formula which deals with the refraction of light.[7] In his posting, Sandy tried to disprove this formula. The engineer, Kim, responded with a biting commentary he'd published in a well-known math journal. Sandy subsequently sued Kim in small claims court for defamation. As the skit opens, the two have agreed to try to resolve the case through mediation, a much less costly procedure.

As mediation role-plays go, this one is unusual in that it relies on mathematics in two subtle ways. First, the reframing in the skit reflects the metaphor drawn from mathematics which I introduced earlier in this chapter, viz., $1 = .999\ldots$. The symbol "1" connotes a sense of finality and authority that comes from absolute unity, but the form ".999 . . ." (although equivalent in meaning) implies a flexibility and openness that "1" lacks. This is the same sense in which we use the delicate craft of reframing in mediation to re-language the conversation so that all parties can better hear the issues being presented. Just as many mediation clients don't initially understand the usefulness of reframing their language, many math novices resist the proven relationship that $1 = .999\ldots$. Several individuals have even posted dis-proofs of the equation on YouTube:

---

7. See chapter 19.

the posting of and response to one such challenge inspired the reframing skit.

Another mathematical subtlety in the skit appears in the actual language of the role-play. Specifically, I compiled almost all of Kim's conversation from real comments made online in response to the actual YouTube video (noted above) which purports to disprove the mathematical notion that $0.999\ldots = 1$. This subject may seem to be a topic that would not draw much serious interest, but in fact this video was uploaded on September 9, 2012, and within a year and a half it had received more than 33,300 views and over 4,000 comments (though it has been replaced since then and no longer seems to be online), most of which point out errors in the argument, and many of which also denigrate the maker of the video.

A number of these caustic comments show up as part of Kim's voice in the skit. Even more were not included in the skit:

> "Someone please shoot this guy!"
> "Blasphemy."
> "You're dumb."
> "How many times do you think this person was dropped as a child?"

To be honest, even I was shocked at the intensity of the responses over something so objective as a mathematical fact. It makes me worry in general about our future as a society and in particular about how our use of various new online technologies is going to contribute to that society. What is it about humans that allows us to so quickly escalate such a supposedly benign conversation to war-like verbiage!

Nonetheless, using math as the presenting issue for a mediation has an advantage because it is rational and rarely found in such simulations; thus it helps us step outside the normal box and see the situation from a different perspective. When I share this skit, I always ask the audience to pay particular attention to the intentional softening of the harshness of the clients' conversations. This effort de-escalates what easily could have developed into ever-more-loaded name-calling and a probable impasse in the mediation. At the same time, the mediator also reframes the language in a way that acknowledges each party's "truth." Thus, the atmosphere changes to one more open to resolution. Mediation is not about compromise; it is about finding an agreement that works for all the clients. Reframing is a tool which supports this effort.

This role-play is similar to ones I've actually mediated, although I did need to stretch my boundaries to encompass a small-claim issue where the presenting issue is a mathematical proof. When initially presented with the mathematics, many individuals resist the seemingly paradoxical ideas embodied in the concept that $0.999\ldots = 1$. Similarly, reframing our conflicts requires both cognitive and emotional energy to grasp and accept the seeming paradox implied. Such work and understanding, however, can empower our spiritual selves to choose the path of less harm and greater good.

A MEDIATION SKIT: THE INVALID MATH PROOF[8]

Mediator (*after introducing the process and setting a few ground rules*): So I'd like to ask each of you to give a brief statement about what brings you to this mediation table and what you hope to have come out of it. Sandy, let's start with you.

Sandy: He has publicly defamed me, and now I have no chance whatsoever for a scholarship because of the article he published in the *Journal of Mathematical News*. Plus he plastered nasty things about me all over Facebook. That's harassment. He has ruined my scholarly reputation and cost me my future. I want restitution. At least six thousand dollars, which is what the scholarship would have been.

Mediator: Thank you, Sandy. We'll explore your goals further, but first I'd like to hear from Kim. Kim, very briefly, what brings you here today, and what do you hope to have come out of this mediation?

Kim: I was just saying the truth. Bringing me to court over this? That's way out of line. I want the case dismissed. Pay him six thousand dollars just for my telling the truth? You've got to be kidding.

Mediator: Thank you, Kim. Let's see if I can sum up what you both have just said. Sandy, you want restitution for things that Kim wrote

---

8. While this skit is fictitious, the derogatory comments actually appeared online in comments associated with another mathematical claim.

THE ART OF REFRAMING 209

about you. (*Sandy nods "yes."*) And Kim, you feel you were just telling the truth and you hope Sandy will drop the case. (*Kim starts to nod yes, and to say something, but Sandy interrupts loudly.*)

Sandy: No way. I'm *not* letting him get away with this. *He's* the dumb-ass if he thinks I'm going to be kicked aside that easily.

Mediator: Sounds as though you've some pretty strong feelings about this. Can you tell me a little more about what happened?

Sandy: Well, how would you feel if someone put on Facebook that you were a dumb ass?

Kim: Ah, come on. He was making a fool out of himself with his YouTube demonstration about Snell's Law, and he didn't even notice it! His proof was reducto ad estupido. I mean, the dislike button isn't enough. There should be a retarded button. I admit I might have gone a little overboard, but I was raging so much at his idea that "trigonometry doesn't see it that way" and "there's no angle that's refracted." That's just completely wrong. I hate these armchair mathematicians who think they can disprove maths. These people belong with creationists. He deserved to be called dumb ass.

Mediator: You do sound upset. Can you help me more fully understand why? This is what I am hearing, that you feel Sandy put an incorrect mathematical proof online and that it really pushed your emotional buttons. Do I have it right so far?

Kim: Yeah, basically.

Mediator: Well, I'm not sure I know enough about the math to make any judgments here. Help me understand a bit why this was so distressing to you.

Kim: I love mathematics. I'm an electrical engineer and I use math all the time in my work. Right now, I'm working on a fantastic new lighting system that will be an amazing asset to advertisers, stage designers, really anyone putting on any sort of show that can be enhanced with special lighting effects. It's the stuff of the future. We need kids coming up to understand the mathematics that makes this work. So, when I see garbage like Sandy here was disseminating to the public, it really makes me see red. I think it will turn people away from this work.

Mediator: So are you saying that you use this mathematics in your work and you are disturbed when someone spreads information that might deter people from becoming involved with it?

Kim: Yeah, that's pretty much right.

Mediator: Is there more you want to say about this?

Kim: Well, just that it was really, really poor stuff he put out. OMG, he did a formal proof that he is retarded!!! It was *amazing*!

Mediator: So it wasn't just that you fear young people might be put off by what he was demonstrating, but it sounds as though you were genuinely upset because Sandy wasn't painting mathematics with a clean brush.

Kim: Yes. I guess I hadn't thought of it that way, but now it does seem like he was kind of denigrating mathematics. Spreading a lot of misinformation, too.

Mediator: Sandy, thanks for listening to Kim's comments. That can't have been very comfortable for you. Still, it does seem that he was pretty worried about what effect your video might have on aspiring mathematicians and engineers. What would you like him to know about how you saw it?

Sandy: Geesh. He was all over me telling me how crazy I was. He wrote something about how I must have been on crack. Said the bug was in my brain, not in math, so everything I see will have a bug. It was humiliating.

Mediator: Respect is important to you, isn't it?

Sandy (*nodding vigorously*): Yes. You know, I'm not great at math, but I'm *not* stupid, in spite of what he said.

Kim (*addressing Sandy*): Your presentation was really boneheaded. I feel bad for you presenting this garbage in public.

Mediator (*addressing Kim*): Are you saying, Kim, that Sandy's presentation was naive? (*Kim shrugs a sort of "yes."*) And that you were concerned that he was putting his naivety all over the video screen?

Kim: Yeah, you know, the video really was actually pretty good for an amateur. One of the better ones I've seen. (He turns to look at Sandy.) That thing you did with the light on the board, that was rather clever. I just don't think you heard how stupid you sounded with the math.

Sandy: Ouch. There's that stupid, again. But at least there was a "clever" in there about the video. Thanks, for that at least. (*This last said bitterly.*)

Mediator: I hear discouragement in your voice, Sandy. Am I hearing this correctly? And if so, would you be willing to say a little more about what that's all about?

Sandy: You bet I'm discouraged. I mean, I deserve some respect, here. I'm pretty inventive and I like tinkering around with math, too. I found Snell's Theorem online when I was trying to figure out that lighting effect. I was really excited when I thought I'd come up with the proof that refutes Snell's theorem. I was proud of myself. And then, all I get is this ship-load of name-calling, spread out for everyone to see it. I mean, that really stung.

Kim (*looking a little abashed*): Well, Sandy, I can see how that might have hurt. Honestly, I've been around too many arrogant young people who just want glamor and don't want to do the work to earn it. I probably over-reacted. I'm sorry for that. But, truly, you are making a lot of errors here. Far too many. Your work isn't mathematically sound and often works as a misuse of trigonometry. But it's good enough that if you pass it on, some gullible and uneducated people will be taken in by it, and that just spreads misinformation. It would help for you to have a stronger foundation of algebra and to have a working knowledge of calculus, too. I assure you that Snell's Law is correct. I highly recommend that you speak to a mathematician in your area.

Sandy: Fat chance of that now. I'll never get a scholarship now. And I can't stay in college without one.

Mediator: This is helpful information. Kim has offered an apology. I want to make sure that you heard that, Sandy, and I'd like to know if that changes things for you at all.

Sandy: Yes, it does, actually. I just felt like I had to defend myself. No one else was, that's for sure.

Kim (*looking at the mediator*): I've had more tunnel vision than maybe I should have had. In a way, it's people like him who make way for awesome ideas and thoughts. People who question can get a lot more things done than people who just accept a certain way of thinking. Is he correct? No. But it's not that he's wrong that's the prize, but the fact that his questioning of this proof serves to further prove it right. We don't get answers trying to conform to the situation or prove something right. We get our answers from attempting to prove things wrong, and when we fail to prove something wrong then we can consider it true. So never stop questioning. (*This last statement is addressed directly to Sandy.*)

Mediator: It seems to me that we have made a lot of progress here. Thank you both for your good work and your willingness to be open. We still have further work to do, though. I suggest we take a short break and then come back and see if we can put together some kind of an agreement that works for both of you. Let's resume in ten minutes.

Chapter 22: Fuzzy Logic in the Health Care Setting[1]

MORAL MATH FOR VALUE-LADEN CHOICES

As a contract chaplain with the pastoral services department at a local hospital, I am often involved with life and death issues that require multi-faceted choices and which sometimes result in ambiguous levels of satisfaction with those choices. For instance, I sometimes visit with patients about using artificial support (e.g., breathing tubes, mechanical respiration, and forced feeding). Most patients elect to forego some or all such support when and if they have lapsed into a persistent vegetative state that is deemed by medical professionals to be terminal in a relatively short duration. The medical staff usually encourage this choice if there is little likelihood that the patient will ever resume a fully aware and high-quality life. Those "if's" are significant qualifiers even in normal situations, but they can become full-fledged stumbling blocks during times of natural disaster, war, epidemic disease, or calamity. Under such extreme conditions, hospital resources may be drastically limited or may even disappear altogether, and decisions about ethical allocation of reduced resources (who gets what treatments?) can essentially turn hospital staff into death squads.

In *Five Days at Memorial*,[2] a 2013 eye-opening book about one hospital's struggles in New Orleans following the 2005 hurricane Katrina,

---

1. Voss, "Fuzzy Logic." I gave a sermon on the topic "How Fuzzy Logic Might Save Souls" on February 15, 2004.
2. Fink, *Five Days*.

journalist Sheri Fink gives a Pulitzer Prize–winning account of the ethical dilemmas which can arise in such life-and-death situations. In the epilogue to her book, Fink notes that failures to adequately plan for triage needs have continued to occur in many other places since Katrina.[3] "Emergencies," she writes, "are crucibles that contain and reveal the daily, slower-burning problems of medicine and beyond—our vulnerabilities: our trouble grappling with uncertainty, how we die, how we prioritize and divide what is most precious and vital and limited; even our biases and blindnesses."[4]

These human vulnerabilities can be challenging. Fink's delicate and sensitive handling of them in her journalism is an attempt to speak of the horse on the dining room table that nobody wants to mention. Since Katrina, federal agencies have begun insisting (as a requirement for certain funding) that state and local health departments in the US develop new triage protocols to address some of these issues, but at best this can be a slow process. These are value-laden considerations. A few of the efforts to address them have included public input, but most have not, even though, as Fink puts it in regard to one program for public engagement, "regular citizens showed they were able to gather, engage, discuss these issues, and learn from one another. They easily grasped ethical concepts that some health officials had assumed were the province of experts only."[5]

This is the point where my own interests and work come into play. Throughout my active ministry, I cultivated a two-fold position which prompts this article:

1. the general public deserves to be informed about and have a voice in the making of important ethical decisions, such as those in the rapidly changing area of health care, and

2. the process of decision making about social and moral issues can often be positively enhanced by concepts which are rooted in mathematics.

To this end, I've developed and led a series of workshops on moral math designed to make mathematical ideas accessible to the lay individual and

---

3. Triage comes from a French term *trier*, meaning to choose, split, or classify. It was first used in the Napoleonic wars and persisted as a way to classify patients in terms of urgency.

4. Fink, *Five Days*, 464.

5. Fink, *Five Days*, 479.

to demonstrate how math can help promote positive social behavior.[6] Fuzzy logic is one such mathematical area; it has, for example, potential as a significant tool in the triage situation mentioned above. To grasp this potential fully, we need at least some understanding of how fuzzy logic works.

WHAT IS FUZZY LOGIC?

The first thing to understand is that some of the ideas stated in this essay are partially true and partially false.

Let me elaborate. Western science—our science—grew up under the strong influence of Aristotle, that ancient Greek philosopher who insisted that truth is a yes or no creature. In the Aristotelian view, a proposition is either true, or it's not-true. A color is red, or else it's not-red. Water boils at 212 degrees Fahrenheit, or it doesn't boil at 212 degrees Fahrenheit. A light is switched on, or it's off. You love mathematics, or you don't love mathematics. In such classical thinking there are no grays, no in-betweens, no partial truths, no middle-ground. For most of its existence, Western science has championed this law of the excluded middle.

Here in the West we tend to believe that when we think rationally or reasonably, we are thinking *logically*, by which we consciously or unconsciously mean we are thinking with crisp Aristotelian logic. In reality, however, about 99.9 percent of everyday human reasoning is not Aristotelian. Most of us think most of the time that most things are partially true and partially false. Our thinking, in effect, is *fuzzy*.

Fuzzy thinking can be fun thinking—like the little boy who was trying to memorize the Ten Commandments. When he got to "Thou shalt not commit adultery," his mother asked him what he thought the commandment meant. The child thought a moment, then replied, "It means you shouldn't want to be an adult."

Traditional logic says there is a right answer and a wrong answer to the mother's question about the commandment, but the little boy picked a middle answer, something that was sort of true. Fuzzy logic pays attention to that excluded middle.

Fuzzy logic can be traced back to 1965 when Iranian-born Lofti Zadeh, then a Berkeley professor of electrical engineering, wrote a

---

6. Voss, "Workshop," 114–28.

landmark paper titled "Fuzzy Sets."[7] Humans, of course, used fuzzy reasoning before 1965, but after Zadeh's paper appeared, this very human thought process acquired a new name and an entirely new mathematical framework.

There is nothing fuzzy or vague or uncertain, however, about the mathematical framework of fuzzy logic. The math of fuzzy logic is as explicit as "Two plus two equals four."[8] It's about as interesting, too. Which necessarily means it's also boring to some degree. Mathaphobes think fuzzy logic is boring to degree 1 and interesting to degree 0. Fuzzy logicians think fuzzy logic is boring to degree 0 and interesting to degree 1. For most of the rest of us it's probably moderately interesting, say, maybe "halfway" interesting, or interesting to degree .5. In fuzzy logic things are assumed to be true *to some degree*, and simultaneously *false to some degree*, where, by mutual agreement, a numerical value between (or including) 0 and 1 is arbitrarily assigned to represent that degree. Because the number selected is purely subjective, the choice sometimes leads to dissension. Generally, however, we can do a surprisingly good job of quantifying vagueness. We can even quantify the fuzziness of purely linguistic notions such as "surprisingly" or "somewhat" or "quite."

A while ago, I asked Joe Doe, my favorite mathaphobe, if he'd help me out with the research for this essay. Joe promptly replied, "Yes." I asked Joe, whom I perceive as somewhat old and quite tall, the following five questions:

1. What age are you?
2. At what age do you consider a person "old"?
3. What height are you?
4. At what height do you consider a man "tall"?
5. On a scale of zero to ten, how handsome are you?

Joe Doe, it turns out, is seventy-nine years old and five foot nine and a half inches tall. That was very helpful. Just what I wanted. In fact, Joe, it also turns out, considers "old" a mind thing, which means he thinks "a person is old when they quit doing things that they want to do." Joe has seen people who are old at fifty and also who are over ninety and still not old. By his own reasoning, Joe is not old, because he can still do things he

---

7. Zadeh, "Fuzzy Sets."
8. Kosko, *Fuzzy Future*, 15.

wants to. "It's just harder," he says. Furthermore, Joe thinks "you are tall if you are over nine and a half inches."

These answers were not at all what I wanted, and I was just about to say Joe Doe was a lost cause when I had an alternative idea. I asked my scientific, biochemist husband Dan how old a person has to be to be "old" and how tall a person has to be to be "tall." Being embedded in Western science, Dan immediately gave me what I wanted. Dan considers a person "old" at age one hundred and "tall" at six feet.

Now, using Joe Doe's factual data and Dan's definitions of old and tall, I pulled out my trusty hand calculator and figured out that Joe is old to degree 79, that is, he is 79 percent old. He is also 85 percent tall, or tall to degree 85. So, you see, with Dan's assistance, we assigned numerical values that are surprisingly consistent with the perception that Joe is somewhat old and quite tall.

It is easy to misinterpret fuzzy thinking as probabilistic thinking because, after all, we are trying to numerically interpret the level of certainty to which, say, Joe is old. However, probabilistic thinking maintains the law of the excluded middle and hence belongs to classical logic, not fuzzy logic. When we say Joe has a 79 percent chance of being old, we are talking about the *probability* that Joe is old, which still means either Joe is old or he isn't. No middle ground here. Just a better chance that he is old than that he isn't. Black and white. But when we are thinking according to fuzzy logic we say that Joe is *partially old*, or, more precisely, that Joe's membership within the set of "old" people is .79. The mathematical rules for operations on fuzzy quantities are different from the rules for operations on probabilities, so while the numerical relationships between probabilistic and fuzzy thinking bear a superficial resemblance to each other, they are still two very different species of math.

Oh, but we're forgetting about Joe Doe's handsomeness. Remember my fifth question to Joe: "On a scale of zero to ten, how handsome are you?" I even gave him guidelines for interpreting the endpoints. *Zero*, I said, means "flat out horrid ugly" and *ten* means "absolute gorgeous hunk of a guy." Now Dan and I immediately agreed that Joe is handsome to degree .98, that is, Joe is very handsome. Thus, fuzzy logic yields the following conclusions: Joe is somewhat old, quite tall, very handsome, and decidedly modest. The modest part is a natural language interpretation of Joe's disinclination to assign himself any value whatsoever on the handsome scale, which is to say that first he totally ignored my question and, when pushed, he assigned himself only "seven."

About now you might be wondering if fuzzy logic is good for anything other than describing Joe Doe as somewhat old, quite tall, very handsome, and decidedly modest. The answer is yes.

The first commercial application of fuzzy logic was the development in 1980 of an improved cement kiln, one which effectively managed the highly complex set of chemical interactions involved in the cement-making process. This improved process, fuzzy though it was, efficiently monitored four different internal states of the kiln and managed four dozen or so rules of thumb about their relationships. To instruct the kiln what to do, the fuzzy system used rules such as "If the oxygen percentage is high and the temperature is *high* then *slightly reduce* the coal feed rate" (emphasis added).[9] "High" and "slightly reduce," of course, were translated into numbers between 0 and 1.

Other early applications of fuzzy logic in engineering include fuzzy control of the extraordinarily smooth Tokyo subway, baggage handling at Denver International Airport, and a meteorological system in China for identifying the best places to plant rubber tree orchards. We find fuzzy thinking in the production of automated cars, traffic light controllers, robot graspers, TV tuners, graphics, automated police sketchers, washing machines (which automatically adjust for size and amount of dirt), self-focusing cameras (which consider multiple targets), "smart" ovens (which provide more uniform cooking), smart weapons (which provide more accurate hits), the thermostat on your air conditioner and the water setting on your shower (which keeps the temperature just right).[10]

Fuzzy thinking is also effective in all sorts of decision-support systems, including financial planning, diagnostic systems for determining soybean pathology, and biomedical applications to diagnose breast cancer, rheumatoid arthritis, post-menopausal osteoporosis, and heart disease. In hospitals, fuzzy logic helps monitor anesthesia, blood pressure, insulin for diabetes, and post-operative pain control. In medical situations there have been new fuzzy protocols developed for such things as reducing overall harm during rescue efforts for natural disasters, for monitoring unattended patients in over-crowded emergency rooms and disaster sites, for automated remote triage on military battlefields, and for assigning triage levels of urgency in a hospital setting. There are also fuzzy applications in geography, ecology, nuclear science, the stock

---

9. See Brulé, "Fuzzy Systems"; and Kosko, *Fuzzy Future*.
10. See Bishop, *Shades*, 114–17.

market, handwriting analysis, and even the weather. Moreover, for the past couple of decades fuzzy logicians have been applying this new mathematical tool to human social behavior and issues of ethics.

INSIDE A FUZZY TEXTBOOK

The mathematical symbolism that fuzzy logicians sometimes use to express these subjective and often non-explicit concepts mirrors the syntax of classical Boolean (i.e., true or false) logic. For example, the definition of a fuzzy set A in a nonempty set X is characterized "by its membership function $\mu_A : X \to [0, 1]$ and $\mu_A(x)$ is interpreted as the degree of membership of element x in fuzzy set A for each $x \in X$."[11] The union of two *triangular fuzzy numbers A and B*, for instance, can be defined as

$$(A \cup B)(t) = \max A(t), B(t) - A(t) \wedge B(t) \text{ for all } t \in X^{12}.$$

However, such notation is commonly supplanted with or even completely replaced by much more intuitive graphics, such as the one shown in figure 22.1 which represents the fuzzy control system for the temperature of a room. This figure shows three overlapping trapezoidal fuzzy sets representing the fuzzy notions of cold, warm, and hot. The vertical line represents a "crisp" number which has simultaneous membership in two of the sets, such that it might be described as being fairly cold and slightly warm.

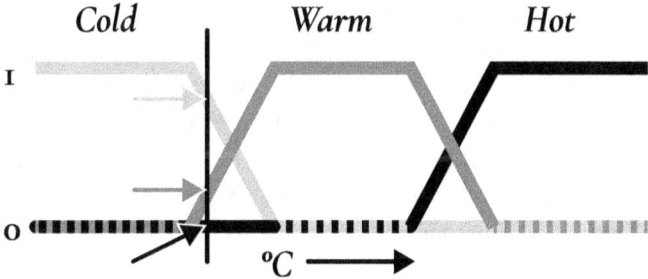

Fig. 22.1. An Example of a Fuzzy Logic Member Function

11. This definition and the notation in the next two sentences are typical of the way fuzzy math is conveyed. See Fuller, "Fuzzy Sets," 6, 15, 22.

12. Non-math readers don't need to worry if this language isn't clear or meaningful. I'm the sort that appreciates knowing what something looks like even if I don't fully understand it. For instance, I once saw the abstract for a paper I'd written which was printed in Russian, about which I know nothing. I didn't recognize *"Capa Bocc"* as my own name, but it was fun to see it anyway.

A variation on this iconic graph which is directly relevant to critical healthcare can be found in "Applying Fuzzy Logic to Medical Decision Making in the Intensive Care Unit," a 2003 article by H. T. Bates and Michael P. Young.[13] In this essay the authors walk the reader through a three-step process designed to aid physician decisions regarding the rate at which intravenous fluids should be given to a selected patient. There are multiple factors which physicians take into consideration in making such a decision, but for purposes of illustration, the authors describe a process which is limited to only two variables, viz., the mean arterial blood pressure and the hourly urine output for the patient. Just as the temperature in the graph presented in figure 22.1 had regions denoted as cold, warm, or hot, the blood pressure and urine output measurements were classified low, normal, or high. The uncertainty regions (e.g., measurements which might or might not be normal) correspond to the overlap areas in the trapezoidal graphs.

In step 1, the possible blood pressure and urine output measurements were "fuzzified." That is, a graph similar to that in figure 22.1 (and/or its set-notation equivalent) was created such that the "overlap" regions had numerical boundaries corresponding to uncertainties about the degree of membership which a particular measurement might have in, say, the category of "normal." In step 2, a table was created to show what action should be taken for every possible combination of the two measurements. In this illustration, the designated action was giving the patient some appropriate level of intravenous fluid. In step 3, the controlled quantity, i.e., the intravenous fluid rate, was similarly fuzzified, in this instance by being divided into five overlapping fuzzy sets, such that the rate of intravenous fluid delivery could be considered low, maintained, moderate, high, or very high. Thus, precise measurements of the blood pressure and urine outputs could ultimately be linked to a precise change in the fluid rate, an outcome which, in principle, could be quickly determined by a computer and implemented completely automatically without human intervention.

For a more complete understanding of the math behind fuzzy logic, interested readers are referred to this article by Bates and Young.[14] One gentle caution: "more complete" is a fuzzy term.

---

13. Bates and Young, "Applying Fuzzy."
14. Bates and Young, "Applying Fuzzy."

FUZZY LOGIC USED AS MORAL MATH

Here are several examples of how fuzzy considerations might impact our ethical and moral choices. I adapted these illustrations from three books, all of which I partially liked and partially disliked. The books are *Shades of Reality*, by Bob Bishop, who from 1992 until his death in 2014 was the "Mr. Logic" of a popular California radio show called the "Thinking Machine"; *The Fuzzy Future*, by Bart Kosko, a professor of electrical engineering at the University of Southern California; and *The Science of Good and Evil*, by Michael Shermer, the publisher of *Skeptic* magazine and a teacher of critical thinking at Occidental College, also in California. Hmmm. Maybe fuzzy writers all live in California! I suppose that conclusion is a little like the guy who ordered a pizza and was asked if he preferred to have it cut into eight or twelve pieces. After a moment of fuzzy thought, the customer opted for the eight-piece-cut, saying he didn't believe he was hungry enough just then to eat twelve pieces. (Yes, that joke was in one of those three books, too.)[15]

My first example of fuzzy morality—oops, make that fuzzy thinking applied to moral choices—is a consideration of the unfairness of our current tax laws. Most of us feel pretty powerless when it comes to our taxes, and quite rightly so, because, even though we theoretically live in a country where we can democratically decide how our tax dollars are spent, few of us believe we actually enjoy such choice. The truth is, as Kosko put it, "The state spends our tax money on what it wants and does not directly ask us to help it choose."[16] Such a process, as the founders of our nation well knew, can lead to a kind of political elitism which oppresses the ordinary individual.

Kosko's suggestion is to use a fuzzy tax form. Such a form would allow ordinary people to select on their IRS forms just what they would like to have their tax dollars spent on. Since there is a certain amount of common need which governments can predict, a portion of the tax money might be set aside for general revenues—perhaps half of our tax dollars, or a third or four-fifths or whatever. (Here's where the dissension comes in.) The remaining amount goes to social categories which you help choose even as you send in your portion of the total tax money. In his book, Kosko provides a sample fuzzy tax form which would clearly help those who pay have a more direct say. "I want_____% of my tax

---

15. Shermer, *Science of Good*, 160.
16. Kosko, *Fuzzy Future*, 49.

dollars to go for _____." Fill in the blank, as in "I want 5 percent of my tax dollars to go for preventative healthcare subsidies."

Just as tax allocation may benefit from fuzzy technology, crime and punishment might become fairer through fuzzy decision making. All of us know of incidents where the rich don't get the same punishments as the poor do, mostly because our judicial system fails to demand across-the-board equal treatment for identical crimes. This class issue can be addressed by carefully matching the severity of the consequences to the seriousness of the crime, i.e., by using fuzzy logic.

Assume, for example, that intoxicated is legally defined as having a blood alcohol content of at least 0.08. As the law currently stands, a driver involved in a car accident can receive a full prison sentence if he has a blood alcohol count of, say, 0.081, while a second person gets virtually no punishment at all if his count is 0.079. Fuzzy theory could smooth out such inequities by offering a sliding scale which matches the degree of drunkenness to the degree of punishment. Two similarly intoxicated drivers would then experience similarly "realistic" law regardless of social, economic, or any other status.[17]

A third example of how fuzzy thinking can assist our moral choices can be found in consideration of the abortion issue. Most of us will find that we are probably already using some version of fuzzy thinking when it comes to issues of life and death. It is helpful here to remember that the line between life and death is fuzzy, not crisp. Avid right-to-lifers[18] are consciously or otherwise using classic Aristotelian reasoning which sees the fetus as passing from 0 percent alive to 100 percent alive in one big jump—no middle ground.

An argument can be made that pro-choicers do the same thing, that they just draw the line between life and no-life at a spot more in that excluded middle ground. In the United States, the legal line according to Roe v. Wade is viability, that is, when a fetus is deemed viable outside the womb (generally in the range of twenty-four to twenty-six weeks).[19] Individual states have different interpretations of course, and to get an abortion beyond the twelfth week is often more complicated. In India,

---

17. See Bishop, *Shades*, 156–58.

18. The abortion issue is controversial even in the labels opposing camps use for themselves and one another. Here I chose to use terms that each camp chooses to use for itself.

19. With changes in legislation made in 2023—after this chapter was written—this fact may no longer be correct.

the line is at twenty weeks. In China, where in the 1990s almost half of all pregnancies ended in abortion, the state forced some abortions as late as the sixth month of pregnancy in order to meet its one-child-per-couple population goal. Regardless of where the line is drawn, fuzzy logic urges us to think proportionally. That is, one factor we could consider in assigning human rights to an unborn fetus is *the degree to which* the fetus is alive. Partial rights for partial life.

In some ways, in our country we currently give full rights for partial life. Once, at the hospital, I was called to be with a young man whose wife was giving birth prematurely. At twenty-four weeks, the baby was born alive but very sick. I watched as this young man, who spoke almost no English, struggled with assorted feelings. Clearly, he wanted this child to be okay, to "make it." When he saw his little girl, he wept with joy that she was alive. But I also saw the grandfather, whose presence was testimony to his support for his son at this difficult time. Again, we shared no common language, but it didn't require a common language for me to see his conflict. Grandpa took one look at his tiny, tiny granddaughter, and shook his head with painful sadness. "Too soon," he said, and even though it wasn't in a language I knew, I understood what he was saying, how he was weighing all the issues ahead for this family trying to raise a child with so many strikes against her.

Were the doctors right to give this partially developed infant full rights to life, that is, to offer every assistance possible, even though it will cost hundreds of thousands of dollars and great hardship, and even then would likely leave a child who was severely handicapped? In general, I believe our protocols take into account the "fuzziness" of life. Yet, even with that confidence in our system, I still have some internal doubt. The only thing about which I had no vagueness in dealing with this family was the prayer I offered, which was as wholehearted as I could make it.

MORAL SUBTLETIES

Like all tools, of course, fuzzy logic is just that—a tool. This tool takes two basic forms: fuzzy technology and fuzzy decisions. It can serve society well or poorly, or, in keeping with fuzzy thinking, to some degree therein. Consider, again, for example, the notion of matching degree of drunkenness to the period of time spent in jail. One problem with this approach is the severity of the crime. One day in jail involves some of the same heavyweight penalties that one year in jail does. In principle, the idea of matching partial guilt with partial punishment seems fair, but fairness does not always ensure justness. Awareness of such moral complexity has led to caution in using decision-based fuzzy logic tools: most are now suggested as decision-making *support* aids. The ultimate moral decision still rests in the collective human mind.

One thing is clear, however. Fuzzy logic adds a new and potentially powerful tool to our toolbox for making moral decisions. Michael Shermer offered an interesting take on this issue when he set forth what he called a theory of *provisional* morality. Provisional morality is not the same as absolute morality, which is what we find in fundamentalist thinking. Holding the Ten Commandments as absolute standards of right and wrong is an example of fundamentalist moral thinking. Provisional morality allows for exceptions. At the same time, provisional morality is not the same as relativistic morality. When I think of relativistic moral thinking, I think of the *Non Sequitur* cartoon by Wiley Miller in which Moses has been reading to his flock from the famous stone tablet. "I don't care what your lawyer said," Moses tells his flock. "They're not called the ten recommendations." Provisional ethics is not the same as relativistic ethics, either. The comparison is more like the bumper sticker "Give me ambiguity or give me something else." As Shermer puts it, scientific facts "are conclusions confirmed to such an extent that it would be reasonable to offer our provisional agreement." Similarly, in professional ethics, "moral *or immoral means confirmed to such an extent it would be reasonable to offer provisional assent.*"[20]

This secular approach to morality is bound to certain principles. Shermer identifies four such principles: "The Ask First Principle," "The Happiness Principle," "The Liberty Principle," and "The Moderation Principle." These four principles of moral behavior translate roughly to a variation of the Golden Rule, an assumption that it is moral to seek happiness with someone else's happiness in mind and never to seek happiness when it leads to someone else's unhappiness, to seek liberty with someone else's liberty in mind and never to seek liberty when it leads to someone else's loss of liberty, and to generally seek moderation over extremism. Using these principles for making ethical decisions is a secular way of being moral . . . to a degree.

---

20. Shermer, *Science of Good*, 167.

FUZZY FUTURE

Fuzzy life issues are becoming more and more complex as new technologies arise. This happens at both ends of the life spectrum, with questions about prolonging life for the aged counterbalancing questions about who owns the rights to genome space. Fairness and justness are concerns inevitably raised in making such decisions. Who gets access to the best of modern medical techniques? Often it boils down to a matter of who has the money to buy them. The poor are usually the losers. The good news is that fuzzy scientists can facilitate non-fuzzy change in matters of equality.

Back in 1999, for instance, Kosko predicted that fuzzy logic would bring about "your own medical software agent." Such an agent, he envisioned, could track your physical condition daily by reading into your personal computer your daily biorhythms and bio-variables, which you would determine through inexpensive personal sensors such as blood and urine tests done at home with the assistance of computer chips. Since your medical agent would really be a set of software programs, it would search and learn, diagnose your problems, and recommend treatment at the best rates and from all available sources, including international ones. The agent would complement traditional medicine, not replace it. Notably, Kosko saw possibilities for increased fairness in the procedure:

> The poor may benefit most as both supply of and demand for cheap smart medical agents swell and help shape health care in the digital age. The poor will be able to afford the personalized and high-quality health care that now only the better-off can afford.... Agents will be the great equalizers of the digital age.[21]

Variations on this idea have since been developed by using fuzzy protocols. The Personal Information Carrier (PIC), for example, is one new project which provides an electronic dog tag that allows "every soldier to carry their entire medical history around his neck."[22] The device is part of an automated triage and emergency management information system that aims to shrink the death rate of soldiers who are killed in action by remotely extending the reach of the medic. The prototype system—which offers a framework for information analysis, information

---

21. Shermer, *Science of Good*, 222.
22. McGrath et al., "ARTEMIS," 7.

movement, and decision support capabilities—may also be used to monitor first responders and casualties in the civilian domain.[23]

With access to the Internet, you can readily find other health care developments based on fuzzy logic. One project in Australia, offering prototype mobile decision-support for hospital triage, uses linguistic terms such as *immediately* or *imminently life-threatening, potentially life-threatening,* or *life-serious* as well as physiological attributes including *mild* or *moderate, pink* or *pale* to help guide a clinician's decisions when a patient presents as an ambiguous triage case.[24] Another uses fuzzy logic and decision trees to make classification of a patient's urgency level in the shortest possible time with minimum error.[25] Yet another provides a "smart" wireless system for monitoring vital signs and locations of ambulatory but unattended patients with the goal of providing improved services at both hospital emergency departments and disaster sites.[26] This is just a sampling.

Many of these new fuzzy protocols deal with smart technologies which do, in fact, contribute to smart (or at least smarter) decisions. Nonetheless, decision-support opportunities in value-laden ethical situations are still in their infancy. Hospitals, as Fink noted, are only beginning to address highly value-sensitive issues such as who is euthanized when medical provisions and care are scarce or nonexistent. All too often, even these attempts do not include the voice of the general public. Fuzzy logic offers a simple way in which that public voice may be included.

For example, hospitals could seek out value-related choices along with the other information which patients (and/or their families) are routinely asked to provide when they are admitted. In the hospital where I work, the pastoral services department has recently implemented a system whereby each admitted patient selects how important a visit with a chaplain is to him/her by checking *very important, somewhat important,* or *not very important*. Chaplain time is limited—we are in demand. Each morning chaplains receive a printed list of patients' responses to these three simple choices, and we use them to help prioritize whom we visit and when we visit them. This is so simple that it doesn't even seem fuzzy, but at its root, it's a logic which can benefit us all, and it is effective.

---

23. McGrath et al., "ARTEMIS," 1.
24. San Pedro et al., "On Development."
25. Mondragon et al., "Patient Classification."
26. Curtis et al., "SMART."

We are only a short fuzzy way from getting public input on more explicitly moral concerns, such as:

> "If medical supplies and services are scarce in an emergency, who should receive them? Prioritize 1–6, where 1 means "gets the highest priority" and 6 means "lowest priority":
>
> _____First to arrive
> _____Sickest
> _____Youngest
> _____Oldest
> _____Those who have DNR (do not resuscitate) orders
> _____Other............(Please specify)

During non-crisis times, hospitals could offer patients and visitors an opportunity to fill out such a survey. If pastoral services had a role in this process, such a tool might even be useful as a doorway to discussing life and death issues that some people are reluctant to pass through, and, as every chaplain knows, such discussions in and of themselves are often spiritually healing. Furthermore, the results of such a survey might not only help hospital staff better prepare for difficult ethical choices in times of triage and other stressful situations, but they would likely have the additional benefit of receiving more implementation acceptance from the public. Even the hardest decisions are likely to have more total buy-in when people feel they've had a voice in making them.

CONCLUSION

The new frontier for making ethical decisions can be decidedly "fuzzy." Fuzzy scientists can do many smart things with fuzzy logic, and that includes providing decision-support for value-laden concerns. To the best of my current knowledge, "smart" moral protocols have been underused as tools in issues surrounding the moral complexities which can arise in various social situations. This is especially the case during hospital triage and other emergency situations. Moral math is part of the solution.

Part 5: Moral Math

"SIMPLE ARITHMETIC: HEAVY ON BUTTER, CREAM, WINE"[1]

Not long ago, the government
of the people for the people
needed 700 billion dollars to help
Freddie Mac and the Mae sisters.

Three hundred million people
lived in the United States then.

If each person put one dollar
into a central pot, the pot
would contain one third
of one billion dollars

not even a pinch of salt
in the bail-out soup.

To fill the pot, each person needed
to contribute $2000, a fantasy
since few have a spare $2000, plus
consider the cost to the 74 million

then under 18 who presumably needn't
think about such obligations, let alone

own them. More than 6.7 billion people
lived in the Mac and Mae global world.
If each person donated $100,
the global pot might have saved

the floundering Maes and Mac
with real rather than virtual money.

1. Voss, "Simple Arithmetic."

but 2.6 billion people lived on less
than $730 per year back then and
half the world's adults made less
than $2200, so at least

half the world's adults were poor sources
for a rescue pot. Still, there's good news!
The richest 1% own 40% of global
assets. High grade butter. Subtracting
the world's 2.2 billion children
from the world's 6.7 billion people

leaves about 4.5 billion adults
in the world, which is a lot.

Collectively, 1%, 45 million, own
40% of the world's coins. Cream.
Imagine that this thriving 1%
donates 40% of the needed dollars.

If the 9% with 45% of global riches
also donates 45% of the 700 billion

the pot would need just another
105 billion, and if the remaining 90%
of the world's adults split that $105
billion evenly, it's only a 2.5 cent

contribution per grown-up. Count me in!
Heck, I'll throw in a whole dollar

and pay for 39 more of the world's
citizens who won't, or can't, contribute
even two cents to a country
whose wealth and mismanagement

are both so blatant. Fine wine
down the drain.

Chapter 23: A Workshop to Introduce Concepts of Moral Math[1]

I AM A RETIRED Unitarian Universalist minister who loves mathematics; I used to teach it. When I gave up my position as the head of the math program at an undergraduate women's college to attend seminary, I took my interest in math with me. Subsequently I wrote about the relationship between math and religion for my doctoral thesis, work later published as *What Number Is God?* Then I began offering math sermons from the pulpit (being always careful not to scare away with the "m" word); I also penned a number of articles for various journals about matheology and related topics. Still later, I became interested in the relationship between math and social behavior, and out of this interest I developed a workshop designed to help individuals explore this connection.

Around the year 2010, I presented this moral math workshop four times in quite diverse settings. One of these was at a conference for women and faith held in San Francisco, and another at a class in public administration held at the University of Nebraska, Omaha (where I reside). Another time, I offered the workshop to a group of mediators affiliated with the Concord Mediation Center in Omaha, and yet another time it was a part of the adult religious education program at the church where I was filling in as pastoral care minister during a period of transition. Up to a dozen participants were present in each of the workshops, which was a relief because I always worry that I'll not have enough people present for the interactive part of the program to be effective. Each workshop drew participants who self-identified with varying levels of math expertise, from low to high, and an even greater relief was that each group

---

1. Voss, "Workshop."

developed an obvious enthusiasm for the subject, regardless of the math skill the participants claimed.

I admit to some bias about the value of this work on math and social behavior. Why is it important? My assumptions are three: that many math-related discoveries have been made in recent years which impact our collective understanding of social equity, justice, conflict resolution, and other issues demanding moral decision-making; that the potential effect of these discoveries is important to all people, not just to those who are mathematically proficient; that many of these ideas may be presented through the use of interactive exercises which demonstrate the math involved in such a way that most people can understand them without actually doing any mathematics.

These assumptions have led me to design a series of five sets of interactive exercises culled from game theory, theoretical complexity, fuzzy logic, basic algebra, and simple arithmetic. The exercises are fun and easy. Two of them I created myself, but the others I pulled straight out of math literature. After presenting each exercise, I relate them by analogy to selected examples of social issues. The expectation is that these ideas mined from math can encourage positive social behaviors. I have found that two-hour sessions, with one break, are just about right to lead the participants through this material in a meaningful way. "Meaningful way" means that the attendees gain an appreciation of how math can be used to stimulate new thinking about solutions to various social ills. People hold differing social and religious beliefs. The differences are important because they sometimes lead to conflict and sometimes to learning and regeneration. Everyone believes something, although not everyone always has full awareness of their beliefs. Sometimes two or more people believe pretty much the same things, such as that two plus two equals four or that there's a higher power that influences the universe. When people share beliefs, they automatically form bonds.

Individuals often believe differently, too, at least over time. When I was a child, I believed I was a child who lived with two parents and two siblings on a farm in Ohio. At some level I still hold that belief, but now it is supplemented by an additional understanding of life as an illusion. My beliefs about myself have changed as I've aged and also as I've experienced a mystic spiritual path.

I am a mystic, a former mathematics professor, a retired minister, an interests-based mediator, and a shaman. The "shaman" part is a new claim, and it only came about after I read Anne Fadiman's mind-opening book, *The Spirit Catches You and You Fall Down*, about cultural clashes between the Hmong immigrants and much of our US society. Toward the end of this book Fadiman quoted renowned anthropologist Dwight Conquergood, who pointed out that:

> Shamans are, first and last, quintessential mediators. They are threshold-crossers, endowed creatures who can go between the earth and the sky. Grand articulators, shamans' special gift and mission is to bring opposites together—to bring the physical and moral worlds into meaningful conjunction. That is why they are identified with archetypal connectors such as images of ladders, bridges, ropes, and cosmic trees that sink roots into the earth while branching towards the sky.[2]

For me, "shaman" has long connoted holy men and women, often with indigenous roots, who enter into trance-like states from which they perform healing rituals. As far as I know I've never entered into a trance-like state (other than the one commonly deemed "human"), but Conquergood's description nonetheless fit me like an old, comfortable glove. For all of my professional ministerial career, I've used mathematics to bridge and bring together two seeming opposites—science and spirit—in the hope that my efforts might help heal those suffering from some sort of spiritual alienation. Meanwhile, I grew older, and now I have reached a point where I wish to share my ideas further in the hope that some younger person will want to pick up and further explore this material, developing it into age-appropriate curricula for formal and informal education. To that end, I will lead you here through one of my workshops.

OVERVIEW OF A MORAL MATH WORKSHOP

Whenever possible, I email all pre-registered participants a list of online videos to watch before the workshop actually convenes. These videos demonstrate ways in which mathematics can be used to illuminate social behavior (specifics are noted in chapter 26) and, thus, set the stage for what we do in the one to two hour session. At the beginning of the workshop I distribute a take-home bibliography and a list of the interactive exercises we will engage in, along with the math source I've drawn the exercise from, plus a list of relevant examples of social behavior that this mathematical understanding might influence:

---

2. Fadiman, *Spirit Catches*, 267.

MORAL MATH WORKSHOP: EXERCISE SUMMARY

Source/Moral Issue	Experiential Exercise	Social Behavior
1. Non-Zero-Sum Game (Cooperation & Trust) cf: Alternative Reality Games (ARGs)	Dollar Auction Chicken for Groups	Nuclear arms race Genovese 1964 murder Cuban missile crisis WWII troops escaping flood
2. Chaos Theory/Emergence (Best Trends &Attitudes)	The Contact Process	Rich get richer Segregation Pig of Happiness
3. Fuzzy Logic (Fairness)	Fuzzy Tax Form Crime and Punishment	Class-free decision making DWI: levels .081 vs .079
4. Algebra (Caring for Others)	Equal Cake Cutting	Division of estates & territory
5. Math for Kids (Generosity & Kindness)	One Grain of Rice	Growth of AI (Singularity) Environmental pollution

As the workshop plays out, I also provide participants with additional handouts for several of the topics. As an example, I've included the one on "The Contact Process" in appendix A.

I usually begin the workshop with the dollar auction, a non-zero-sum game in which a dollar bill is auctioned off to the highest bidder. This exercise works like a normal auction except for one small difference: the runner-up bidder also pays the auctioneer whatever he/she bid, but receives nothing in return. In my experience, people usually hesitate when the bidding reaches about one dollar (a complete wipe out, except, of course, for the second bidder who is about to lose close to one dollar). The bidding normally stops around $1.40, when someone realizes that the game has changed from the opportunity to get a great bargain to the need to minimize their potential loss, and then to the recognition that there is no way out of the game except to stop it. At this point, I bring up the similarities between this game and, say, a nuclear arms race. The obvious conclusion, and the hope, is that education might have at least some kind of modifying effect on whether or not people even engage in such a process.

The second exercise, like the first, is drawn from non-zero-sum game theory, but this one is an example of a social dilemma where one player is actually an entire group. Chicken for Groups is a short exercise where everyone gets a chance to win either one dollar or ten cents, simply by writing that amount down on a piece of paper. If at least one person writes ten cents, then everyone gets what he or she wrote. However, if everyone writes one dollar, no one wins anything. This is a Volunteer's Dilemma, where it is desirable for one person to volunteer for the common good. A classic example is the 1964 murder of Kitty Genovese, who was stabbed to death in the courtyard of her New York City apartment while thirty-eight neighbors watched and heard her cries, but did nothing to assist her. Another is the 1962 Cuban missile crisis where the Soviet Union (via Krushchev) and the United States (via President Kennedy) were engaged in an increasingly dangerous game of chicken leading to nuclear war until one of them (Krushchev) publicly volunteered to back off.

After doing these two exercises, we discuss participants' reactions, and I distribute a handout with additional explanation about the theory behind non-zero-sum games, including an introduction to the classic Prisoner's Dilemma and some brief examples of what happens when the relative weights of the options (Temptation, Reward, Punishment, and Sucker payoffs) are switched around, plus a list of some of the conclusions that have been drawn from non-zero-sum game theory regarding cooperation. All of this is written in user-friendly language, so that those with little math expertise won't become discouraged. I end this section by referring to the list of resources in the bibliography I distributed earlier, and by talking a little about how some alternate reality games are potential sources to raise the quality of life and to help ordinary people by curing disease, stopping climate change, spreading peace, ending poverty. The way to change the future is to play with it first.[3]

Next, I introduce the Contact Process, which is an interactive exercise I developed to illustrate concepts from self-organizing emergence and network theory.[4] This exercise is based on a few simple action rules which involve an element of randomness. To begin, I distribute the handout I've prepared for this exercise, which includes a little background

---

3. See Challenge:Future, "Impact."
4. See also chapter 18, "Exercise from Network Theory."

about relevant ideas from complexity theory (starting with the butterfly effect, which many of the participants will have already encountered in popular culture) and an overview of the exercise, along with the game rules we use. In this exercise, participants wave colored cards to see how patterns self-emerge over time when the action is determined by a few simple rules. Most players are initially astounded when clusters of red or blue appear and sometimes even tip at some point so that one color essentially emerges as dominant in the room. I then ask such questions as "what happens if a newcomer to the room entered with a preference for, say, red? Where would they choose to sit?" In the ensuing discussion, we eventually summarize outcomes of self-organizing emergence.[5]

The third set of exercises is drawn from fuzzy logic, and, once again, I begin with a handout. This one includes, first, an income tax form that would allow taxpayers to have partial say in how their taxes are spent[6] and, secondly, a list of recommended prison terms for abortion based on number of weeks that have elapsed since conception,[7] thus illustrating partial punishment depending upon degree of crime.[8] This notion is easily appreciated when applied to DWI offenses, where our current system of testing for drunkenness suggests that one person might be deemed totally drunk and a second not drunk at all (and punished accordingly) when the alcohol readouts in their respective systems are only a fraction different. I give a little background on the mathematics involved in fuzzy logic, but time limitations usually mean that I can't do much more than offer these examples of how fuzzy logic can be an aid to social decision-making. Participants usually aren't necessarily convinced that these particular ideas are the ones they want to champion, but they quickly see that fuzzy math can lead to out-of-the-box thinking, with the possible outcome being more fairness and equity in social behavior.

The fourth exercise is drawn from an algebraic algorithm showing one method of cutting a square cake into an odd number of equal pieces (see also chapter 25).[9] I am quick to point out that there are other, more sophisticated mathematical devices for dividing material things fairly. The math in this exercise, however, is simple—simple enough that I am always tempted to go through the algebraic proof with the group, but past

 5. See also chapters 18, 25, and 26.
 6. Kosko, *Fuzzy Future*, 16.
 7. Bishop, *Shades*, 187.
 8. See chapter 22, "Fuzzy Logic in the Health Care Setting."
 9. Eastaway and Wyndham, *Why Do Buses*, 82–83.

experience with anxiety on the part of those who are less mathematically sophisticated has taught me to restrain myself. The math details are all there on the handout for anyone interested, and, of course, I'm happy to help them through it at some other time. Instead, I demonstrate the actual steps involved in locating the places to cut the cake, and then I bring out the cake—or cakes if there are a lot of people—and send them off in odd-numbered groups to duplicate the procedure. I use frozen, name-brand cakes that come in five inch squares, and I'm the extra person who ensures that the number of participants cutting each cake remains odd. This exercise is always a popular one, and there's never any cake left to lug home, either.

The fifth and final exercise shows how ideas adapted from math and applied to social behavior can be introduced to children at very young ages. To accomplish this, I have the participants act out the children's story *One Grain of Rice*,[10] to which end I provide appropriate props and garments to clothe two volunteers. One volunteer plays the role of the Raja, a mighty but unwise leader in the East who rules his country with an iron fist and little generosity. The other plays Rani, a young girl under the Raja's rule.

When the country suffers a bad drought, the Raja keeps the court storehouses filled with rice while the people go hungry. Rani, whom the Raja takes to be well-intended but not very clever, works out a deal with him to give her a single grain of rice on the first day of the month, two pieces on the second, four pieces on the third, eight on the fourth, and so on for one entire month.[11] By the end of the month the Raja has completely emptied his stockpiles and would be ruined except for the generosity of the young girl, who gives the rice back to him upon his promise that he will be a good ruler henceforth and will make sure to care for his people properly.

The two volunteers act out the story as I read it, and also read their own parts aloud (from a script I give them) whenever I give the proper clue. Rani pulls out of a bag (the storehouse) varying sizes of lightly checkered cloth to represent the various amounts of rice she's given. The final one is lengthy enough for Rani to carry it out the door. The rest of the workshop participants (i.e., the "people") make grumble sounds whenever something goes wrong for them and joyous sounds when

---

10. Demi, *One Grain*.
11. See chapter 7, and also chapter 13 on "Doubling."

things get better. Although some groups have initially been somewhat reserved, by the time the story is finished everyone is having a great time, and the only thing lacking is the real children.

Although there are many other such stories that could be substituted, *One Grain of Rice* is a lovely note on which to conclude the workshop. Two social activities that I introduce that are representative of this exponential-like growth include modern computer technology, particularly artificial intelligence, and environmental pollution. The handout I send home after this exercise is an excerpt from *The Singularity Is Near*, by Ray Kurzweil;[12] it includes a lovely parable about a lake owner who wants to stay home and tend the lake so that it doesn't become totally covered with lily pads, which are said to double every few days. He waits for months and months without anything significant happening to the lake, then takes a vacation only to find that the last seven doublings have completely smothered the fish in the lake. Kurzweil then applies this mathematical parable to information-based technologies, thus setting up the possibility that "by the end of this century, the nonbiological portion of our intelligence will be trillions of times more powerful than unaided human intelligence."[13]

It's a nice moral issue to ponder after the workshop is finished. At my most recent workshop I also solicited written feedbacks, two of which I quote below with permission. One woman said, "I love the social implications in which these mathematical models can 'normalize,' 'naturalize,' and 'neutralize' particular social behaviors . . . . This was fun!" By some unbelievable coincidence this woman is a ministerial colleague less than half my age who also holds an undergraduate degree in mathematics, thus proving (at least to me) that there are others who can marry math and spirituality.

Another participant, a computer programmer, wrote, "The pacing of the talk was excellent. We covered two hours of material in two hours, not too fast and not too slowly. It was the right level for the audience, and rich enough so both beginners and people experienced in math and complex systems got something from the presentation . . . . For each area of math you covered, the triple of a little theory, plus exercises, plus real-world examples was very effective."

---

12. Kurzweil, *Singularity*, 7–9.
13. Kurzweil, *Singularity*, 9.

Overall, my experience with this moral math workshop has been highly challenging and extremely rewarding. Nearly everyone who has been through the session leaves it with an "aha!" attitude, and I leave it with great gratitude for the social wisdom we can gain through mathematical tools.

Chapter 24: *Out of Statistics, Hope[1]

You can lie effectively, or you can tell the truth.
You may know which you are doing.

To see things in the seed, that is genius.—Lao-Tzu

READING

Invocation

Out of nothing, this world.
Out of chaos, form.
Out of Adam, Eve.
Out of wonder, stories.
Out of explanations, science,
Our of imagination,
guppies, puppies,
schools, gatherings,
ice cream, stars.
Out of the present, poetry.
Out of the past, wisdom.
Out of our prayers, hope.[2]

Chant: "Free the heart. Let it go. What we reap is what we sow."

---

1. This is a slightly modified variation of the sermon "Out of Statistics, Hope," which I presented to the Community Church, New Orleans, on March 24, 1996.
2. Voss, *Out of Prayers*, 1.

SERMON

For this morning's opening words, I shared the first poem in a collection of poem-prayers called *Out of Our Prayers, Hope*. I wrote this little chapbook back in 1991 when I was still in seminary and was doing my clinical pastoral experience, or, more simply, the hospital training ministers typically undergo. My sermon title today is a play on this book title, one which seems particularly fitting for a mathematician turned minister: *Out of Statistics, Hope*.

Statistics is what I used to teach to one of my classes. Some of my students called it "sadistics." We can guess why. Statistics deals with hard facts. It crunches numbers out of elaborate, sometimes mind-boggling equations and spits out expectations in the form of probabilities. Statistics isn't particularly easy. But, then, neither is hope. Hope is what I try to experience in my ministry. I'd like to say it's what I teach in my ministry, but that seems a bit presumptuous since I'm still struggling to learn hope. Hope deals with soft facts. Hope crunches courage out of disappointments and setbacks, and it spits out expectations in the form of faith.

Of the two—statistics and hope—hope is the harder to master. Over the years, humankind has evolved a variety of methods to help us gain and retain trust in the divine. Prayer is certainly one of them. Psychoanalysis is a more recent method. Being in community, seeking the support of friends, medication, even legislation to ensure fair treatment and/or open opportunity—all these are ways in which we have sought through the ages to secure hope. Nonetheless, I think we've traditionally overlooked a potential way, and it is to this error of omission that I speak today. Out of statistics, we can find hope. On the whole, finding hope is a much more demanding challenge than learning statistics—even sadistic statistics. There is much to be discouraged about in this life. If the world were a village, then predictions for the future of our village would not only be discouraging, they'd be downright alarming. Where is the hope in such statistics?

First, statistics can bring us new perspective—something essential to those who are without hope. Sometimes, our problems seem so overwhelming that we feel impotent and helpless in the face of them. The world, for instance, currently seems to be riding a rapid road to disaster. Even the size of the human population is problematic. Did you know that of all the people who have ever lived on earth, over half lived during the twentieth century? That's a lot of people we're talking about. It's hard enough to get a sense of such a big number, let alone feel that we're anything more than one insignificant, faceless creature in this vast impersonal sea. Yet, with the aid of certain statistics, suddenly we dwell in a village of, say, a hundred people. We can relate to a village. In a village, we can really grasp what is going on. Better yet, in a village, we have an identity. We *are* somebody. We make a difference. In a village, it matters what one person does. If only one more person becomes a doctor in our village of one hundred,[3] suddenly the number of doctors has doubled. If you become a doctor, you make a 200 percent difference in the quality of health care. With statistics we can change our perspective and, in the process, recognize that we are not so powerless as we thought.

Second, statistics can suggest avenues of action. I found an article in a *Menninger* report about people who have lost their jobs, or, more specifically, about people who have not lost their jobs *yet*, but are afraid they might. The employees who remain after cutbacks—the survivors—also face increased stress. According to statistical studies, however, survivors are better off if they use control (problem-focused) rather than escape (emotion-focused) coping strategies. "Control coping involves proactive actions and assessments, whereas escape coping consists of those action and assessments that involve avoidance. . . . Unlike those using escape coping, survivors who used control coping reported much greater organizational commitment, higher job performance, and less intention to leave the organization.[4] On the basis of such statistical studies, if your company is downsizing, it's clear that your most hopeful line of action is control coping.

Statistics suggests other best paths. Another *Menninger* report, for instance, indicated that spouse abuse may be related to a prior head injury. "Head injury alone, of course, does not cause spouse abuse. But studies of its aftermath suggest that it can impair the ability to control aggressive impulses. . . . [Men] who suffer a head injury—in childhood or afterward—may be at risk of becoming aggressive toward their partner." In such cases, the researchers recommend preventive positive

---

3. Today there are lots of versions of this idea. Here is just one video: Knovva Academy, "If the World."

4. Menninger, *Menninger Letter* 3:9. The ideas I'm referring to in this and the next three footnotes all came from two of Menninger's letters, but I was informed via email by the Menninger Foundation that "Menninger publications . . . are in a digital format that cannot be opened with existing platforms. Hard copies no longer exist after this much time has passed."

action—premarital counseling.⁵ Similarly, through statistics we discover hopeful possibilities for early determent of other violent crimes. Did you know that:

> the early detection of two specific circumstances in a child's life birth—complications and early maternal rejection—may help identify persons who are more likely to commit violent crimes at some point in adulthood. But appropriate interventions with these children and their parents, according to researchers from UCLA and the Institute of Preventive Medicine in Copenhagen, Denmark, may help prevent violent crimes later on. . . . [In particular], they suggest two possible ways to help reduce the prevalence of violent crime: Provide better prenatal care to reduce birth complications. Help new parents learn better caregiving skills.⁶

In the process of reshaping our perspectives and offering guidance regarding our best paths of action, statistics often provides us much needed reassurance and encouragement. Your happiness involves (1) an ability to adapt to changing circumstances, (2) a view of the world as benevolent and controllable, and (3) values and goals that provide a sense of direction.⁷ Yes, chances are, you'll be at least a little reassured. Happiness really is attainable: just concentrate on these three factors.

Still, the statistics of encouragement can be quite subtle. For instance, a March 1996 issue of *Newsweek* carried a report of an elegant study concluding that Alzheimer's disease may be more frequent among those who demonstrate something called low "idea density" and "grammatical complexity." Specifically, if your writing style is dense and complex, you may have some sort of built-in resistance to encroaching dementia.⁸ Now, in my own personal family history, Alzheimer's has sometimes been a problem. So, if you tell me later on that this sermon I've written for you today was too difficult and convoluted to follow, how can I help but be encouraged!

And here's one more item I ran across only a few days ago which, I admit, has already provided me with an inordinate amount of reassurance and encouragement. The title tells it all: "Whiners May Be Better Off, Study Finds." "Go ahead and complain," invited the article. "Whine

---

5. Menninger, *Menninger Letter*, 3:9, 4.
6. Menninger, *Menninger Letter* 3:9.
7. Menninger, *Menninger Letter* 3:7.
8. Snowden, "Linguistic Ability."

if you must. Expressing your discontent could help you live longer than your quiet, inner-suffering pals."[9]

Finally, here's an interesting statistic reported last year in *Science News*:

> People whose religious beliefs give them feelings of *strength* and comfort and who regularly participate in a social activity markedly improve their chance of surviving at least 6 months after undergoing heart surgery.[10]

This last illustration points to a fact so significant that it warrants being counted as a separate way in which statistics can help us find hope. In particular, *statistics* suggest that we enhance our religious commitment. A recent article in the *Wall Street Journal* insists that "the potential of churches and synagogues to improve the quality of health care in America has made 'Congregation-Based Health Ministry' the hottest topic within virtually all the denominations of every religion."[11] And a report in Focus on the Family *Citizen* says it even more succinctly: "For Good Health, Go to Church." Statistics show that, as a group, religious folk live longer than non-religious folk and that, in addition to lengthening your life, religion can also help lower your chances of getting sick. "Infrequent religious attendance," warn these researchers, "should be regarded as a consistent risk factor for morbidity and mortality of various types."[12]

Now, as a minister wanting to minister, that data gives me hope! How do we find hope in statistics? With apologies to Elizabeth Browning, let me count the ways. Statistics gives us new perspective. It suggests new paths, brings encouragement and reassurance, and, finally, leads us straight to church, where, as everyone knows, hope hides in empty pews, just waiting for someone to catch it, carry it home. Months later, it reappears as impersonal worlds that have become friendly, healthy villages . . ., as raw statistics that have grown into new cures or abandoned guns or emptied iron cages . . ., as blooming marigolds in discarded coffee cans lining the decaying wooden steps.

Statistics convince. Mathematics as a whole is renowned for its reliability and certainty. Yes, that same certainty is elusive. Just when you think you know what's coming next, the best numerical statements turn

9. University of Nebraska Omaha, "Whiners" 8.
10. Science News Editors, "Behavior," 124.
11. *Wall Street Journal*, "Congregation-Based Health Ministry."
12. Hartwig, "Good Health."

into marigolds planted in coffee cans. For years, Euclidean geometry assured us that the angles of any triangle always add up to 180 degrees. That fact was routinely used to demonstrate the truth of such things as the existence of God. Then one day, non-Euclidean geometries were discovered and, poof, triangles with angles that totaled more than 180 degrees. And less than 180 degrees.

It's like that with statistics, too. Today, we look to statistics for truth with a Platonic faith that mathematical reality is the ultimate reality—more real, to some, than God. Two plus two is four. Period. The truth, the absolute truth and nothing but the truth. In a study titled "The Impact of Religion on Men's Blood Pressure," psychiatrist and former National Institute of Mental Health researcher David Larsen determined that, statistically speaking, "even smokers benefit from religion."[13] Truth. Absolute truth. Statistics convince. Yet, somehow we suspect that these same statistics can be used to mislead, to delude, to lie. Statistics may give us truth, but can we trust it? What a paradox of thought we have here!

Edward MacNeal, in *Mathsemantics*, relates how he asked 196 job applicants to solve the following addition problem: What is the sum of two apples and five oranges? Fifty-two applicants answered "7 fruit." Forty-six answered just seven, not seven of anything. Thirty-six answered "2 apples + 5 oranges," which, MacNeal observed, didn't seem to solve any problem in addition. Twenty-seven applicants refused to "add unlike values." Fifteen responded "7 apples and oranges," fifteen waffled, and five gave clear-cut wrong answers such as "7 oranges." All in all, the 196 applicants answering the question gave 56 digitally different responses. How can anyone find hope in the mathematics of such a slippery process?

What MacNeal is getting at is the notion that there is nothing wrong with our mathematics—it's our math *semantics* that cause us difficulties. If I hold up a red pencil and a green pencil and ask you to add them, chances are you'll say "two pencils." "But, no," I say. "This is a reddie and this is a greenie. You can't add greenies and reddies."

"But they're both pencils," you protest.

"So," says MacNeal, "whether you can add things together depends on what they're called, is that right? If I call them 'fruit,' you can add them together, but if I call them 'apples' and 'oranges,' you can't. That makes it a question of who will do the naming, doesn't it?"[14]

13. Hartwig, "Good Health."
14. MacNeal, *Mathsemantics*, 6.

Traditional schooling, contends MacNeal, does little to put math and semantics together and hence to address the seeming problem. Instead, it yields adults who are afraid to use numbers, who fear that "math is a powerful mystery they're not privileged to know."[15] This mystery creates a chasm which, for many adults, becomes a hopeless pit. Math anxiety is one term frequently used to define the condition. Escapist coping is perhaps more accurate.

I will illustrate with another example from MacNeal's book. Here's a little test for you. What year do you think the capital of Burma was founded? I'd like you to answer this. In fact, I'd like you to jot your answer down. Some of you may be uncomfortable with this little exercise. Some of you may even refuse to give an answer. Perhaps your inner dialogue is something like this—and I quote again from *Mathsemantics*:

> McN: When do you think the capital of Burma was founded?
> *You: I've no idea.*
> But you must have some idea.
> *No, really, I have no idea at all. I don't even know what the capital of Burma is. Is it Rangoon?*
> Sorry, but the question isn't "What is the capital of Burma?" It's "When do you think it was founded?"
> *Well, I can't say if I don't even know what city it is, can I? I just have no idea.*
> Please, stop giving me false information about yourself. You must have some idea, and I'm asking you for it.
> *You want me to guess? Is that it?*
> Not at all. I want you to use what you know to make an estimate.
> *But I don't know anything about Burma.*[16]

Now, if your self-talk, or your actual talk, was somewhat along these lines, then, rest assured, you are among the majority. Most people, MacNeal discovered, refused to make an estimate. They fear being wrong. MacNeal suggests that that fear impedes our knowledge acquisition by discouraging what he calls "our least expensive and most valuable learning technique, trial and error."[17] I believe he is right. But I also believe he has inadvertently lifted up a most valuable lesson for all of us who quest after hope.

15. MacNeal, *Mathsemantics*, 7.
16. MacNeal, *Mathsemantics*, 219.
17. MacNeal, *Mathsemantics*, 220.

In order to enjoy hope, we have to be willing to risk something. In particular, we have to be willing to risk being wrong, to risk failing. R. H. Macy failed seven times before his now-famous store in New York caught on. English novelist John Creasey acquired 753 rejection slips before he published 564 books. Babe Ruth struck out 1,330 times, yet he also hit 714 home runs.[18] Abraham Lincoln was defeated for public office four times, failed in business, couldn't get into law school, went bankrupt, lost his fiancée to death, had a total nervous breakdown and was in bed for six months, and received fewer than one hundred votes when he sought the vice-presidential nomination at his party's national convention. Lincoln didn't let failure stop him. He took a chance. And then another and another.[19]

Herein is perhaps the most valuable lesson of all which we can glean about hope from statistics. Statistics is all about probabilities—about chance.

I have here a package of marigold seeds. Each one of these seeds is a miniature math program. We can read about it in chemistry and biology texts where it's typically called "genetic coding." If we plant one of these seeds, we have a good sense of the probable outcome—especially if we water and nurture it. It is not a certainty that this seed will produce a brilliant marigold. But the chances are pretty good.

Whenever we plant a seed like this—or any seed—we are taking a chance. We are risking. We are trusting in probabilities and statistics. And what we reap, ultimately, is hope. Take a chance today. Plant a seed. Grow hope.[20]

---

18. Canfield and Hansen, *Chicken Soup*, 233–35.

19. Canfield and Hansen, *Chicken Soup*, 236–37.

20. The capital of Burma is Rangoon, probably founded in the sixth century, and until the eighteenth century a small fishing village. It was named the capital in 1753.

Chapter 25: Generating Trust through Moral Math[1]

Do unto one side as you do unto the other.

Therefore all things whatsoever you desire that men should do to you, do you even so to them.
—New Testament, Matt 7:12, from the Christian tradition, ca. 30 CE[2]

While most of us recognize theoretical mathematics as a source for many of the advances humankind has made in science and technology, fewer of us are aware that some of these same mathematical ideas can be and are being applied to issues of social behavior. This essay explores several of these ideas. Specifically, it examines concepts drawn not only from simple algebra, but also from the theory of complexity (and its offshoots), from fuzzy logic, and from game theory, particularly non-zero-sum game theory. An underlying assumption of this essay is that we generate trust whenever we engage in the Golden Rule. Many of us have seen various formulations of this rule, but there is one version, drawn from the world of mathematics, which you may not recognize.

---

1. Voss, "Generating Trust." I offered a summary of this essay in Seattle, Washington, January 27–30, 2005, at the International Conference of Unity and Diversity in Religion and Culture. Many of the ideas in it began as a series of three sermons presented in January, February, and March 2004 at the First Unitarian Church of Sioux City, Iowa. The essay was also the basis for an intensive course I offered in ethics, in January 2007, at Meadville Lombard Theological School in Chicago.

2. Unless noted otherwise, citations herein of religious expressions of the Golden Rule were found on "Quotes of Wisdom."

> **The "mathematical" golden rule states that for any fraction, both numerator and denominator may be multiplied by the same number without changing the fraction's value.**
>
> —Weisstein, Mathematical Golden Rule[3]

For example, one half equals three sixths, (½ = ³⁄₆), an equality derived by multiplying both numerator and denominator by the same number—in this instance, by "3"—i.e., by doing unto the "one" (1) as you would do unto the other (2). While it seems to take a lifetime (or more) for us to learn to practice this golden rule in our social and spiritual lives, it only takes a few years of elementary school for most of us to grasp the concept through mathematics. Despite the simplicity of this observation, contemporary social scientists have only recently begun to consider mathematics as a source for ethical guidance.

Even then there can be subtle underpinnings when it comes to ethics. For example, results from decision psychology have shown that we often don't treat these fractions as equivalent. A phenomenon called ratio bias means that the same small probability is perceived as larger if the numerator and denominator are larger. Thus, if a jar contains red and white balls, and you win money if you randomly draw a red ball, many subjects will feel that ten red balls (or even eight or nine red balls) out of one hundred total balls gives a better chance of winning than one red ball out of ten total balls. Mathematics combined with social science can increase the depth of our decision-making strategies.[4]

Today the concept that we can make better moral decisions with the help of theoretical mathematics seems to be spreading: scholars are using mathematical ideas and techniques, for instance, to better understand the social behavior of cooperation, fairness, and altruism. Consider the issue of slicing a pan of newly baked brownies into equal pieces for an *odd* number of people. Sharing the brownies fairly with an *even* number of people is a trivial problem, rapidly done by some combination of halving, quartering, and re-halving the baked batter. A slightly more complicated situation is, say, dividing an eight by twelve-inch cake into five equal pieces. To do this, mark off the forty-inch perimeter into five equal segments of eight inches each (40 ÷ 5 = 8), then slice along the imaginary line which connects each of the resulting eight marks on the perimeter

---

3. Weisstein, "Golden Rule."
4. Dan Levine, personal communication.

of the pan to the center point of the dish. The five pieces formed by these slices will be the same size, a fact readily verified by using the familiar algebraic formula for the area of a triangle, A= ½ bh (see figure 25.1).[5] By extension, this process will work for any number (odd or even) of individuals.

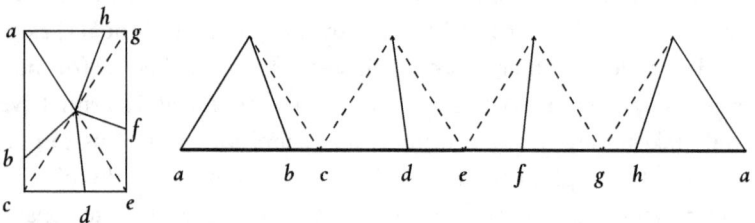

Fig. 25.1. Cutting a Cake into Equal Pieces

Although an eight by twelve-inch brownie cake would obviously yield sparse refreshment for a large quantity of people, the principle behind this exercise nonetheless introduces what's been called the "mathematics of envy."[6] In fact, mathematicians have developed intricate algorithms for cutting a cake of any size into any number of pieces in a manner which reassures the recipients that the split was fair. Such cake-cutting algorithms might seem frivolous or even insignificant were it not that these strategies are being successfully adapted to the resolution of tricky conflict situations such as property division after a divorce, allocation of an inheritance, or the division of territory following a war.[7]

This is the sum of duty. Do not unto others that which would cause you pain if done to you.

—MAHABHARATA 5:1517, FROM THE VEDIC TRADITION OF INDIA, CA. 3000 BCE

Another mathematical area that has stimulated recent scholars to think creatively about social behavior is complexity theory. Formally known as nonlinear dynamic systems theory, complexity theory is popularly

5. See Eastaway and Wyndham, *Why Do Buses*, 83 for a similar diagram.
6. Eastaway and Wyndham, *Why Do Buses*, 85.
7. See Browne, "Biologists Tally"; Hill, "Mathematical Devices"; Peterson, "Formulas for Fairness," 284–85.

identified with one of its offshoots, chaos theory. An easy introduction to one of the major ideas in complexity theory can be found simply by watching a 2004 movie: in *The Butterfly Effect*, small changes in initial conditions lead to substantially different outcomes in the life-story of the main character. The movie takes its name from a similar concept found in the mathematical theory. Tagline: "Change one thing, change everything."

Two additional related ideas also drawn from complexity theory are the notions of *self-organizing emergence* and *strange attractors*.[8] Somewhat over-simplistically, self-organizing emergence refers to the self-generation of repetitive patterns of order within chaos. This process is ubiquitous in our universe, found in everything from weather patterns to genetic DNA. In biological systems, self-organizing emergence is often referred to as the process of *autopoiesis*, from two Greek roots meaning "self" and "making."

Similarly, strange attractors are points or spaces in a system where significant changes in the basic structure of the system occur. Strange attractors may be loosely identified with certain other mathematical concepts called bifurcation points, phase transitions, and critical or threshold points, some or all of which are present in more popular contexts. When Malcolm Gladwell defined the title of his recent book *The Tipping Point* as "that magic moment when an idea, trend, or social behavior crosses a *threshold*, tips, and spreads like wildfire," he was essentially speaking of strange attractors.[9] Strange attractors generate sudden, all-at-once change.

The butterfly effect, self-organizing emergence, and strange attractors are all computer-dependent ideas. Without the dramatic ability of the computer to solve complex nonlinear equations and then print the results out in colorful, meaningful patterns, we would never have identified any of the behavior we now understand as chaotic determinism. Chaos, in this newer computer-generated understanding, is not entirely random; it is, instead, "an occult, 'hidden,' or implicate *order* within nature."[10]

Psychologists, physiologists, and neuroscientists have begun to explore the human dimensions of complexity theory, noting, for example, strange attractor behavior in human trauma and healing. Thus, while

---

8. See chapter 18.

9. Gladwell, *Tipping Point*, back cover (emphasis added).

10. Miller and Swinney, "Human Dimensions" (emphasis added). Mathematicians associate these patterns with yet another offshoot of complexity theory called fractal geometry.

one traumatic event may shape a life, it may only take one intense therapeutic event to reshape it. In the words of two such theorists, "Healing spreads out through the individual life like ripples on a pool of water. This changeability is the prime characteristic of many chaotic systems. It is not harmful to the brain. In fact, it may be the very property that makes perception possible."[11] Or, again and to be more explicit, "Mathematical metaphors help us visualize the bigger picture."[12]

Hurt not others in ways that you find hurtful.
—Tripitaka, Udanga-varga 5, 18, from the Buddhist tradition, ca. 525 BCE

Another important branch of mathematical complexity is *network theory*, which is based on a view of reality in which everything is inseparably connected. Abstract laws of network theory help us understand more about the diverse ways in which we can be connected and reveal dynamics about relationships which previously have been poorly understood or totally overlooked. Some of these laws suggest new, more altruistic approaches to human relationships.[13]

Consider, e.g., the variation on a procedure or game known in mathematical network theory as the "Contact Process."[14] This game is a concrete way of illustrating the abstract principles at work in a network. In recent years, researchers have applied these abstract laws of self-emergence to a variety of real-life arenas. In inanimate systems such as economics, the rich do, in fact, tend to get richer. In computer systems, the Internet gets viruses. In engineering systems, electric power grids collapse like dominoes. In health systems, disease spreads in epidemics. In social systems, fads prevail.

The latest system being explored is that of human social behavior. Consider, for instance, a growing social community such as a church or residential area to which a newcomer arrives with a strong preferential attachment for the color of human skin. According to network theory, that person naturally searches the community for others with the same

---

11. Miller and Swinney, "Human Dimensions."

12. Miller and Swinney, "Human Dimensions."

13. Several recent books appropriate for the lay reader are excellent references regarding the application of network theory to social behavior: Barabási, *Linked*; Buchanan, *Nexus*; Johnson, *Emergence*; Watts, *Six Degrees*.

14. See chapters 18, 23, and appendix B.

attachment preference—he or she finds the like-minded hubs and joins them. And the hubs in this case can grow into segregation. This is one way racism emerges in such a social system.

Similar conclusions have been drawn about the growing prevalence of various kinds of cheating in America. For instance, without any direct reference to formal networks, social strategist David Callahan nonetheless describes a contemporary societal situation consistent with the "rich get richer" aspect of network theory.[15] Cheating is becoming pervasive at all levels of American society, Callahan maintains, and the growing gap between winners and losers in our country is having a lethal effect on personal integrity. Network theorists would say that the idea of cutting corners has become a strange attractor. Callahan's extensive list of practical ways to transform this trend may be arguable, but they are also all potential methods of reducing the temptation to cheat by lessening the rewards that support the strange attractor behavior of this moral decline.

Do not do to others that which would anger you if others did it to you.

—SOCRATES, CA. 470-399 BCE

Another area of mathematics which researchers are adapting to social behavior is that known as fuzzy logic. While our world currently uses a plethora of practical applications of fuzzy logic,[16] most recently and perhaps most importantly for this discussion are the ways in which fuzzy logicians are applying this new mathematical tool to human social behavior and issues of ethics. Sometimes they are simply showing us our unrecognized biases.

According to Bart Kosko, for instance, some people would resist a fuzzy tax form because they "think most people are too dumb to choose wisely."[17] Kosko points out that there is a prejudicial IQism behind such a reaction, where the smart think less of the less smart. "Smart" and "less smart" are, of course, vague terms; all of us are smart to some degree and not smart to some degree. Nonetheless, IQism is prevalent in today's society—it's right up there with racism and sexism and ageism, except IQism is more politically correct. In Kosko's words, "Intelligence is a

---

15. Callahan, *Cheating Culture*.
16. See the section in chapter 22 "What Is Fuzzy Logic?"
17. Kosko, *Fuzzy Future*, 61.

form of power. The smart find little comfort in letting the less smart have power. They find even less comfort in letting the less smart have power over them. Who wants to take orders from someone with a lower IQ? And just about everyone sees themselves as smart."[18]

Fuzzy thinking can assist us in our moral choices by suggesting alternatives to yes-or-no, black-or-white thinking. In confronting the abortion issue, a fetus might be viewed as alive to some degree, and also not alive to some degree;[19] some fuzzy logicians are suggesting an extension and refinement of this notion in the form of partial rights for partial life. In deciding who owns the rights to genome space, fuzzy logic might help us more methodically identify and weigh the many various concerns about pre-birth DNA programming. In considering issues of euthanasia, fuzzy thinkers see potential value in quantifying the degree of aliveness. In determining fairness and justness about who gets access to the best of modern medical techniques, fuzzy scientists predict equality not only through fuzzy decision-making, but also with the aid of fuzzy technology, as in the form of a fuzzy computer chip which tracks your physical health. Similarly, crime and punishment might be made fairer through fuzzy decision making, where the severity of the consequences can be more precisely matched to the seriousness of the crime.[20]

Like all tools, fuzzy logic is just that—a tool. It can serve society well or poorly.[21] Here, the Golden Rule appears to be golden to a degree, and also not golden to a degree. Perhaps it is enough to be charitable.

Be charitable to all beings, love is the representative of God.
—**Koran, Sunnah, from the Islam tradition, ca. 620 CE**

One last mathematical area of particular note for its social implications is the study of non-zero-sum games. *Zero*-sum games are those in which someone wins and someone else loses; the sum of their "scores"

---

18. Kosko, *Fuzzy Future*, 62.

19. For more on this topic, see chapter 22.

20. These examples are also discussed in Kosko, *Fuzzy Future*. Another source on similar material is Bishop, *Shades*.

21. Computer-enhanced data mining techniques which draw on network and order theory allow "Mathematicians [to] help in [the] global war on terror" (headline in the *Omaha World-Herald*; Associated Press, "Mathematicians"). The emphasis in this article is less on the uses of mathematics for facilitating trust and cooperation than on developing sophisticated procedures for defense.

adds up to zero. Tic-tac-toe, Scrabble, chess, and Trivial Pursuit are common illustrations of zero-sum games. The lead sentence in a recent front-page news article, "Aristide Choice: Flee or Die," indicates a typical adaptation of this mathematics to the global political scene: "For President Jean-Bertrand Aristide, all the international pressure to step down had an impact, but what really forced his quick exit Sunday was the lethal reality of Haiti's *zero-sum politics*."[22]

The promise of *non*-zero-sum strategies is the hope of more cooperative, fairer, win-win solutions to problems which initially seem to lead only to someone's victory at the cost of others' punishment and/or "sucker" status. The classic illustration of a non-zero-sum game is the Prisoner's Dilemma, a game wherein two conspirators in crime are arrested and the police, lacking enough evidence to convict either of them, offer them both a deal. Confess and, if your partner doesn't confess, you go free. If you both confess, you both serve some small amount of prison time. If neither of you confesses, you both serve a larger amount of prison time. If you don't confess but your partner does, you serve the maximum prison sentence allowable.

There are several variations on this dilemma, the ramifications of which mathematicians have carefully mapped out. One of the easiest ways to comprehend the collective possibilities of these games is to consider a version of the Prisoner's Dilemma known as the dollar auction.[23] In this variation, we auction off a dollar bill, starting with a bid of two cents and increasing by increments of ten cents or less. There is one special rule: the auctioneer must be paid not only by the highest bidder, but also by the second-highest bidder. The highest bidder pays what he bid and takes the dollar. The second-highest pays what *he* bid but gets nothing. Whenever this auction is held, someone nearly always bids more than one dollar, and the game therefore degenerates into a non-cooperative effort to avoid loss. This happens even when people *know* the potential outcome; the fever of the game (or the nuclear weapons race or the genetic-engineering quest) gives rise to irrational decision-making. The only way out of the game is for someone to just cut their losses and stop.

There are a number of general conclusions suggested by research into non-zero-sum-game theory. For one thing, cooperation is optimized when the individuals involved are nestled in a network of cooperators.

---

22. Hansen, "Aristide Choice," 1 (emphasis added).
23. See also chapters 23 and 26.

Not everyone has to be nice for niceness to evolve, but there must be at least some cooperators in order for the nice guys to benefit from their own niceness. Otherwise, cooperators are suckers who eventually disappear.[24] Furthermore, those inclined to cooperate in one context usually do so in other contexts.[25] Cooperation is also more likely in small groups than in large ones. In small groups, bad apples are more transparent, personal efficacy is greater, expectations of reciprocity are higher.[26] Likewise, in non-zero-sum games, most players defect (decline to cooperate) most of the time, even when they are permitted to communicate about their strategies. Some defection is stimulated by the impulse to compete. This impulse might be modified if people initially (i.e., as children) learn how to play non-zero-sum games, rather than the zero-sum games so pervasive in our culture.[27]

Political liberals (as the term is commonly used in the US) tend to be cooperators, making the assumption that it is better to risk that someone may cheat if it means society as a whole could benefit. Political conservatives are usually defectors. They place a high priority on personal autonomy, feel that they shouldn't be forced to cooperate if they'd rather not, and believe that by pursuing private gain, an individual frequently also promotes the public good.[28] Moreover, trust is an important factor in playing non-zero-sum games in a win-win manner. "Technologies of trust" (ranging from governmental laws to non-zero-sum games played online by many people living many miles apart) foster cooperation so that it can culturally evolve.[29] Finally, ethical prescriptions such as the Golden Rule or Immanuel Kant's "categorical imperative" address Prisoner Dilemma–like conflicts by urging us to set aside our self-interests for the common good. The bottom line is this: if we follow the Golden Rule, we automatically terminate the Prisoner's Dilemma.[30]

What is hateful to you, do not to our fellow man. That is the entire Law; all the rest is commentary.—Talmud, Shabbat 31a,

24. Barash, *Survival Game*, 139.
25. Poundstone, *Prisoner's Dilemma*, 177.
26. Barash, *Survival Game*, 139.
27. Poundstone, *Prisoner's Dilemma*, 174–75.
28. Barash, *Survival Game*, 135.
29. Wright, "Nonzero Hour," 343.
30. Méro, *Moral Calculations*, ch. 4.

from the Judaic tradition, ca. 1300 BCE

The suggestions explored above are all lifted from the research of others; none of them is original to this author. The originality of *this* redaction is two-fold. First, this essay collects these ideas into a succinct *beginner's guide* to ways in which we can utilize mathematics as a tool for ethical decision-making. Second, the treatment of these ideas is intentionally *slanted toward the more trust-engendering aspects of social interaction*, that is, to practices and attitudes which foster such behaviors as cooperation, fairness, and altruism. May the success of this essay be measured by the degree to which the reader is inspired to use and/or explore these mathematical tools in greater depth. After all, to extend the role of trust in our global society, we must . . .

Regard your neighbor's gain as your gain and your neighbor's loss as your loss.

—Tai-shang Kang-ying P'ien, from the Taoist tradition, ca. 500 BCE

Chapter 26: Moral Mathematics

Its Development and Potential for Social Benefit and for Spiritual Growth[1]

MORAL MATH CAN BE understood as the collection of ideas culled from mathematics and used (often metaphorically) to support and foster positive human social action. While this is not a new idea, it is relatively new in this form and in this nomenclature. In short, math can help us lead more altruistic, moral lives. Some of the essentially spiritual ideas presented here are based on recently developed math concepts such as game theory, theoretical complexity, the science of networks, and fuzzy logic. Other concepts, such as statistical imaging, are more traditional. All stretch math into a tool for exploring and teaching concepts usually relegated to the more humanistic realms of philosophy, religion, and social studies.

While ideas drawn from math can help individuals in their own personal quest for spiritual growth (as demonstrated, for instance, in the math testimonials by McFarlane and Voss quoted in the section "Potential for Spiritual Healing" below), the main outreach for this work is more social in nature. Ten examples of math used as a tool to impact social behavior illustrate ways to interpret moral math. These range from a television series about helping catch criminals, to support for educators who use math to help students understand and overcome social injustice and

1. Voss, "Moral Mathematics." Because this essay was an invited chapter in the *Handbook of the Mathematics of the Arts and Sciences* (a living reference work by Springer), I wrote it in third, rather than first, person. It is a part of a section on "Mathematical Influences and New Directions," edited by Ken Valente.

inequity, to directly applying fuzzy logic as a valuable aid in reducing the problems of human sex trafficking and illegal immigration. All of these may be considered issues of morality. Two other examples are given in vignette form at the beginning and end of the chapter.

DOLLAR AUCTION VIGNETTE

At the opening of a writers' retreat held in late 2018, poet, minister, and moral math pioneer Sarah Voss mentioned to the small group of writers assembled around a dining table that she would be working on an article about moral math for a handbook on mathematics and the arts and sciences. The other attendees, all with limited mathematical backgrounds, asked what moral math was, and, after a brief explanation, Voss demonstrated the concept by holding what is known in mathematical game theory as the dollar auction. She held up a crisp one-dollar bill, explaining that she would auction it off to the highest bidder in an auction identical to any other, with one caveat: while the highest bidder pays the auctioneer his winning bid and receives the desired dollar bill, the second-highest bidder (by entering the play) agrees to pay her last bid, even with no return on it.

"Who will give me twenty cents for this dollar bill?" Voss asked, and one person quickly raised a hand. "Thirty cents?" The bidding began then in earnest. Everyone was involved. Everyone had fun. (It was only a dollar, after all.) Around eighty cents, the bidders began to realize that someone was going to lose "big" and when the bidding finally stopped at $1.50, it was clear that even the winner was a loser. Then Voss asked them to compare this experience with that of a nuclear weapons race, and the discussion turned more serious as the writers/witnesses to this dollar auction saw the similarities.

"So how do you avoid something like this?" someone asked.

"You don't get into the game in the first place," someone else observed.

Voss adapted this dollar auction from current math literature and presented it in an experiential, user-friendly way so that even non-mathematicians could get the sense of the mathematical idea behind it. Then it was related by analogy to a social situation, where the resulting new insights held the promise of significant contribution to future moral behavior.

Occasionally, additional surprises emerge. A week later, at the conclusion of the writers' retreat, one poet, a newly retired English teacher, commented that triangles, parallel lines, and other metaphors from mathematics were somehow showing up in her newest poems.

HISTORY OF MORAL MATH

Voss, the first to claim the moral math title for this work, originally heard the term in private conversation with Sal Restivo, a leading contributor to the sociology of mathematical knowledge. Voss, a Unitarian Universalist minister and former math teacher, subsequently used the term in a presentation on "Moral Math and the Golden Rule" at the 2004 joint annual meeting of the Society for the Scientific Study of Religion and the Religious Research Association. The first known printed use of the phrase occurred in "Generating Trust through 'Moral' Math," a variation on the earlier presentation.[2]

An underlying assumption of her presentation was that we generate trust whenever we engage in the Golden Rule: Do unto others as you would have them do unto you. Versions of this rule exist in most of the world's religions, although some of us need many years to really incorporate the principle into our daily living. The basic principle, however, is easily understood through a mathematical Golden Rule which even children can grasp: for any fraction, multiplying (or dividing) both the numerator and the denominator by the same number will result in a fraction of equivalent value. For example, 1/3 = 2/6. You need only do unto the "1" (in this case, multiply by 2) as you do unto the "3" (again, multiply by 2). In this sense, mathematics is a tool to help children grasp the basic moral concept and to enhance their sense of fairness.

The foundations of moral math are informed by histories of both morality and mathematics, where strong cases have been made for the social nature of the two concepts. According to Sal Restivo, mathematics and mathematical objects are best understood in terms of a natural history or an ethnography of a cultural system. It is "math worlds," social networks of cooperating and conflicting human beings, that produce mathematics, not individual mathematicians or the minds or brains of individual mathematicians.[3] Moreover, in many cultures, those who

---

2. Voss, "Generating Trust."
3. Restivo, "Social Life," 250.

understand the prevailing mathematics are positioned to have a social advantage. The ancient Egyptian priests, for example, were powerful precisely because they could do such amazing calculations as those needed to predict the floods of the Nile, knowledge of which was the crux of economic advantage. A little mathematical insight has often been enormously empowering for those who hope to lead society.

Similarly, in *Purity and Danger*, noted anthropologist Mary Douglas linked the roots of moral decision-making to efforts to reduce ritual pollution in the *social* community, i.e., to the control/elimination of "dirt" in society. This, she pointed out, was as true for modern society (with its emphasis on pathological hygiene and the absence of any religious connection) as it was for primitive societies (where pollution rules about such potentially "dirty" things as certain dietary and sexual behavior were often conveyed through religious injunction). But while moral situations often are unclear and contradictory, Douglas maintained that pollution rules are unequivocal in a given culture and can "serve to settle uncertain moral issues." Moreover, dirt (defined as "matter out of place") implies both a set of ordered relations and a contravention of that order. Thus, dirt in society "is the by-product of a systematic ordering and classification of matter, insofar as ordering involves rejecting inappropriate elements. This idea of dirt takes us straight into the field of symbolism and promises a linkup with more obviously symbolic systems of purity."[4] To the moral math practitioner, mathematics assumes precisely such a symbolic role of purity.

The explicit use of math to understand, engage, and foster social ethical behavior, such as that illustrated in the dollar auction vignette, is only now fully coming into societal consciousness. However, the practical use of math for social regulation and benefit is not new at all. An examination of an antique math text is insightful here. Consider, for example, a math book linked to society that was used by Grandpa Williams, who represents a compilation of several of the author's relatives.

Grandpa Williams was a rural postman who lived his entire life in middle Ohio and who delivered the country mail by horse and buggy and did a little farming and a lot of carpentry on the side. When Grandpa Williams was in his seventies, he even built a house almost entirely by himself. In the late 1800s, when he was still a teenager, he studied from a

---

4. Douglas, *Purity and Danger*, 34–35, 129–39.

book called *Ray's New Higher Arithmetic*.[5] According to its introduction, this book was "adapted to the wants of classes in High School, Academies, Normal Schools, Commercial Schools and Colleges, as well as to private students," and it gave special attention to "modern business transactions" in such a manner that the pupil was "taught to think for himself correctly, and to attain his results by the shortest and best methods."[6]

As might be expected, this text is so outdated that it is fascinating. In the introductory section, important terms are precisely defined. *Science* is "knowledge properly classified," *principles* are "the primary truths of a science," *mathematics* is "the science of quantity," *art* is "the practical application of a principal or the principles of science." In a later chapter, *evolution* refers to a substantial chapter with algorithms dedicated to extracting roots of numbers. The accompanying "examples for practice" ask the student to find, for instance, the square root of the fraction 6/7 and the cube root of 7301384.[7]

"Word problems" included in the text seem quaint by current standards: "A man buys 32 3/4 pounds of coffee at 17 5/8 cents a pound: if he had got it 4 2/3 cents a pound cheaper, how many more pounds would he have received."[8] The answer (11 247/311) is printed immediately following the question, a consistent pattern so the reader knows the task is clearly more than getting a correct solution. In this section, the goal is to learn how to handle common fractions—any attempt to replicate this today without the assistance of a calculator virtually guarantees a new appreciation of the cognitive skills demanded of students in this era. This generation of learners could be amazingly facile when it came to doing mental calculations.

There are no pictures in this math text—no enticing stories to draw the reader into the situation. There are, however, various instructive *Remarks*. One typical example: "A *perch* of stone is a mass 16 ½ ft. long, 1 ½ ft. wide, and 1 ft. high and contains 24 3/4 cu. ft." Similarly, "Round timber will lose ½ inch being sawed, hence 50 cubic ft. of round timber is said to be equal to 40 cubic ft. of hewn timber, which is a *ton*."[9] There are also some four hundred pages of clear arithmetical explanations, followed by long lists of word problems for the students to solve. Students

5. Ray, *Ray's New*.
6. Ray, *Ray's New*, iv, iii.
7. Ray, *Ray's New*, 353.
8. Ray, *Ray's New*, 97.
9. Ray, *Ray's New*, 139.

were expected to drill until they learned the procedures, and, presumably, learned to do them quickly. The underlying goal, nonetheless, was to enable the student to function successfully in the social world. A couple more word problems will illustrate this point.

From a section on *Partial Payments* for loans:[10]

> $1480. Woodstock, VT. April 12, 1879. For value received, I promise to pay John Jay, on order, fourteen hundred and eighty dollars, with interest annually. James Brown. Indorsed: July 25, 1879, $40; May 20, 1880, $50; June 3, 1881, $350. What was due April 12, 1882? (Ans. $1291.95)

Added to this section are various historical and legal data, including specifics of a decision known as the "United States Rule" in which the Supreme Court of the United States detailed the proper way to make an *Indorsement* (viz., by writing the date and amount of payment on the back of the note). Also noted were rules for partial loan payments that applied only to Connecticut and Vermont, of which, presumably, the above problem was a relevant example.[11]

Interestingly, in one accompanying remark in this section, the reader learns that "the whole *aim* and *tenor* of legislative enactments and judicial decisions on questions of interest [due on partial payments], have been to favor the debtor, by disallowing compound interest, and yet *this very rule* fails to secure the end in view, and really maintains and enforces the principle of compound interest in a most objectionable shape . . . [in that] *the closer the payments are together, the greater the loss of the debtor*, who thus suffers a penalty for his very promptness."[12]

A second illustration is from a section on *Simple Proportions:*[13]

> A grocer has a false gallon, containing 3 qt. 1½ pt.: what is the worth of the liquor he sells for $240, and what is his gain by the cheat? (Ans. $225, and $15 gain)

Not only are practical social concerns lurking in these problems, but there are specific suggestions of moral issues as well. Grandpa Williams's math book is proof that mathematics has long been a social tool.

---

10. Ray, *Ray's New*, 265.
11. Ray, *Ray's New*, 261–66.
12. Ray, *Ray's New*, 261–62.
13. Ray, *Ray's New*, 180.

When Grandpa Williams was in his mature years, Aldous Huxley wrote what was to become his famous dystopia, *Brave New World*. In this novel, a caste society of the future produced a world of contrived happiness: the totalitarian government bred a carefully regulated number of people in the society to predetermined lifestyles, which they were conditioned from birth to enjoy. Peace reigned and nobody feared death. Such a brave new world looked desirable at first glance, but under Huxley's pen it proved to drastically limit human freedom, growth, and dignity. Though future-oriented, the novel reflected issues and concerns of the early twentieth century. Mass production had reinvented the world. With the arrival of the industrial age, amazing new feats and forms of communication were inexpensive and available to the entire developed world. At the same time, the Russian Revolution of 1917 and the first World War had stimulated widespread political, cultural, economic, and sociological unrest.

By the middle 1940s, the Third Reich had developed a substantial eugenics program which was only narrowly refuted at the end of World War II. Atomic energy had been utilized, a mixed blessing at best. But the child growing up in the United States then was largely unaware of these dynamics. Life was sweet. The immediate social world was interesting and safe, and children largely enjoyed freedom to explore the physical environment in ways children of 2020 will never know. Television and airplanes opened exciting new vistas. Grandpa Williams's grandson landed a lightweight plane in a nearby field. In many ways, fortunate children of this era lived in a Norman Rockwell painting—somewhat utopian, yet nonetheless filled with a steady dose of wry, reflective humor. Little did they know, or care, that the US Army's erection of the first electronic digital computer in 1946 had already begun the reign of computers and that the industrial era was already giving way to the age of information. Nor did they realize in 1953 that Francis Crick and his colleagues had discovered the great helix of DNA which would lead to Dolly and cloning, genetically modified food, and, in October 2018, the controversial birth of human twins whose genes had been embryonically altered.

But above all, children of Grandpa Williams's era did not understand that what was changing most was the speed at which everything was changing. In 1958, Huxley wrote *Brave New World Revisited*, a nonfiction work in which he concluded that the brave new world was becoming a reality much more rapidly than even he had suspected. Whether or not this world would/will truly become a dystopia is still an open question, but the "more rapidly" part of Huxley's concern is trackable. Math books call it "exponential."

Today we are faced with the results of ever more rapidly expanding human ability to tinker with hybrid, artificial, genetically altered, and "ordinary" life-forms, the last of which is likely the most vulnerable to extinction. At the very least, value-oriented and/or morally-inclined life forms (including ordinary human beings) must act with discretion in using current and future abilities. This suggests the need for innovative approaches to social behavior, in the broadest sense of the phrase. Math is one tool which is increasingly used to help guide this social endeavor. Mathematicians and non-mathematicians both can access the potential value of this tool and put it to good use.

LIMITATIONS, RESISTANCE, AND CAUTIONS

Moral math developers encounter some fairly predictable difficulties. On the one hand, scientists and other scholars sometimes resist or downplay the metaphorical and experiential nature of much of this work out of concern that it might water down scientific facts and thus negatively impact actual science. As the 2001 Templeton Science and Religion Prize Laureate Arthur Peacocke put it, "The trouble with using metaphors taken from science and used in non-scientific settings is that people tend to distort their true meaning."[14] Although Peacocke, a physical biochemist *and* an Anglican priest, referred here to metaphors from science, he clearly intended his statement to embrace metaphors from mathematics (mathaphors) as well.

On the other hand, some of the non-mathematicians whom moral math enthusiasts hope to include in this conversation are culturally predisposed to fear or avoid math—so much so that whenever the "math" word comes up, some individuals shut down before they ever start a real exploration of the topic. The essential idea behind the concept of moral math—that mathematics can be intentionally utilized to foster certain kinds of social behavior—is an ambitious one in that it assumes an egalitarian opportunity for *all* people to utilize the ideas, not just those trained in mathematics. But the math anxiety which some non-mathematicians claim interferes with this goal. Moral math presenters are therefore

---

14. Arthur Peacocke, personal conversation, Oxford, August 23, 1997.

challenged to pay extra attention to the venue in which ideas are shared and to the user-friendliness with which the math involved is presented. Fortunately, many of the relevant mathematical ideas *can* be framed in metaphorical (or other) ways such that it is not necessary for the receiver to be fluent in the language of mathematics to understand the concept and its possibilities.

An interesting and inspiring case study is Tara Westover. Westover was the daughter of a man who didn't believe in public education and so she was home-schooled or no-schooled throughout her childhood. In her 2018 memoir, *Educated*, she captures some of the struggles with math which she had to overcome after she'd decided to pursue a formal college education. One day, she recalls, she realized that to become college educated she would need to score well on an ACT test:

> The next day, I drove forty miles to the nearest bookstore and bought a glossy ACT study guide. I sat on my bed and turned to the mathematics practice test. I scanned the first page. It wasn't that I didn't know how to solve the equations; I didn't recognize the symbols. It was the same on the second page, and the third.
> I took the test to Mother. "What's this?" I asked.
> "Math," she said.
> "Then where are the numbers?"
> "It's algebra. The letters stand in for numbers."
> "How do I do it?"
> Mother fiddled with a pen and paper for several minutes, but she wasn't able to solve any of the first five equations.

So Westover bought herself a large algebra text. In her memoir she remembers some of the angst she experienced:

> I hadn't studied math since long division, and the concepts were unfamiliar. I understood the theory of fractions but struggled to manipulate them, and seeing a decimal on the page made my heart race.

A little later, she also acknowledged the lack of parental support she'd experienced for her educational ambitions:

> When I'd told Dad that I planned to go to college, he'd said a woman's place was in the home and that I should be learning about herbs—"God's pharmacy" he'd called it, smiling to himself—so I could take over for Mother. He'd said a lot more, of

course, about how I was whoring after man's knowledge instead of God's, but still I decided to ask him about trigonometry.

Somewhere during this journey, Westover grew to trust and appreciate math in ways she had not thought possible:

> I began to study trigonometry. There was solace in its strange formulas and equations. I was drawn to the Pythagorean theorem and its promise of a universal—the ability to predict the nature of any three points containing a right angle, anywhere, always. What I knew of physics I had learned in [my father's] junkyard, where the physical world often seemed unstable, capricious. But here was a principle through which the dimensions of life could be defined, captured. Perhaps reality was not wholly volatile. Perhaps it could be explained, predicted. Perhaps it could be made to make sense.[15]

Westover was born in 1986 and while most of her peers, at least in the Western world, would not have known such extreme limitations in their schooling, many of them, regardless of gender and background, would surely be able to relate to "the decimal on the page" which made her heart race. Overcoming this angst is a challenge both for the untrained math novice and for those who are trying to promote math as a tool to enhance positive social behavior.

That math can be used as such a tool is both a gift and a limitation of the work of moral math. Moral math is a supplement to, not a replacement for, ethical instruction. While math is proving to be a useful social tool, it is still a tool, just a tool, and, like all tools, it can be used for good or ill. Moral math is designed for the well-intentioned, but those intentions are obviously not guaranteed. Not by humans nor, as some worry, by future robotics and advanced artificial intelligence (AI).

A full exploration of this latter topic is beyond the scope of this article, but for those interested, a good starting place is "The Ghost in the Machine: Can Mark Zuckerberg Fix Facebook before It Breaks Democracy?"[16] Even if efforts to expand moral math ideas succeed, this should happen only with appropriate attention to careful checks and balances on its use.

---

15. Westover, *Educated*, 124–25.
16. Osnos, "Ghost."

TEN EXAMPLES OF MATH USED AS A TOOL TO IMPACT SOCIAL BEHAVIOR

Below are short descriptions of some moral math efforts. The selections are intentionally varied in nature and technique to show the range of ways to interpret moral math.

1. **An early illustration from popular media is** *Numb3rs*, a six-season television crime drama series which ran on CBS from January 2005 to March 2010. According to data from several online sources (e.g., Wikipedia, and TVSeriesFinale), the series averaged more than ten million viewers per season and is still accessible through online streaming (e.g., Hulu, Amazon). In this award-winning series, each episode involves a crime solved through the efforts of an FBI field office agent with the help of the agent's brother, a mathematical genius associated with a fictional institution of science called CalSci. The mathematics displayed is always accurate, though often not easily understood, and sometimes the connection to the plot is also less than transparent. To accommodate those with interest beyond screen time, Keith Devlin (known to millions of NPR listeners as the *Math* Guy on NPR's *Weekend Edition* with Scott Simon) and Gary Lorden (the principal *math* advisor to *Numb3rs*) published *The Numbers behind Numb3rs: Solving Crime with Mathematics*, a 2007 book detailing the math behind each episode. The mathematics involved includes statistics, math modeling, Bayesian inference, networks theory, and game theory.

Numb3rs, like some other recent efforts to use math to alter social behavior, focuses almost exclusively on *bad* behavior, thus turning this use of math into something of a correctional or policing tool. Nonetheless, it is significant that this fiction turned into reality after the series ended, at least in Los Angeles, where "UCLA mathematicians working with the Los Angeles Police Department to analyze crime patterns have designed a mathematical algorithm to identify street gangs involved in unsolved violent crime."[17]

2. **The online, peer-reviewed** *Journal of Humanistic Mathematics* (*JHM*) is an intentional home for reflections about "the aesthetic, cultural, historical, literary, pedagogical, philosophical, psychological, and sociological aspects of mathematics." On their website, the editorial board allows

17. Wolpert, "Can Math."

that the term *humanistic mathematics* "could include a broad range of topics; for our purposes it means 'the human face of mathematics.' More broadly, we aim to provide a forum for both academic and informal discussions about matters mathematical."[18]

Far-ranging in subject-matter, essays in *JHM* have nonetheless included specific work on the relationship between math and social behavior.[19] According to co-editor Gizem Karaali:

> JHM publishes articles about the state of the mathematical profession (both in research and in education), underrepresentation issues within the world of mathematics, and mathematics across national and cultural boundaries, as well as other types of writing which may stimulate discussion among its readers. As such, the values of mathematics and mathematics education, the ethical obligations of mathematicians and mathematics instructors, and moral math have been explored in past issues, and the JHM editorial team encourages further explorations of similar themes in future contributions.[20]

3. A second example from print media is a single volume book, *The Mathematics of Behavior*, by Earl Hunt, professor emeritus of psychology and adjunct professor of computer science at the University of Washington. As the title implies, Hunt's work, unlike that of the *JHM*, is very *narrowly* focused on social behavior and math. Yet within that focus it uses examples from psychology, sociology, economics, ecology, "and even marriage counseling," to provide a survey of how "mathematical thinking may be applied to problems in the social and behavior sciences."[21] The mathematic areas involved include calculus, probability, and statistics.

4. In the last few decades, mediation has become a valued method for resolving social disputes. In 2008 the Werner Institute for Negotiation and Dispute Resolution, a part of Creighton University in Nebraska, hosted a first-of-its-kind conference which applied chaos theory, complexity, and emergence to the field of conflict resolution. Stated goals of this conference were:

18. Huber and Karaali, "About This Journal."
19. See Voss, "Workshop."
20. Gizem Karaali, personal communication, April 11, 2019.
21. Hunt, *Mathematics of Behavior*, book description.

> To create a cross-disciplinary community of academics and practitioners interested in the intersection of complexity theory and conflict resolution
>
> To create a forum to promote integration of complexity principles into the field of conflict resolution and engagement in order to improve effectiveness of Alternative Dispute Resolution (ADR) practices in complex systems
>
> To share theories of conflict engagement, group dynamics, human factors and decision-making with experts in complexity science and chaos theory
>
> To develop strategies for day-to-day use of complexity principles to improve practice and education in conflict resolution so that: (1) the highest quality decisions emerge; (2) effective feedback loops are established; and (3) emergent phenomena are integrated organically with processes designed to foster engagement and resolution of conflict.

The International Conference on Chaos, Complexity and Conflict, according to then faculty member Bernie Mayer, "brought together practitioners, researchers and theorists in a creative dialogue that looked at issues on the cutting edge of both conflict theory and conflict practice."[22]

5. From the arena of educational pedagogy we find emerging interest in teaching mathematics in order to further social justice. One confirmation of this trend is found in *Teaching Mathematics for Social Justice: Conversations with Educators*, a book in which the authors, Anita Wager and David Stinson, have assembled a collection of fourteen essays by scholars/teachers/activists interested in the important role that mathematics teaching plays in helping students to understand and overcome social injustice and inequality. This collection "is the start of a compelling conversation among some of the leading figures in critical and social justice mathematics, a number of teachers and educators who have been inspired by them and who have inspiring stories of their own to tell—and any reader interested in the intersection of education and social justice."[23]

Collectively, these new pedagogical suggestions are designed to promote equity in mathematics teaching. That is, they intentionally teach children from diverse backgrounds, races, and cultures. However, they go beyond this goal in that they also explore how to help students use math to learn *about* social justice. Put elsewise, they intentionally teach

---

22. Nogg, "No Dispute."
23. Wager and Stinson, *Teaching Mathematics*, cover description.

children how to recognize social injustices and promote more equity themselves. This approach is a major digression from the treatment of social concerns in Grandpa Williams's math book.

6. Fuzzy logic, or the mathematics of uncertainty, has now been adapted to social concerns with provocative results and considerable potential. For instance, fuzzy logician John Mordeson (emeritus mathematics professor and director of the Center for Mathematics of Uncertainty, Creighton University) has cowritten two books[24] and several papers on the subject of human trafficking, modern slavery, and illegal immigration. Mordeson and his cohorts have also successfully used the mathematics of uncertainty to investigate concerns such as the challenge of keeping youth in the US foster care system safe from human trafficking,[25] and the determination of countries which have the most problematic trafficking routes into the States.

As Mordeson puts it:

> Accurate data concerning flow of trafficking in persons is impossible to obtain due to the very nature of the problem. The goal of the tracker is to be undetected. The size of the problem also makes it very difficult to obtain accurate data. There are many reasons for the scarcity of data. Among the most important are the victims' reluctance to report crimes or testify for fear of reprisals, disincentives, both structural and legal, for law enforcement to act against traffickers, a lack of harmony among existing data sources, and an unwillingness of some countries and agencies to share data. Thus concepts from mathematics of uncertainty provide a valuable way to study the problems of human trafficking and illegal immigration.[26]

A related area which promises significant aid from fuzzy logic is the medical field. The assumption here is that ethical decisions which hospital staff and others sometimes have to make involve value-laden choices which lend themselves to "fuzzy" or "smart" protocols.[27]

7. Certain video clips show how math can help render moral issues more accessible. Available online, they teach social concepts through

---

24. Mordeson and Mathew, *Advanced Topics*; and Mordeson et al., *Fuzzy Graph*.
25. Robinson et al., "Foster Care."
26. Mordeson et al., "Dialectic Synthesis."
27. Voss, "Fuzzy Logic."

demonstration. Voss has collected a beginning source list for such videos, which is replicated here.[28]

- "Visualizing Obama's Budget Cuts": This video uses visuals to enhance our comprehension of large numbers and help increase our insight into social issues around the national budget.[29]
- "Immigration, World Poverty, and Gumballs": This video offers another visual demonstration regarding number-size; this one attempts to clarify issues linking immigration to reducing world poverty.[30]
- "Teaching Game Theory with Video Clips": This is a blog post that introduces various resources across the net, including five movie clips, which can be used to gain understanding of real business situations.[31]
- "Direct Network Flow Problem on *Numb3rs*": This video is an example of how the six-season television series known as *Numb3rs* portrays mathematical topics as useful tools for solving various crimes.[32]
- "How Algorithms Shape Our World": In this TED talk, Kevin Slavin shows how algorithms of Wall Street can be digitally reshaped to shed insight on the vicissitudes of the Dow Jones index and how the topography of algorithms offers a metaphor with teeth to rethink the role of contemporary mathematics.[33]

8. The Survival Game, an interactive exhibit at the San Francisco Exploratorium lets museum visitors "play with concepts like trust, fairness, and equity through exhibits that highlight social tensions and dilemmas, including the Prisoner's Dilemma and the Tragedy of the Commons." Designed to experientially engage visitors in making generous social decisions about those in need, this exhibit is based on an East African society where the primary medium of trade is cows. It is noted as a "new

28. Voss, "Fuzzy Logic."
29. Wimp.com, "Visualizing."
30. Numbers USA, "Gumball Video."
31. Aje, "Teaching Game Theory."
32. SuperJustimagine, "Direct Network."
33. Slavin, "How Algorithms."

frontier in exhibit development."³⁴ The Survival Game was designed by The Human Generosity Project, a group of scientists studying mutual aid systems around the world.

9. A sermon makes an unusual and interesting arena for moral math, as Voss discovered in what she's called her math sermons. Two examples illustrate. In one, first offered in 2014 at a Unitarian Universalist church in Sioux City, Iowa, Voss talked a handful of volunteers from the congregation through a kind of dance which illustrated how light refracts or bounces back in various situations. This exercise came from an online article on teaching Snell's Law of Refraction (see chapter 19, footnotes 6 and 7).³⁵ After the volunteers physically demonstrated the math idea which is found in Snell's formula, Voss related the process to the spiritual issue of redemption. A variation of this sermon was subsequently published in *Still Points Arts Quarterly*, a journal focusing on art and spirituality.³⁶

In another sermon first given in Omaha, Nebraska, in 2019, Voss explored the social justice topic of intersectionality by using Venn diagrams, a notion first defined by the English logician John Venn in 1880 in an attempt to demonstrate the logical relationship between groups of things, or sets (see chapter 20, 196–201). Each Venn diagram is a circle and the circles overlap where there is a commonality. Intersectionality is the interconnected nature of social categories such as race, gender, and class as they relate to a given group or individual, and as they are subject to social bias and/or discrimination.

10. A "statistical poem" is what editor Roger Hodge once termed an intriguing compilation of figures and facts published faithfully every month since 1984. Others just call it "Harper's Index"³⁷ and note that it is a popular feature of *Harper's Magazine* which reports sometimes funny, often sobering political and social realities through statistics and unusual figures. A couple of recent examples:

---

34. McDonald, "Exhibitizing Cooperation."
35. Henderson, "Marching Soldiers."
36. Voss, "Redemption."
37. *Harper's Magazine* was first published in June 1850 by the New York City publisher Harper & Brother. Harper's Index has been a monthly feature since 1984.

> Percentage of Americans aged 13 to 17 who cite texting as their favorite way to communicate with friends: 35
> Who cite talking in person: 32
> Number of "two-hundred-year floods" Houston has suffered since 2015: 4
> Percentage of Americans who have had to evacuate their homes because of a natural disaster: 22
> Distance, in feet, by which the Earth's axis of spin has shifted since 1899: 34
> Estimated percentage of that shift that is due to climate change: 40.[38]

Like all good poetry, the Index can stimulate enough emotive energy to translate into action. Here, selectively, are more statistical tidbits from *Harper's*. Together they might constitute a mathematical equity notebook:

> World-wide, 54% of all people fall into the "middle and upper classes" and 46% fall into the "lower classes." Of those 46% lower classes, 700 million live in slums, 150 million have essentially no shelter whatsoever, 500 million are on the verge of starvation, 100 million are supported by garbage, 93 million are beggars. The total income of this "lower" 46% is 900 billion U.S. dollars annually. By contrast, the food and property destroyed by rats amounts to $400 billion per year; $700 billion each year would provide those in poverty with adequate food, water, education, and health. Today in the United States, 60% of adults with incomes less than half the poverty standard are women, the greatest cause of elderly abuse is financial exploitation, and ethnic groups comprise only a quarter of our population but over half of our AIDS cases. Seventy-one percent of black Americans believe that Arabs and Arab Americans should be singled out from other ethnic groups for special security precautions at U.S. airports; 57% of whites believe this.[39]

Simple math facts help clarify social inequity and can help inspire justice and contrition.

---

38. *Harper's Magazine* Editors, "Harper's Index," 9.

39. *Harper's Magazine* Editors, "Harper's Index," 9. Note that some of the statistics in this paragraph are from subsequent Indexes that I was unable to access later, even with help from *Harper's*.

EXPERIENTIAL PRESENTATIONS

While efforts to positively impact social behavior often take traditional forms (e.g., research, lecture, or demonstration), a communication strategy that uses *experiential* exercises plus social analogy warrants further investigation. Early techniques which incorporate such experiential teaching methods have successfully challenged people to resolve conflicts, treat each other fairly, be more cooperative in their interactions, and, generally, engage in moral behavior.

These exercises differ from other attempts to motivate moral development in that they are all culled from mathematics. Response has been enthusiastic, even from self-identified mathaphobes (who respond best when reassured that the math is user-friendly). The perceived neutrality of math seems to make moral math an avenue where individuals from different walks of life and different religious perspectives can find common ground to work together.

Descriptions of some of these efforts can be found in "A Workshop to Introduce Concepts of Moral Math."[40] The fifth and final exercise in this article uses a math fable to show how ideas adapted from math and applied to social behavior can be introduced to children at quite young ages. To accomplish this, two volunteers act out a children's story, *One Grain of Rice*. Using simple but appropriate props, garments, and guided prompts, these two children (or two young-at-heart adults) play the role of the Raja, a mighty but unwise leader in the East who rules his country with an iron fist and little generosity, and Rani, a young girl under the Raja's rule.[41] It's an apt moral issue to ponder after the workshop is finished. It's worth noting that the kinds of *experiential* involvement that this aspect of moral math encourages were first developed in the therapeutic setting, where they have proven to be effective tools for dealing with a wide range of social needs (see, e.g., Onsite).[42]

---

40. Voss, "Workshop."

41. See chapter 23 for how this story plays out.

42. Onsite is a program based in Tennessee offering experiential therapy workshops designed to help individuals and couples discover a better future. https://www.onsite-workshops.com.

FIVE (OF MANY) AREAS TO TARGET FOR CONTINUED MORAL MATH DEVELOPMENT

1. Stop Sadistic Statistics; Practice Paradisiacal Possibilities

Mathematics has long been both a forecaster of doom and a prophet of progress. Adversity warnings drawn from statistics can pave the way for positive new trends. For instance, a couple of decades ago researchers predicted big problems from overpopulation. The world population is now increasing at the alarming and potentially disastrous rate of one city the size of Los Angeles per month. Yet, because of the forewarning provided by statistical analysis, we may, with conscientious planning, reach population stability within a handful of decades.[43]

2. Live Better on the (Chaotic) Edge

In a 2019 *New Yorker* cartoon by Hanbin, two butterflies sit on neighboring bar stools. One says to the other, "Remember that hurricane a thousand miles away? That was me." When a study of weather patterns led Edward Lorenz to unveil this science of complexity and chaos theory in the 1960s, he opened the door to ideas which would make professional organizational communicators take note. The key phrase in the new communication dynamic is "self-organizing emergence." And the key place to find such a thing is right there in that murky, messy, uncomfortable space between order and total chaos.

3. Get a (Moral) Brain!

Mathematics and human brains are intricately connected, and not just because the brains somehow allow humans to "do" mathematics. In the late 1970s, scholars suggested that the human brain carries out its functions by using a kind of mathematics itself: the brain interprets all the data it receives as bioelectric frequencies, upon which it performs complex calculations. "Softness" or "greenness" or the smell of freshly baked cookies are only frequencies when the brain encounters them. The brain interprets, or calculates, these frequencies and stores them as abstract relationships. In this sense, as neuroanatomist Paul Pietsch put it, "mind is a mathematic."[44]

Investigators have since used ever-more-sophisticated imaging techniques to track which parts of the brain do what, a knowledge which

---

43. Elgin, *Promises Ahead*, 22–23.
44. Ferguson, *Aquarian Conspiracy*, 179. (Also see chapter 17.)

has significantly impacted and improved, for instance, various medical and health practices. New exploration of the brain often involves formal computer modeling which is focused on moral judgment and decision making. For example, researchers have started outlining new neural connections in the human brain in order to understand how the human brain can accentuate tend/befriend behaviors (instead of or in addition to fight/flight tendencies) when things aren't going so well.[45] Others have built mathematical models to help understand conflicts between, say, profit and harm. One new study, for example, shows that formal mathematical modeling can improve prediction of moral behavior.

This has clear legal and policy implications. If researchers can discover a set of parameters that can describe decision making across a variety of contexts, these could be used to design incentive schemes that promote moral behavior and discourage antisocial behavior.[46]

As UTA psychology (and former mathematics) professor Dan Levine put it in an article about lessons gleaned from neuroscience and experimental psychology, "Mathematics is a powerful tool for making sense of a confusing set of influences and for overcoming conventional wisdom to get to the truth."[47]

4. How Fuzzy Logic Might Save Souls

Although we've long suspected that Aristotle's law of the excluded middle might be overly restrictive, the Western world zealously embraced it—until 1965, that is, when Lofti Zadeh wrote a paper introducing "fuzzy" logic.[48] Fuzzy logic holds that not everything is black and white, right/wrong, true/false, or (in computerese) 0/1. Today, the world often focuses on "gray"—partially true and partially false, or (in computerese) values that fall in the numerical interval between 0 and 1. Fuzzy logic has already proven productive. We now have "smart" machines that better regulate everything from traffic flow at stop lights to pain control in the postoperative hospital room. Most recently, fuzzy logic has been applied to human behavior, with the idea that we might learn better ways of voting and paying taxes, of rewriting the abortion debate, of dealing with class issues, and of conducting "smart" wars.[49] The result may be less

45. Eisler and Levine, "Nurture, Nature"; Levine, "Lessons."
46. Crockett, "Formal Models," 85–90.
47. Levine, "Lessons," 15.
48. Zadeh, "Fuzzy Sets"; Zadeh, "Sets and Systems," 29–30.
49. Voss, "Fuzzy Logic."

ignorance, government, poverty, death—plus more power to the people and better ways of determining just how ethical someone really is.

5. Cantorian Religion Can

Matheology (short for mathematical theology) uses math metaphors to inspire and guide our spiritual lives. Thus, Georg Cantor's set theory ideas have been used to describe a religious inclination that is structurally new and doctrinally pluralistic.[50] In "Matheology and Cantorian Religion," Voss abstracts from seven set-theory insights seven metaphorical counterparts of traits which might be associated with this new religious structure. For instance, Voss discusses Cantor's notion that there exists a set of all sets which contains itself and metaphorically implies that a "Cantorian religion draws on all other religious views and also contains itself. One of the chief characteristics of this new religion is therefore understood as an emphasis on the acceptance of diverse religious perspectives.[51]

A related idea comes from computational neural-network-theorist Dan Levine in his work supporting a partnership society. As Levine puts it, a partnership (as opposed to a dominator) approach to religion

> falls between, and bridges, the two traditional extremes of theism and secular humanism. It seeks spiritual depth and transcendence but relies on the individual's inner experience and intuition rather than on outside authority. It accepts a diversity of theological beliefs and ritual observances, so that none of the world's current major religions would "win" over the others. As a recent bumper sticker says, "God is too big to fit inside one religion." Yet it incorporates beliefs about how people should treat each other.[52]

POTENTIAL FOR SPIRITUAL HEALING

Moral math contains within it the capacity for spiritual healing. Of course, an argument can be made that anything that positively impacts social behavior can promote spiritual health, but mathematics can carry this deeper, into the realm of epistemological insight.

---

50. Voss, *What Number*, 111–46.
51. Voss, "Matheology and Cantorian." (See also chapter 10, footnote 11.)
52. Levine, "Lessons," 20.

Today, many people tend to think of math and spirituality (if they think of it at all) as something which the ancient Greek Pythagorean society used in the effort to find and promote harmony on earth and in the heavens. The worldview of this society was nowhere near as informed as that which modern cosmology offers us, so it is likely that much of Pythagorean philosophy would have eventually lost its influence even without the help of the discovery of irrational numbers, a concept which radically upset the perceived harmony in society. Throughout succeeding ages, there have always been some mathematicians drawn to spiritual metaphors from mathematics,[53] but by the middle of the twentieth century, there was a kind of rejection of such satiny thinking in favor of a more rigid logic that was compatible with humanism, but more so by far with secular humanism than with religious humanism. For spiritual well-being, individuals went to a pastor or a guru or a shaman, but almost never to a mathematician. To a large extent the same thing may be said of today's society, but the moral math proficient sees new possibilities already arising.

In the twentieth century, perhaps the person most notable for his belief that math can further spiritual development was the American mystic and philosopher Franklin Merrell-Wolff. Born in California in 1887, he grew up Methodist, was educated in mathematics and philosophy at Stanford and Harvard, and taught mathematics very briefly in 1914 at Stanford, after which he immersed himself in mystical teachings and ultimately followed the Advaita Vedanta school of Hindu philosophy. He spent much of his nearly century-long life in the Sierra Nevada mountains in an ashram which he and his first wife, Sheriffa, founded. His thought and teachings have been collected into several printed volumes and voice recordings.

In one of his published works, Merrell-Wolff describes his appreciation of mathematics as a vehicle for transcendence from normal consciousness (which all humans have when they are not dreaming) to a consciousness that is of a higher order, a consciousness without an object. While he recognizes effective modes of approaching this transcendence in the esoteric traditions of the Orient, he nonetheless chose the mathematical road as the one of pre-eminent power for Western culture:

> Now the validity of mathematics is established upon a basis that is quite impersonal and universal. Its authority is not dependent

---

53. Voss, *What Number*, 71–109.

upon the name of any writer of any mathematical treatise. In its purity, it deals only with the transcendental or ideal objects of the very highest order of thinkable abstraction or universality.... Herein is revealed the power of pure mathematics as an instrument of consciousness-transformation on a very lofty level.[54]

Although first-hand resources are still accessible today, an online summary by physicist and mystic Tom McFarlane is an excellent source for a quick (or quicker) understanding of Merrell-Wolff's work in connecting spirituality and mathematics. In "The Spiritual Function of Mathematics and the Philosophy of Franklin Merrell-Wolff," McFarlane recaps how math acts for Merrell-Wolff as a bridge between the relative and transcendent states of consciousness:

> It [math] serves, on the one hand, as a vehicle for crossing from the transcendent to the relative by providing a highly subtle and precise language for expressing the immediate contents of transcendent states with minimal distortion. On the other hand, it also serves as a vehicle for crossing from the relative to the transcendent by providing highly abstract and universal symbols for generating insights through contemplation. Wolff emphasizes, however, that although the structure of this mathematical bridge is provided by the highly subtle forms of thought, an actual crossing of the bridge requires the motivating power of love and devotion.[55]

Merrell-Wolff, according to McFarlane, notes that mathematics is so well suited for this task of cross-translation because it constitutes our most abstract language, and therefore has the potential to carry the purest revelation of truth. Mathematics "is not only a thread by which we may know the Beyond, but also a means by which we may commune with it."[56]

Other mathematicians also point out how deeply intertwined mathematics and ultimate truth are. In "Spirit-Wise Math," we read about two of particular interest. One is the British mathematician G. Spencer-Brown, who, in 1969, published *Laws of Form*, a small mathematics text, which used mathematics as a sort of universal language of mysticism. Forty-five years later, MIT physics professor Max Tegmark published *Our Mathematical Universe*, in which he, too, offers a strong argument for

---

54. Merrell-Wolff, *Experience and Philosophy*, 394.
55. McFarlane, "Spiritual Function."
56. McFarlane, "Spiritual Function."

how math is the basis of reality. The works of these two math scholars are both spiritually intriguing. Taken together, these two authors (Tegmark and Spencer-Brown) point to a world formed of recursive, self-repeating, self-reproducing units which are to some extent self-aware and which are based on and/or equivalent to various mathematical structures. These math structures reveal themselves through tokens, marks, symbols, and, sometimes, through mathaphors.[57]

In this collection Voss has also written a bit about her own spiritual growth through mathematics: "When I first encountered Euler's formula, I already knew about the mathematical importance of 0,1, e, i, and π, but I'd entertained not a clue about their possible interconnection. It was a startling and mystifying insight. At the time, I was still an atheist…. It was a bad time for me when I … was leery of everybody and everything. Somehow, mathematics—with all its numbers in all their multitude of forms—was the exception, and in my eventual embrace of a new spiritual outlook, trust in math was a bridge for me."[58]

In a similar vein, Tom McFarlane, author of *Einstein and Buddha: The Parallel Sayings* and founder of a Silicon Valley patent firm, shares (expressly for this essay) a story from his own journey:

> I have a vivid memory from my first or second year of college when discussing mathematics with an older student. I don't remember the specific topic, but at one point he pointed out to me that mathematical truths are only true relative to particular axioms and definitions that we have assumed, and that they are not true independently, in and of themselves. Moreover, the axioms are merely assumed to be true, and do not rest on any deeper foundation. This may not have been the first time I considered this, but in this particular instance the insight was especially profound for me. None of our mathematical theorems is true in any context-independent way. And yet, mathematics is the paradigm of certain knowledge. On the one hand, once we clearly specify a particular set of axioms and definitions, there is no ambiguity or doubt or uncertainty about what statements are and are not true relative to that context. (For example, no postmodern critique or skeptic can ever show that there is a largest prime in the natural numbers, or that the Pythagorean theorem is not true in Euclidean geometry.) On the other hand, in mathematics we are free to choose any axioms and definitions we

57. Voss, "Spirit-Wise Math," 239. And see chapter 16 for more details.
58. Voss, "Miraculous in Number(s)," 82.

like, and true statements will change accordingly. (Finite fields can have a largest prime, and the Pythagorean theorem is false in non-Euclidean geometry.) So there is no absolute, context-independent truth.

For me personally, this insight had implications far beyond mathematics. For example, in situations where I would find my own ideas in conflict with the ideas of someone else, instead of following the impulse to prove myself right and them wrong, or figure out who is "really" right, I would instead seek to understand in what sense each is true in its own context. How do our assumptions or definitions differ? Of course, there is always the possibility that we do share common assumptions and definitions but one of us is simply being inconsistent. But the effect of the insight was to give others the benefit of the doubt, to look at apparently conflicting positions as alternatives that can be true in their own context instead of as opposed to each other in a dogmatic battle for truth. Many years later, I wrote a playful parable about this insight.[59]

I think it is fair to say that this insight from mathematics has had for me a moral dimension, insofar as it has helped to support personally an attitude of openness and interest in superficially conflicting ideas and opposing viewpoints. This kind of openness is essentially a form of love. The golden rule would have us consider the perspectives of others not as opposed to our own but as another possibility to be understood on its own terms, on equal footing with our own.[60]

CLOSING VIGNETTE

This essay opened with a moral math vignette and it closes now with another one. It shows the potential of moral math to heal old wounds.[61]

It was 2005 and I had prepared a presentation on moral math as a tiny part of a three-day UNESCO–type event in Seattle. My "track" was on trustworthiness and justice, and, right before I presented, a middle-aged gentleman shared his personal story about the terrible difficulty he'd had growing up Jewish in Austria after World War II. Another man in our group was

---

59. McFarlane, "Counting on Truth."
60. McFarlane, "Morality."
61. See Voss, "Generating Trust."

also from Austria, and his family had been part of the resistance movement. This second man suggested that the first person's story was one-sided, and the conversation took off from there, with the result that very raw emotions were ignited and one of the facilitators was even choking back tears. Being unable to bring resolution to the situation, the facilitators finally decided just to move forward with the agenda, which was fine with me except that the next item on the agenda was my highly cognitive presentation on moral math. Oh, no, I groaned inwardly. What on earth was I supposed to do next?

Winging it, I told the group a little about my interest in healing and how I found mathematics a fruitful place to glean fresh, out-of-the-box ideas. Then I led them through an experiential exercise called the dollar auction which I'd found in the literature on mathematical game theory and, after that, through a network-theory exercise which I'd developed to illustrate the way self-organization can emerge from the apparent randomness of chaos theory. To my surprise, I not only conveyed how math might work to promote trust, but I also showed them that it did. As one observer put it, genuine healing took place in the room.

Even the Jewish presenter told me later that he'd found my presentation powerful and personally healing, particularly the part which dealt with the random nature of self-organized emergence, which he related to the situation of the Holocaust. The fact that the Holocaust might have emerged randomly (rather than deliberately) seemed to be a comfort to him—though I wish now I'd had more time to unpack/clarify my interpretation with him. His feelings were echoed in various ways by other participants so that, all in all, it was extraordinarily exciting for me. I had assumed that my work could lead to healing, but this time I actually saw it happen.[62]

CONCLUSION

There is room for optimism, in spite of possible misuse of math, particularly in the realm of artificial intelligence. A recent *New Yorker* cartoon by Farley Katz shows a small airplane-shaped drone hovering over a flowering plant on the ground of a barbed-wire fortress. Two guards watch as the drone waters the flower from a can attached to it. One guard says to

---

62. Voss, "Mathematics, Ministry, Mediation."

the other, "Unfortunately a tiny percentage of the drones are opposed to violence."

Tongue-in-cheek, but nonetheless hopeful!

Indeed, as this essay has pointed out, moral math offers out-of-the-box approaches to social behavior issues. There are still many discouraging social problems in human society—disease epidemics, climate change, political cheating, power hoarding, cast-iron stands on abortion, terrorist attacks, and discrimination against minorities or the transgender community, or the poor, the elderly, the disabled, anyone not a man, or an individual who's black *and* poor, or black, poor, *and* disabled, or . . . . Moral math enthusiasts won't necessarily have immediate answers, but they unquestionably have tools that, used thoughtfully, can help the discernment process involved in solving these problems and promoting generosity, equity, fairness, sharing, caring, helping.

Chapter 27: Do No Harm: Math and Ethics[1]

Mathematics is the handwriting on the human consciousness of the very Spirit of Life itself.—Claude Bragdon

Throughout this *Math Mystic's Guide to Creative Spirituality* I have attempted to show mathematical underpinnings that relate to and can assist our spiritual journeys. In the process I have intentionally drawn on past work which I have published, a task that turned out to be challenging and sometimes difficult, but also personally rewarding in that it's helped me review my own individual spiritual journey. While Lewis Thomas has called mathematics the universal language of the future, I have found it to be a welcome language of mysticism. Because of its ability to transcend our three-dimensional world and to show us realities that go beyond the scope of our technology, mathematics offers a trustworthy vehicle for exploration of a reality where mystical notions can be addressed in ways other than as purely revealed truth. At the same time, math is also a language which addresses our ordinary reality, the one in which I am sitting in my modest office at a desk which holds my computer, typing as fast as my thoughts (and aging hands) will permit.

Mathematics, then, is a guide to both the ordinary and the mystical realms, one or the other and sometimes both at the same time. Or maybe always both at the same time, in much the same sense that, for example, Dan Levine writes about how urgently our current reason-emotion split

---

1. Voss, "Exploring Moral Math," 5B. The sermon I drew from for my second example was titled "Nature of Love in a World Where Dolly Gives Birth to Herself." I presented it to the Second Unitarian Church of Omaha on February 13, 2000.

needs to be healed.² Levine is a neuroscientist and a professor of psychology at the University of Texas at Arlington. His earlier career was as a professor of mathematics. In his words:

> The difficulties we have with systems are a sign that [the] Communications Revolution is in full swing but the Compassionate Revolution has not yet arrived. In other words, we have the rapid technological advances but our systems for interpersonal and institutional relationships are still rooted in older norms based on competition, domination, and lack of trust, and consequently the technology has not been made as user friendly as possible.³

Levine offers a further note of caution in his comments:

> Almost any activity can be helpful, harmful, or neutral for human relations, depending on the context. Judgment of whether an activity is ethical or unethical cannot be made simply from knowing the behavior that the activity involves. Rather, such a judgment also requires knowledge of the spirit in which the behavior is performed.⁴

His caution echoes my own. As I have put it elsewhere in this guide: While math is proving to be a useful social tool, it is still a tool, just a tool, and, like all tools, it can be used for good or ill.⁵ It is, thus, with growing awareness of the need to do no harm that I put together this final chapter in my guide. Culling through my past writings, I find two examples that expand this idea.

The first is a six-hundred-word editorial, "Exploring Moral Mathematics," which I wrote in 2019 for the *Omaha World-Herald*'s Midlands' Voices.⁶ Since I began my study of the relationship between religion and math/science in the late 1980s, I have come to recognize ever more intensely a growing need for ethical considerations in moral math. In this editorial, I take several examples from an earlier (but still 2019) edition of my local newspaper to lift up this concern. Here are all 619 of those "six hundred" words:

---

2. Levine, *Healing*.
3. Levine, personal correspondence, March 31, 2021.
4. Levine, *Healing*, 79.
5. I've said something like this often in this manuscript. See chapter 26: "Limitations, Resistance, and Cautions" for these exact words.
6. Voss, "Exploring Moral Math," 5B.

DO NO HARM: MATH AND ETHICS 289

Twentieth-century developments in mathematics have created 21st-century tech concerns that deserve increased societal attention and more thoughtful ethical guidelines to bring forth a cohesive, productive and just future. A trendy new direction in math, dubbed "moral mathematics," seeks to add wisdom and discernment to math-based ideas affecting human social behavior.

Several examples that warrant dialogue and examination can be found in the Oct. 13, 2019, *Omaha World-Herald*. For instance, the newspaper that day included a *Washington Post* article detailing how Russian disinformation agents have used online methods to influence real-world events through social media: it predicts likely political innovation which Russian operatives and others might use to manipulate various outcomes in upcoming U.S. elections and to otherwise create discontent among the populace.

In that day's Living section, Molly Cavanaugh writes in her column on parenting that modern technology isn't a parent's best friend. "I've tried my hardest . . . to avoid being too much of a helicopter or lawnmower parent," Cavanaugh writes. "However, this school year seems to be electronically compelling me to hover and attempt to clear the path for my (now fourth grade) son for the first time ever."

In a movie preview, we read that in *Gemini Man*, Will Smith plays a 51-year-old version of a government assassin who faces off against a computer-generated version of his 24-year-old self. Smith says that cloning "ultimately pans out to be poison honey. It will be a reach that potentially comes back to bite humanity in ways we are not considering fully."

World-Herald staff writer Reece Ristau writes about how Nebraska's "Silicon Prairie" is having a powerful and hopefully productive impact on the local economy. "I have no idea what the data center world looks like in 10 years," says Andrew Rainbolt, director of the Sarpy County Economic Development Corp., "but I don't think our demand for the Internet or cloud computing is going to go away anytime soon."

Each of these articles showcases issues explored under the moral math umbrella, the specific intent of which is to make social behavior more just, fair, caring, altruistic. . . .

However, these *World-Herald* examples show some of the worrisome aspects of using this umbrella. Similarly, the *Guardian* recently carried an article in which Hannah Fry, associate professor of mathematics at University College London, calls for mathematicians and computer engineers to heed a Hippocrates oath similar to the one that physicians honor. "First, do no harm."[7]

Says Fry: "We've got all these tech companies filled with very young, very inexperienced, often white guys who have lived in math departments and computer science departments.... They have never been asked to think about ethics, they have never been asked to consider how other people's perspectives of life might be different to theirs, and ultimately these are the people who are designing the future for us."

Though accurate, I wish to carry Fry's point further. I first considered the ethics involved in mathematical/scientific decision-making in the early 1990s (about when Dolly was being cloned) at a Templeton-sponsored conference where a female representative of a major drug company shared advances her company was making in biogenetic engineering. She pointed out the total lack of any mandatory ethical oversight for this whole process. The drug companies themselves were creating such regulatory boards; even then they could see the need for ongoing ethical input.

Though uncertain about the status of such ethics committees these days, I am sure of two things. First, we need ethical boards, and second, they need to include ordinary people, not just specialists. The ethical decisions of today will shape the decisions of tomorrow, and they will be far-reaching. J. Doe needs a voice in them.

That was my caution in 2019. My second (and final) example is a portion of a sermon on biogenetics which brings up ethical issues which I was only just beginning to pay attention to some thirty years ago. I share excerpts from this sermon now in part to trace my own response to ethical issues related to mathematics. You will see that I have moved from a place of minimal awareness of the need for ethical input/guidance in moral math decision-making to a place where I intensively wish to call wide attention to this need. So here, culled from a 2000 sermon titled "The Nature of Love in a World Where Dolly Gives Birth to Herself," is the history behind my current call for stronger ethical deliberations:

In early 2000 I attended a conference on religion and science held in the San Francisco area. As part of this conference, we were invited to visit one of the research facilities at the University of California at Davis. I chose to tour the large animal facility in what no doubt was once part of the school's agricultural college. There I encountered two sets of two

---

7. Fry, "Hippocratic Oath."

goats. The first set was a mother goat and her baby. They were cute. They looked, smelled, and acted like any other mommy/baby goat pair. What was unusual about them was that they had both been cloned from the same egg cell. More specifically, a fertilized egg, cloned from another goat, was divided, producing two identical twin eggs. One of these twin eggs was frozen and the second was implanted in a surrogate mother, who subsequently produced a female baby goat. When the baby goat grew to reproductive maturity, the first cell was unfrozen and implanted in the now mature other one. The two goats were both cloned from identical genetic material; thus, in essence, the mother goat had given birth to herself.

As I understood it, the impetus for this experiment was to test a hypothesis regarding a mother's willingness and ability to nurture her infant. One theory held that a mother "mothers" because at some level she perceives foreign material in her, i.e., material not of her own makeup. However, in this case the baby was genetically identical to the mother, and, since the mother did all the normal things that mothers do—nursing, tending her offspring, etc.—the experiment showed that the presence of foreign genetic material is *not* the trigger that causes a female to perform the mothering function.

Whether this hypothesis was of enough significance to justify the experiment I cannot say. What I can report is that my own personal reaction to this situation was one very close to repugnance. I generally consider myself pretty open to new ideas, so it surprised me that I had such a negative reaction. I note it here simply as a fact, but I must observe that it is a very common fact. Traditionally, we humans do not *like* change, at least not initially. In most cases we overcome any initial resistance and adapt to the change. Sometimes this is appropriate, sometimes inappropriate. But, clearly, the emotional weight of change cannot and should not be the deciding criteria regarding whether or not it is a right change.

The second set of goats—both mature females, both very pregnant—were not cloned, but transgenic animals. Transgenic means they were in some way a mixture of two species, as in *trans*, or crossing, *genes*. Actually, in this instance, they were mostly goats. They certainly appeared to be goats, normal goats even, poking their heads out of the pen at anyone close enough to nudge, grabbing at whatever you were carrying. Goats. Well, almost goats. What was different about these goats is that they had each been implanted with a single human gene. So, transgenic, in this case, meant a combination (albeit minimal) of goat and human. Now I've known the occasional individual (usually male, I'm sorry to say) who acted like an old goat, but that's really not quite the same thing. These goats were the subject of a very new kind of experiment, one that is loaded with ethical questions that take us to, and beyond, the stated purpose of the experiment, which, in this case involved the potential medicinal uses of the milk these goats might produce. In truth, my emotional reaction to this transgenic situation was just as negative as it was to the goat who gave birth to herself. Here was a world I didn't want to confront, a world of the future, except that the future was now.

I should point out that the title I finally chose for this sermon is technically incorrect. Dolly, the famed sheep, did not literally give birth to herself. Dolly was cloned, yes, but cloning of animals, to say nothing of plants, is something that was going on long before Dolly was born in 1997. What was unique about Dolly is that she was cloned from a mature adult cell, not from embryonic material. This was a breakthrough that, again, has definite medicinal implications, which I will draw out more finely a little later. For now, let me point out that the current raging controversy over biogenetic research stems largely from questions about the source of *embryonic* material. In all likelihood, however, much of the material necessary to continue such research may soon be scientifically produced in laboratory culture. In fact, my understanding is that it already *is* produced in this fashion, although not yet in sufficient quantity to meet the increasing research needs. It seems to me, therefore, that ethical issues surrounding the use of donated fetal tissue in general, and aborted fetal tissue in particular, will eventually no longer carry as much weight in religion and sexuality conversation. Which is not to say that no ethical issues remain, only that the current popular focus may be shortsighted.

Today, various cloning studies have been successfully conducted on plants, on animals, on human embryonic material donated from terminated pregnancies and from IVF (in vitro fertilization) clinics, and on human material that comes from adult brain tissue which has been surgically removed for treatment of epilepsy. Yet, there's a bit of a slippery slope in the use of the term *cloning*. What is expressly forbidden by law is the type of cloning that leads to the reproduction of humans—basically a kind of non-sexual procreation. What is expressly banned by law is the use of public funds for such research. Nonetheless, virtually everyone in both the public and private research sectors currently argues against human reproductive cloning. No human Dollys allowed in the foreseeable future![8] Furthermore, from theological considerations of the dignity of personhood, reproductive human cloning would be an ethical disaster.

On another level, however, on the level of what is called somatic cell nuclear transfer, human cloning offers the possibility of significant and impressive medical breakthroughs. Without doubt, there exists now new hope for reducing human suffering and improving human health and wellbeing. To name only one of a multitude of examples, consider a person suffering from heart disease. Using somatic cell nuclear transfer, a mature adult cell from the patient could be fused with an enucleated donor egg cell which could then be developed into entirely new—and healthy—heart muscle cells. If these healthy cells were subsequently reintroduced into the patient, the risk of rejection would be virtually eliminated since the material transplanted would be genetically identical to that of the patient. From theological considerations of beneficence, this clone-your-own-organ transplant process is essentially a good idea. Furthermore, the beginnings of a technology for it are already present in laboratory culture.

The main problem: What's in the petri dish? Is it property or is it person? This is a question which our theology of sexuality must eventually address in new and thoughtful ways. If what is in the petri dish is in any sense person, then the theological implications of issues of procreation need to be reexamined. Procreation is no longer a province of heterosexual marriage alone, for example. And what about test-tube babies that have been genetically altered in some way? Why stop at test-tube manipulation, for that matter? Consider the recent case of the Down's syndrome fetus which doctors surgically "fixed" while still in the womb. Or what about the possibilities that homosexuality is genetically determined—is that something our theology tells us we should "fix" if we have the technology to do so?

There are more questions still. Is it possible, for instance, to be respectful toward something, such as fetal tissue—or animals—which you intend to destroy? Who should give consent for donated research material, and under what conditions? Our Western tradition subtly assumes a kind of private ownership of bodily parts (including fetuses) which has led us to set various standards for informed consent, to say nothing

---

8. Remember, this sermon was written more than two decades ago. A Chinese researcher, Jiankui, apparently accomplished this gene editing for humans when twin baby girls, known by their pseudonyms Lulu (Chinese: 露露) and Nana (娜娜), were born in October 2018.

of allowing us to justify such donation on the basis that such informed consent has been obtained. But might this just be an abdication of responsibility? Other cultures, for example, question whether the donating individuals have *any* right of decision in such matters. Are we reacting to subtle cultural biases that are no longer appropriate? Since research is now done entirely in the private arena, does that mean that we do not need to be publicly accountable for it? Or have we lost control, so that we have nothing to say about it? Have we, as a collective community, allowed scientific advances to drive theological stances? Should we, for that matter, even engage in efforts to eradicate the effects of aging cells and disease? Should we use illness and suffering as a measure of who we are as a community? How, in a pluralistic society, will we achieve public consensus on future action? How can we ensure that all research is conducted in the context of concern for global justice?

As I revisit the three decades I've invested in the study of mathaphors, matheology, and moral mathematics, I realize how indebted I am to a handful of people and organizations which have supported and encouraged this exploration. One of the organizations is the Templeton Foundation, which has offered opportunities, constructive substance, and on occasion financial support which I badly needed. One small (yet hugely relevant) example is the Templeton-sponsored conference I attended many years ago where I heard my first real ethics discussion about biogenetics. What the lecturer said about the need for ethical oversight has influenced me and my work ever since. At the time of her lecture, she was working for a big-industry company and sat on their self-formed ethical board. The reason she was part of an ethical board for this company was that no one else was taking the responsibility to form such a board and so the company, in an unprecedented effort to make ethical choices about sensitive issues, felt obligated to form an ethics review board themselves rather than to ignore the issue, or to allow decisions to be made purely on the basis of economic profit.

Oh, I realized. There is no J. Doe, no ordinary person who will have any say on these important, life-influencing changes—changes likely to materialize even without such input. And who is most likely to be affected by these choices? None other than J. Doe.

To a huge extent, that revelation has guided my work since. Instead of opting for a formal, scholastic research approach to my efforts, I have tried hard to find ways of raising J. Doe's consciousness. Hence my math sermons. My "coming out of the 'math' closet" and dealing with math microaggressions. My classes for seminary students. The experiential workshops I've offered. The attempts (unsuccessful) to put together a museum exhibit on math and religion. A dedicated website. My editorials. This book, which contains my collected work. My mistakes. My revisions. Throughout these years I have experimented with different ways to step away from the well-insulated Scholar's Room and into the lives of ordinary people who have a right and a responsibility to be involved in the shaping of our collective human future.

Have I been successful? Well, I am certainly not alone in this effort. But only time will track any emergent "strange" attractor.

"FOR SOME ODD REASON"

That's why, says Book Angel
to explain how "Math" ended up
in the name of his non-math press

same as the seminary student
who, years ago, enrolled
in my class on math and religion,
later confided that when
she'd arrived on Day 1
she'd almost kept right on
going out the other door
but didn't

same as the friendly,
enthusiastic, finally-going-
to-college older student
I met (even more years ago)
at a social engagement
who instantly iced
when she discovered
I was the math teacher
for the remedial class
she'd start next week,
and yes, she aced the class

same as Stephen Hawking
whose editor told him he'd
lose half his audience
for every equation he used,
so he used only one

same as

same as

same as me, who couldn't
figure out why math hounded
like a faithful dog that knew
something important.

Appendix A: Twenty Loosely Spiritual Insights Drawn from Mathematics

1. $n_1 \sin\theta_1 = n_2 \sin\theta_2$ (Snell's Law)
When light travels from one medium to another, it generally bends or refracts. Something similar happens to the human spirit during redemption.

2. $E^{\pi i} + 1 = 0$ (Euler's formula)
Everything important is connected.

3. Definite integral of calculus
The one is equivalent to the many. Yes, that's paradox. Yes, that describes relationship. Yes, that's how God is.

4. $1 = .9999999$ (repeating continuously)
Things that appear to be very different may really be the same.

5. Gödel's incompleteness theorem
You can have consistency or completeness, but not necessarily both at the same time.

6. Real number line
There's more irrationality than rationality.

7. Number Stories
We can use mathematical tools to help describe the spiritual realm beyond Copernicus.

8. Real, complex, and transfinite numbers
The real always has zero imaginary component, the complex is more fun, and the Infinite is strangely ordered.

9. Chaos theory
Chaos and order is a chicken and egg dilemma, but chaos deserves fresh PR.

10. Mathematicians
There's a little mathematician in each of us, and in other "lesser" creatures, too. God is a mathematician. God is love, and other stuff, too. But God is definitely a mathematician.

11. Network theory
To make a difference, target the hubs.

12. Statistics
You can lie effectively, or you can tell the truth. You may know which you are doing.

13. Thirteen
is just another number; nonetheless I'm definitely not going to stop here.

14. Inequalities
Some things are greater than other things.

15. Entanglement
Weird things happen. Nonlocality. Miracles. Non sequiturs. Grace.

16. Reducing fractions
(as in 6/8 = 6/8 = 6/8)
Humor makes everything easier.

17. N-dimensions, hyperspace
Abbot had it right: a flatlander can't fully comprehend Sphereland. But math, a mystical language, helps us grasp dimensions of existence that otherwise we'd mostly deny.

18. Beginning algebra
Algebra is an under-recognized source for comprehending the Golden Rule. Do unto one side as you do unto the other.

19. Set of all sets
A "religion of all religions" is just as flawed and just as true as any other religion, but it is structurally different and refreshingly interesting.

20. "42"
The answer to everything is pretty simple.

Appendix B: The "Contact Process" for Self-Organizing Emergence and Networks[1]

OVERVIEW

The Contact Process is an interactive game which illustrates the concepts from self-organizing emergence and network theory. By playing it, we *experience* the abstract mathematical foundations of emergence and how it can impact social behavior.

RELEVANT IDEAS FROM COMPLEXITY THEORY

1. Small changes in initial condition make big changes in outcome (cf. the butterfly effect).
2. Self-organizing emergence refers to the tendency of order to appear out of chaos.
3. Strange attractors (closely related terms include bifurcation points, phase transitions) are points or places where significant changes in the basic nature of substance occurs.
4. Collectively, such ideas belong to what is formally called the theory of nonlinear dynamic systems and is informally referred to as complexity or chaos theory. The initial development of these was completely dependent upon the emergence of the computer.

[1]. Adapted by Sarah Voss for interactive learning.

5. Chaos theory, network theory, and the theory of fractals are all intertwined; it's a little like looking at the same picture which has been depicted in different artistic mediums. The emphasis in each is different.

6. Network theory is based on a view of reality which holds that everything is inseparably connected. Scholars are currently trying to flesh out abstract laws of network theory in order to understand more about the diverse ways in which we can be connected.

ACTION RULES FOR THE CONTACT PROCESS

1. Arrange chairs like on a checkerboard grid and allow participants to choose where to sit so that at least some of them are close together (neighbors). The group has a stockpile of red and blue cards.

2. Each participant chooses a red *or* a blue card from the stockpile, and then picks a number between 1 and 6 (or 1 and 4 for a small group) which will be that individual's special number for the duration of the play.

3. The leader rolls a die, and everyone with that number stands up. Those standing will have either a red card or a blue card.

    A. Each participant standing up who holds a *red card trades it for a blue card* from the group store.

    B. Each participant standing up who holds a blue card does one of the following:

        i. Trades it for a red card if one or more neighbors have a red card (the shifting probability).

        ii. Keeps the blue card otherwise.

4. Wave cards to see the patterns developing, then repeat step #2. Continue indefinitely.

Alternative Versions

The game changes if the shifting probability changes. Imagine a big room of people playing the contact process. What happens if three people

THE "CONTACT PROCESS" FOR SELF-ORGANIZING EMERGENCE

(instead of one) are needed to exchange blue cards for red cards? What happens if six people are needed? (A: The shifting probability decreases as the percentage of neighbors increases and change is more gradual.)

SUMMARY OBSERVATIONS

1. The colors shift over time, either rapidly or gradually. There may even be several shifts over time. Note: a kind of color-order emerges out of what was initially a purely *random* distribution. This is a simplified example of how self-organization emerges out of randomness.

   That is, self-organizing emergence arises from randomness on the basis of *simple action rules* and a given, though arbitrary, *shifting probability*.

2. If the shifting probability is high enough, a threshold (or critical point) is reached. One color might take over. This is an example of an abstract law. Another law: If a community is *growing* and newcomers have an *attachment preference* (maybe they like red), they gravitate to form clusters which reflect that preference. In our contact process, an attachment preference ensures that eventually there will be several large clusters of red and some of blue and not much mix or diversity. In our example, these clusters are linked to the people who initially stood up; these individuals (randomly selected) become the focus of a *hub* and may turn into *strange attractors*. Like the Pied Piper, they collect more and more of whatever it is they are collecting. Sometimes the behavior or identity of a community tips out at some critical point (or *threshold*) and a cascading action results somewhat as water becomes steam when it reaches the boiling point.

3. The computer allows researchers to study patterns in order to make sense of this abstract game. As the process plays out, the bigger picture becomes clearer and more such *laws emerge*.

SELECTED OUTCOMES OF SELF-ORGANIZING EMERGENCE

- In inanimate systems (such as economics): the rich get richer
- In health systems: disease spreads in epidemics

THE "CONTACT PROCESS" FOR SELF-ORGANIZING EMERGENCE

- In engineering systems: electric power grids collapse like dominoes
- In computer systems: the Internet gets viruses
- In cellular systems (such as the neural network of the brain and life itself): self-making occurs
- In social systems: fads prevail, racism develops, cooperation spreads

Note: To bring about social change, redirect the hubs.

Appendix C: An Interview with Sarah Voss on Mathematics, Ministry, Mediation

Fig. B1. Sarah Voss, 2009

Introduction[1]

The text below is a record of written correspondence between Thomas McFarlane and Sarah Voss during 2009. This document is copyright © 2009 by Sarah Voss and is published here with her kind permission.

---

1. This interview originally appeared in *Holos* and included the following biographic details: "In the course of her diverse life, Sarah Voss has been a mathematics professor, a Unitarian Universalist minister, a mediator, and a police chaplain. She holds a Doctor of Ministry from the Meadville Lombard Theological School in Chicago." See Voss, "Mathematics, Ministry."

Tom McFarlane: Thank you for agreeing to this interview. I'm very glad to have this opportunity to learn more about your life and work because you have a very unique background as both a professor of mathematics and, later, as a Unitarian Universalist minister. Perhaps most importantly, though, you have worked to explore some fascinating connections between these two fields of knowledge, such as in your book *What Number Is God?*

Before we get into these very interesting topics, however, I'd like to first ask if you would share with us some of your personal background. Perhaps you could start by telling us a bit about your upbringing, for example, where you grew up and what your childhood was like. Were you raised in any particular religious tradition?

Sarah Voss: Thanks for asking, Tom. I appreciate the opportunity to become a *Holos* interviewee. It's an honor to be asked. I'm happy to share a bit about my personal background—and most everything else, too.

I was raised on a dairy farm in the northeastern corner of Ohio. We lived about seven miles from Lake Erie, but visited it only rarely and in the summer, usually when my cousins from Kansas came for a visit and then never after early August when the danger of getting polio seemed (according to my mother) to increase significantly. Mine was a pretty conventional rural upbringing—quite conservative as I look back on it, with 4-H every summer (sewing and showing my Guernsey heifer) and every Sunday the Congregational church (youth choir once a month and confirmation by the time I was eleven). I've just finished writing all about my upbringing (and more) in a book whose working title is *Self-Making: Autopoiesis of Woman*. It's my personal story, written with a mathematical underpinning. *Autopoiesis* is translated variously as self-emerging, self-forming, or self-making, so the subtitle is redundant. I suppose that's another rule I've broken.

Tom: What drew you to the study of mathematics in college? And, later, what motivated you to seek a career in academia as a mathematician? Did you have an interest in religion during this period of your life? Did you have a sense of the connection between the two back then?

Sarah: I was good in math. I was good in English, too. I was also insecure about a ton of things, especially finding a husband—which was the golden goal of every girl I knew back then. In college I majored in math because (1) I qualified to participate in a unique undergraduate honors program in mathematics and (2) I thought there'd be more opportunity to meet my future husband if I went into math. Not exactly the most admirable reasons, I admit, but I was young.

I always wanted to write, but mathematics kept finding me one way or another. Like the time after I'd quit teaching math to ninth-graders and never wanted to teach anything to anyone else ever again, and I applied for a position as a public relations director at a small community college in Maryland (my home at the time). I wrote a great cover letter which got me an interview, but the personnel department quickly scoped out my total lack of qualifications for the position I wanted and offered me a job teaching math instead. That sort of thing happened to me all of my life, the second twenty years of which (to address the last part of your question, Tom) I called myself an atheist. So, yes, I had a strong interest in religion during that period of time; it was just highly negative. Not the same thing at all as apathy. As for a connection between math and religion back then? Nada. Not a bit. Not that I could see, anyway. I never ventured out of Plato's cave back then.

Tom: Could you elaborate a bit about how you came to identify yourself as an atheist? When did that transition take place? Was there some specific dissatisfaction or negative experience that drove you away from religion?

Sarah: Perceptive questions, Tom. I think my atheism probably started when I was a teenager and was super-sensitive, super-critical, and super-insecure. As a young teen I also had a close call with death which took me through a "life-review," but didn't seem to get me to that "light at the end of the tunnel" stage. Emotionally, I felt rejected and distrustful, both in my social and spiritual lives. Somehow I eventually translated that into a strong intellectual conviction that life was purely material. That conviction lasted into my late thirties, and was not easily shattered even then.

Tom: During your time as a professional mathematician, what was the relationship for you between mathematics and religion? How did your interest in relating these two areas of knowledge emerge for you?

Sarah: At first there wasn't any connection for me. At that time I considered religion a bad word, while mathematics represented something I could trust—like the rest of the scientific world. I had a strong desire to avoid what I considered the hypocrisy of the religious world, and I certainly didn't want to subject my young, impressionable children to it! My world didn't have a lot of hope in it then, and none that was non-material.

Then I had what I refer to (depending upon my audience and/or mood) as a mid-life crisis or the dark night of a mystic journey. That story is too long to tell here. Anyway, one day not long thereafter when I was mathematics program director at an all-women's Catholic college, I began to tell my five female calculus students how God was like the definite integral of calculus. I watched myself telling them this, and even I thought it was a little odd. Soon after that, however, I began to seriously investigate the relationship between mathematics and religion. It was a hard go. Most of my contemporaries didn't think there was a relationship between mathematics and religion.

Tom: Although you've indicated it is a long story, could you say something more about your transformation from an atheist to a mystic? Did mathematics play a part in your mystical transformation during this period?

Sarah: I go into more detail about this in *Self-Making*. Let me just say here that an ex-priest was the catalyst for my transformation and that a messed-up surgery left me withering in enough pain that for a short period I'd have welcomed any form of relief, even death. I think that my inner willingness at that point to give up my material life helped prepare me psychologically for the major spiritual change which would follow in the next few years. Mathematics definitely accompanied and supported the intellectual part of this transformation, but it was not causal.

Tom: What prompted you to change your career from mathematics to ministry? What drew you to the Unitarian Universalist (UU) tradition?

Sarah: After my mystic conversion, I felt a strong call to the ministry. I pretty much felt compelled to become a minister. I don't think anyone should become a minister if they can possibly do anything else. When I was enmeshed in my dark hour, I'd found Unitarian Universalism. On a liberal-to-conservative continuum of religions with Protestant origins, Unitarian Universalism was at the far left end, a bit more religiously liberal than Congregationalism. It was a good fit for me in my aspiring search for truth. It still is. There is a great deal of freedom (and a less immediately obvious demand for responsibility) in UUism to pursue this search.

Tom: Did you begin your ministry with the idea to relate mathematics and religion, or did that emerge later? How has your work relating mathematics and religion developed over the years?

> *I'd realized that mathematics, like poetry, was one of the languages historically used to try to communicate the mystic experience. . . . I went to seminary wanting to find out more about how that language worked.*

Sarah: When I went to seminary, I intentionally took mathematics with me. I knew I wanted to explore the relationship between math and religion more intensively, and I believed (more or less correctly) that I could do so through the UU faith tradition. I entered theological school with a profound desire to write my doctoral thesis on the topic. By this time I'd realized that mathematics, like poetry, was one of the languages historically used to try to communicate the mystic experience. Think of Abbot's *Flatland*, for example, where poor A. Square journeyed into Sphereland and was forever changed. I went to seminary wanting to find out more about how that language worked. I figured maybe then, by some gift of God's grace, I might find myself in a situation where I might actually be able to assist someone else in finding the hope I myself had found in and through mysticism.

As for how this work (relating mathematics and religion) developed over the years, the short answer is amazingly well. I was able to accomplish 51.388 percent of what I hoped to do. I'm kidding. I just like the sound of precision in 51.388 percent! Precision has been conspicuously absent in "how my work developed over the years." But, somewhere around "half of my expectations and endeavors were realized" is probably pretty descriptive. I've developed and taught an award-winning class about the relationship between math and religion. I've written extensively about the subject. I've offered workshops, lectures, and have even preached about it. Not long ago I accompanied a science and religion class from Rensselaer Polytechnic Institute as guest faculty on a two-week trip to Italy. I've also had some disappointments, such as a class on moral math which I was very excited about offering at my seminary but which didn't get enough students to "make," and a traveling museum display which I spent hours of time and vast amounts of energy developing but which I was never able to get funded, and an online journal which I sort of let slip away quietly into the zone of a personal website. There's just not been very much money—either to live on or to bring some of my ideas to fruition. But the inner rewards have been bountiful, and, probably, more to the point of your question. Over the years, I've enlarged the focus of my work to include not only matheology, but something I refer to as moral math, an umbrella term (not original to me—I think I first heard it from Sal Restivo of RPI) to include ways in which mathematics can help inform everything from conflict resolution to how we vote. I see this as a ripe arena for further exploration. The possibilities are exciting.

Tom: You once offered to the church you were serving five sermons based on different mathematical metaphors. What prompted you to give these sermons and what were the metaphors? How were these sermons received?

Sarah: Oh, goodness, I can't even remember which sermons those were, only that they were five of the early ones. What prompted me was that I'd discovered (in researching my thesis) that a major way in which the language of mathematics was historically used to expand our understandings of spirituality was through the use of what I call *mathaphors*—i.e., metaphors drawn from mathematics. Mathaphors, in other words, were hugely important to what I've called *matheology*. That's the main premise of my book *What Number Is God?* (which, not coincidentally, started out life as my doctoral thesis). Was it surprising that I'd want to share mathaphors from the pulpit? Not to me. I wanted to share these ideas any way I could, just as any other (overzealous?) mystic might.

Mathaphors, however, have current as well as historical importance. Today's culture is largely caught up in the truths of science, which consistently uses mathematics as the primary language for both exploration and communication. To me, that means mathematics is also an exquisite candidate for *contemporary* spiritual exploration. Lewis Thomas, author of many books on science, medicine, language, and philosophy, once referred to mathematics as the universal language of the future. So, sure, I've spoken mathematics from the pulpit. How? Well, carefully. And not all the time, either. I remember early on in my professional ministry how I announced that I would be giving one of my math sermons on an up-coming Sunday. One person, whose math anxiety was extreme, stayed away altogether. For quite a while after that I gave the sermon first and then told them what it was!

Here are the names of some of my "math" sermons. "Coming Out" of the *Math* Closet; The "Strange Attractor" of Hope; Reflections about Nothing; Out of Statistics, Hope; Prayers That Count; Our Electronic Church; Gödel on Evil; Our Entangled Web (that one was a bust); God and Quantum Transitions; Computers and Consciousness; Toward a Cantorian Religion; How Fuzzy Logic Might Save Souls. That's probably half of them. I tried to interest a publisher in putting together a book of them, but, alas, without success. You need a lot of resilience to be a pioneer in this field!

Tom: Although it may sound surprising to modern ears, in your book you say that mathematics has been used throughout human history as a connecting device between metaphysics, theology, and religion. Who are some of the historical precursors to this perspective that mathematics has some relevance for religion? Do you have in mind Pythagoras? Nicholas of Cusa? Cantor? Others?

Sarah: Yes. Yes. Yes. Others include Plato, Galileo, Novalis, Jacobi, Kronecker.

Tom: In your book you write about how mathematics provides a metaphor for understanding metaphysics, and you describe a metaphor as a way of seeing. Could you elaborate on this idea a bit, and perhaps provide a simple example of what you mean? Do you think there is something special or fundamental about mathematics as a metaphor for viewing reality?

Sarah: Feminist theologian Sallie McFague once defined a metaphor as "seeing one thing as something else." We "see as." For example, we see God as Father, and we act accordingly. We see God as Mother, and our actions are likely to change somewhat to fit this alternative way of seeing. In this sense a metaphor is a way of seeing. Mathematics provides not just "a" metaphor for understanding metaphysics, but lots of them. Some offer better ways of seeing than others.

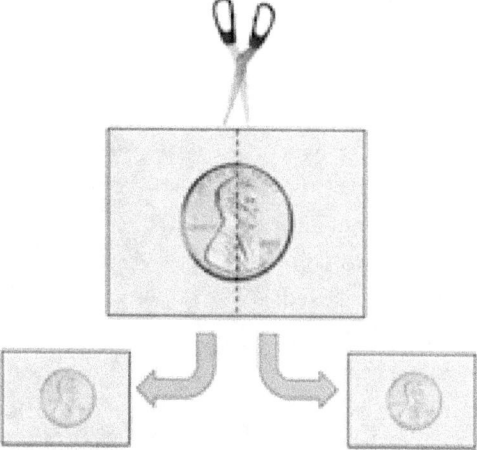

Fig. B2. Cutting a Hologram in Half: Cutting a hologram in half yields two smaller holograms, each containing a complete image of the whole. Each half thus contains the whole.

Take holography, for instance. In one math and religion class I taught, I invited a skilled physics professor to demonstrate the characteristics of holography—particularly, the surprising property that each part of a holographic image is in some sense equivalent to the whole. The professor arrived in our classroom equipped with an appropriate piece of "film" and all the other tools he needed to produce a holographic image. He then took a holographic "picture" of an ordinary penny. When he was done, he passed the film around so that all of the students could see for themselves what the image looked like. It looked just exactly like what all of us who have seen both a hologram and a penny might expect it to look like—something a little on the order of a "ghostly" one-cent coin. After everyone in the class had seen the image, the professor used a pair of scissors to snip the "picture" right down the middle, in effect splitting the penny into two parts. Everyone gaped in surprise after examining these two separate pieces of film because *each one* showed the penny in its entirety. Each part was equivalent to the whole.

The physics professor was demonstrating science, not mathematics, but the thing about holography is that the whole process was spelled out clearly in mathematics maybe twenty years or so before the technology (i.e., the laser) was invented to turn the theory into a material reality. The mathematics came first. Then came the technology to make images we could hold in our physical hands. Then, still later on, came the idea that we could use the notion of holography to see something else as if it were a hologram. David Bohm, Einstein's coworker, was probably the first to identify the metaphorical possibilities of holography. Bohm developed a model of reality that sees each part of energy and matter as a microcosm that enfolds the whole. Later Michael Talbot and Stanislav Grof (to cite two contemporary examples) used Bohm's ideas to create their own metaphysical versions of reality, each revealed, respectively, in their books, *The Holographic Universe* and *The Holotropic Mind*. The titles of those two books alone illustrate what I mean about how mathematics can be used as a metaphor for viewing reality.

Tom: Physicist Eugene Wigner once famously wrote about the "unreasonable effectiveness of mathematics in the physical sciences." What are your thoughts on this mystery? What explanation would you propose to understand how it is that mathematics works so well in physics?

Sarah: I am awed by this mystery. How would I propose to explain this wonder? I wouldn't. I just enjoy it. That's pretty much how I feel about the mystery of life, too. The best I can do is describe it, or at least the part of it I'm familiar with, and I'm apt to do that with mathaphors. In fact, that's what I just did in my book, *Self-Making: Autopoiesis of Woman*. I looked at my life as though it were an autopoietic process and used nine of the characteristics

Fig. B3. Jonesy: This is Jonesy. She keeps Sarah company in her office these days. She's wearing a T-shirt that illustrates a contemporary mathaphor. It reads: "And God said: [Maxwell's equations] . . . and there was light!" Jonesy first appeared in Sarah's article "Mathematical Theology."

of this process to structure my story. I think chaos theorists, to name one potential audience, will be interested. If others are interested, too, then maybe it will find a publisher. (There *is* hope!)

Tom: In one place in your book you write that "nature is just mathematics that you can touch" [p. 42]. Could you elaborate on what you mean by this? It sounds similar to Galileo's view that the book of nature is written in mathematics but you seem to go further by saying that nature is not merely described by mathematics, but is mathematics.

Sarah: There does seem to be a mathematical structure undergirding nature. Is nature mathematics? I guess my answer is yes and no. Does a human need a human skeletal structure in order to be a human? Yes. Is a human its skeletal structure? No, not really. It's something like that, I think, between math and nature.

Tom: A series of quotations in your book [p. 76] seem to suggest that the very existence of things is essentially mathematical. For example, Philolaus says that "All things have a number, and it is this fact which enables them to be known." Philo says number was "the basis of the design of the Creator" and "the number itself, rather than its concrete representation, is considered the ultimate reality." Dionysius the Areopagite wrote that "to the best of our ability, we use symbols appropriate to things Divine, and from these again we elevate ourselves, according to our degree, to the simple and unified truth of the spiritual visions." Can you explain in what sense numbers are built into the very nature of reality?

Sarah: This is tricky, Tom, and I'm not sure how well I can answer your question. I can tell you that it is possible to understand the very existence of things as essentially mathematical. That is one way of seeing. I think the quotes which you refer to on page 76 indicate that a variety of individuals throughout history seem to have engaged in that kind of perspective. It is not the only way. And even seeing the very existence of things as essentially mathematical is open to a variety of interpretations. In fact, the whole section of my book around page 76 refers to number symbolism, which is more popularly known as numerology. I confess I'm not much of a numerologist, although I can remember applying one such system to my own birth name and determining that I was an "8"—or something like that. I recall avidly reading what it meant to be an "8." It felt a lot like reading my horoscope: no matter what I read, it fit. Numerology can be fun. But true? The Enneagram is a more recent variation of numerology and I know some folks who put great stock in it. What the heck, Augustine put great stock in number symbolism, too. He thought it was a way to discover the "mysteries of God which are set down in Scripture." More recently, Michael Drosnin set forth a highly popular (and controversial) variation of Augustine's position in *The Bible Code*. It, also, was fun reading, but it's not exactly what really gets *me* going.

Tom: The quote above from Dionysius suggests that mathematics actually can be used for more than merely gaining intellectual understanding. He seems to suggest that mathematics can actually help to attain a mystical illumination. Kurt Gödel also seemed to hold this view. For example, Hao Wang from his book *Reflections On Kurt Gödel*, p. 196, writes, "He [Gödel] also looked for (but failed to obtain) an epiphany (a revelation or sudden illumination) that would enable him to see the world in a different light. (In his conversations with me, he repeatedly said that Plato, Descartes, and Husserl all had such an experience.)" What are your thoughts on (or experiences with) mathematics as a way of mystical illumination?

Sarah: To the best of my knowledge, any efforts I've made to illuminate the mystical way for someone else haven't gone very far. I actually don't spend much effort trying to be a guiding light. It feels presumptuous and a little arrogant. I *have* sown lots of thought-seeds, though, and many of them are mathematical in nature. Who knows what will happen to those seeds in the future?

Mathematics, however, has played a *fundamental* role in the way I claim my *own* mystical insights. Math has provided ways for me to grasp things that I couldn't comprehend in any other fashion. One example (which I mentioned earlier) is the way the part can be equivalent to the whole; the mathematical theory of holography helped me accept this contradiction. Because I trust the mathematics, I am comfortable saying to myself that perhaps something similar is true in the mystic world. That is, my mathematical knowledge both supports and expands my mystic understanding that the divine in each of us is a microcosm of a much greater divine.

Tom: In theology there is the paradox that God is not merely the sum of everything but in some sense transcends everything and is more than the sum of the parts. You have related this paradox to mathematics with the metaphor "God is a definite integral." Now this is certainly meaningless to anyone who has not learned calculus, and even to those who know calculus its meaning is probably not self-evident. Could you briefly explain the definite integral and in what sense it is God?

Sarah: Briefly? You jest, Tom!
All right, I'll do my best. In its simplest form, the definite integral of calculus is a complex, sophisticated process of adding up many, many geometric areas—so many different areas that there is no end to them.

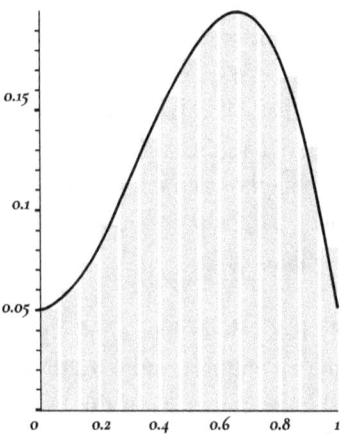

Fig. B4. Approximating the Area under a Curve: The area under a curve can be approximated by adding the areas of rectangles. As the width of the rectangles decreases, their area more closely approximates the area under the curve. The definite integral calculates the area exactly by taking infinitely many rectangles of infinitesimal width. (Note that, online, the image "moves" to show the concept.)

Imagine a stack of paper of various sizes and shapes which is so high it disappears from sight. Some of these sheets of paper are like the ones you put in your computer printer, the ones which are about 8 by 11 inches, or (roughly) 88 square inches in area. Others may be the size of, say, a 3 by 5 inch postcard, or roughly 15 square inches in area. Your task is to add all of them up and come up with the exact number of square inches in the whole bunch. You don't even know how many areas you're adding together, because this is a never-ending process and there are always more. An infinity of areas. Summing up all these areas of this never-ending column of paper is surely impossible, but—and this is a huge "but"—a special mathematical technique called the definite integral allows you to transcend this problem and discover the total sum—the whole column, even though you can't see it. That's not exactly the way the concept is presented in a calculus text, but it's roughly the idea. What this process taught me is how the one and the many are the same.

Mystics like to talk about the unity of everything. There are lots of ways of saying this. Sometimes I think of how many different souls there are in the reality I am experiencing, and how different they all seem to be one from the other. Yet when you add them all up, you just get God.

Tom: In the modern world we are faced more than ever with the confluence of different cultures and religions. It is challenging for many people to understand how these different religions, which appear to be mutually exclusive, can be reconciled. You suggest that Cantor's mathematics of infinity can help to understand the relationship between religions. Could you elaborate on this metaphor and explain a bit about the mathematics of the infinite and how it can help provide a useful understanding of the relationship between religions?

Sarah: You'd probably like this in half a page or less, right? I'm afraid, Tom, that I'm going to cop out here and refer those who are interested to the thirty-five-page chapter called "God the Definite Integral and Cantorian Religion" which appears toward the end of *What Number Is God?* The metaphor about God as a definite integral dealt with ultimate reality—how everything is related to everything else. The metaphor about Cantorian religion was not so much about ultimate reality as it was about the different kinds of religions which try to deal with that ultimate reality. Some people think, for example, that, while there are many approaches to the top of the spiritual mountain, there is only one right one—that only one will actually get you there. Others think there are several possible routes which will get you to the top, but they prefer one over all the others, and that one is their religion of choice. In modern times, greater ease of travel and better communication technologies have increased the world's awareness of this religious pluralism. I suggest in this last chapter of *What Number Is God?* that a totally new kind of religion is emerging, one that is made up of the set of all these religions. This is not a better religion than the others. It is just a different kind of religion. It is structurally different from the others in the same sense that the mathematician Georg Cantor's "set of all sets" was structurally different from all the rest of the other sets. At the same time, this new, highly pluralistic religion that is emerging is also just another religion, subject to all the problems and limitations that any other religion might encounter.

For those who are interested in knowing more about how this structural difference impacts this emerging religion, I refer you to "Matheology and Cantorian Religion," an article I wrote for the *Journal of Religious Humanism* (Winter/Spring 2004). In this essay I identify seven specific ideas about mathematics which, thanks to Cantor's legacy, are now known to be true, and also seven ways in which these mathematical ideas can be adapted to our spiritual lives. As one example, I write in this article that the structure of this Cantorian religion lends itself to the acceptance of religious contradictions and paradox. One such paradox is that a Cantorian God both is and is not an infinite God.

Tom: The metaphors discussed above seem to have primary relevance for the abstract understanding of God and the relationships between religion. How can we apply the metaphors in our personal religious lives? Can these metaphors help transform us from self-centeredness to Reality-centeredness? If so, how? Can you share any examples from your life?

> *Anything that helps to demonstrate how we are all related to each other is a spiritual asset. Personally, I have found fertile ground in mathematics for demonstrating many such concepts.*

Sarah: Excellent questions! I guess if I were to write *The Math Mystic's Guide to Creative Spiritual Living*, it would probably contain a large section on how behavior and belief inform each other. If the "many" truly believe that they are "one," then, barring duress or other interference, the many are likely to relate together with ease, tolerance, acceptance, and the almost automatic expectation of working for the good of the whole, much as a person's two separate hands naturally work together to benefit the larger body. Similarly, when I act as though I am related to everyone else, I come to believe that I truly *am* related to everyone else. If I act as though I love my enemy, over time I am likely to do so. I tend to think that anything that helps to demonstrate how we are all related to each other is a spiritual asset. Personally, I have found fertile ground in mathematics for demonstrating many such concepts.

If, however, duress and other interference inhibits this otherwise natural progression from self-centeredness to Reality-centeredness, then

I'd pull out the second section of the *Math Mystic's Guide*—the part about "moral" math. This is the section that culls from the math literature all the possible ways in which mathematics offers insight into conflict resolution, fairness, equity, and so on.

Tom: In *What Number Is God?* you write that "It is the responsibility of the liberal religious leader to promote such exploration [between mathematics and metaphysics]." What are some of the ways (in addition to your book, of course) that you have done this?

Sarah: I think I've largely addressed these ways in my earlier comments, but I'd like to mention here one of the most meaningful experiences I've had in my attempt to promote exploration between math and metaphysics. It was 2005 and I had prepared a presentation on moral math as a tiny part of a three-day UNESCO event in Seattle. I had assumed that my work could lead to healing, but this time I actually saw it happen. It was God's grace that I could experience that healing, even once—such a wonderful affirmation of my work.[2]

Tom: Since writing your book *What Number Is God?* in what ways have your thoughts on this topic developed? In what ways have others developed these kinds of ideas?

Sarah: I have definitely moved more in the direction of action. Now retired, I recently trained to be a mediator in what is known as "interest-based mediation." This is a fabulous process, geared toward helping the dissenting parties make their own decision about how to resolve their differences. In the last few years I've taken something of a sabbatical from my own active work on math and religion—no workshops, no lectures, no research of any sort. Still, the possibilities of moral math seem to be calling me, so when I underwent mediation training, I did so with the sense that this new work would at least be compatible with my former

---

2. Aside from some email conversation with a conference convener, the first place I ever wrote about this lovely event was in this interview. However, if you, welcome Reader, have processed everything I've collected and put into this *Guide*, you will have already seen the tale in chapter 26, all of which was drawn from my contribution to the new Springer living reference work called *Handbook of the Mathematics of the Arts and the Sciences*. Hence, I'll not repeat it here. However, should any of you kind readers have experienced healing of some sort by way of this *Guide to Creative Spirituality*, I hope you will share your experience with me. (See www.piZine.org for ways to contact me.) I promise to write about that, too.

work on moral math. To my great excitement I discovered that the mediation centers with which I am affiliated had recently offered a continuing education program that involved chaos theorists from a nearby university. They were demonstrating the very kinds of things I've been preaching about all my ministry.

When I first began studying the relationship between math and spirituality, it was hard to find other people who were involved in the area. In the twenty-plus years since then, that has changed dramatically. Mining mathematics for spiritual inspiration has become a much more recognized and better understood practice.

Tom: You have written that "a renewal of this divine aspect of mathematics will contribute to the overall spiritual health of our contemporary religious institutions" [p. 161] and that "Our wider social community stands now at the edge of a new way of thinking, of a paradigm shift" [p. 160]. Moreover, you have proposed that "The root of renewal lies in our willingness to embrace mathematics as a metaphorical language" [p. 162]. How do you envision this unfolding in the future? How would you like to see it unfold?

Sarah: Like a hope-flower blooming.

Tom: That's a beautiful image. Would you venture to envision some features of this flower when it has bloomed? How would you hope it might contribute to or change the way people think and act and live?

Sarah: Thanks. Your questions here bring out the Platonic idealist in me. I don't know that we will ever achieve universal peace, serenity, fairness, equity, altruism, unconditional love, and so forth, but I contend that it is worth striving for these things. Life without this intent is of dubious value. Moreover, mathematics is a wonderful mind-opener, as in "thinking outside the box." Where else (besides through a "mystic moment") can we find the tools to help us envision, say, a fourth or fifth or nth dimensional existence? Mathematicians (especially those interested in string theory) seem to do this with (relative) ease, and sometimes they can even translate what these tools lead them to see so that those of us still inside Plato's cave can get at least a partial glimpse of their vision. Of course, it is possible that a hope-flower in full bloom (where conflict and controversy always manifest respect and loving care) would be boring beyond bearing, but that's a risk I'm willing to seed.

Tom: Thank you for taking the time for this interview! I hope that this will be of benefit to people and help bring about the changes you envision.

Sarah: Thank you, Tom, for offering me the opportunity to let more people know of this work.

Appendix D: Final "Mathaphorical" Wave

Math as a Literary Tool and a Hope for the Future[1]

Thirty years ago, I stopped teaching calculus to Nebraska undergraduate students, attended theological school in Chicago, and wrote a ministerial doctoral thesis which, in 1995, became *What Number Is God?*—a volume in SUNY's series on Western esoterism. That title was short for *What Number Is God? Metaphors, Metaphysics, Metamathematics, and the Nature of Things*. It opened doors for my work on math and spirituality. It also marked the place and time when I first began to understand that metaphors drawn from mathematics could be effectively employed as literary tools, an endeavor I have loved. In this book I used metaphors drawn from mathematics to show that they can help even those who are not math specialists gain insightful understandings of the spiritual world and social behavior. After SUNY published this work, I coined the term "mathaphor" to indicate a metaphor drawn from mathematics. I have used it in many applications since.[2]

I am not the first person to use mathaphors as a literary tool. For instance, two variations on holography occur in the titles (and content) of Michael Talbot's book *The Holographic Universe* (1991) and Stanislav Grof's volume on *The Holotropic Mind* (1990). Another appears in the content of Frank Tipler's *The Physics of Immortality* (1995) where the author holds that the human soul "is nothing but a program being run

---

1. Voss, "Mathaphor as Literary Tool." Portions of this essay are drawn from "Context and Compassion," a math sermon which the author initially offered on October 24, 2021, to the First Unitarian Church of Sioux City, Iowa.

2. See also Voss, "Workshop"; "Moral Mathematics"; and "Mathematics and Theology."

on a computer called the brain," and that the universal wave function is bounded by an Omega Point which he describes as "an omnipresent invisible field, guiding and creating all being, and ultimately Personal"—all mathematical features which Tipler claims as traditional defining properties of the Holy Spirit.[3] There are many more such uses of mathaphor which, together, span the human presence on earth. The Pythagoreans (ca. 530–520 BCE), for instance, said that number rules the universe, and Plato (429–348 BCE) held that God ever geometrizes. Many of these metaphorical expressions were used to validate philosophical treatises that we might today link to the ethereal realm of theology.

Not everyone has accepted the use of mathaphors. After I was ordained in 1992, I began to offer math sermons from the pulpit. After one of the first, I discovered that that four-letter "m" word frightened some self-defined mathaphobes. In a class I taught to seminarians ("Math, a New Language of Theology"), one of my students later told me that when she had first passed through the classroom door, the math she'd expected to encounter in the class had tempted her to go right out the other. She turned out to be a wonderful student who was glad she had signed up for the course. On the other end of the spectrum, Episcopalian priest and biochemist Arthur Peacocke once told me that he became concerned when people took metaphors from science and used them in popular literature because he felt it was too easy to misuse the science involved.[4]

Peacocke, who some years later would receive the noted Templeton Prize for Science and Religion, was correct, of course: it is easy to misrepresent the science and/or the related mathematics. Nonetheless, I have found that (if done gently) introducing the math/science with a metaphor can ultimately give non-mathematicians a better feel for what the math that lies behind it means and how it applies to the spiritual notion(s) involved. Similarly, as long as the metaphor is not abused, most scientifically oriented individuals are happy to know that those who find math/science less than friendly can actually become more willing to try out the math.

An illustration of the way I've used mathaphor in workshops is the dollar auction, which is an experiential example I culled from game-theory literature about the Prisoner's Dilemma. In this mathematical game, a dollar bill is auctioned off according to the normal procedures of an auction where the highest bidder takes the whole dollar, but in the dollar

3. Tipler, *Immortality*, 185.
4. Private conversation, Oxford, August 23, 1997.

auction the second highest bidder has to pay his/her/their last bid as well. Those who agree to participate in the game soon realize the snare they've encountered. Invariably, the procedure turns into a lose-lose situation. Nobody really wins. With discussion, players and observers recognize that in actual practice more attention to the initial rules of the game is the best and perhaps only way to avoid a real-life counterpart of, say, a nuclear weapons race or, for another instance, questionable gene editing. Sometimes it's wisest just to NOT engage in the game. The dollar auction is one example of how a metaphor drawn from mathematics can help us learn about and even change moral behavior.

My efforts to develop and use such resources have been personally challenging, highly satisfying, and on occasion even spiritually rewarding, but largely this work has been that of a single, committed pioneer—i.e., me. And then I found acclaimed author Colum McCann and his brilliant 2020 novel *Apeirogon*. Suddenly, I was not alone! This prize-winning author intentionally uses a mathaphor not just occasionally, but as the essential structure to tell an entire tale of spiritual triumph over discord, heartbreak, disaster, and hatred.

An apeirogon is a term used in mathematics: it refers to a generalized polygon—a many-sided figure with a countably infinite number of sides.

Fig. B5. An Expandable Facsimile of a Three-Dimensional Apeirogon

An expandable facsimile of a three-dimensional apeirogon shows a science toy which illustrates a many-sided polygon with a limited number of sides. The view through the spaces it forms is flexible and interesting. An artistic rendition of an apeirogon offers a two-dimensional version of a generalized polygon,[5] but an actual apeirogon has infinite dimensions, and thus one's imagination clearly is the best visualization! Imagination also helps in understanding how an infinitely sided geometric figure is also perfectly real, sort of like God is in our ordinary vision—real and beyond real, both.

Apeirogon (the book) tells the true story of a Jew and a Palestinian, each of whom lost young daughters to the violence in the Middle East, who then turned their grief into an organization called Combatants for Peace.[6] Both the organization of McCann's book and its title are paradoxes. Welcome paradoxes! The book is a symbol for how we can turn grief and pain into something vibrating with true compassion.

Apeirogon contains 1,001 "chapters"—some long, some only one line, and some seemingly unrelated to the main story. All of them, taken together, help us examine the notion of compassion from many different perspectives and contexts. There are constant surprises in this book, some small and numerical, such as the ones about "amicable" numbers (a pair of numbers whose sum of their proper divisors equal each other, such as 220 and 284),[7] or the way the first half of McCann's "chapters" are labeled from 1 to 500, followed by a chapter numbered 1,001, and then a second set of chapters declining in number from 500 back down to 1. Some of the surprises are large, too, such as how all of this weird structure encourages the reader to suspend normal responses and actually believe that we can change as a collective body of humans and learn to be a more compassionate species.

These are the crucial facts of *Apeirogon*:

Bassam Aramin's ten-year old daughter Abir is shot by a rubber bullet fired from an M-16 rifle that had been manufactured in the town of Samaria, North Carolina. The bullet left the gun at more than one hundred miles per hour and traveled fifteen meters through the air before it smashed into the back of Abir's head, crushing the bones in her skull. Abir had gone to the grocery store to buy candy. Two hours later—while

---

5. Baez, "Diary."

6. McCann, *Apeirogon*, 238.

7. The proper divisors of 220 are 1, 2, 4, 5, 10, 11, 20, 22, 44, 55, and 110; of 284 are 1, 2, 4, 71, and 142.

stalled in an ambulance near a checkpoint, Bassam reaches into his daughter's school bag and finds the candy beneath her schoolbook. The border guard who fired the shot is eighteen years old.

Then, about ten years later, Rami Elhanan's thirteen-year-old daughter Smadar is killed while walking arm-in-arm with her girlfriend near an outdoor restaurant in Jerusalem. The bombers are dressed as women, explosive belts wrapped around their stomachs, wearing headscarves to hide their faces. They are all from a village in the West Bank. For two of them, it is the first time they had ever been in Jerusalem. The force of the blast on Ben Yehuda Street knocks Smadar high in the air. Smadar. From the Song of Solomon. The grapevine. The opening of the flower.

And so, Colum McCann gradually unfolds the story of these two grieving men, so different one from the other, yet so much the same, too. The book *Apeirogon* tells it all. And it tells it from many different perspectives. That's where the metaphor of the title comes in, and, in essence, it says it all. It's not just a metaphor: it's a mathaphor, a literary tool with increasingly recognized impact.

Here is how my friend Steve Skinner, a retired high school physics and chemistry teacher, describes the book:

> The word "Apeirogon" is from a Greek word meaning infinite sides, and since the story line is about two very different points of view in the Mideast conflict, using an infinite-sided polygon means that the view is different looking at the whole problem from the point of view of any face, literally any human face or any issue face [sic].[8]

To be sure, not everyone cares for this literary tool as much as Steve and I do:

> McCann has formatted his book like the geometric oddity for which it's named, in a sequence of brief, disconnected sections that threaten to go on eternally. . . . Reading it is like listening to an erudite conspiracy theorist explain their thesis of the universe, the thesis being that just about every meaningful thing that has ever happened is connected, and connected specifically to Israel and Palestine. The idea that those places are by nature capital-M Meaningful [sic] too often substitutes for an attempt to really see, or question, what that meaning might be. McCann, in "Apeirogon," has taken that substitution to a new extreme.[9]

---

8. Personal correspondence, October 17, 2021.
9. Zax, "Fascinated."

But others get it:

> *Apeirogon* is structured as 1,001 individual chapters, some as short as a sentence, some comprising Sebald-like photographs, some merely blank spaces (a reflection of one of the mathematical theorems that underlie the novel). . . . I kept thinking as I read it about all the ways that *Apeirogon* could have failed, about the ammunition it might have provided to all of those who claim that no one should write a novel that reaches beyond their own particular experience. It could have been maudlin, tawdry, exploitative, trite. Instead, it's a masterpiece, a novel that will change the world, and you don't hear that very often.[10]

Such different responses echo the tension in using metaphors drawn from mathematics to which I referred earlier. Necessary, perhaps, to bring about more creative change.

To read *Apeirogon* is to embrace the power of compassion. Some of this book is fiction. Some is true. It doesn't matter. These two men came together in their grief, then helped form a group they called Combatants for Peace; they are now showing us how compassion can champion everything else. Today, Aramin and Elhanan travel the world together, sharing their stories, promoting peace. McCann, with his innovative writing, is helping us all walk through these new doors. Indeed, with his careful selection of a geometric term to mold and then unfold the story of the Mideastern conflict, McCann has broadened the literary toolbox while simultaneously evoking a sweet compassion of the human spirit. What more can we ask of a mathaphor?

10. Preston, "Apeirogon."

Bibliography

Abraham, Ralph. *Chaos, Gaia, Eros.* San Francisco: HarperCollins, 1994.
Acattinei, Ciprian. "A Review of Mikael Stenmark's Scientism: Science, Ethics, and Religion." *Metanexus: Views* (ListServ) Oct 7, 2002. URL no longer available, last accessed November 2002.
Aczel, Amir D. *The Mystery of the Aleph: Mathematics, the Kabbalah, and the Search for Infinity.* New York: Washington Square, 2000.
Adams, Cecil. "Did a State Legislature once Pass a Law Saying Pi Equals 3?" The Straight Dope, Feb 21, 1991. https://www.straightdope.com/columns/read/805/did-a-state-legislature-once-pass-a-law-saying-pi-equals-3.
Adams, Douglas. *The Hitchhiker's Guide to the Galaxy.* New York: Del Rey, 2005.
Aje. "Teaching Game Theory with Video Clips." *The Filter^* blog, Oct 29, 2008. http://thefilter.blogs.com/thefilter/2008/10/teaching-game-theory-with-video-clips.html.
Anderson, Bernhard W. *Creation Versus Chaos.* New York: Association, 1967.
Anjruu. "Euler's Identity. So What?" ScienceForums.net, Jul 24, 2005. https://www.scienceforums.net/topic/11718-eulers-identity-so-what/.
Applied Science. "Lab—Physics (5A)." https://www.msnucleus.org/membership/html/k-6/as/physics/5/asp5_2a.html.
Associated Press. "Mathematicians Help in Global War on Terror." *Omaha World-Herald*, Oct 17, 2002, 6A.
———. "Trust: Social Media Could Turn Things around, If Not for Hackers, Viruses, Hateful Posts." *Omaha World-Herald*, Dec 2, 2013, 8.
Azad, Kalid. "Intuitive Understanding of Euler's Formula." Better Explained. https://betterexplained.com/articles/intuitive-understanding-of-eulers-formula/.
Baez, John. "May 2015 Diary." https://math.ucr.edu/home/baez/diary/may_2015.html.
Barabási, Albert-László. *Linked: How Everything Is Connected to Everything Else and What It Means for Business, Science, and Everyday Life.* New York: Penguin, 2003.
Barash, David. *The Survival Game: How Game Theory Explains the Biology of Cooperation and Competition.* New York: Times, 2003.
Barbour, Julian. *The End of Time: The Next Revolution in Physics.* Oxford: Oxford University Press, 2001.
Barrow, John D. *The Constants of Nature.* New York: Pantheon, 2002.
Bates, Jason H. T., and Michael P. Young. "Applying Fuzzy Logic to Medical Decision Making in the Intensive Care Unit." *American Journal of Respiratory and Critical*

Care Medicine 167:7 (2003) 948–52. https://www.atsjournals.org/doi/full/10.1164/rccm.200207-777CP#.VwxFkodBnIU.
BBC News Online. "Biological Computer Born." Jun 2, 1999. http://news.bbc.co.uk/1/hi/sci/tech/358822.stm.
Beckmann, Peter. *History of Pi*. 19th ed. New York: St. Martin's, 1976.
Begley, Sharon. "Science Finds God." Special reprint. *Newsweek*, Jul 1998, 2.
Bell, E. T. *Numerology*. Vol. 3. Westport, CT: Hyperion, 1933.
Bennett, Charles H., et al. "Teleporting an Unknown Quantum State via Dual Classical and EPR Channels." *Physical Review Letters* 70 (1993) 1,895–99. https://doi.org/10.1103/physrevlett.70.1895.
Bishop, Bob. *Shades of Reality: How the New Fuzzy Philosophy Will Change Your World View*. Lakewood, CO: Glenbridge, 1998.
Bogomolny, Alexander. "Square Root of 2 Is Irrational." Interactive Mathematics Miscellany and Puzzles. https://www.cut-the-knot.org/proofs/sq_root.shtml.
Bohm, David. *Wholeness and the Implicate Order*. New York: Routledge, 1980.
Bois, J. Samuel. *The Art of Awareness*. 3rd ed. Dubuque, IA: Brown, 1983.
Bonting, Sjoerd L. *Chaos Theology*. Ottawa: Novalis, 2002.
Boston University. "The Reflection and Refraction of Light." Jul 27, 1999. https://physics.bu.edu/~duffy/py106/Reflection.html.
Browne, Malcom W. "Biologists Tally Rewards of Generosity." *New York Times*, Apr 14, 1992, B5.
———. "Lively Computer Creation Blurs Definition of Life." *New York Times*, Aug 27, 1991, C1.
Brulé, James F. "Fuzzy Systems: A Tutorial." Fuzzy Logic: The Net's Original Fuzzy Logic Archive. https://wiki.eecs.yorku.ca/course_archive/2010-11/W/4403/_media/fuzzytutorial.pdf.
Buchanan, Mark. *Nexus: Small Worlds and the Groundbreaking Theory of Networks*. New York: Norton, 2002.
Burton, David M. *The History of Mathematics: An Introduction*. Newton, MA: Allyn and Bacon, 1985.
Callahan, David. *The Cheating Culture: Why More Americans Are Doing Wrong to Get Ahead*. Orlando: Harcourt, 2004.
Canfield, Jack, and Mark Victor Hansen. *Chicken Soup for the Soul*. Deerfield Beach, FL: Health Communications, 1993.
Capra, Fritjof. *The Web of Life*. New York: Anchor, 1996.
Challenge:Future. "Impact—The Best Way to Change the Future Is to Play with It First." Vimeo video. 2001. https://vimeo.com/26827357.
Chase, Gene B., and Calvin Jongsma. *Bibliography of Christianity and Mathematics: 1910–1983*. Sioux Center, IA: Dordt College, 1983.
Cheng, Eugenia. "Curing Procrastination with Calculus." *Wall Street Journal*, Mar 13–14, 2021, C4.
Chopra, Deepak. *How to Know God*. Abridgement, Philadelphia: Running, 2001.
Connor, Steve. "Scientists Prove It Really Is a Thin Line between Love and Hate." *Independent*, Oct 29, 2008. https://www.independent.co.uk/news/science/scientists-prove-it-really-is-a-thin-line-between-love-and-hate-976901.html
Crockett, Molly J. "How Formal Models Can Illuminate Mechanisms of Moral Judgment and Decision Making." *Current Directions in Psychological Science* 25:2 (Apr 6, 2016) 85–90. https://doi.org/10.1177/0963721415624012.

Curtis, Dorothy W., et al. "SMART—An Integrated Wireless System for Monitoring Unattended Patients." *American Medical Informatics Association* (2008). https://www.ncbi.nlm.nih.gov/pmc/articles/PMC2274866/.

Dantzig, Tobias. *Number: The Language of Science*. New York: Macmillan, 1930.

Davies, Paul. *The Mind of God: The Scientific Basis for a Rational World*. New York: Simon and Schuster, 1992.

Davis, Philip J., and Reuben Hersh. *Descartes' Dream: The World According to Mathematics*. San Diego: Harcourt Brace Jovanovich, 1986.

Demi. *One Grain of Rice: A Mathematical Folktale*. New York: Scholastic, 1997.

Dennett, Daniel C. *Kinds of Minds: Toward an Understanding of Consciousness*. New York: Basic, 1996.

Devlin, Keith J., and Gary Lorden. *The Numbers behind Numb3rs: Solving Crime with Mathematics*. New York: Plume, 2007.

Diggins, Julia E. *String, Straightedge, and Shadow*. New York: Viking, 1965.

Douglas, Mary. *Purity and Danger: An Analysis of Concepts of Pollution and Taboo*. New York: Routledge, 1988.

Downey, Tika. *History of Zero: Exploring Our Place-Value Number System*. New York: Rosen, 2004.

Drosnin, Michael. *The Bible Code*. New York: Simon and Schuster, 1997.

Dyson, Freeman J. *Infinite in All Directions*. New York: Harper and Row, 1988.

Eastaway, Rob, and Jeremy Wyndham. *Why Do Buses Come in Threes? The Hidden Mathematics of Everyday Life*. New York: John Wiley, 1999.

Eckhart, Meister. *Meister Eckhart: The Essential Sermons, Commentaries, Treatises and Defense*. Vol. 2. Translated by Edmund Colledge. Classics of Western Spirituality. Mahwah, NJ: Paulist, 1981.

Eisler, Riane, and Daniel S. Levine. "Nurture, Nature, and Caring: We Are Not Prisoners of Our Genes." *Brain and Mind* 3 (2002) 9–52. https://doi.org/10.1023/A:1016553723748.

Elgin, Duane. *Promises Ahead: A Vision of Hope and Action for Humanity's Future*. New York: William Morrow, 2001.

Eliot, T. S. "Little Gidding." In *Four Quartets*. New York: Harcourt, Brace, and Company, 1943.

Ensign, Robert. "From Engineering to Apocalypse: Scientific Creation as Rhetoric." *Journal of Interdisciplinary Studies* 1–2 (1993) 93–112.

Eves, Howard. *An Introduction to the History of Mathematics*. New York: Holt, Rinehart, and Winston, 1964.

Fadiman, Anne. *The Spirit Catches You and You Fall Down: A Hmong Child, Her American Doctors, and the Collision of Two Cultures*. New York: Farrar, Straus and Giroux, 1998.

Ferguson, Marilyn. *The Aquarian Conspiracy: Personal and Social Transformation in the 1980s*. Los Angeles: J. P. Tarch, 1980.

Fink, Sheri. *Five Days at Memorial*. New York: Crown, 2013.

Foor, Daniel. *Ancestral Medicine: Rituals for Personal and Family Healing*. Rochester, VT: Bear, 2017.

Franzen, Torkel. *Gödel's Theorem: An Incomplete Guide to Its Use and Abuse*. Natick, MA: A. K. Peters, 2005.

French, Kimberly. "After the L, G, and B." *UU World* 33:1 (Spring 2019) 30–35.

Fry, Hannah. "Math and Tech Specialists Need Hippocratic Oath, Says Academic." Edited by Ian Sample. *Guardian*, Aug 16, 2019.
Fulghum, Robert. *It Was on Fire When I Lay Down on It*. New York: Ivy, 1989.
Fuller, Buckminister. *Synergetics*. New York: Macmillan, 1975.
Fuller, Robert. "FS I: Fuzzy Sets and Fuzzy Logic." Lecture notes, Óbuda University. https://web.archive.org/web/20221004000535/https://uni-obuda.hu/users/fuller.robert/nfs1.pdf.
Gamelin, Theodore William. "What Really Are Real Numbers?" https://studylib.net/doc/5871454/what-really-are-real-numbers%3F---ucla-department-of-mathem.
Garrett, Michael. "Einstein's Formula for Success." https://www.success.com/einsteins-formula-for-success/.
Geertz, Clifford. *The Interpretation of Cultures*. New York: Basic, 1973.
———. *Myth, Symbol, and Culture*. New York: Norton, 1971.
Gladwell, Malcolm. *The Tipping Point: How Little Things Can Make a Difference*. Boston: Little, Brown, 2000.
Gleick, James. *Chaos: Making a New Science*. New York: Viking Penguin, 1987.
Goldberg, Stephen. *Jonah: The Anatomy of the Soul*. Miami: MedMaster, 1990.
Goswami, Amit. *The Self-Aware Universe: How Consciousness Creates the Material World*. New York: Tarcher, 1993.
Graham-Rowe, Duncan. "Half Fish, Half Robot." *NewScientist Online*, Jun 10, 2020. https://www.newscientist.com/article/mg16622420-400-half-fish-half-robot/.
Grandy, David. "The Musical Roots of Western Mathematics." *Journal of Interdisciplinary Studies* 5:1–2 (1993) 3–24.
Green, Alex. "Quantum Mind." Quantum Mind Conference ListServ Discussions. 1998–2001. https://web.archive.org/web/20011225224432/http://listserv.arizona.edu/archives/quantum-mind.html.
Greengrass, Joel, and Rick Mueller, dirs. *Life, the Universe and Douglas Adams*. Greater Talent Network, 2011. YouTube video. https://www.youtube.com/watch?v=OHJLNrDzYmo.
Grof, Stanislav. *The Holotropic Mind: The Three Levels of Human Consciousness and How They Shape Our Lives*. San Francisco: Harper, 1992.
Groothuis, Doug. *The Soul in Cyberspace*. Grand Rapids, MI: Baker, 1997.
Guillen, Michael. *Five Equations That Changed the World*. New York: Hyperion, 1995.
Hampden-Turner, Charles. *Maps of the Mind*. New York: Macmillan, 1981.
Hansen, Matthew. "Aristide Choice: Flee or Die." *Omaha World-Herald*, Mar 1, 2004, 1.
Harper's Magazine Editors. "Harper's Index December 2018." *Harper's Magazine*, Dec 2018.
Hartwig, Mark. "For Good Health, Go to Church." *Focus on the Family Citizen*, Jun 21, 1993.
Hawking, Stephen W. *A Brief History of Time: From the Big Bang to Black Holes*. New York: Bantam, 1988.
Henderson, Tom. "The Marching Soldiers Analogy, Refraction and the Ray Model of Light, Cause of Refraction." The Physics Classroom. https://www.physicsclassroom.com/class/refrn/u14l1c.cfm.
Hersh, Reuben. *What Is Mathematics, Really?* Oxford: Oxford University Press, 1997.
Hick, John. *An Interpretation of Religion: Human Response to the Transcendent*. New Haven, CT: Yale University Press, 1989.

Hill, Theodore P. "Mathematical Devices for Getting a Fair Share." *American Scientist* 88 (Jul-Aug 2000) 325–31.

Hofstadter, Douglas. *Gödel, Escher, Bach: An Eternal Golden Braid.* 20th anniversary ed. New York: Basic, 1999.

———, and the Fluid Analogies Research Group. *Fluid Concepts and Creative Analogies: Computer Models of the Fundamental Mechanisms of Thought.* New York: HarperCollins, 1995.

Hopper, Vincent Foster. *Medieval Number Symbolism: Its Sources, Meaning, and Influences on Thought and Expression.* Norwood, PA: Norwood, 1977.

Houghton, John. "Where Is God Thinking in More Than Three Dimensions." In *God for the 21st Century*, edited by Russell Stannard, 159. Philadelphia: Templeton Foundation, 2000.

Huber, Mark, and Gizem Karaali, eds. "About This Journal." *Journal of Humanistic Mathematics.* https://scholarship.claremont.edu/jhm/about.html.

Hunt, Earl. *The Mathematics of Behavior.* Cambridge: Cambridge University Press, 2006.

Huxley, Aldous. *Brave New World.* New York: Harper and Brothers, 1932.

———. *Brave New World Revisited.* New York: Harper and Brothers, 1958.

IMDB. "2001: A Space Odyssey. Douglas Rain: HAL 9000." https://www.imdb.com/title/tt0062622/characters/nm0706937.

Jacobi, Jolande. *The Psychology of C. J. Jung.* New Haven, CT: Yale University Press, 1973.

Johnson, Steven. *Emergence: The Connected Lives of Ants, Brains, Cities, and Software.* New York: Simon and Schuster, 2001.

Kaku, Michio. *Hyperspace: A Scientific Odyssey through Parallel Universes, Time Warps, and the Tenth Dimension.* New York: Doubleday, 1994.

Kapitan, Alex. "What It Takes to De-Center Privilege: The Failure of this Week's UU World Article." *Roots Grow the Tree* (blog), Mar 6, 2019. https://rootsgrowthetree.com/2019/03/06/what-it-takes-to-de-center-privilege/.

Khan Academy. "Euler's Formula and Euler's Identity." YouTube video. May 17, 2011. https://www.youtube.com/watch?v=mgNtPOgFjeo.

Keyser, Cassius Jackson. *Mathematics and the Question of the Cosmic Mind with Other Essays.* New York: Scripta Mathematica, 1935.

Knill, Oliver. "Mathematics in Movies." Last updated December 2022. https://people.math.harvard.edu/~knill/mathmovies/.

Knovva Academy. "If the World Was Only 100 People." YouTube video. Global Citizenship, Mar 2, 2018. https://www.youtube.com/watch?v=A3nllBT9ACg.

Kosko, Bart. *The Fuzzy Future: From Society and Science to Heaven in a Chip.* New York: Harmony, 1999.

Kurzweil, Ray. *The Age of Spiritual Machines: When Computers Exceed Human Intelligence.* New York: Viking, 1999.

———. *The Singularity Is Near: When Humans Transcend Biology.* New York: Viking, 2005.

Larson, David, et al. "The Impact of Religion on Men's Blood Pressure." *Journal of Religious Health* 28 (1989) 265–78. https://doi.org/10.1007/BF00986065.

Lawlor, Robert. *Sacred Geometry.* London: Thames and Hudson, 1989.

Leary, Timothy. *Chaos and Cyberculture.* Berkeley: Ronin, 1994.

Lederman, Leon, and Dick Teresi. *The God Particle: If the Universe Is the Answer, What Is the Question?* Boston: Houghton Mifflin, 1993.

Len, Patrick M. "Online Reading Assignment: Total Internal Reflection, Polarization." *P-Dog's Blog*, Jan 29, 2020. https://waiferx.blogspot.com/search?q=total+internal+reflection.

LeShan, Lawrence, and Henry Margenau. *Einstein's Space and Van Gogh's Sky: Physical Reality and Beyond*. London: Macmillan, 1982.

Levine, Daniel S. *Common Sense and Common Nonsense: A Conversation about Mental Attitudes, Science, and Society*. Arlington, TX: Mavs Open, 2018. E-book. http://hdl.handle.net/10106/27541.

———. *Healing the Reason-Emotion Split: Scarecrows, Tin Woodmen, and the Wizard*. New York: Routledge, 2021.

———. "Lessons from Neuroscience and Experimental Psychology for a Partnership Society." *Interdisciplinary Journal of Partnership Studies* 2:2 (2015) art. 4. https://doi.org/10.24926/ijps.v2i2.111.

Lightman, Alan. *Ancient Light: Our Changing View of the Universe*. Cambridge, MA: Harvard University Press, 1991.

Liversidge, Anthony. "Father of the Electronic Information Age." Interview with Claude Shannon. *Omni* 9:11 (Aug 1987) 60–67.

Livio, Mario. *Is God a Mathematician?* New York: Simon and Schuster, 2010.

Loewe, Michael. "China." In *Divination & Oracles*, edited by Michael Loewe and Carmen Blacker, 34–62. Boulder, CO: Shambhala, 1981.

MacNeal, Edward. *Mathsemantics*. New York: Viking, 1994.

Maher, Jimmy. "Eliza, Part 1." *The Digital Antiquarian* (blog), Jun 15, 2011. https://www.filfre.net/2011/06/eliza-part-1/.

Manganiello, Dominic. *T. S. Eliot and Dante*. New York: St. Martin's, 1989.

Maor, Eli. *e: The Story of a Number*. Princeton, NJ: Princeton University Press, 1994.

Mariah, Katelyn. "It Is Never Too Late to Have a Funeral . . . ." Blog, Sep 2, 2012. https://magneticbusinesswoman.wordpress.com/2012/09/02/it-is-never-too-late-to-have-a-funeral/.

"Many Boomers Left Churches in Confusion." *Omaha World-Herald*, Jul 4, 1992, 38.

May, Andrew. "Mathematics and Mysticism." British Mensa's *Aquarian*, Feb 2006. https://www.andrew-may.com/mm.htm.

May, Herbert G., and Bruce M. Metzger, *The New Oxford Annotated Bible with the Apocrypha, Revised Standard Version*. Oxford: Oxford University Press, 1973–1977.

McCann, Colum. *Apeirogon: A Novel*. New York: Random House, 2021.

McDonald, Hugh. "Exhibitizing Cooperation." *Human Generosity Project* (blog), Aug 19, 2017. https://www.humangenerosity.org/exhibitizing-cooperation/.

McFague, Sallie. *Metaphorical Theology: Models of God in Religious Language*. Philadelphia: Fortress, 1982.

McFarlane, Thomas J. "Counting on Truth: A Parable on the Multiple Forms of Truth." *True Nature* (blog), Jan 1, 1993. https://integralscience.wordpress.com/1993/01/01/counting-on-truth-a-parable-on-the-multiple-forms-of-truth/.

———. "Morality and Mathematics." *True Nature* (blog), Aug 18, 2018. https://integralscience.wordpress.com/2018/08/18/morality-and-mathematics/.

———. "The Spiritual Function of Mathematics and the Philosophy of Franklin Merrell-Wolff." 1995. http://www.integralscience.org/sacredscience/SS_spiritual.html.

McGrath, Susan P., et al. "ARTEMIS: A Vision for Remote Triage and Emergency Management Information Integration." Report, Nov 30, 2003. https://www.researchgate.net/publication/228608664_Artemis_A_vision_for_remote_triage_and_emergency_management_information_integration.

Menninger, Karl Augustus. *Menninger Letter* 3:7 (Jul 1995).

———. *Menninger Letter* 3:9 (Sep 1995).

Méro, László. *Moral Calculations: Game Theory, Logic, and Human Frailty*. New York: Springer-Verlag, 1998.

Merrell-Wolff, Franklin. *Franklin Merrell-Wolff's Experience and Philosophy: A Personal Record of Transformation and a Discussion of Transcendental Consciousness*. New York: State University of New York Press, 1994.

Miller, Iona, and Graywolf Swinney. "Human Dimensions of Chaos Theory: Consciousness, Physiology, Perception, and Psychology." *On The Human Dimensions of Chaos Theory* (blog), 1992. https://web.archive.org/web/20090211141948/http://www.geocities.com/iona_m/ChaosTheory/chaostheory1.html.

Miller, James B. "From the Garden to Gauss: Mathematics as Theological Metaphor." 7th European Conference on Science and Theology, Durham, England, March 31–April 4, 1998.

Mishlove, Jeffrey. *Thinking Allowed: Conversations on the Leading Edge of Knowledge*. Tulsa, OK: Council Oak, 1992.

Mondragon, Norbeto, et al. "Patient Classification Algorithm at Urgency Care Area of a Hospital Based on the Triage System." *Journal of Medical Informatics & Technologies* 22 (Oct 2013) 255–63. https://web.archive.org/web/20170809095351/http://jmit.us.edu.pl/cms/jmitjrn/22/19_Mondragon_3.pdf.

Mordeson, John N., and Sunil Mathew. *Advanced Topics in Fuzzy Graph Theory*. Studies in Fuzziness and Soft Computing 375. New York: Springer Cham, 2019. https://doi.org/10.1007/978-3-030-04215-8.

Mordeson, John N., et al. "Dialectic Synthesis: Application to Human Trafficking." *New Mathematics and Natural Computation* 15:3 (2019) 395–410. https://doi.org/10.1142/S1793005719500224.

Mordeson, John N., et al. *Fuzzy Graph Theory with Applications to Human Trafficking*. Studies in Fuzziness and Soft Computing 365. New York: Springer Cham, 2018. https://doi.org/10.1007/978-3-319-76454-2.

Musser, George. "A Pixelated Cosmos." *Scientific American* (Oct 2002) 18.

My Schoolhouse. "Reflection and Refraction." http://www.myschoolhouse.com/courses/O/1/36.asp.

Nadeau, Robert L. *Mind, Machines, and Human Consciousness*. Chicago: Contemporary, 1991.

Nagel, Ernest, and James R. Newman. *Gödel's Proof*. New York: New York University Press, 2001.

Nahin, Paul J. *An Imaginary Tale: The Story of "i"—the Square Root of Minus One*. Princeton, NJ: Princeton University Press, 1998.

Nebelsick, Harold P. *Circles of God: Theology and Science from the Greeks to Copernicus*. Edinburgh: Scottish Academic Press, 1985.

Nogg, Ozzie. "No Dispute: Werner Institute Fills Major Role in the Burgeoning Field of Conflict Resolution." *Creighton University Magazine*, Fall 2008, 16–19. https://www.creighton.edu/fileadmin/user/creighton-magazine/archive/PDFs/2008_creightonfall2008.pdf.

Norman, Jeremy. "The First Book Written by a Computer Program." HistoryofInformation.com. https://www.historyofinformation.com/detail.php?entryid=3806.

Numbers USA. "Gumball Video: Immigration, World Poverty and Gumballs—Updated 2010." Dec 1, 2015. https://www.numbersusa.org/msp/gumball-video.

O'Murchu, Diarmuid. *Quantum Theology: Spiritual Implications of the New Physics*. New York: Crossroad, 1997.

O'Neill, Michael. "Euler's Formula." S.O.S. Math. http://www.sosmath.com/complex/number/eulerformula/eulerformula.html.

Osnos, Evan. "The Ghost in the Machine: Can Mark Zuckerberg Fix Facebook Before It Breaks Democracy?" *New Yorker*, Sep 17, 2018, 33–53.

Otoshi, Kathryn. *One*. Novato, CA: Ko Kids, 2008.

Pederson, Olaf. "Christian Beliefs and the Fascination of Science." *Physics, Philosophy, and Theology: A Common Quest for Understanding*, edited by Robert J. Russell et al, 124–39. Vatican City: Vatican Observatory, 1988.

Peterson, Ivars. "Formulas for Fairness: Applying the Math of Cake Cutting to Conflict Resolution." *Science News* 149:18 (May 4, 1996) 284–85.

———, and Carol Ezzell. "Crazy Rhythms: Confronting the Complexity of Chaos in Biological Systems." *Science News* 142:10 (Sep 5, 1992) 156–59.

The Physics Classroom. "The Cause of Refraction." https://www.physicsclassroom.com/class/refrn/u14l1c.cfm.

Pickover, Clifford. *The Loom of God: Mathematical Tapestries at the Edge of Time*. New York: Plenum, 1997.

Polkinghorne, John. *The Way the World Is*. Grand Rapids, MI: Eerdmans, 1983.

Poundstone, William. *Prisoner's Dilemma*. New York: Anchor, 1992.

Prendergast, Kate. "Time Out of Mind: A New Vision of Temporal Reality." *Science & Spirit* 11 (Mar/Apr 2001) 19–21.

Preston, Alex. "Apeirogon by Colum McCann Review—a Beautifully Observed Masterpiece." *Guardian*, Feb 24, 2020. https://www.theguardian.com/books/2020/feb/24/apeirogon-a-novel-by-colum-mccann-book-review.

"Quotes of Wisdom: The Golden Rule." Diamond Helpers. https://web.archive.org/web/20040810212417/http://www.diamondhelpers.com/loveandlife/famousquotes/goldenrule.shtml.

Raatikainen, Panu. "Review of Gödel's Theorem: An Incomplete Guide to Its Use and Abuse, by Torkel Franzén." *Notices of the American Mathematical Society* 54:3 (2007) 380–83.

Radha, Chime. "Tibet." In *Divination and Oracles*, edited by Michael Loewe and Carmen Blacker, 33–37. Boulder, CO: Shambhala, 1981.

Rational Wiki. "Indiana Pi Bill." Last updated May 1, 2019. https://rationalwiki.org/wiki/Indiana_Pi_Bill.

Ray, Joseph. *Ray's Mathematical Series: Ray's New Higher Arithmetic*. New York: Van Antwerp, Bragg, 1880.

Reinhold, Arnold G. "Math in the Movies." Last updated June 16, 2011. http://world.std.com/~reinhold/mathmovies.html.

Restak, Richard. *The New Brain*. New York: Rodale 2003.

Restivo, Sal. *Beyond New Atheism and Theism: A Sociology of Science, Secularism, and Religiosity*. New York: Routledge, 2023.

———. "The Social Life of Mathematics." In *Math Worlds: Philosophical and Social Studies of Mathematics and Mathematics Education*, edited by Sal Restivo et al, 247–78. New York: State University of New York Press, 1985.

———. *The Social Relations of Physics, Mysticism, & Mathematics, Part 2*. Boston: D. Reidel, 1983.

Riktw. "The Answer to Life, Universe and Everything." YouTube video. May 9, 2008. https://www.youtube.com/watch?v=aboZctrHfK8.

Robinson, Jessica R., et al. "Foster Care Deficiencies and Human Trafficking." *New Mathematics and Natural Computation* 15:2 (2019) 215–30. https://doi.org/10.1142/S1793005719500121.

Rosen, Robert. *Life Itself: A Comprehensive Inquiry into the Nature, Origin, and Fabrication of Life*. 1st ed. 1991. New York: Columbia University Press, 2005.

Roy, Arundhati. *Public Power in the Age of Empire*. Transcription of speech, 99th annual meeting of the American Sociological Association, August 16, 2004. New York: Seven Stories, 2011.

Rucker, Rudy. *Mind Tools: The Five Levels of Mathematical Reality*. Boston: Houghton Mifflin, 1987.

Saffarti, Jack. "Quantum Mind." Quantum Mind Conference ListServ Discussions. 1998–2001. URL no longer available. Last accessed 2006.

San Pedro, Jocelyn C., et al. "On Development and Evaluation of Prototype Mobile Decision Support for Hospital Triage." Paper, 38th Hawaii International Conference on System Sciences, Monash University, Australia, January 2005.

Schimmel, Annemarie. "Numbers: An Overview." In *The Encyclopedia of Religion*, edited by Mircea Eliade, 2. New York: Macmillan, 1987.

Schulman, Frank. "Axioms of Theology." *The Price of Truth*. Chicago: Meadville-Lombard, 2006.

Science News Editors. "Behavior." *Science News* 147.8 (Feb 25, 1995) 124.

Shermer, Michael. *The Science of Good and Evil*. New York: Henry Holt, 2004.

Shrader, Douglas W. "Seven Characteristics of Mystical Experiences." Presentation, Sixth Annual Hawaii International Conference on Arts and Humanities, 2008.

Sirag, Saul-Paul. "Consciousness: A Hyperspace View." Appendix in *The Roots of Consciousness*, by Jeffrey Mishlove, 327–65. Tulsa, OK: Council Oak, 1993.

Slavin, Kevin. "How Algorithms Shape Our World." TEDGlobal, Jul 2011. https://www.ted.com/talks/kevin_slavin_how_algorithms_shape_our_world.

Smith, Karl J. *The Nature of Mathematics*. Monterey, CA: Brooks/Cole, 1984.

Smoot, George, and Keay Davidson. *Wrinkles in Time*. New York: William Morrow, 1993.

Snowden, David, et al. "Linguistics Ability in Early Life and Cognitive Function and Alzheimer's Disease in Late Life: Findings from the Nun Study." *Journal of American Medical Association* 275:7 (Feb 21, 1996). 528–32. doi.org/10.1001/jama.1996.03530310034029.

Somé, Malidoma Patrice. *Of Water and the Spirit*. New York: Penguin, 1995.

Spencer-Brown, G. *Laws of Form*. New York: E. P. Dutton, 1979.

Stacey, Ralph D. *Complexity and Creativity in Organizations*. San Francisco: Berrett-Koehler, 1996.

———. "Management and the Science of Complexity: If Organizational Life Is Nonlinear, Can Business Strategies Prevail?" *Research-Technology Management* 39:3 (May/Jun 1996) 8–10.

Stenger, Richard. "Robo-eels, Critters on Chips Lead Cyborg Pack." CNN, May 8, 2001. https://www.cnn.com/2001/TECH/science/05/08/brains.robots/.

SuperJustimagine. "Direct Network Flow Problem on Numb3rs." YouTube video. Apr 8, 2011. http://www.youtube.com/watch?v=_fitfJfF46Q.

Talbot, Michael. *The Holographic Universe*. New York: HarperCollins, 1991.

Tarbox, Elizabeth. *Life Tides*. Boston: Skinner House, 1992.

Tegmark, Max. *Our Mathematical Universe: My Quest for the Ultimate Nature of Reality*. New York: Knopf, 2014.

Thomas, Lewis. *Et Cetera Et Cetera: Notes of a Word Watcher*. New York: Little, Brown, 1990.

Tikkanen, Ay, and Alex Spe. "Epimenides." *Encyclopedia Britannica*. Last revised February 25, 2011. https://www.britannica.com/biography/Epimenides.

Tipler, Frank J. *The Physics of Immortality*. New York: Doubleday, 1995.

Tiwari, Maya. "Episode 150: Honoring Ancestors." Women's Power to Heal Mother Earth, Jun 9, 2023. Podcast. https://podcasts.apple.com/in/podcast/episode-150-honoring-ancestors/id1507256948?i=1000616315008.

Torkel, Franzén. *Gödel's Theorem: An Incomplete Guide to Its Use and Abuse*. New York: CRC, 2005.

Turkle, Sherry. *Life on the Screen: Identity in the Age of the Internet*. New York: Simon and Schuster, 1995.

University of Missouri Kansas City. "Proof—There Are More Real Numbers Than Natural Numbers." YouTube video. May 29, 2009. https://www.youtube.com/watch?v=mEEM_dLWYog.

University of Nebraska Omaha. "Whiners May Be Better Off, Study Finds." *The Gateway* 16:18 (Mar 8, 1996) 8.

Unknown author. "In the Beginning." The Online Book of Genesis. https://www.oocities.org/dpleache/humor/genesis.html.

Unwin, Stephen. *The Probability of God: A Simple Calculation That Proves the Ultimate Truth*. New York: Three Rivers, 2003.

van Geert, Paul. *The Development of Perception, Cognition, and Language: A Theoretical Approach*. Boston: Routledge and Kegan Paul, 1983.

Voss, Sarah. "Book Review: Robert Rosen's 'Life Itself.'" Metanexus, Apr 6, 2000. https://metanexus.net/book-review-robert-rosens-life-itself/.

———. "Depolarizing Mathematics and Religion." *Philosophia Mathematica: An International Journal for the Philosophy of Modern Mathematics* 2:5 (1990) 129–41.

———. "Exploring Moral Math." *Omaha World-Herald*, Nov 2, 2019, 5B.

———. "Fuzzy Logic in Health Care Settings: Moral Math for Value-Laden Choices." *Journal of Humanistic Mathematics* 6:2 (Jul 2016) 161–78. https://doi.org/10.5642/jhummath.201602.12.

———. "Generating Trust through 'Moral' Math." In *Unity and Diversity in Religion and Culture: Exploring the Psychological and Philosophical Issues Underlying Global Conflict*, edited by Liubava Moreva et al., 578–89. International Readings on Theory, History and Philosophy of Culture 22. St. Petersburg: Eidos, 2006.

———. "Going beyond Copernicus." In *Rocking the Ages: The Pulse of Continuity and Change*, edited by Carol S. Lawson and Robert F. Lawson, 7:165–77. West Chester, PA: Swedenborg Foundation, 2000.

———. "Mathapor as a Literary Tool." *Journal of Humanistic Math* 13:1 (Jan 2023) 232–38. https://doi.org/10.5642/jhummath.FHPM8098.

———. "Mathaphors and Faith Understandings of Consciousness." *Journal of Interdisciplinary Studies, Science and Religion: The Missing Link* 17:1/2 (2005) 88–104.

———. "Mathematical Theology." *Spiritual Information: 100 Perspectives on Science and Religion*, edited by Charles L. Harper, Jr., 221–27. Philadelphia: Templeton Foundation, 2005.

———. "Mathematics and Theology: A Stroll through the Garden of Mathaphors." *Theology and Science* 4:1 (Mar 2006) 33–49.

———. "Mathematics, Ministry, and Mediation: An Interview with Sarah Voss." *Holos: Forum for a New World View* 5:2 (2009). https://www.centerforsacredsciences.org/index.php/Holos/holos-voss.html.

———. "Matheology and Cantorian Religion." *Journal of Religious Humanism* 37:1 (Winter/Spring 2004) 14–16.

———. "The Miraculous in Number(s): The Hidden Meaning of Mathematics." *Parabola: Myth, Tradition, and the Search for Meaning* 43:2 (Summer 2018) 78–83.

———. "Moral Mathematics." In *Handbook of the Mathematics of the Arts and Sciences*, edited by Bharath Sriraman et al., 2,729–51. New York: Springer Cham, 2021. https://doi.org/10.1007/978-3-319-70658-0_79-2.

———. "Old Pythagoras Would Be Pleased: Theological Reflections on Dyson's Mathematics." Center for Theology and the Natural Sciences: Templeton Conference on the works of Freeman Dyson, Omaha, Nebraska, October 2000.

———. *Out of Our Prayers, Hope*. Omaha, NE: Immanuel Medical Center, 1991.

———. "Redemption." *Still Point Arts Quarterly* 23 (Fall 2016) 60–66.

———. "Sacred Qualities." *Parabola: Myth, Tradition, and the Search for Meaning* 24:3 (Fall 1999) 32-37.

———. "Simple Arithmetic: Heavy on Butter, Cream, Wine." *Journal of Humanistic Mathematics* 10:1 (Jan 2020) 472–74. https://doi.org/10.5642/jhummath.202001.26.

———. "Spirit-Wise Math: Two Examples from a Collection of Mathaphors." *Journal of Humanistic Mathematics* 9:1 (Jan 2019) 224–44. https://doi.org/10.5642/jhummath.201901.13.

———. "Ten Ways Contemporary Mathaphors Are Shaping Our Spiritual Lives," Klein 2000 Lecture, First Unitarian Church, Ann Arbor, Michigan, October, 2000.

———. *What Number Is God? Metaphors, Metaphysics, Metamathematics and the Nature of Things*. Western Esoteric Traditions. New York: State University of New York Press, 1995.

———. "A Workshop to Introduce Concepts of Moral Math." *Journal of Humanistic Mathematics* 2:2 (Jul 2012) 114–28. https://doi.org/10.5642/jhummath.201202.10.

———. *Zero: Reflections about Nothing*. Photos by Dan Sullivan. Notre Dame, IN: Cross Cultural, 1998.

Wager, Anita A., and Stinson, David W. *Teaching Mathematics for Social Justice: Conversations with Educators*. Reston, VA: National Council of Teachers of Mathematics, 2012.

Waldrop, M. Mitchell. *Complexity: The Emerging Science at the Edge of Order and Chaos*. New York: Simon and Schuster, 1992.
Wall Street Journal. "Congregation-Based Health Ministry." Jul 1994.
Walter, Katya. *Tao of Chaos*. Shaftesbury: Element, 1994.
Walton, Christopher L. "Our Story Hurt People." *UU World*, Mar 6, 2019. https://www.uuworld.org/articles/apology-spring-2019.
Watts, Duncan J. *Six Degrees: The Science of a Connected Age*. New York: Norton, 2003.
Weisstein, Eric W. "Euler Formula." *MathWorld*—A Wolfram Web Resource. https://mathworld.wolfram.com/EulerFormula.html
———. "Golden Rule." *MathWorld*: A Wolfram Web Resource. https://mathworld.wolfram.com/GoldenRule.html.
Westley, Marian. "Science Finds God." *Newsweek*, Jul 20, 1998. https://www.washingtonpost.com/wp-srv/newsweek/science_of_god/scienceofgod2.htm.
Westover, Tara. *Educated: A Memoir*. New York: Random House, 2018.
Wheatley, Margaret J. *Leadership and the New Science*. San Francisco: Berrett-Koehler, 1992.
Wikipedia. "Absolute Infinite." Last updated October 21, 2023. https://en.wikipedia.org/wiki/Absolute_Infinite.
———. "John Wallis." Last updated September 22, 2023. https://en.wikipedia.org/wiki/John_Wallis
———. "Natural Logarithm." Last updated October 13, 2023. https://en.wikipedia.org/wiki/Natural_logarithm.
———. "Zermelo–Fraenkel Set Theory." Last updated October 4, 2023. https://en.wikipedia.org/wiki/Zermelo%E2%80%93Fraenkel_set_theory.
Wimp.com. "Visualizing Obama's Budget Cuts." Apr 29, 2009. https://www.wimp.com/visualizing-obamas-budget-cuts.
Wolpert, Stuart. "Can Math and Science Help Solve Crimes? UCLA Scientists Work with L.A. Police to Identify and Analyze Crime 'Hotspots.'" *UCLA Newsroom*, Feb 20, 2010. https://web.archive.org/web/20170502151021/http://newsroom.ucla.edu/releases/can-math-and-science-help-solve-153986.
Woolley, Benjamin. *Virtual Worlds*. Cambridge: Blackwell, 1992.
Wootters, William. "Current Issues in Physics." Lecture at Templeton Summer Workshop, Chicago, June 1998.
Wright, Robert. "Nonzero Hour: Cooperation, Evolution and Destiny." Interview by Mary Lacombe. *Science and Spirit*, online exclusive. URL no longer available. Last accessed August 2000.
———. *NonZero: The Logic of Human Destiny*. New York: Pantheon, 2000.
Zadeh, Lotfi A. "Fuzzy Sets." *Information and Control* 8:3 (1965) 338–53.
———. "Fuzzy Sets and Systems." In *System Theory*, edited by Jerome Fox, 29–30. Brooklyn, NY: Polytechnique, 1965.
Zax, Talya. "Fascinated by the Israeli-Palestinian Conflict—and Exploiting It." *Forward*, Feb 25, 2020. https://forward.com/culture/440450/apeirogon-colum-mccann-israel-palestine-rev iew-bassam-aramin-rami-elhanan/.
Zeki, Semir, and John Paul Romaya. "Neural Correlates of Hate." PLoS ONE 3:10 (Oct 29, 2008) e3556. https://doi.org/10.1371/journal.pone.0003556.
Zohar, Dana. *The Quantum Self*. New York: William Morrow, 1991.

www.ingramcontent.com/pod-product-compliance
Lightning Source LLC
Chambersburg PA
CBHW071226230426
43668CB00011B/1320